FIRST KNOW YOUR ENEMY
COMPREHENDING IMPERIAL GERMAN WAR AIMS
& DECIPHERING THE ENIGMA OF *KULTUR*

John
in alter Verbundenheit

John Moses

The ANZAC Cenotaph in Atherton,
North Queensland, unveiled 25th April 1924

FIRST KNOW YOUR ENEMY
COMPREHENDING IMPERIAL GERMAN WAR AIMS
& DECIPHERING THE ENIGMA OF *KULTUR*

JOHN A. MOSES
WITH
PETER OVERLACK

AUSTRALIAN SCHOLARLY

© John A. Moses 2019

© Chapters 8–10, Peter Overlack 2019

First published 2019 by
Australian Scholarly Publishing Pty Ltd
7 Lt Lothian St Nth, North Melbourne, Vic 3051

Tel: 03 9329 6963 / Fax: 03 9329 5452
enquiry@scholarly.info / www.scholarly.info

ISBN 978-1-925801-60-6 HB

ISBN 978-1-925801-61-3 PB

Cover, clockwise from top left: Kaiser William II (King of Prussia and Emperor / War Lord of Imperial Germany, 1888–1918); George V (r. 1910–1936) King of the United Kingdom and of the British overseas Dominions and Emperor of India; Count Maximilian von Spee, Vice Admiral of the Imperial German East Asia Squadron (1912–1914); Rear Admiral William Rooke Creswell KBE and First Naval Member of the Royal Australian Navy (1912–1919)

Cover design: Wayne Saunders

'No sane man can pretend that the Government of Germany, mainly directed by a disguised autocrat, or, at most, by a disguised oligarchy, is any fit instrument for securing the truest happiness for the greatest number.'

– Professor T. G. Tucker, 'British and German Ideals' in *Public Lectures on the War*, George Robertson & Co., Melbourne, 1915, p. 10

'The ideology of the uniqueness (*Besonderheit*) of the German spirit and the political mentality that corresponds to it has been expressed most accurately in the writing of German academics. Indeed, it is from them during the first months and years of the war that the quintessence of German self-perception as articulated by leading political and cultural personalities can be best deduced.'

– Professor Kurt Sontheimer, 'Der deutsche Geist als Ideologie' in *Demokratie und Diktatur: Geist und Gestalt politischer Herrschaft in Deutschland und Europa,* Manfred Funk et al. (eds.), Droste Verlag, Düsseldorf, 1987, p. 36

'[The Great War] was an act of incredible political and moral irresponsibility perpetrated by a small group of men around the German Emperor at the instigation of a fatalistic Prussian general [von Moltke] who was at the end of his tether.'

– Volker R. Berghahn in *No Man's Land*, review of *The Pity of Way* by Niall Ferguson, *New York Times*, 9 May 1999

Contents

Appendices

Acknowledgements

There are two kinds of acknowledgement, namely institutional and personal. First and foremost I am greatly indebted to the Deutscher Akademischer Austauschdienst (DAAD) for enabling me to study in Germany as a post graduate student from 1961 to 1965, and then later to the Alexander von Humboldt Foundation which, after I joined the staff of the University of Queensland, strongly supported my research projects over many years. Both these institutions made my academic career possible.

On the personal side, during my studies in Germany I became greatly indebted to Professors Franz Schnabel in Munich, 1961–62, and Waldemar Besson, my *Doktorvater* in Erlangen, 1963–65, as well as to his eminent colleagues, Walter-Peter Fuchs and Karl-Heinz Ruffmann. Later I became associated with Professor Fritz Fischer in Hamburg and a number of his *Assistenten* among whom was at that time Dr Imanuel Geiss. In addition, while on study leave, Professor Werner Jochmann, also at Hamburg, welcomed me into his Institute for the Study of the German Labour Movement. All of these men, now deceased, proved to be both most hospitable and encouraging to their Antipodean junior colleague.

Elsewhere I enjoyed collegial dialogue and collaboration with Professor Klaus Bade in Osnabrück. Also at that time I met the notable Paul Kennedy, then at Oxford, an association that yielded a most valuable results. Further, my long friendship with the late Professor Georg G. Iggers at the State University of New York at Buffalo proved immensely instructive in furthering my understanding of German intellectual history. About the same time I also met and got to know very well the Austrian-Israeli Professor Walter Grab when we were both on study leave in Hamburg. In addition I met and corresponded with over many years with Professors

Volker Berghahn, Hartmut Pogge von Strandmann as well as John Röhl when they were well established in academic posts in England. Through this association and my publications I became very much identified with the 'Fischer School.' In North America, the long associations I enjoyed with John Conway at the University of British Columbia in Vancouver as well as with the late Professor Gerry Feldman at Berkeley have been extremely important. Another American who had moved to Australia whose collegiality over the years has been much appreciated is Professor Joseph Siracusa, now at RMIT.

Former Queensland students who proceeded to academic careers of their own include the late Roger Fletcher, Peter Overlack, Gregory Munro, Julian Jenkins and Anthony Cooper. All of these produced highly significant work which became internationally recognised and with whom the subsequent scholarly association has proved mutually beneficial. Next, I owe and immeasurable debt of gratitude to the late Professor Gordon Greenwood because it was he who launched me on an academic career through his dedication to the discipline and his wise counsel. He made my academic post at Queensland possible in the first place.

With regard to the technical challenges posed by getting a manuscript into publishable form I owe an immense amount to the expertise and magnanimity of the Reverend Graham Lindsay of Canberra. The index was very professionally and generously executed by Alison Sloper to whom I am most grateful.

Finally, I would have accomplished very little were it not for the understanding and support of my German-born and educated wife, Professor Ingrid Moses neé Heise and our two high achieving sons Professor Dirk Moses, now at the University of Sydney, and Rolf Moses who is CEO of the Queensland Law Society. To all of them I extend my heartfelt thanks.

Foreword

Today university academics are increasingly internationally networked, with instantaneous communication over the Internet, and many enjoy regular international and conference travel. Fifty years ago, this was not as easy it is now. While there were well-established networks between Melbourne and Sydney on the one hand and Oxbridge and London on the other, some scholars pursued less well-trodden paths. In the history of twentieth-century Australian historians' international scholarly careers, John A. Moses' journey from Atherton in Northern Queensland to Munich and Erlangen in post-war West Germany stands out as one of the more unusual trajectories.

John Moses has written about this life story in an autobiographical essay ('My History is Not Your History, or How an "Ethnic" Australian views our National Past', in 'The Lucky Country 50 Years On'. *Proceedings* of the Independent Scholars' Association of Australia, 2014). It is a remarkable account of his road from being an apprentice radio technician from Atherton, to training for the Anglican priesthood, to pursuing postgraduate research in a Munich still scarred from the Second World War and then Erlangen University near Nuremberg. In the early 1960s West Germany, as he describes in this present work, Moses found himself propelled into some of the most consequential debates among German historians in the twentieth century, analysing how German history took the road to Nazism, war and the Holocaust, and grappling with the elements in German society that made that path possible. Moses' teachers in Munich and the formerly Nazified Erlangen university wrestled with these questions in their teaching and their scholarship. During his researches in Germany, Moses witnessed the storms of controversy over Fritz Fischer's work on

German war aims in the First World War, became acquainted with Fischer himself, and then became one of the foremost interpreters of the Fischer controversy to English-speaking readers (notably through his book *The Politics of Illusion*, 1975). His work on Fischer was just one facet of his very productive career as a historian of Germany, with his *oeuvre* including a standard two-volume history of German trade unionism from its origins to the advent of the Nazi regime, pioneering works on international imperial history, including a significant collection on Germany and the Pacific edited with Paul Kennedy, historiography, trade-union theory from Marx to Lech Wałęsa, Dietrich Bonhoeffer, and much else besides. This prodigious scholarly output has continued unabated since his retirement from the University of Queensland over two decades ago. I would also like to record here that John Moses has also long been a generous supporter of and mentor to younger Australian scholars working in the field of German history.

In his formative years as a student of German history in the 1960s, John Moses saw how the Hamburg historian Fritz Fischer was virulently attacked by many of the most conservative members of the old German historians' guild for suggesting that the German elites were largely culpable for unleashing the First World War, that there was a degree of continuity in German foreign policy from the period of Kaiser Wilhelm II to Hitler, and that foreign policy had to be understood in the context of domestic social and political conflicts. These arguments were heretical to the German historical establishment of the day. It is therefore a subject of some bafflement and perhaps vexation for Moses that theses which in Germany are now applauded by the conservative-nationalist right – for example, that the German elites were no more culpable for outbreak of 1914 than any other government of that time (or perhaps than the unruly Serbs) – have found wide acceptance and approval among Australian historians, including among some of a 'left-nationalist' persuasion.

This book is in some ways an attempt to deal with this problem, on which Moses brings his intellectual resources and his scholarly experience of over half a century to bear. A few factors seem to play a role in what may seem to be a cognitive dissonance among some Australian historians, as they embrace historical interpretations that are also congenial to the right in Germany. There is a degree of insularity among some practitioners of Australian history. It is possible to progress from an Honours degree in Australian history at our universities to a PhD in the same field, without in-depth work in another field of history, and unlike the situation at universities in the best European or North American universities, our history students can get away without reading foreign languages, even at PhD level. No wonder that there is sometimes a self-referentiality about debates in Australian history. It is true that recent Australian Historical Association conferences have embraced the concept of transnational history, but the comparative or transnational studies in these fora have often involved other English-speaking countries, or parts of the British Empire.

Secondly, the secular formation of many of the younger generation of Australian historians leaves many unaware of, or uninterested in, the role of religion in Australian history, which means that some miss the profound sectarian divisions in Australian society that persisted well into the 1960s (at least). Here, John Moses' theological education equips him to uncover the importance of religious belief in aspects of Australia's past, such as the origins of the commemoration of Anzac.

Thirdly, John Moses perceives a degree of 'presentism' in much of our historical writing. The fact that we have developed a much more critical perspective on the history of the British Empire than many of our predecessors espoused (not least because of our growing awareness of the injustices meted out to Australia's Indigenous population) does not mean we cannot try the leap of historical imagination to try to reconstruct the attitudes of Australians in government positions in 1914. At this time, Australia was thoroughly integrated into the economic, security and political systems of the Empire, even if many writers today wish it had been otherwise.

At the same time, it is important to note that John Moses stresses that it is necessary to air historical disagreements without impugning the integrity of other scholars, and there is no doubt that much of the critical historical writing questioning Australian participation in the First World War comes from honourable motives, such as revulsion against the horrors of the war, and a desire for more self-reliant national policy in the present and future.

In the present work, John Moses seeks to stress that the German Empire in the form it had adopted by 1914 was not just a run-of-the-mill rival for trading markets, but represented a threat to the international *status quo* as it then existed and thus to peace. It has become fashionable among some historians of Germany to treat the concept that German history followed a 'special' or 'peculiar' path of development as old hat. In part, this is because the approach of the 1970s 'critical social historians' who followed in the wake of Fritz Fischer and the upheavals of the 1960s in West Germany has been partly replaced by more emphasis on new kinds of cultural history less attentive to social structural approaches or political-constitutional issues. Many theses have been written about middle-class reform movements in *fin-de-siècle* Germany, or about the ways in which German technology, industry or the arts could be seen as embracing 'modernity'. But at the same time, there were persistently pre-modern and anti-democratic features in Imperial Germany: the rigorous discrimination against the Social Democratic labour movement, the major force pressing for democratization of Imperial Germany; the ways in which the large Prussian landowning aristocracy (known as the 'Junkers') were able to entrench themselves behind a virtually unreformable constitution to stave off pressure for structural reforms; and the thorough-going militarism throughout the German middle and upper classes.

John Moses (with the assistance of his former doctoral student Peter Overlack in the sections dealing with naval strategy) seeks to challenge a number of prevailing views on Australia's role in the First World War and especially on Australia's confrontation with the German Empire. No doubt the author is expecting that some of this work will meet with disagreement in some quarters. But history lives from debate: the great

Dutch historian Pieter Geyl famously described history as an 'argument without end'. And there is much to be learned from John Moses' long scholarly journey from Atherton to West Germany and back to Australia again.

Andrew G. Bonnell

Professor in History, University of Queensland.

Editor (History), Australian Journal of Politics and History

Preface

Every work of historical scholarship is to some degree autobiographical. One cannot 'jump over one's own shadow', meaning to escape one's identity, as the Germans say. So then, I make no apology for the use of the first person singular in the prose that follows. As an Australian born in North Queensland 10 June 1930 I grew up at a time precisely when the Anzac movement had struck deep roots throughout society. Returned Diggers from the Great War lived and worked among us in considerable numbers. I saw them marching every Anzac Day. By the time I can remember some of these men would have been only in their forties, and by 1939–40 not few of them had enlisted again. Others, of course, were older and lived through the Second World War as senior citizens.

Since I knew many of them personally and heard some of their stories I quite early received a boy's impression of war and soldiering. What I remember above all was the solidarity of these men who, I appreciated later, had been through the grimmest of battle experiences. All seemed to have been scarred by it in some way. Indeed the effects of *shell shock* were still very evident in a number of cases. None of them could have believed that war was a glorious thing; rather it was the scourge of humanity, but it engendered in these men a deep loyalty to their comrades and to their country. Neither did I at any time hear any of them speak contemptuously of the enemy. I think they appreciated that the Turkish and German soldiers were men like themselves who believed that they had no choice but to fight for their country. That, in any case, was the impression they left on me.

At that time, of course, and through the rest of my school days never did I think I would ever find the means to travel overseas, let alone become a post-graduate student in Germany. The impact of the Great Depression and the isolation of the Atherton Tableland had made any idea of foreign travel illusory to most people except the few among the professional and propertied classes. I remember that our family doctor who ran a small private hospital where I and all my siblings came into the world, took his wife on a trip to England for the Coronation in 1937. That was truly exceptional but it meant that at least some of our community were able to demonstrate that we were all members of the British Empire.

With the passing years, however, circumstances decreed that by 1956 I was actually able to enrol at the University of Queensland from where I was launched into the ever challenging world of learning, first in Brisbane and ultimately in Munich and then in Erlangen where I had completed a doctorate in 1965.

Ever since my return to Australia after those five years post-graduate study in the then West Germany (1961–65) I had tried to pass on to my students what I learned from my German mentors. My main professor in Munich was the notable Roman Catholic liberal opponent of the Third Reich, Franz Schnabel (1887–1966); while in Erlangen next to my supervisor Waldemar Besson, it was the leading Reformation historian Walter Peter Fuchs (1905–97). Understandably in the years I was there the West German professors of modern history had been preoccupied with the question that challenged all intelligent people, namely how the catastrophe of the Third Reich became possible in a supposedly civilised and predominantly Christian nation.

In the 1960s the evidence of the total humiliation of Germany was still overwhelmingly obvious. There were still many streets in all cities in which there were ugly charred allotments where once handsome buildings had stood, recalling the era of 'carpet bombing'. As well, the presence of the United States Army obtruded itself on the population. 'Amis' (pronounced: *am-ees*, that is, Americans) were everywhere. It was also the peak of the Cold War when some twenty Russian divisions were stationed a couple of hour's drive away in East Germany. Then, by October 1962 the Cuban missile crisis had engendered in many West Germans a state of existential anxiety. Could Germany be devastated again, this time in a nuclear holocaust? Novelists such as Hans Helmut Kirst wrote graphically about it.[1]

It was almost two decades since the conclusion of the Second World War and by then the universities had been well and truly de-Nazified. *Vergangenheitsbewältigung,* meaning 'coming to terms with the legacy of the past', had become the intellectual/spiritual/pedagogical challenge of the day. Significantly, my professors had been in no doubt that the two principal factors had been first the political culture of Prussian militarism, and second, related to it, were the circumstances of the founding of the Prusso-German Empire in 1871 by the Prussian minister-president, Otto von Bismarck (1815–98). The 'Iron Chancellor' as he was called, had succeeded in imposing an authoritarian, anti-parliamentary constitution which was in reality a skilfully disguised form of monarchical absolutism. In short, Bismarck had imported into 19th century Germany a constitution which was essentially an up-dated version of that which had operated under the famous war-lord Frederick the Great (r. 1740–86). Bismarck had imposed on modern industrial Germany a constitution that was designed to sustain the social-political relationships of a by-gone agricultural economy. It was bound to become dysfunctional in a modernising industrial society. In 1871 all Germany was covered in a blanket of stifling Prussianism and that meant the permanent militarisation of the country. Added to that the Prussian School of historians at German universities functioned like a Greek chorus applauding the achievements of Prussia in creating the German Empire as quasi a law of history.[2] In short, Prussianism (*Borussismus*) had become the unofficial national German ideology although it was not welcomed enthusiastically by all sections of society. Subjects of different persuasions such as Social Democrats, Liberals and many Roman Catholic were never at ease under the Prussian solution to the German Question. These disgruntled burghers were decried often as Germans of questionable allegiances. In fact, it was considered a form of disloyalty for Germans to embrace political ideas which had their source outside the country. And that meant socialism, liberalism and Roman Catholicism.

In the post-1945 era, certainly by the mid-1960s at the latest, all these issues could be subjected to critical historical examination practically for the first time. Students began at last to learn that the Bismarckian solution to the German question had really been a disaster of world political proportions although many students still clearly resisted this assessment. But there was no gainsaying the fact that the Bismarckian Reich enshrined military virtues as representing the noblest values in society, and these influenced both domestic and foreign policy in seriously divisive ways. In all other respects, though, Germany had become an ultra modern society. With regard to industry, economics, commerce, science, education and culture the Bismarckian-Wilhelmine Reich led the world; only politically had it been saddled with an antediluvian constitution. As a survey of both domestic politics as well as foreign policy during the Second Reich shows, Germany had become a Great Power (*Grossmacht*) of the most volatile character. It was a powder keg that could be ignited at any time as a study of Bismarck's chancellorship illustrates.[3] By the beginning of the 20th century, German foreign policy, expansionist colonial policy (*Kolonialpolitik*) and especially naval policy (*Flottenpolitik*) were the most pressing issues exercising the mind of all European statesmen in varying degrees.

Even in the far flung Pacific region, the dominions of the British Empire were becoming increasingly concerned about the German naval presence at that time. So then, the question of German war aims as comprehended by our then leaders must be squarely confronted and evaluated.[4] A survey of the fledgling Commonwealth's defence awareness shows that there was considerable concern about Anglo-German relations. When the Great War came German policy and military behaviour confirmed all the fears that had been evolving over the previous decades. Prusso-Germany was an empire led by militarists who operated, as the outbreak of war in 1914 illustrated, with complete disregard for international law and humane principles. This was the image of the enemy (*Feindbild*) at that time. The self-perception of the Australian and New Zealand governments and most of the populations was that the dominions had to fight to ward off the possibility of a German victory over the British Empire.

In recent times, however, this self-perception has been subjected to bitter criticism by some historians who, for reasons best known to themselves, would prefer it to have been other wise. They say in effect, 'We do not approve of what happened and disapprove of the decisions taken at that time. They should have been different.' This explains what at the present time, during the centenary of the Great War, a number of writers have focussed on the phenomenon of Anzac with the aim either of explaining or of denigrating it to the current generation. Understandably, in any open society, it is to be expected that authors from a variety of conflicting ideological persuasions will raise their voices in an effort to convince the population to accept their version of events and their relevance to us today.

No one can complain about that because it is everybody's right to say virtually whatever they please and to go into print and tout their views in the market place of ideas. That is democracy at work and is simply the result of the basic right to freedom of expression. There are, of course, some reasonable restrictions on this which, for example, forbid the airing of racist views or other forms of calumny against people for their ethnic origins or religious beliefs. Tolerance, like egalitarianism, is, however, a widely accepted Australian value, indeed, as is sometimes said, it is in our DNA as Australians, past intolerance of Aborigines and 'New Australians', notwithstanding.

In a pluralist society one may expect disagreement among writers over anything and everything that concerns the nation. Anzac is certainly one such topic over which personalities and minds clash. That being so, it is important that there is an on-going dialogue about this uniquely Australasian issue. So in the light of our cultural tolerance a variety of views and opinions will inevitably be encountered. It is recognised that no one would venture into print if s/he did not think s/he had something valuable to add to the discussion no matter how under-researched or ideologically chaotic. However, my academic training, first at the University of Queensland and then in Germany has encouraged me as a historian to 'look over the fence' especially into the German back yard to become aware of other people's perceptions.

In a word, I experienced a comparative dimension through which I became attuned to the crucial differences between my education as an Australian and the cultural formation of Germans of all classes and regions. My relatively long sojourn in Germany was indeed a rare privilege. In Munich with Professor Schnabel I was made more acutely aware of the unique political-pedagogic influence that history professors once exerted on their students and through them as future teachers themselves, on the education of school children.

Schnabel understood very well that the rise in the 19th century of the Prussian school of historians had functioned to inculcate the notion that Germans of all regions of the country should accept the 'Prussian solution to the German question' and to revere Otto von Bismarck as founder of the new Reich which he led as Chancellor from 1871 until his dismissal by the Kaiser, Wilhelm II, in 1890. Bismarck's administration, however, had bequeathed an undeniably controversial legacy to the nation. First, he had imposed a constitution on the new federation which prioritised Prussia's political culture within the leadership of the Reich. In a word, as already stressed, he had *Prussianised* Germany. That meant, although the Kaiser was called a constitutional monarch Bismarck's constitution allowed him to choose the national government which was responsible solely to him and not to the elected lower house, the Reichstag. In short, the *Kaiser* who as Emperor of Germany and King of Prussia, continued virtually as a constitutionally disguised absolute monarch and war lord who had at his disposal a highly trained army to enforce his will both domestically and externally.

So, from Franz Schnabel I learned what genuine militarism really was. It had the most deleterious effects on the German people who were constitutionally barred from replacing their militaristic leaders with democratically minded statesmen, and of these, there was no shortage. In a real sense the Reich government was *de facto* an instrument of the Prussian army and the aristocratic capitalist classes that supported it. As well, opinion makers such as the professors of history at the time never tired of teaching their students about the Prusso-German mission to the world.

For this reason it is untenable in any explanation of world politics in the 19th and 20th centuries to ignore the blatantly anti-democratic character of the Bismarckian-Wilhelmine Reich. It made its first bid for world domination (*Weltherrschaft*) in the early 20th century, but when that failed, tried it again only 35 years later with the *furor teutonicus* of Nazi Germany. These herculean efforts to re-shape the world in a Prusso-German image had to provoke a response in particular from the democratic Anglo-Saxon world of which both Australia and New Zealand were part. The British Empire which had developed into the Commonwealth of self-governing, independent nations had become what the Germans called, a *Kriegsverein*. That is incidentally a word like *Zollverein* which means 'customs union' and in trade terms that is what the British Commonwealth also used to be. And in times of international crises which threatened the security of the Commonwealth, it also became a *Kriegsverein*, meaning an *ad hoc* association of sovereign states who joined forces to resist a common enemy. That, in a word, sums up why our leaders well before 1914 had decided to declare solidarity with the British Empire in order to resist the expansionist ambitions of the German Empire. On this subject there is no shortage of scholarly studies.

More recently it has been said that had the world been constituted differently, Australia and New Zealand would never have felt obliged to be involved in any wars at all. Our natural preference was for a peaceful planet on which, as it says in the Bible, the nations had turned their 'spears into pruning hooks and their swords into ploughshares and not learn war any more'. These sentiments were expressed in at least two books of the Old Testament and are thus of great antiquity. Sadly, however, that state of international affairs has never been attained and so the world is still waiting for universal peace. But instead of peace, nations have repeatedly engaged in conflict and conquest as the late medieval Italian scholar, Niccolo Machiavelli (1469–1573) had described in his famous tract for rulers, *The Prince*. He observed that war was endemic to the human condition.

The rulers of all nations believed in the necessity of armed force both to subjugate internal opposition to the rule of the princely house on the one hand and to defend the country from potential invaders on the other. The prince was automatically a warrior; it was his vocation. And still today, in order to be able to assert the right to exist, each sovereign State regardless of its system of government is obliged to maintain the most efficient armed forces it can afford.

That said, understanding the world has proved curiously difficult for not a few Australians and New Zealanders because they have long laboured under the illusion that distance from the world's flash points somehow ensured that we would not be affected by other nations' conflicts. The Great Powers and their disputes were a long way off, hence there was no reason to become involved. This attitude will of course change if it has not already done so in the mind of many especially those who remember the Japanese threat to our security 1940–45. But now there are other Great Powers and 'rogue states' such as North Korea who by reason of geography and political culture have changed the foreign policy equation especially for countries of the Asia-Pacific region. And the Peoples' Republic of China looms as a Great Power which only acknowledges international law when it suits her.[5]

The thought of Australia exerting a hegemony in the South-Pacific is rarely expressed. Nevertheless, by virtue of her resources and geographical location she quasi automatically fulfils that role in a restricted way. She has, with some notable exceptions, respected the aspirations of former colonial peoples to attain to and maintain their own sovereignty.[6] And this stance post 1945 has on occasions led to military involvement in such places as Malaysia, East Timor, the Solomon Islands and Iraq, Iran and Afghanistan. But these forays abroad have been essentially peace-keeping exercises, and they have proved to be necessary and in the long term beneficial to the local communities although there are some citizens who do not share this view. For this reason alone, however, Australia and New Zealand maintain armed forces. The world is a dangerous place because of the persistent warlord-ism of some countries which often derives, apart from secular nationalism, also from religious fanaticism. It was extremely dangerous in 1914, indeed existentially so.

This book will show why the ability to stand up and fight when national security is challenged, is still an urgent necessity. Nations driven by religious fanaticism of whatever provenance, like totalitarian dictatorships, will never leave the world in peace until they have imposed their will on all free nations or have been persuaded to abandon their expansionist ambitions. It ought not to be forgotten that fascism and totalitarian communism are forms of state religion. Australia and New Zealand as successor states to the British Empire have evolved as responsible peace-promoting middle powers. These two nations have developed their own unique ideological ethos at the core of which is the dedication to freedom and the rule of law. May it remain so.

Introduction

One of the surest ways to court defeat in sport or war, in the friendliest or the most deadly competition, is to undervalue the strength of our opponent. [...] Even from the most materialistic of motives it is necessary for us to discover what resources the enemy possesses ...

— Professor William Alexander Osborn,
'Germany's Intellectual Strength and Weakness' in
Public Lectures on the War

What One Needs to Understand

1. History is about comprehending the past and how it has affected the present. We cannot change the past but we can try to find out as far as humanly possible, *how it actually was* (von Ranke).

2. For this reason one must investigate the past on its own terms and not apply the values of today to the people of decades and centuries ago, otherwise one falls victim to the fallacy of *presentism*.

3. We need also at the same time to remember that we all view the past through the lens of our own formation, that is one's family up-bringing, one's political allegiance and one's church and school experience, and the like. This awareness needs to inform all our assessments and judgments about the past. In short, while being conscious of all this baggage, we strive for as

much objectivity and impartiality as possible. Again, one-sided interpretations of the past may not be used as a party-political weapon to promote a present-day agenda.

Our aim is to try to understand the war-aims of an enemy which, in 1914, was out to inflict the greatest possible damage on *all* British possessions. Imperial Germany showed no interest whatsoever in collaborating with other Powers in securing peace for the long-term. This was well understood by our political leaders at the time. Consequently, appropriate defensive measures had to be taken. All national policy makers as well as the general public were obliged to reflect why such desperate and costly steps were necessary, as they are at the present time. Prior to the First World War, a famous English journalist and Labour politician named Norman Angell (1872–1967) wrote a remarkable book entitled *The Great Illusion* in which he argued that nations would shrink back from war because of the cost in men and materiel, *even to the victor*.[1] Of course, he did not argue that such reflections would rule out the possibility of war entirely because the decision-making process is not always rational. Nations are composed of people of differing cultures and among these there are those who harbour delusions of imperialist grandeur and these may indeed outweigh all rational reflections about the cost of war. Such delusions may be the consequence of nationalistic ideology or a religious sense of mission to impose a putatively superior culture on backward or culturally different foreign neighbours. But while they are essentially delusions they are still very effective and dangerous since they motivate political will. This book argues that in order to understand the 'seminal catastrophe of the twentieth century' (George F. Kennan) one needs to explore especially the inner motivation of the Prusso-German *Machtelite* (power elite). In a word, we must ask from where did the ruling classes derive their ideas of nationhood? What, indeed, was the driving force behind their seemingly relentless will to expand at the expense of neighbouring nations both small and great?

As indicated, I have learned, particularly at German universities, to understand the discipline of history as a so-called *Geisteswissenschaft*, that is literally a 'mental science' as opposed to natural sciences like physics and chemistry. It means simply that the practice of history as a discipline has to be rigorous; sources have to be verified; no guess work is permitted and the narrative derived from the facts has to be 'objective', free from emotion or propaganda. One had to try as far as humanly possible, to show 'how it actually was', as Leopold von Ranke had memorably written. Since then, there has been considerable reflection on von Ranke's influence on the discipline, and of course, it is now widely accepted that there can be no such thing as a *true* re-creation of the past 'how it actually was' because inevitably the personal view point and value system of the writer will obtrude themselves into the narrative.[2]

Nevertheless, that is not a licence to draw absurd or unsupportable conclusions from the evidence, in short to the force the data into a Procrustean bed of one's personal preferences. Neither may one disregard sources that do not support the argument one prefers in order to make a case for one's own firmly held convictions. Indeed, one must keep oneself out of the story and grasp one's role as a historian as a dispassionate communicator. However, in highly emotion-charged topics such as 'war-guilt' even the most even-tempered scholars find it extremely difficult to remain *au-dessus de la mêlée*. There often occurs a slippage between the objective ideal on the one hand and on the other hand the desire to convert the reader to one's own point of view. Consequently, it is a case of *caveat emptor*, buyer beware, when trying to digest historical narratives.

It has to be conceded, then, that clinical objectivity is beyond the capacities of human beings to achieve. An individual's outlook on the world, one's intellectual/spiritual formation or world view derives from a range of influences and these will impinge on what and how one writes. In one's interaction with colleagues and fellow citizens generally one has always to bear in mind that everyone is different in varying degrees and one must take these differences into account in assessing one's relationships. For example, one may not be over hasty in one's judgements of others because there may be factors, the existence of which one is unaware. It is always wiser to reserve judgement, to give people the benefit of the doubt and to make allowances for their situation.

In this context it must be observed that in spite of the increasing ethnic diversity evident throughout the Australian community during the 20th and 21st centuries the political culture was/is that of the British Empire. If one was born well before the Second World War one grew up in a vigorous parliamentary democracy in which equality before the law was constitutionally enshrined and loyalty to the house of Windsor was a given. I do recall, however, that I knew families of Irish-Roman Catholic origin who clearly were resentful of British political culture at the time. They nevertheless chose to participate in it in order to advance their own particular agendas.

As a result, one became aware at an early age of sectarianism, for example, and of party-political differences. But if asked to nominate the abiding memories of those pre-World War II years it would have to be the annual Anzac Day march. The reason is that on these occasions, returned service men and women from the Great War of 1914–18 were still marching, and children as Scouts, Guides, Cubs or Brownies marched with them. The march went up the main street accompanied by the town brass band, finishing at the war memorial in the middle of town where there was a plinth on top of which was/is the life-sized statue of a defiant digger, actually in combat.[3]

The names of the fallen from the district are inscribed on marble plaques, now up-dated with those from later conflicts. When the assembled marchers and citizens gathered at the war memorial, the ensuing ceremony included speeches by local municipal dignitaries and padres representing the Church of England, the Presbyterian and Methodist Churches. Only Roman Catholic clergy were absent because of the ban imposed by the Papacy at that time which prohibited 'Catholics' from participation at public events where prayers might be said by heretical and schismatic Protestant 'ministers', or when hymns of non-Roman provenance might be sung. Times have changed because Roman Catholic padres certainly now take part in Anzac Day services.

4

The question to ask is why did people think it was important to be part of such an event? The answer was supplied in the speeches made by the aforementioned dignitaries. Our soldiers fought and died for *God, King and Empire*, that is for British freedoms. That was the phrase used in the 1930s and it still resonates in my ears as it was often enunciated by padres speaking in all the brogues then present among us, namely educated southern (Oxford) English, Scottish, Welsh as well as educated and broad Australian. In this way we became very aware of the mixed composition of our community but also of the reasons for the great and costly conflict in which we as an outpost of Empire had been so sacrificially involved. All the speakers at that time were clearly aware of the fact that had the British Empire not prevailed against the German Empire in 1914–18, our freedoms would have been jeopardised. Consequently, there was no argument; one had to stand up for and support the imperial cause because if the mother country had gone under it was only a matter of time when a triumphant, anti-democratic Prussianism would have exerted its oppressive influence on our life. Germany certainly had the means and the will to do so, provided she had been successful in executing her ambitious war-aims program.

This appraisal was not uncontested; there were people of decidedly left-leaning and /or Irish nationalist persuasion who opposed supporting the war effort. All this emerged especially in the two great Conscription debates as well as in movements decidedly hostile to the imperial connection.[4] Indeed, in the light of our observations about the ethnic composition of Australian society, it was not surprising that there would have been conflicting interpretations of our participation in the Great War. It is argued here, however, that an in-depth knowledge of Prussianism is essential to enable one to come to a satisfactory explanation of the kind of political culture that made two world wars possible. One is at a distinct disadvantage if one is, as the Germans archly phrase it, 'unprejudiced by any expert knowledge of the subject'.[5] In short, before one can make a comment, one needs to be aware of what German war aims were and how they were perceived by people living in the overseas Dominions of the British Empire. Otherwise any scholarly dialogue is frustrated from the outset.[6] In a word, those writers who venture to discuss the Anzac tradition without a clear appreciation of the implications of *Weltpolitik* will be unable to say anything that will further our understanding.

It will surely not be surprising that already prior to 1914 there were informed Australian commentators on world affairs who had in particular first-hand experience of imperial Germany.[7] Contrary to what commentators such as the German-Australian Dr Gerhard Fischer has written, both Australian academics and politicians were well informed about the political culture of the Kaiser's Germany and to what extent it differed from British political culture and was thus inimical to everything that the Australasian Dominions stood for.[8] On this subject many leading Australian politicians and academics had made extensive comment. Their self-perception was that they had an obligation by virtue of their knowledge of world affairs to inform the wider community. This they did in public lectures and articles in the daily press. As well, there were Australian chapters of the *Round Table* in all State capitals which consisted of discreet groups of men in high positions throughout the country who made it their business to follow the course of international relations and make recommendations to the Commonwealth government on questions of national security. It is untenable to believe that the government was composed of men subservient to bureaucrats in London. It so happened that most Australian academics and public servants as well as the Anglican bishops were very well informed about the world situation and the Dominions' role in it.[9] Professor Stuart Macintyre of the University of Melbourne emphasizes this in the 1994 biographical study of his distinguished predecessor in the chair of history there, namely the notable Ernest Scott (1867–1939). Macintyre makes the point very strongly, as I had done in 1991 regarding Professor George Arnold Wood at Sydney University, that leading historians and other academics who were knowledgeable about the power politics of the day perceived an obligation to inform both the federal government and the general public about the impact that great power rivalries was having on the Dominions. These men were sufficiently well educated to realise that the 'tyranny of distance' in the age of great navies was no defence against a determined hostile Great Power bent on despoiling the British Empire.

The present argument is straight forward enough: when Imperial Germany made her bid for world power in 1914 the other Powers, Britain, France, Russia and finally the United States of America were directly threatened. There was no choice but to oppose the 'Prussian Menace' with all the military and naval resources that could be deployed. It represented an ideology totally inimical to the liberal West. Prussianism was brutally anti-labour, anti-parliamentarism, racist (anti-Semitic) and militaristic. It should be borne in mind that it was precisely because of these characteristics and the possibility that imperial Germany could defeat the Western parliamentary nations of Britain and France that the United States was finally persuaded that she, too, after some hesitation, had no choice but to do her utmost to oppose Prusso-German war aims in order, in the words of President Woodrow Wilson, 'to make the world safe for democracy.'[10] This knowledge should at least heighten awareness of the reasons why the Pacific Dominions of the then British Empire became so sacrificially involved in the Great War of 1914 which, as Professor Ernest Scott phrased it, was 'the pivotal event' in Australian history.[11]

Finally, it is imperative that Australian students understand the Prusso-German *self-perception*. This means simply to become aware of how the German intellectual community (*Bildungsbürgertum*) in general believed their nation should behave with regard to the rest of Europe and the world. In short, we need to comprehend what the Germans called their *Sendungsbewusstsein*, their sense of mission. And to do this one must come to grips with Prusso-German notions about the nature of the State, of government and especially of the role of the military in defending and promoting what the Germans called their *Kultur*.

The latter concept is, essentially, what distinguished Germans from other Europeans. It was cultural nationalism taken to the highest philosophical level, and on this subject there exists a considerable literature. Establishing what made the German a special kind of European exercised the mind of leading German historians, theologians and philosophers especially from the time of the French Revolution right through the 19th and into the 20th century when under the National Socialist dictatorship it issued into the most grotesque form of racism in human history. So the question of how a great cultural nation could descend into the abyss of such barbarism as was perpetrated by the State and the army during both the Great War and the Third Reich is one of the most challenging issues confronting both historical and theological scholarship ever since the end of the Second World War.

All this comes under the heading of 'the continuity thesis' in German history and it is centrally relevant to our topic which is focussed on understanding the nature of the enemy. And since this book is intended primarily for an Australasian audience, it begins with a chapter that explains the origins of the practice of solemn commemoration of the fallen that began as a consequence of the losses incurred by our forces engaged as part of the British Empire's war effort against imperial Germany and her allies, chiefly the Ottoman Empire. Consequently, after the first question of civil or civic religion, specifically the origins and nature of Anzac commemoration has been dealt with, there follows a chapter which sketches the formation of the Prusso-German Empire in order to illustrate its 'peculiarity' in comparison, especially with the Anglo-Saxon West.

The third chapter draws attention to the existence of the German intelligence gathering network in Australasia in order to show that it is absurd to imagine that the Australasian part of the British Empire was somehow by virtue of its remoteness from Europe invulnerable to aggression. This is followed by a chapter which elaborates on Prusso-German political culture while chapter five investigates the German ideology of *Historicism* and its political implications. Chapter six compares German and Australian perceptions of war while chapter seven investigates how the Australian academic community assessed the need to be involved in the titanic struggle with imperial Germany. There then follow chapters by Dr Peter Overlack on the role assigned to the German cruiser squadron in the Pacific in the event of war between Germany and the British Empire. His in-depth investigation of the imperial German naval archives has enabled him to reconstruct a phase of naval history that illustrates the long-term German war aims in the Pacific, and in particular the Australian government's response to them. His unique ability to investigate the official German archival sources here allows Australians for the very first time really to appreciate the danger the fledgling Commonwealth had to face in 1914–18.

The Appendices combine five items containing relevant information and comment. The first summarises German war-aims 1914–18 and reproduces the text of the 'September Program'. The second Appendix gives a translation of an account of the events leading to the German decision to urge Austria to attack Serbia. This was composed by Dr Bernd Schulte of Hamburg based on the most recent archival research. Appendix 3 reproduces a pamphlet composed in March 1915 by a leading member of the Australian chapter of the *Round Table*, Archbishop St Clair Donaldson of Brisbane on why it was essential to combat German expansionism. Appendix 4 provides a list of both the German and Australian warships operating in the Pacific by August 1914. And finally the portraits of those German politicians and historians who have both criticised German militarism and the decision for war in 1914, that is *Der Flucht nach vorne*, meaning 'flight into war'.

Finally, what do we expect to learn from the above? In the first instance it is the fact that each nation has been formed by its peculiar historical experience and that this is an educative process that imparts to the nation its unique and inimitable characteristics. Each people is consequently also imbued with the will first to preserve its cultural identity; some will try to impose their putatively superior civilisation on weaker nations in the conviction that their culture (*Kultur*) is really better for the world. That is, of course, *imperialism*. But not all imperialisms are the same. The contrast, say, between the ideal manifestation of British imperialism and that of the Germans is instructive. Agents of both, of course, committed atrocities against their subject peoples such as the Amritsar riots in India and the Irish troubles for the British while for the Germans their genocidal policies in S.W. Africa (Namibia) and in Tanganyika are significant examples.

However, in the British case these outrages were roundly condemned by liberal and Christian elements while for the most part bourgeois Germans endorsed the project of forcibly imposing on the so-called *Naturvölker* (native peoples) the superior culture of the *Kulturnation,* Germany. Social Democrats, Roman Catholics (Centre Party) and progressive liberals certainly condemned all this in the Reichstag. And in 1907 the government responded by appointing a distinguished civilian, Dr Bernhard Dernburg (1865–1937), to lead the Colonial Office and oversee reforms.

Other imperial powers, past and present, operate(d) in similar ways. Once an imperial power subdues a weaker nation the complex process which results from the clash of cultures begins to have a *Wechselwirkung,* meaning that neither culture can remain as it was; both the invader and the invaded undergo learning experiences that result in deep-seated changes, some not entirely unwelcome. One thing is clear: the nations are still a long way from living in harmony with each other because the problem of religious-cultural friction appears ineradicable, at least for the foreseeable future.

CHAPTER 1

'Lest we Forget' – Christianity and Australian Culture

It should not surprise the attentive reader and politically aware citizen that there is something undeniably religious about Anzac Day ceremonies. It has to do with 'civil' or 'civic' religion which is a concept used to describe solemn public events in the history of the nation. These are acts of commemoration and they occur in all nations regardless of their historically dominant religious culture. They may or may not be officially endorsed by the religious denominations but whether the ceremonies are held within or outside a sacred building, they are nevertheless examples of civic religion. Anzac Day is the major Australasian manifestation. In Britain it is Armistice Day, 11 November. In France and elsewhere on the European Continent the war dead are commemorated on the Church's All Souls' Day, 2 November. There the link with the Christian faith is, of course, explicit. And when one attends the dawn service, for example, at the Australian War Memorial in Canberra the religious character of the ceremony is overwhelming. First of all there are padres present from the main stream churches, namely Roman Catholic, Anglican and Uniting Churches, who take turns in leading the prayers and there is always the singing of hymns of at least theistic content. That is to say there is a general acknowledgement of the existence of a deity who may or may not be the holy and undivided Trinity of Christianity but simply the Creator God, the author of the universe.

What is very evident to the perceptive observer at all Anzac Day ceremonies is that the citizens who attend them are united in some form of devotion which presumably in the first instance is to the memory of those who have paid the supreme sacrifice in the service of their country. People who have lost their kinsfolk in war as well as citizens generally come out on Anzac Day to declare their solidarity with the nation. So it is a patriotic event which unites citizens beyond their different religious denominational beliefs for one day of remembrance. The mantra 'Lest we forget' sums it up. These words originated in a hymn composed by Rudyard Kipling in 1897 called the 'Recessional' and this hymn is invariably sung on Anzac Day. Of course, Kipling in that poem was not thinking of the fallen in battle but of the evanescent and temporary nature of imperial power. The full text rewards closer study. In short, the words, 'lest we forget' have been creatively misappropriated to mean something different, namely the sacrifices made in the service of one's country.

In the planning of the Day, the first Anzac Day Commemoration Committee (ADCC) in Australia was the one that was inaugurated in Brisbane at a public meeting on 10 January 1916 in the city's Exhibition Hall, presided over by the then state governor Sir Henry Goold Adams and the Premier the Honourable T. J. Ryan (see the photo between pp. 200–1). That is the event which laid the foundation for the Anzac Day as we now know it. The meeting unanimously elected Canon David John Garland to be its secretary because of his high profile as a very public-spirited Anglican priest in Queensland who had an established reputation for getting things of national or municipal importance done with efficiency and aplomb.

The Brisbane committee was of course only one of many such committees throughout the Commonwealth who had convened more or less spontaneously with a view to establishing a day of commemoration. Understandably, very soon after the news of the Gallipoli landing and its aftermath had reached Australia the press began to publish information and commentary about the significance of what was happening. This unleashed a variety of responses.

The news of the fallen was received in the community with a mixture of shock and pride, especially after the reports of the British journalist Ellis Ashmead Bartlett had been digested. The reports by Charles Bean had been delayed by Army censorship and were only released later.[1] Paradoxically there was both sadness and jubilation. Consequently, in a number of cities celebration committees, driven by pride in the Anzac's achievements were formed to mark the event. The result was that there developed a variety of forms of celebration such as sports days, concerts and other forms of public entertainment. In the Churches, on the other hand, particularly in the Church of England, where bishops and clergy were more mindful of the sacrifice of young lives in defence of the Empire, there began a series of commemorative services in all cathedrals throughout the country. The very first one recorded was a Requiem Eucharist (Mass), held in St John's Cathedral Brisbane on 10 June 1915 celebrated by the Archbishop St Clair Donaldson himself. The Service Register documents that it was attended by some 600 mourners on a Thursday morning and these included the State Governor as well as the consuls of both France and Russia, their presence making it a state occasion.

It should not go unobserved that of all the Anglican dioceses in Australia, that of Brisbane and indeed the entire province of Queensland, consisting of five dioceses at that time, was defined by its alignment with the Anglo-Catholic or High Church branch of the Church, a tradition that had no Protestant reservations about services commemorating the dead. The Roman Catholics on the other hand, being predominantly led by a hierarchy originating from Ireland, was still pre-occupied with the 'troubles' being experienced there over English rule to be overly concerned with the great imperialist struggle between the British and German Empires. It found initially little resonance among them. This, of course, was to change. But the fact is that solemn Anzac commemoration was led by the Anglican Church. And Canon Garland from his status as secretary of the Brisbane ADCC was determined to advocate his concept of commemoration throughout both the Commonwealth and New Zealand. In our sister Dominion Canon Garland had already become very well known throughout the length and breadth of the country due to his secondment (1912–15) to the New Zealand bishops for the purpose of leading a campaign in the community to amend the NZ Education Act to allow Bible Study in government schools. The specific cultural-educational reasons for this will be explained below.

Canon Garland (1864–1939) in his new role as secretary of the Queensland ADCC, since January 1916, quickly began an energetic public relations exercise to promulgate his ideas for a solemn commemoration of the fallen at Gallipoli. It was a campaign that lasted from 1916 until 1930 during which time Canon Garland assiduously lobbied Federal and State premiers as well as municipal officials throughout both Dominions advocating the Brisbane form of solemn commemoration. Step by step each state following the New Zealand example passed legislation establishing Anzac Day as a solemn day of commemoration. The passage of the legislation in New Zealand was, of course, relatively straight forward since there was only one government concerned, whereas in the Australian Federation there were seven jurisdictions to bring into line, that is the six States and the Commonwealth. Consequently, the achievement of relatively uniform commemoration service in each took longer.

Nevertheless, Canon Garland worked so tirelessly from the beginning in Brisbane that he became known as the 'Architect of Anzac Day'. What is also noteworthy is that the proposal of the date 25 April, the day of the landing to the Brisbane ADCC came from Mr Thomas Augustine Ryan, not to be confused with the then state Premier Thomas Joseph Ryan. Mr T. A. Ryan was a prominent Brisbane auctioneer who had a son fighting in the Dardanelles who thankfully survived. In this regard Mr Ryan had resolved the question of what was the most appropriate date for the commemoration.

As will be obvious from noting the composition in the surviving group photograph above of the Brisbane ADCC in 1921 Church leaders clearly predominated. The Anglican and Roman Catholic Archbishops are readily recognisable seated in the front row with Canon Garland standing on the extreme left of the picture. The other members include former chaplains from all denominations as well as army officers and municipal leaders. Given the presence of high-profile representatives of all denominations it was indeed a striking example of early ecumenism. The hitherto competing and theologically incompatible denominations are seen here collaborating in the common cause of remembrance of the fallen. Remarkable is the fact that all these churchmen as well as army personnel deferred to Canon Garland's well-known organisational ability as well as his negotiating skills and above all to his knowledge of liturgy. This is of key importance. A leader was needed who understood how a solemn public service of commemoration should be appropriately organised and performed. Providentially, he appeared in the form of a man who had been born in Dublin into the Church of Ireland. So what is the Church of Ireland? While most Irish people were baptised and confirmed members of the Roman Catholic Church there existed and exists a much smaller number of Irish people who are either members of the Presbyterian Church or the Anglican Church in Ireland. The latter is still called the Church of Ireland in full communion with the Church of England. Strong cultural links are to be found in places one least expects.

The history of the Church of Ireland is an eventful one indeed. The main reason was that in the 19ᵗʰ century when all of Ireland was legally part of Great Britain Parliament voted to reduce the number of Anglican bishoprics from 22 to 12 on grounds of redundancy. The move unleashed a vigorous protest in which leading Oxford theologians contested the right of the secular government to interfere with the organisation of the historic Church. The closures nevertheless proceeded. Indeed, the Church of Ireland continued to experience other internal difficulties mainly because of the strong Calvinist dogmatism of many of its adherents who were traditionally opposed to broad and/or high church Anglicanism. It was also influenced to a great extent by *Orange-ism*, namely the very strong Irish Protestant movement that originated in the ill-conceived campaign of William of Orange to assert Protestantism over Popery in Ireland. And to this day Irish history continues to be dominated by the virulence of the conflict between Protestantism and Roman Catholicism as is evidenced in the frequent 'troubles' experienced in Ulster (Northern Ireland) in recent times. Orange-ism, however, spread throughout the world wherever Irish people have migrated, and there are Orange Lodges to be found in all these countries such as in the British Commonwealth and the United States of America.

The point of mentioning this at all is that Canon David John Garland grew up in Dublin strongly influenced by Orange-ism. This meant that in his youth he had imbibed all the teaching about history and theology that distinguished and plagued the domestic life of the Church of Ireland. This educational experience was of central significance for his biography. In short, David John Garland was a very Protestant Anglican Irishman brought up in the Orange tradition when he migrated to Queensland in 1884 and settled initially in Toowoomba where he found work in a law firm and became a member of the Masonic Lodge. However, providentially, the Anglican Church he attended, was that of St James', the second parish of that city. It was then under the incumbency of one Thomas Jones, a priest of determined Anglo-Catholic persuasion and a man of energetic entrepreneurial temperament.

It was certainly providential that the young Garland made this encounter because such was the character of 'Tommy' Jones (as he was always known) that he was able to convert the Dublin immigrant from his Orange influenced Biblical fundamentalism to becoming a fervent, convinced and crusading Anglo-Catholic. Jones persuaded Garland that the Church to be truly Catholic did not require submission to the See of Rome whose Bishop was simply the same as any other foreign Bishop. What made a Church Catholic was the Apostolic Succession of Bishops which the Church of England carefully retained, as well as the Biblical sacraments of Baptism and the Eucharist. In addition, it was/is an Anglican tenet to comprehend the Bible as containing all that was necessary for salvation. That in a nutshell was what the Church of England stood for, and David John Garland in Toowoomba under the guidance of 'Tommy' Jones, became a vigorous champion of Catholic Anglicanism which understood itself as the progressive and dynamic element of the Church. As well, of course, the Church of England at that time in the Antipodean colonies was the largest Church, and it was also the Church of the most powerful Empire the world had ever seen. 'Tommy' Jones, must be regarded, then, as the most significant personage in Garland's biography. It was he who convinced the young Garland that he had a vocation to the priesthood. The passionate young Irishman needed to be personally convinced. His undoubted knowledge of Holy Scripture was a promising start, albeit from a very Protestant or fundamentalist standpoint. It remained for 'Tommy' Jones to educate him in the history and mission of the Church. With Jones' guidance, then, David John Garland became a *catechist*, that is a lay teacher in the parish, and was prepared for ordination by Jones as was the practice in the days before theological colleges. Garland was duly made deacon in Grafton in 1889 and served in country parishes in that diocese until he moved to Perth, WA in 1892 where he was ordained priest. Garland served in the West with distinction where he proved to be a clergyman of great administrative and entrepreneurial skill, quickly gaining advancement. Of great significance, however, was his acquisition of an army chaplain's posting at the time of the Boer war when he ministered to troops encamped and training in Fremantle before embarkation to South Africa (see the photo between pp. 200–1). Here Garland manifested his deep pastoral concern for recruits which he retained all his life, serving actively as he did in the Middle East on a special chaplain's licence for almost two years from late 1917.

If this background is not understood, making sense of the Anzac ceremonial that was devised by Canon Garland will be difficult. The point is that although the Gallipoli campaign inspired many models of celebration or commemoration throughout Australia, it was the one devised by Canon Garland in collaboration with the ADCC which was finally officially adopted or adapted by all states, the Commonwealth and New Zealand. The central element in all this which drove Garland and most other chaplains who served in the AIF during the Great War was the conviction that the young men who fell in the service of the imperial cause had died defending Christian values. They were modern day crusaders against the scourge of Prussianism. The British Empire, as many at the time were convinced, stood for genuinely Christian values against the putatively pagan values of the German Empire. And to this conviction many sermons from the Anglican hierarchy throughout the Empire bore eloquent witness. Indeed, for all the British-based churches at that time the war was a crusade against the ruthlessness of Prussianism symbolised by the vain glorious Kaiser (Wilhelm) William II.[2] And here we are challenged to understand something which the secular mind has difficulty in comprehending, namely the fact that nations are conceived of as essentially spiritual entities or at least driven by a spirit of patriotism. This does not exclude the commercial element. If nations perceive that their economic existence is threatened, and /or, importantly, as in the case of imperial Germany where their future development is obstructed, they will resort to warfare. That is the lesson of history.

As well, in all countries the armed forces are honoured and the fallen remembered. This universal phenomenon of solemn remembrance of the members of the national armed forces who have died in defending the nation may, of course, take different forms from country to country depending on national traditions. The German-Jewish scholar George Lachman Mosse made a perceptive analysis of this in several studies in which he pointed out that the general commemoration of the nations' war dead is a phenomenon that became fashionable only as a consequence of the French revolutionary wars when for the first time volunteer soldiers, that is citizens, formed an army to fight for the cause of the nation, in short to secure liberty, equality and fraternity.[3] This was a consequence of the nationalism of the masses. For the first time in history, the common man had a fatherland worth fighting for because in it he had rights in the modern sense. Prior to that armies were manned by conscripts raised by an absolute monarch of paid mercenaries. Mosse's point was that once absolutist monarchs were disposed of and replaced by democratically elected, parliamentary governments the character of the State had changed radically. The winning of citizenship gave people for the first time a stake in their own country and its values. Of course, Napoleon Bonaparte exploited this by his *Levée en masse*, that is by requisitioning able bodied men to fight in his campaigns of conquest.

In Australasia and other parts of the British Empire, the recruitment of troops for defence purposes was left to volunteers. Conscription did not occur until the Second World War when the Japanese invasion seemed a distinct possibility and so Australian troops both conscripts and volunteers fought in Malaya, the Dutch East Indies and New Guinea. Australian soldiers who fought in the First World War were all volunteers. The two conscription referenda (1916 and 1917) were both lost. And here is a point in our narrative to explain why the Pacific Dominions became involved in the Great War, so named by the Germans simply because it means the big war, that is *Der grosse Krieg*. The term is only a description of the extent of the conflict as it involved the entire British Empire as well those of France and of Russia, plus, on the enemy side, the Austro-Hungarian Empire and then the Ottoman Empire. It was not a mere trade war as some of its Australian opponents affected to believe, but an existential conflict in which the German war-aims prioritised the destruction of the British Empire as well as those of France and Russia. That is why the Kaiser and his naval advisers, led by Grand Admiral Alfred von Tirpitz (1849–1930) wanted to build a first-class navy that could threaten the Royal Navy in the North Sea and directly attack British coastal cities. This ambitious aim was in reality beyond the reach of the Germans as the famous naval battle of Jutland (called in German, *Skaggerak*) 31 May to 1 June 1916 was to demonstrate. That great naval contest ended effectively in a draw, after which the German navy never ventured out again to engage the Royal Navy in another set battle. Instead reliance was then placed largely in unrestricted submarine warfare which in the end was a bad decision since it guaranteed Germany's ultimate defeat by provoking the United States' entry into the war on the side of the British and French.

As Australian politicians and commentators well knew at the time, had the German war-aim against Britain succeeded, namely to eliminate the Royal Navy and threaten British coastal cities, it would have been just a matter of time before the overseas Dominions were placed under political pressure by a victorious imperial Germany. As my collaborator in this book, Australian historian, Dr Peter Overlack, in numerous research articles, has demonstrated, the German navy had been building up its bases in the Pacific in the region to enable its cruiser squadron (*das Ostasiatische Geschwader*) under Vice Admiral Count Maximillian von Spee (1861–1914) for the purpose of attacking shipping plying between Australia and New Zealand to Britain.[4] And that included the intention as well to destroy harbour installations. These actions had been long planned prior to the war and were based on intelligence gathered by a network of German operatives who were controlled out of the various German consulates in all capital cities.

Since the Commonwealth security police had been carrying out surveillance on these operatives for some time they were quickly arrested and interned on the outbreak of war. It is therefore quite irresponsible of those Australian historians and publicists who argue that this country was in no danger from imperial Germany 1914–18.[5] There was indeed a long-standing imperial German threat to the security of the Australasian Dominions, first indirectly had the Germans succeeded in destroying the Royal Navy and, secondly, directly had the German cruiser squadron in the Pacific been able to carry out its war plans in 1914. The argument that Australia and New Zealand were too remote from the flash points of Europe and were therefore never going to be endangered by Germany and hence had no stake in the Great War is consequently untenable.

It should, therefore, be noted that there is an on-going struggle among Australian historians and publicists to dominate the historical-political consciousness of citizens. The arguments of the ill-informed and ideologically biased who seem only to believe what they want to believe need to be countered by conscientious scholarship. It has, therefore, to be thoroughly understood, that historiography is an on-going argument among scholars who compete in the market-place of ideas for the hearts and minds of the reading public. As has often been said, Australia and New Zealand are free countries in which everyone is entitled to publish his or her views without fear or favour. The number of divergent intellectual universes which people in open societies inhabit is legion. Achieving reciprocal understanding among them is naturally never going to be easy.

This means, however, that everyone has to accept critical challenges to their findings and to their philosophy of history. Indeed, to re-iterate, history is pre-eminently an ideologically driven discipline. Each author is entitled to her views provided the integrity of others is not maligned. For example, it is no secret that a number of writers on the subject of Anzac commemoration are deeply hostile to the very idea. That is their perfect right, but it is suggested here that their hostility derives from an impoverished comprehension of the essentially civil religious aspect of Anzac commemoration. This means that they are insufficiently aware of the Christian culture of our ancestors.[6] And here attention is drawn to the religious formation of Canon Garland.

Coming as he did from an Orange family in Dublin David John Garland had grown up in a community riven by serious sectarian rivalries. As a family that was always passionately loyal to the Orange cause in Ireland the Garlands were essentially fundamentalist Protestants, extremely hostile to Popery as they understood it. Their conviction in the Protestant cause in Ireland and their loyalty to the British throne was unshakable. Being intensely *Bible-believing Christians* they cultivated a literal but largely uncritical knowledge of Holy Scripture which formed the basis of their spirituality and thus informed their religious consciousness. Roman Catholicism or Popery was regarded as both theologically an abomination and as extremely disloyal to the British throne. There is a considerable literature on this phenomenon which has blighted Anglo-Irish history for centuries.[7]

As recounted above David John Garland, after his arrival in Toowoomba was converted to Anglo-Catholicism by Canon Tommy Jones who was able to steer the young Garland's Biblical enthusiasm into other channels and employ it in the service of the Church, in short to harness it together with the liturgy in the traditional Anglican way, which as felicitously formulated by notable 16th century theologian, Richard Hooker (c.1554–1600) claimed that the Church of England was based on three key pillars, namely *Scripture, Reason and Tradition*. This meant that the Church (Tradition) was based on the Bible (Scripture) and communicated to the faithful by means of a liturgy enshrined in the *Book of Common Prayer* (Reason). As well, it needs to be appreciated that the history of the British peoples was intimately bound up with the Church as was, of course, the case in all other European countries. The English State always existed in a symbiotic relationship with the English Church. This did not change at the Reformation which occasioned the rift with Rome. Indeed, the self-perception of the English bishops still at the end of the 19th century was that the Church was the *conscience of the nation*. Without the moral anchorage of an established Church to restrain it the State would become a raging monster devouring all in its path.[8]

The English constitution is still intimately bound up with the Church; in Britain the monarch is supreme governor of the Church of England whereas in the dominions there is religious–political pluralism. There has been no established church since the days of Governor Burke who in 1836 dissolved the nexus of Church and State in the colony. Incidentally, Governor Burke was an Irishman and a member of the Church of Ireland. Informally, however, Church of England bishops in both colonial and post-colonial Australia did enjoy a privileged social relationship with State and Commonwealth governors, and clergy such as Canon Garland were not shy in frequenting the 'corridors of power' to exert what ever influence they could for the causes they espoused. Garland was an unusually forceful and persistent personage in his day, active on behalf of many public causes, the most notable and continuing one being Anzac commemoration.

This energy derived from Garland's perception of the State and Empire.[9] It was widely held among church dignitaries as well as 19th century statesmen such as William Ewart Gladstone (1809–98) that the British Empire had a vocation from almighty God to plant the seeds of parliamentary democracy among the peoples of the world over which it held sway. It was an idea that flourished among the champions of imperial federation and was behind the formation of the *Round Table* movement.[10] All nations have invoked the sanction from the deity for their existence and their vocation in the world. It is very odd, however, that whereas some nations regard the Almighty as a God of peace, others regard him/her as a God of battles very much as is encountered in some of the books of the Old Testament. There exist enlightening studies of this phenomenon.[11]

In this opening chapter it is necessary to explain for the edification of the secular mind just how seriously religion and the Bible during the 19th and early 20th centuries were taken in broad sections of the community, that is, right across the Christian denominations. This is documented by the very energetic campaigns undertaken by all non-Roman Catholic churches in both Australia and New Zealand to have the Education Act in various States amended to allow both Bible reading in government schools as well as to permit clergy to enter schools weekly to conduct religious instruction for the children of their respective flocks. Indeed, the Bible in Schools movement was a phenomenon of the British Empire generally. British-based missionaries first of all regarded the fact that almighty God had allowed Britain to extend her sway throughout the world and this implied an obligation to bring the liberating message of Holy Scripture to all the peoples who lived wherever the Union Jack flew and upon which the sun never set.[12]

This raises the interesting question about how religion was appropriated to justify imperialism. As mentioned above, all the Great Powers in the Age of Imperialism claimed that in extending their power throughout the world they were implementing the will of the Creator. Hence there occurred throughout the nineteenth century an explosion of missionary movements driven by the respective churches of the European nations. Each denomination established their missionary enterprises to convert the native populations under their control, a movement which was fraught with sectarian rivalry such as one could witness in microcosm for example in Western Samoa where French Marist priests had early begun to compete with the London Missionary Society missionaries for the hearts and minds of the Samoans. This situation posed a virtually insoluble dilemma for the German colonial administration when the islands were ceded by international agreement to German control in 1900. On the hoisting of the German imperial flag every effort was made to replace the French RC clergy with Germans. The Kaiser had even endorsed the establishment of a Marist house in Meppen, Westphalia, to train future missionary priests. This would eventually take care of the Roman Catholic section of the population while the replacement of the personnel of the London Missionary Society with German Protestant staff proved more problematic.[13]

In a word, it was deemed important to have missionaries who ran the schools and maintained hospitals who were loyal to the colonial power and functioning as virtual agents of that power to make the native peoples into pliant and obedient subjects in accordance with the imperial power's cultural-political ideals. It did not matter whether the missionaries in each case perceived themselves as having been instrumentalised in the service of their political masters; the missionaries had willing placed themselves in that role in the belief that they were serving the will of God. In short the political culture of the imperial power was propagated willingly by the missionaries. In the case of the self-perception of a priest like Canon Garland all clergy serving overseas were agents of the imperial power because like William Ewart Gladstone they perceived the mission of the British Empire not only to spread liberal political values such as the rule of law, basic rights and freedom from oppression but also the Gospel of Christ from which they believed all these values were ultimately derived. In short, the propagation of Bible-based Christianity went hand in hand with British political culture. Indeed, in an emphatically Whig-ish manner British missionaries had claimed the Bible as the virtual handbook of Empire. And although Canon Garland was never formally a member of any missionary society he nevertheless perceived himself as serving in a virtual mission field which both Australia and New Zealand, at least in his view, constituted. The citizens of these self-governing Dominions needed to be aware of the source of their cultural-religious values, which was without any doubt the Holy Bible.

This is where the secular historian hits the wall although all honours students in modern history at our universities were presumably trained to try to re-experience the past by entering the mind of the protagonists in the drama which they were trying to explain. And it is precisely here that the historian who is unacquainted with the world of ideas of, say, an Anglican priest who was a champion of the Oxford Movement, must encounter an insurmountable difficulty. In such instances the would-be writer is automatically disqualified from even imagining that s/he could offer a plausible explanation. And of course, the problem of tooling up to enable one to enter the world of ideas of a chaplain like Canon Garland makes any attempt by the outsider illusory from the beginning. One needs a broad-based and multicultural spiritual-intellectual formation in order to be able to unravel the past in a way commensurate with the strict historiographical standards of internationally acceptable scholarship.

Finally, turning now to what may reasonably be called Canon Garland's 'war theology' and its origins, two factors stand out: first the role of the Church as the agency throughout history for propagating the Gospel (good news) of Jesus of Nazareth for *sacralising* the world, and secondly, the propagation of Biblical knowledge as the means of achieving this. As he would have imbibed from his Anglo-Catholic mentor Tommy Jones, it was the Church's obligation to convey its healing message to *all peoples*. And since the time of the apostolic Church, that is the Church in the first one hundred years, it had done this first by evolving a liturgy (the Eucharist or Mass) and then by compiling the Bible, a task not completed until the early fourth century. This was the key world-changing cultural event of human history.[14] And since the early 19th century when the British Empire had been granted, in the words of Rudyard Kipling, 'dominion over palm and pine'[15] it was its duty to facilitate the proclamation of the Gospel to all peoples and to defend them against the depredations of such misguided imperialist Powers as the Prusso-German Empire under its vain-glorious Kaiser. Here again it must be noted that Garland had imbibed a very Gladstonian understanding of Empire in the same way as had virtually all Anglican bishops throughout the world at that time.

CHAPTER 2

Towards Understanding the Rise of the Prusso-Germany: The Unknown Empire

If Germany were to develop into a democracy and carry on a democratic foreign policy, we would have peace in Europe.

– Alfred Fried, 1911[1]

In all attempts to explain conflict in human affairs and our part in it, the necessity of examining causal connections is unavoidable. Australia and New Zealand would never had become involved in the Great War of 1914–18 had it not been for the Kaiser's Germany and her aggressive imperialism and consequent war-aims program which both directly and indirectly affected the Pacific Dominions. Any explanation of Antipodean involvement in that conflict demands investigation and understanding of the expansionist policies of imperial Germany.

That nation/empire (Reich) had been founded in 1871 as a result of the military victories of the leading Teutonic kingdom of Prussia. There is now no longer a political entity known as Prussia because it was abolished at a conference of the victorious Allies held at the Prussian city of Potsdam near Berlin which had been the location of the residence of the kings of Prussia from the 14th century. There between 17 July and 2 August 1945 it was decided that since Nazism had grown out of the matrix of the Prussian militaristic political culture the kingdom of Prussia should be expunged from the map of Europe.

The decision was essentially based on the assessments of historians such as the Englishman AJP Taylor and the Frenchman Eduard Vermeil who had both independently published surveys of German history in which they focussed on the authoritarian, militaristic political culture of Prussia as being incompatible with the egalitarian, liberal and democratic political traditions of the West.[2] Before them, however, there were a number of British and American historians who had identified the peculiar nature of Prussia going back to Sir John Robert Seeley, author in 1878 of a three volume biography of Baron vom Stein (1757–1831), a high ranking Prussian official who had tried valiantly to re-shape the constitution of Prussia after the Napoleonic Wars. Seeley who became Regius Professor of history at Cambridge in 1869 was essentially a liberal but he did not hide his admiration for the discipline and order which characterised the administration of Prussia at the time leading up to the unification of Germany under the Prussian Chancellor Otto von Bismarck in 1871.[3] Later British commentators such as James Marriot (1859–1945) and Charles Grant Robertson (1869–1948), William Harbutt Dawson (1890–1948) and the Norwegian-American Thorsten Veblen (1857–1929) were far more critical.[4] During the Great War of 1914–18 many more professorial voices were raised pointing out the dire consequences of Prussian militarism. Not least among these were the Professor of History at the University of Sydney, George Arnold Wood (1865–1928) and his counterpart in Melbourne, Professor Ernest Scott (1867–1939) and Professor Archibald T. Strong (1876–1930) also of Melbourne. All of these men contributed immensely to strengthening liberal democratic values in the Australian education systems and were especially well informed about Prussian political culture.[5]

In retrospect it is not difficult to discern the great gulf that existed between Prussian political values that were behind imperial Germany's war-aims 1914–1918, and the values for which the Anzacs had fought. This bears reflecting upon. One may justifiably contrast Prussianism with the values of the Anzacs. There are two factors which account for this. First, Australia was colonised by the British at a time when Enlightenment ideas were well established. This is evident from the time of the first Governor

Arthur Philip who discharged that office from 1788 until 1792. It was continued by his successors, particularly by Governor Lachlan Macquarie from 1810 to 1821 who was the last autocratic governor of the colony. As the colony developed more and more as a place of settlement for free immigrants from Britain rather than a dumping ground for convicts, so the administration took on an increasingly more consultative character and in the passage of time established British institutions were transferred to the tiny but growing Antipodean population.

By the time of the great gold rushes in the 1850s when the population trebled within a decade from the influx of shiploads of sanguine miners from around the world, it became increasingly clear to the powers-that-be that Australia was going to develop a very democratic political culture. In a word, the ideas of equality and representative government became deeply entrenched in the colonial outposts that were established in the later settlements. These were located at Hobart, Melbourne, Adelaide, Brisbane and Perth. An essential part of this development was the transfer of trade unionism from Britain and so the colonial working class became early imbued with the ideology of workers' rights (Chartism).[6] Government should no longer be determined by the interests of the propertied classes but for all men and women without distinction. So the Australasian colonies developed the reputation of being the world's workshop of democracy. Both workers' rights and the emancipation of women were issues written large on the political agenda of Australasians. For example the winning of the eight hour day already in the mid-1850s for the Stonemasons in New South Wales and Victoria was a historic milestone in the struggle for more equitable labour relations. And the right of women to vote, first established in 1893 in New Zealand and then in Victoria in 1902, was indicative of the advanced democratic spirit of our ancestors. This degree of Enlightenment clearly did not yet extend to the aboriginal inhabitants of the country.

In a word, people in Australasia very early acquired a reputation for being radical democrats. That spirit became engrained in our political culture. And in this regard, the observations of a forgotten Swiss immigrant named Henry Alexis Tardent (1853–1929) confirmed this. Why should this be significant? The answer lies in the fact that the Swiss have a very long history of struggle for democracy. They have very different political experiences from their German and Austrian neighbours to the north and east as well as from their Italian neighbours in the south. In the west, of course, the influence of the French by contrast was very strong. The point is that Henry Tardent knew a democrat when he saw one. He had certainly had a very colourful career and in one of his incarnations he was a journalist who specialised in commenting about the character of his chosen Antipodean countrymen. As a young man Tardent had spent many years living in Russia. He had gone to Bessarabia as part of the Tsarist Empire to live and work in a Swiss enclave, and it is there that he met his future wife, so Henry Tardent was through his foreign travels a man of distinctly cosmopolitan character but also one driven by a unquenchable *Wanderlust*. In 1887 he had decided with his young family to emigrate to Queensland where he became distinguished as an entrepreneur in various agricultural enterprises as well as journalism. Henry Tardent was a gifted linguist whose democratic credentials were strengthened by the fact that he became one of the founding members of the Labor Party in Queensland.[7] Given his French-Swiss background augmented by his years of living in Tsarist Russia Henry Tardent became an acute judge of national character. This was revealed in a comment he wrote about returning Diggers from the First World War. He recorded his impressions of these young men and commented on their demeanour that they fought as 'free' men, by which he meant not as mercenaries, but as democrats who had enlisted voluntarily as citizens to fight against tyranny and oppression.[8] In modern terms Tardent might have observed that because these men were born and bred in a free country the DNA of democracy was at the core of their being. Australia is a very different place from any part of Europe so the people here were bound to grow up with values and outlook on the world peculiar to the unique environment. And by 'environment' one includes not only the physical-geographical-climatic factors but also the intellectual-spiritual-cultural elements that were transplanted here from the British Isles and Europe generally. All these elements combine to produce a *new species-being* to adapt an expression taken from Karl Marx. It is an observation made also by other thoughtful writers such as the historians, George Arnold Wood, Ernest Scott down to Manning Clark, and of course much, much earlier than any of them, Henry Tardent, as a Swiss democrat, was clearly sensitive to this and so was able to comment on Australasian national character with insights derived from his own European origins and experience. And among these characteristics were clearly egalitarianism, individualism and self-reliance which included a sense of solidarity with one's mates. Obviously, these are generalisations but they are borne out today in our political life. Scoundrels will turn up in every society but always in the background there are those values of decency and egalitarianism that are ineradicable and which form an essential part of the national character. Thereby they contribute to the uniqueness of our Antipodean identity.

In what follows one must bear in mind the above observations of Henry Tardent. It certainly becomes clear to all Australians and New Zealanders who travel abroad that we are not only made to feel different, even from our Canadian and American cousins; we are different. Our differences, also from our kinsfolk in the British Isles, have become even greater with the passage of time, the basic common values notwithstanding. And of course, the differences between ourselves and the various European peoples are manifest. And here the contrast with the Germans against whom we have been involved sacrificially in two most costly world wars becomes very marked indeed. The roots of this difference must now be explored because without knowledge of the political culture that produced the phenomenon of Prussian militarism and Nazism we will not be able to comprehend why we had no choice but to fight as part of the British Empire against the German Reich.

As a student in two West German universities (Munich and Erlangen) from 1961 to 1965, I was confronted daily with the differences between myself as an Australian and the variety of Germans, both university staff and students with whom I was associated. I say 'variety' advisedly because very soon I became sensitized to the internal differences among Germans themselves. At the universities in particular one encountered students from all over the country because of the German tradition that encouraged students to spend semesters at different universities all through German-speaking Europe until they found a professor with whom they wished to deepen their studies further and eventually to work towards a doctorate. In Munich, for example, there were obviously a majority of Bavarian students, but even these represented regional differences such as those from Franconia (Nuremburg region) in the north or those from the west around Augsburg. Beyond the Bavarian borders were the Swabians from around Stuttgart and the Rhinelanders from around Cologne and many other cities and regions. All were distinctive, especially in their various dialects. However, the biggest differences were between Bavarians and north Germans where one was confronted with the historical rivalry between Prussians distinguished by their generally strict and formal behaviour and the Bavarians who were more *gemütlich,* that is their more relaxed and jolly disposition. But there was one factor which became crucial in relationships with all Germans across the board, and that is the question of party-political allegiances. Those of Social Democratic persuasion were always easier to get along with than conservatives. That accounts for the fact that in my own studies I investigated the history of social democracy and in socialism its various manifestations, and wrote my doctoral thesis on the German Social Democratic trade union leader, Carl Legien (1861–1920), the father of modern German trade unionism.[9]

Carl Legien was one of the most effective leaders of democratic socialism in Germany along side his party friend, the pioneer revisionist Eduard Bernstein (1850–1932). Legien's personal motto for the working-class struggle for emancipation was *Organisation ist alles.* In short, a disciplined, well organised trade union movement would achieve its aims against an authoritarian state in a far more practical and civilised way than by violent revolutionary confrontation such as advocated by the Bolsheviks at that time. That explains why Lenin regarded Legien as the enemy of revolution as he did all German social democratic revisionists. And here is where life experience accounts for the difference. Legien had done military service in the Prussian army where he became an officer's batman. In that role he learned the importance of command, discipline and organisation. He would apply these principles to the working class in its struggle for emancipation from wage slavery. Most importantly Legien understood that it was pointless for the working class to encourage wild strikes against the Prussian state because he knew only too well how it would react, namely by calling out the army to suppress any manifestations of worker insurgence. This was especially important given that the army by then had machine guns at their disposal, a fact that led Friedrich Engels to observe that this invention had made old style revolutions illusory. Legien had also internalised this lesson. In a word, Prussianism could only be resisted by adapting Prussian methods into the class struggle; hence *Organisation ist alles*!

Our next task is to examine the origins of Prussianism in order to be able to critique it and come to an understanding of what made Germany so different from its European neighbours. What has been termed the 'peculiarities' of German history needs here to be explained because failure to comprehend Prussianism will cripple our ability to understand the Anzac tradition. One is challenged here to think both laterally and vertically. In a word, if we do not comprehend Prussianism we will not understand Australian political culture. This is not drawing as long a bow as one might first be tempted to think.

In coming to and understanding Prussianism one is best advised to turn to the notable German historian Franz Schnabel. What people did not know then about Schnabel was that he was actually half French through his mother. He was known, of course, to have been a Roman Catholic, but a liberal one of moderate views who supported the Weimar Constitution of 1919–33. As the professor of modern history in post-war Munich he fitted in very well.

Under the Nazi regime, Schnabel's liberal democratic convictions had led to his dismissal in 1936 from the chair he held in Karlsruhe. By that time he had already acquired distinction through the publication of his most influential work, an unfinished four volume history of Germany in the nineteenth century which appeared between 1929 and 1936. This has since been re-issued (1987) indicating that its pedagogic influence is still potent because at its core it highlights the baleful influence of Prussia and Bismarck on German political culture. In it he acknowledged with apparent magnanimity, that the foundation of the Prussian state was the most important political fact in German history, *die grösste staatliche Tat der deutschen Geschichte*. The key statements which follow discuss the 17th and 18th century origins of Prussia and these bear translating here in full because they reveal those essentially reactionary and militaristic features of the kingdom which were strenuously retained until the revolution of 1918–19:

> From the top down everything was regulated. Individual initiative of subjects was discouraged or forbidden because they might conflict with regulations imposed from above; unconditional obedience was essential so that the machine functioned efficiently. Indeed the Prussian military state evinced all the characteristics of the modern state, [...] any shred of individuality was sucked out of the organised masses through the rationalisation of the machine of state. All human relationships as well as all social and economic differences disappeared in the face of the hierarchy of duties, and in Prussia that meant the hegemony of the differences of military rank. The arrogant tone of command guaranteed the certainty and uniformity of all procedures so that the machine functioned smoothly. As well, the insularity of the army and in particular of the officer corps erected a barrier against outside influences while the commanding officers always had at their disposal a reliable and ever ready instrument with which to answer all questions of civilian life strictly in accordance with their military priorities.

Schnabel went on to make a particularly subtle point:

The rationale for all this Prussian 'militarism' was not any lust for conquest or even the idea of national defence *because it was not the state which created the army but the army that created the state.* [emphasis added] In fact the creator of this system, the Elector, Frederick William I (1688–1740) was in all questions of foreign policy peace-loving to the extent of weakness. But his son, Frederick the Great (1712–1786), placed himself outside the norm of both state and dynasty because he proceeded to employ the army in reckless, self-glorifying campaigns. [...] Of course it was a fact of life in a state created by an army that with each campaign everything would be set on one card so that the value which such a glittering weapon possesses for the entire existence of the state acts as a restraint on any decision to risk it in a campaign. So if the tone of the barrack square predominated that was to be expected *because the state was one big military camp.* [Emphasis added.] The rattle of weapons permeated the atmosphere as accompanying music bearing witness to a predominantly martial mentality which inevitably was transferred to the bourgeois population. Obviously, the civil service (*Beamtentum*) was subservient to the authority of the army, schooled as it was in military discipline. Civil servants may have received only modest remuneration but that was made up for in social prestige. And, of course, the civil service functioned exclusively to maintain and increase the army.[10]

The students of Franz Schnabel were privileged and not infrequently surprised to hear the voice of a most erudite scholar who, in the years he taught at Munich (1947–62), had ventured to swim against the mainstream historical opinion concerning the role of Prussia in the course of German history. Conservatives such as Professor Gerhard Ritter (1888–1967) strove in the post-1945 years to dissociate Prussian history from the rise of National Socialism. Indeed, at that time there was a veritable struggle among historians for the hearts and minds of German students. Ritter and the majority of conservatives tried energetically to attribute the advent of Adolf Hitler and the Nazi movement to the consequences of the forced introduction of the allegedly culturally alien parliamentary constitution of Weimar in 1919. It was, so they alleged, inappropriate for the German people to be governed by a multi-party democratic system because it opened up the opportunity for political adventurers to disrupt the smooth running of a bureaucratic monarchy such as the Reich supposedly had been under Kaiser Wilhelm II. So Germany had fallen foul of the enforced abdication of the Kaiser and the subsequent introduction of parliamentarism based on a democratic electoral system. This had opened the floodgates for the demagoguery of Adolf Hitler's party. Such a thesis was, of course, a clever piece of historical sleight of hand intended to absolve the highly authoritarian Prussian political culture from any blame for leading Germany into war in 1914 and for what had happened as a consequence.

Professor Schnabel adamantly refused to accept this version of events. Instead he astutely pointed out that the Germans had been ill-served by the so-called Prussian solution to the German question that had been accomplished by the Prussian Minister-President Otto von Bismarck after his three wars of unification in 1864, 1866 and 1870, against Denmark, Austria and France respectively. Bismarck's Prussianisation of Germany had been intended to prevent the rise of true democracy for all the Germanic peoples. One may not forget that Germany was united solely on Prussian terms and that meant the imposition of a federal constitution devised by Bismarck to perpetuate Prussian domination of the other 36 principalities and city-states. This was ensured essentially by the fact that the Kingdom of Prussia had permanent domination of the upper house, the *Reichsrat*.

As well, in Prussia, although there was universal adult male suffrage for federal elections, a property bias had been imposed on the franchise. It divided men over thirty into three tax categories. Those who paid the most tax were entitled to three votes, those in the middle range got two votes while the majority who were mainly working men received one vote only. And because Prussia was by far the largest German principality (larger than

France) it could never be out voted by the *Reichsrat* because it had the absolute majority of upper house votes. It was like a federal senate or house of lords that because of its ultra conservative composition influenced the political agenda for the entire Reich.

A legislature period was set at five years. But the most subtle anti-democratic feature was the arrangement for the army budget, the biggest item of federal responsibility. This was known as the *Septennat* which meant that the army budget was voted on only every seven years. This removed debate on the heaviest section of the national budget from effective parliamentary control. It made up 4/5 of the total budget, but Bismarck could always rely on the support of the conservative parties against the Social Democrats and Liberals who naturally wanted it abolished as the main obstacle to genuine parliamentary control of the Executive. Although this provision in the constitution was removed in 1893 and replaced by a *Quinquennat*, meaning the army budget came up for debate every five years, it still made little difference to the fact that the new Prusso-German Reich was a military monarchy designed to sustain and promote the strength of the army which drew upon its own internal budget thus making it a state within the state. Failure to grasp this fact will render full comprehension of the nature of Prusso-German politics impossible. It was the concrete political expression of why Prusso-Germany was so different from all the other Powers.

Neither should it go unnoticed that there were numerous dire predictions about the consequences of the Prussianisation of Germany. These came from high-profile contemporary observers such as the famous Swiss historian of the Renaissance in Italy, Jakob Burckhardt (1818–87) who wrote on 27 September 1870, that is, during the Franco-Prussian War, that it had to result in the *permanent militarisation of Germany* and certainly a future war with Russia. Similarly, none other than Karl Marx predicted after the annexation of Alsace-Lorraine that it would lead to what he called a 'race war' in which the French and the Russians would be allied against Germany. But the most perceptive critic of the Prussianisation of Germany was the German Social Democrat, Wilhelm Liebknecht (1826–1900). In

1872 he voiced his opposition to the annexation of Alsace-Lorraine by applying a combination of analysis and prognosis, commenting as follows:

> A state such as that of Bismarckian Prusso-Germany is destined to collapse with fatalistic necessity by virtue of the circumstance of its creation. [...] Having been born on the field of battle, the consequence of a *coup d'état*, of war and revolution from above, it must lurch from crisis to crisis from war to war and either be decimated on the battlefield or by revolution from below. That is a law of nature.[11]

As many commentators since the end of the First World War have observed, looking back over the circumstances of the founding of the Bismarckian Empire, it was then that the conditions for future conflict were already set in place. Bismarck had laid down the ground rules for Prusso-German diplomacy and these were based on the doctrine that in order to maintain the balance of power in Europe, Germany had to be à *trois*, that is to say, allied with two other monarchist European powers in order to maintain the diplomatic isolation of France. These were initially, Austria-Hungary and Russia. Italy was later included but had to withdraw before the outbreak of the Great War.[12] Consequently, the German Empire as it was constituted under Bismarck as a military-monarchy-cum-class-state (*Klassenstaat*) contained the seeds of its own destruction. As such it chose to try and live in a world of enemies, beginning externally with the permanent alienation of France and then internally of its own working class. It may not be forgotten that Bismarck had declared war on the *inneren Feind*, 'internal enemy', namely the organised working class in the form of the free trade unions and the Social Democratic Party. This was done by the infamous anti-Socialist law of 1878 (*Das Sozialistengesetz*) that lapsed only after Bismarck's dismissal in 1890. It was an abject failure because it did not make the socialists go away; on the contrary they developed the trade union movement to become the strongest in Europe. As well the Social Democrats (SPD) in spite of an occasional set back, kept winning electoral successes until 1912 when it became the largest single party in the Reichstag with 110 out of a total of 397 mandates. These were spread over 18 parties. The next largest party was the Roman Catholic Centre Party with 91 seats. Then came the Conservatives and National Liberals with 45 seats each followed by the Progressive People's Party with 42. The remainder comprised a number of splinter parties with only a handful of seats each. Clearly, Germany was far from being an internally united nation; rather it was deeply divided on class and denominational lines, being described as only 'negatively integrated', meaning that there was a massive class division making it internally into a veritable powder keg. The only thing that prevented the explosion of revolution was the political restraint of the socialist trade unions whose leadership realised, as pointed out above, that provocation of the ruling classes by the use of mass strikes would only result in brutal reprisals.[13]

The *Kaiserreich* suffered, then, from serious and virtually insoluble internal tensions resulting from the massive discrepancy between the above-mentioned modern economic basis on the one hand and the residual reactionary social-political structures on the other. In the midst of this problem was, of course, the fact of the continued and vigorous growth of the labour movement which the powers-that-be could not deal with in any satisfactory way.

Consequently, in trying to achieve a clear understanding of the belligerency of its foreign policy this needs to be kept in mind. In order for the Reich leadership to maintain internal stability, it felt compelled to pursue an energetic foreign and colonial policy. In short, the diversion from internal tensions by means of pursuing a politically adventurous overseas policy was the course taken especially in the period after Bismarck's dismissal, that is in the 1890s, which is when the ill-advised German naval policy known as the Tirpitz Plan was conceived. It may be conjectured, of course, that had Bismarck been retained in office then all risky overseas ventures would have been abandoned, but that presumed the possibility of coming to an amicable arrangement with Britain. This, however, was never going to be realised because of the Kaiser's, and Tirpitz' obsession to build a battle fleet to rival that of England.

The upsurge in German imperialistic ambition expressed in such movements as Pan-Germanism frustrated any hope of implementing a policy of supposed Bismarckian restraint. It will be recalled that after the founding of Reich Bismarck had warned against an adventurous overseas policy because it would expose the new nation to dangers with which it could ill-afford to cope. In the event, however, it proved impossible even for Bismarck to keep a lid on the nation's newly fired up colonial enthusiasm. Ironically, though, the first serious beginnings of German overseas expansion occurred precisely during Bismarck's watch. Then, after the Iron Chancellor's dismissal the elements within Germany who desired to force the tempo of imperialistic expansion increased their influence enormously. The warning voices of the few pacifists, Social Democrats and Liberals were effectively drowned out. And with hindsight it may be observed that it was precisely the Pan-German lust for overseas expansion that hastened the ultimate dismantling of Bismarck's life's work. In short, a German world power in central Europe driven by a militaristic elite, by definition incurably authoritarian and opposed in principle to the adoption of liberal or social democratic reforms, was destined to self-destruct. The strategy of trying to shore up the monarchical-militaristic constitution of the Reich by pursing an expansionist overseas policy, that is *Weltpolitik,* simply hastened this result.

The consequences materialised quickly. Domestically there were subterranean intrigues from Pan-German inspired elements who in particular were convinced that the Reich Chancellor, Theobald von Bethmann Hollweg who had been nominated by the Kaiser in 1909 was insufficiently aggressive in his conduct of policy, especially with regard to the 'loyal' opposition, namely the Social Democrats. In foreign policy, especially since the first Balkan war (1912) there was from late in the year a clear move towards planning an ambitious war which would be unleashed at the first favourable opportunity. What has gone down in history as the War Council of 8 December 1912 gives clear indication of the mental preparedness for war among the key members of the power-elite meaning the Kaiser and his military and naval advisers as observed already by Fritz Fischer in 1969.[14] It is argued here that this meeting confirmed Germany's intention to launch a war in Europe at the next favourable opportunity. The source is from the diary of Admiral Georg Alexander von Müller one of the participants in the secret meeting called by the Kaiser. The admiral wrote:

> Sunday summoned to the palace to see His Majesty at 11 o'clock along with Tirpitz, Heeringen (Vice Admiral) and General von Moltke. H.M. [the Kaiser] with a telegraphic report on the political situation sent by the ambassador in London, Prince Lichnowsky. As Grey's spokesman, Haldane informed Lichnowsky that if we attack France, England will come to France's aid, for England cannot tolerate a disturbance in the European balance of power. H.M. welcomed this message as providing the desired clarification for all those who have been lulled into a false sense of security by the recently friendly English press.

H.M. painted the following picture:

> Austria must deal firmly with the Slavs living outside its borders [the Serbs] if it does not want to lose control over the Slavs under the Austrian monarchy. If Russia were to support the Serbs, which she is apparently already doing (Sassanow's remark that Russia will go straight into Galicia if the Austrians march into Serbia), war would be inevitable for us. But there is hope that Bulgaria, Romania, and Albania – and perhaps even Turkey – will take our side. Bulgaria has already offered Turkey an alliance. We really went to great lengths to persuade the Turks. Recently H.M. also tried to convince the crown prince of Romania, who stopped here on his way to Brussels, to come to an agreement with Bulgaria.

If these powers ally themselves with Austria, it will free us up to throw our full weight behind a war against France. According to His Majesty, the fleet will naturally have to prepare for war against England. After Haldane's statement, the possibility of a war against Russia alone – as discussed by the chief of the Admiralty in his last talk – will not be considered. So immediately submarine warfare against English troop transports on the Scheldt River or near Dunkirk, mine warfare up to the Thames. To Tirpitz: rapid construction of additional submarines, etc. A conference is recommended for all interested naval officers. Gen. von Moltke: 'I consider a war inevitable – the sooner, the better. But we should do a better job of gaining support for a war against Russia, in line with the Kaiser's remarks.' H.M. confirmed this and asked the secretary of state to use the press to work towards this end. T[irpitz] called attention to the fact that the navy would gladly see a major war delayed by one and a half years. Moltke said that even then the navy would not be ready, and the army's situation would continue to worsen, since due to our limited financial resources our opponents are able to arm themselves more rapidly. That was the end of the meeting; there were almost no results.

The chief of general staff says: the sooner war comes, the better; however, he hasn't concluded from this that we should give Russia or France, or even both, an ultimatum that would trigger a war for which they would carry the blame. I wrote to the Chancellor in the afternoon about influencing the press.

Professor John Röhl, late of Sussex University in England, has written in his three-volume biography of the Kaiser on the War Council of 8 December 1912 as follows:

Was the World War really 'deferred' on the morning of Sunday 8 December 1912 as Fritz Fischer claimed in his controversial book, *War of Illusions*, until the work on the Kiel Canal had been completed in the summer of 1914? Did the Kaiser ... only consent 'reluctantly' to 'postponement'? Did he continue to think in terms of 'racial struggle' between *Germandom* and *Slavdom* that was inevitable and would probably start in one or two years? The violent criticism which Fischer's 'deferred war' thesis gave rise in the 1960s is to some extent understandable if one recalls those years in which professional historians in the Federal Republic still thought in terms of a general 'slithering over the brink' into war that no power wanted. But times change and historians change with them. Today the prime responsibility of the German and Austro-Hungarian governments for precipitating the Great War in July 1914 is no longer seriously questioned; and the 'war council' of 8 December 1912 no longer appears as merely the inexplicable and inconsequential aberration of a particularly insignificant and not quite rational monarch. As has been shown the military-political discussions on that Sunday morning fit seamlessly into a decision-making process whose origins went far back, and which finally led to the Armageddon in the summer of 1914. Fischer's opponents would have found it easier to refute his 'deferred war' thesis if the world war had not broken out at the very time that was singled out in December 1912 – immediately after the completion of the Kiel Canal – and on the pretext of a long-anticipated racial war between Austria and Serbia.[15]

During the following year there occurred a dramatic constitutional crisis which illustrated beyond any doubt the militaristic nature of the *Kaiserreich*. This has gone down in history as the Zabern affair of November-December 1913 which precipitated the very first vote of no-confidence by the elected parliament against the Kaiser's chosen government. At the centre of the issue was whether the army should be controlled by the parliament as in Western States. The no-confidence vote was, however, refuted by the Chancellor on the grounds that the House had no constitutional control over the army. That was the sole prerogative of the Kaiser. Thereby it was confirmed that the ruling classes, in particular the army, had unconcealed contempt for the representatives of the people and that Prusso-Germany was essentially a military state.[16]

The background to this remarkable crisis was that a twenty-year-old second lieutenant in the garrison town of Saverne, Alsace-Lorraine, named Freiherr (Baron) von Forstner on 28 October 1913 instructed his men to treat the local population, contemptuously called *Wackes*, with violence if called for. Arrogant behaviour on the part of the garrison became rife, provoking the local civilian authorities to protest to the German authorities. In this confrontation, however, the army stood firmly behind the errant second lieutenant thus precipitating a series of further civilian demonstrations. The case was seized upon by the now numerically superior Social Democrats and liberal minded deputies in the Reichstag who together precipitated the historic vote of no confidence in the government. The army, however, was jubilant at the result.[17] It illustrated quite dramatically that the power structures of Reich, the keystone of which was the army, were considered unacceptable by large sections of the population. Indeed, the army had become so unpopular that its officers felt that they now needed an opportunity to demonstrate its presumed indispensability to the existence of the Reich and the honour of the monarchy. The question being posed was when could a war be started without appearing to be the aggressor was soon to be answered.

With the assassination of the Austrian Archduke and his spouse in Sarajevo on 28 June 1914 circumstances seemed most favourable for unleashing a war provided that the diplomats were sufficiently adroit at their task. The army appeared confident that it would triumph in a short, sharp blitzkrieg for which it had a long-prepared plan, and 'the sooner the better'.

Given the peculiarities of the German command structure at the centre of which was the mercurial Kaiser it is not surprising that there is now much divergent opinion expressed about the historical significance of the above mentioned war council of December 1912. The many explanations, which range on the one hand between whether Germany really planned the war or, on the other, whether the war simply erupted by accident, are staggering. The latest on offer is that by Christopher Clark who argues that the war simply resulted from an unintentional diplomatic breakdown among the Powers. This view is very popular among German conservatives at the present time but is sharply criticised by liberals and social democrats in Germany as shall be seen. Certainly, nothing that Clark has written has provided a satisfactory explanation for the German will to war as soon as the constellation of forces seemed favourable, namely to allow Germany to open hostilities without seeming to appear as the aggressor. On the contrary, the extremely diligent archival work of Dr Bernd Schulte of Hamburg has discovered documentation that confirms the significance of the memorandum of 8 December 1912.[18]

It is not surprising to learn that Bernd Schulte was a doctoral student of Fritz Fischer's. And while John Röhl was not a student of Fischer's he was closely associated with a group of former Fischer *Assistenten*, colleagues who later became well known in Britain and the United States such as Hartmut Pogge von Strandmann and Volker Berghahn. In 2012 Röhl together with a German-American colleague, Guenther Roth, had edited and published a collection of 117 private letters of Kurt Riezler to his fiancée, Käthe Liebermann covering the period 1914–15 when Riezler was personal assistant to the Chancellor, Bethmann Hollweg. He was present at all key cabinet sessions and so had intimate inside knowledge of Reich policy. The effect of this new source has been to render totally irrelevant the widely proclaimed thesis advanced by Christopher Clark which is dealt with below in chapter 5.[19]

Riezler's career was remarkable in so far as he had been like Thomas Mann a deeply convinced and patriotic *Bildungsbürger* who believed in the innate superiority of *Kultur*. Then after the war he began to become more distanced from those values and for the sake of his Jewish wife, daughter of the famous painter Max Liebermann, also took refuge in the United States.[20] There in New York Riezler became a professor at the *New School for Social Research* where he gained a reputation for his liberal commitment. Again like Thomas Mann, Riezler in exile became yet another 'German counter German'.[21]

Finally, here, the question of who in the end was essentially responsible for unleashing the Great War becomes secondary in the light of the fact that it enabled imperial Germany to set about realising war aims which various pressure groups in the army, navy, heavy industry, mining and finance had long been advocating. And as far as the Pacific region was concerned Germany had two objectives. First it was intended to destroy all merchant shipping plying between the United Kingdom and the Pacific Dominions and second, once the German navy in the North Sea had established superiority over the Royal Navy, as was clearly intended, it was the German aim to dictate peace terms, also to Britain's overseas Dominions. Occupation by German forces would not have been necessary if the fledgling Dominions could have been isolated by superior German naval force in the South Pacific. Awareness of the militaristic nature of imperial Germany in 1914 is, therefore an essential prerequisite to comprehending why it was impossible to remain neutral in 1914–18.[22]

CHAPTER 3

German War Aims
in the Pacific

*History cannot be written unless the historian can achieve some
kind of contact with the mind of those about whom he is writing.*
— E. H. Carr, *What is History*

There is a well known saying in German that comes from a poem written
by Christian Morgenstern in 1910: *Nichts sein kann, was nicht sein darf.* It
means literally, 'nothing can be that may not be,' or 'that which should not
be, cannot be.'[1] People use it to complain about circumstances of which
they do not approve or if some information is revealed that challenges a
formerly passionately held belief. A relevant example would be that the
Germans were not guilty for the outbreak of the Great War which was
the justification for the imposition of massive crippling reparations on
Germany at the Treaty of Versailles in June 1919. They believed they were
not guilty; *ergo* the Reparations were a miscarriage of international justice.
Australian historians and publicists use the same device to lament the
nation's involvement in the Great War in the first place. Some seem to
believe in all seriousness that since Germany was so far away it could not
possibly have posed a threat to Australian security; consequently we should
have resisted British pressure to contribute men and treasure because it
was pointless and cost so many lives; it really did not concern us. So the
question to answer is: Did the Germans really have aggressive war-aims
towards Britain's overseas Empire in the Pacific as they unquestionably did

towards Britain herself? The answer is emphatically YES, they certainly did. Incontrovertible documentary evidence for this has already been disclosed in German archives by two Australian based historians, namely Dr Peter Overlack and Dr Jürgen Tampke, both of whom are fluent German speakers.[2] Obviously, it is essential to be able to consult the original German sources. However, A. W. Jose, author of volume IX of the *Official History of Australia at War* (1928) had done very well in his reconstruction of German naval operation in the Pacific and Indian Oceans. Now his pioneering work has been augmented by Overlack and Tampke.

In this chapter the aim is to account for the development of German naval operation plans which were to be implemented in the event of a war with Britain, and to report the activities of the German intelligence gathering network which provided information relevant for the navy. We need to be conscious of the fact that the presence of a German cruiser squadron based at the German treaty port of Tsingtao on the Shantung Peninsula in the far north of China was part of a grand imperial design called *Weltpolitik*. And Germany already had by the mid-1880s colonial possessions in the Pacific which included German New Guinea and the islands of New Britain (*Neu-Pommern*) and New Ireland (*Neu-Mecklenburg*), Nauru, the Micronesian Islands (Caroline, Marianas and Marshall groups) and finally Western Samoa. Prior to the acquisition of these islands some German principalities had maintained consulates in most Australian colonial capitals. After 1871 their duties were taken over by consuls representing the new German Empire. Most of these were honorary consuls who were local German-born residents except, of course, the Consul General and his staff in Sydney who were *Beamter*, that is career public servants of the Reich. At that time the Australian colonies did not have diplomatic missions, hence there was no exchange of ambassadors with foreign powers. The German ambassador in London was in both theory and practice the senior diplomatic official of Germany to the entire British Empire. Nevertheless, after the founding of the Reich, the German Federation, the Imperial German Consuls General in Sydney and sometimes also in Melbourne functioned in practice as quasi ambassadors. From the Australian side some colonies did have for a time immigration agents posted in select German cities.

With the advent of German unification under Bismarck it did not take long for colonial enthusiasts to emerge, and during his chancellorship Germany began to join the scramble for overseas colonies. This endeavour Bismarck left to chartered companies whose ostensible purpose was to establish plantations overseas in tropical zones for such crops as cacao, copra and spices which the Germans still call *Kolonialwaren*. It has been argued by the late Hans-Ulrich Wehler in his pioneering study, *Bismarck und der Imperialismus* (1969) that Bismarck, initially did not think it wise for Germany to acquire colonies because it exposed the newly forged nation to potential friction with other colonial powers. Ultimately, however, he came to the view that it might help to channel the turbulent energies within the population into focussing on patriotic ventures abroad. This, so argued Professor Wehler, would enable the government to keep the growing social unrest at home under control, the doctrine of *Social Imperialism*. It was primarily intended as a tool for stabilising domestic politics. However, once it was launched with the acquisition of protectorates in Africa and the Pacific, Germany became, albeit somewhat reluctantly on Bismarck's part, another colonial power jostling also for a *Platz an der Sonne* – a place in the sun. Pressure groups had begun to flourish such as *der Kolonialverein* (Colonial Association, 1882), *der Alldeutscher Verband* (the Pan German League (1891) followed by other patriotic associations such as the *Flottenverein* (Navy League 1898) and the *Wehrverein* (Army League 1912). These organisations have been termed 'secondary systems of social power' or as in the case of the Pan German League, a 'Holding company of militant pre-war nationalism, an organisation intimately tied to important interest groups and other propaganda organisations; the function of all these was the "mobilisation of plebicitary approval" for certain government policies both during and independent of electoral campaigns'.[3]

Bismarck's tentative entry into the race for colonies is a text book example of how social movements at home which are well organised and enjoy popular support can lead to a direction in politics not originally envisaged or at least considered less than prudent by the government. Another important factor was the personality of the young Kaiser, Wilhelm II who had acceded to the imperial throne in 1888, the 'year of the three Kaisers' (*Dreikaiserjahr*) when Wilhelm I having died, 9 March, was succeeded by his ailing son Friedrich III who followed his father to the grave already on 15 June.

The accession of Wilhelm II certainly ushered in a new era in German, European and world politics. His mercurial personality and impetuousness combined to lead him to embrace what with hindsight can be seen to have been very dangerous enthusiasms, in particular his ambition to build a navy that would rival that of Great Britain. Wilhelm's relationship to Queen Victoria, his maternal grandmother, had apparently always been warm, but he certainly developed a deep-seated hostility towards England because it stood in the way of German imperial expansion both on the Continent and overseas by insisting on maintaining the so-called balance of power. Indeed, it is fair to say that the Kaiser was aided and abetted in his enthusiasms very strongly by Admiral Alfred von Tirpitz who became obsessed by the idea of outbuilding the Royal Navy in battleships. With hindsight it can now be seen that it was the bitter rivalry between the kindred nations over naval construction that led to the ultimate alienation that culminated in the Great War.

One cannot be precise in setting a date for the fateful onset of the Anglo-German antagonism (Paul Kennedy, see the photo between pp. 200–1). It was something that was gradually building up during Bismarck's chancellorship partly because the more critical liberal elements in Germany lent towards the kind of parliamentary constitutionalism that had developed in the course of the 19th century in England.

For Bismarck, however, this was an unacceptable idea. He could not endorse the democratic convention that a government should be dependent upon the majority in parliament. His reasoning was based on the possibility that when governments changed at election times treaty arrangements entered into by the previous government could be easily overturned by the in-coming government. This, he believed, would put all alliance obligations at risk and so international stability which Bismarck desired above all on German terms would be endangered. Inevitably in constitutional matters the Iron Chancellor found himself at loggerheads with the Kaiser Friedrich III and his English wife, Victoria, who made no secret of the fact that they would prefer a constitutional monarchy such as existed in England. It is one of the great 'could-have-beens' of history had Friedrich lived to effect his envisaged modernisation of the Prusso-German constitution. But since he died prematurely of throat cancer and was succeeded by his vain and temperamental heir, Wilhem II, history took a completely different path from the more stable and peaceful one envisaged. Above all Wilhelm wanted to rule himself, determined to play a major role on the world stage. Already in 1892 he said: *Zum Grossen sind wir noch bestimmt und herrlichen Tagen führe ich Euch entgegen* (We are destined for great things to come and I will lead you to glorious days ahead). Certainly, *Weltpolitik*, the German version of imperialism, took off under Wilhelm II, especially naval building.

Centrally relevant to our narrative is the afore-mentioned German acquisition of the treaty port of Tsingtao in 1898 on the Shantung peninsula which was built up as a naval base for the cruiser squadron and which had in the hinterland copious coal reserves without which no navy could function long overseas; hence the need of all navies at that time to have reliable coaling stations around the world.[4] The history of the German East Asia Squadron impinges significantly on the history of Australasian defence because in German naval planning the eventuality of a war with England was always on the agenda and so appropriate measures needed to be put in place. These were always updated in accordance with the changes in the diplomatic situation. Well one might ask what could operational plans in the Pacific against Australian ports and shipping possibly have to do with defeating England in the North Sea?

To comprehend this one must appreciate the nature and purpose of cruiser or trade warfare called in German *Kreuzerkrieg* – or often *Kaperkrieg* – which is effectively a form of government-sponsored piracy. The objective is to prevent raw materials essential for the war effort from reaching their intended destination. This means that cruisers operating alone or in small groups should engage all enemy cargo vessels, plunder their cargo and coal and then scuttle them, having allowed crew and passengers to abandon ship in life boats or be taken on board as captives. There is no intention in such warfare to engage enemy warships in a sea battle unless a confrontation proved unavoidable. The main thing was for the cruisers to prevent raw materials from reaching their destination in the metropolitan country thus weakening its capacity to wage war. Consequently, the cruiser warfare could cause critical shortages both of food and raw materials. In the case of exports from Australasia to the United Kingdom the Germans were very well informed as to precisely what kinds of goods were being shipped regularly. How they obtained this knowledge will be dealt with below.

Cruiser warfare, so the doctrine went, was an extremely important means by which to diminish the enemy's ability to conduct a regular land war. It must be stressed that it was the chief means of denying the import of critical goods both in the form of foodstuffs and such commodities as were vital to the survival of the population in the British Isles, especially the working class. Secondly, strategic materials such as wool and wolfram and other key commodities which the Antipodean dominions supplied in large quantities would be lost to the British war effort. Added to this the Royal Navy would be required to send flotillas to remote shipping lanes in the hope of locating a sole enemy cruiser. This, however required the deployment of resources on costly expeditions when they would otherwise be needed in home waters. For the enemy, then, cruiser warfare was a factor of considerable tactical and strategic significance.

A further factor in the equation was the German use of so-called auxiliary cruisers. They were armed merchantmen which were especially useful as bunkering ships, that is for their ability to supply much needed coal to warships stationed overseas. As well, auxiliary cruisers had because of their coal reserves a greater range than even regular cruisers, and with their light armament could deal with most enemy cargo vessels. Too little is known and understood about the German war-aims in the Pacific and the part they played in the overall scheme to dislodge England from her status as the world power of the time.[5] But when the focus is on the function of the German intelligence gathering network in Australia and New Zealand we get some idea of the extent of German ambition and determination to do great damage to the British. Given that a number of high profile Australian-based historians and publicists have either denied the existence of such a network or bagatellised its nefarious purpose, it is surely time a century later, to set the record straight. So what was the purpose of this network and how did it function as an agency of the German navy?

Dr Overlack's research has shown (see below) that the German cruiser squadron in the Pacific was required, as its professional duty, to devise plans for warfare against all possible enemies, and this meant all existing great powers with colonies in the region. Consequently, war plans in case of hostilities with Russia, France, Japan, the United States, and of course, Britain, had continually to be up-dated. This meant that in all these countries and their colonies, German agents were at work gathering intelligence relevant to both defence and commerce. Shipping movements and the nature of cargoes was high on the list of priorities. The objective in each case was to keep up the supply of data of this nature so that it would be available for evaluation in case of war. In short, the plan in each case had to be readily available awaiting activation.

The German intelligence gathering network in Australia and New Zealand was gradually built up from the earliest days of the establishment of consulates. This was far from an easy project for the Germans since they needed people on the spot who had reliable knowledge of defence and commerce matters or who had access to persons who did. Such information had to be gathered without arousing the suspicions of the host country. What was needed then were so-called *Vertrauensmänner* meaning individuals who were known to be pro-German, utterly discreet, trustworthy and loyal to the Kaiser. Some of these people would have been naturalised British subjects of German birth or sympathy along side those native born, unnaturalised German subjects. Obviously, in that case, some were technically traitors. This phenomenon was relatively widespread and has been the subject of reliable research. Persons who were in effect spies reported initially, of course, to the German consulates where the consul himself would be the *Berichterstatter,* that is the chief reporter in each of the port cities from Fremantle to Brisbane and Auckland or Wellington, who then had the task of collating the information for the German Foreign Office. This was done by handing the material to the captain of one of the German cruisers that made regular visits to the main Australasian ports.

As indicated, this was not as straightforward a task as it might seem. It has to be kept in mind that foreign consulates in British possessions did not have diplomatic immunity as do embassies. This meant that the police could at any time enter and demand inspection of all activities of the consuls regardless of whether they were honorary (British subjects) or official German public servants. So there was always a problem concerning where to conceal intelligence material until it was collected by the visiting naval officer.

Nevertheless, the intelligence gathering continued along these lines from prior to Federation and then with increased intensity up to the outbreak of war. This activity was, of course, not unnoticed by Commonwealth security officers who as soon as war was declared arrested all German personnel and known sympathisers who were then destined for internment. It explains as well why no incriminating material was found; it had not in any case been filed in the consulate premises but discreetly deposited in the private homes of German sympathisers who then would have had adequate time to destroy any compromising material.

The Presentism in Left Wing Thought

The historians of the ideological Left in Australia hesitate to investigate the essential reasons for the draconian government policies towards enemy aliens and labour dissenters. The genuine threat to national security by imperial Germany tends to be ignored. Clearly, this is not acceptable because it deliberately brackets out of the equation the facts behind German belligerence. This is precisely what those publicists do who are perennially disgruntled with the social and political culture of Australia and argue that the allegedly exaggerated cult of Anzac hinders progress towards 'independence'.[6] It is argued, in short, that it tends to make Australians more and more attached to the imperial connection and this is portrayed as a bad thing as Douglas Newton argues in his contribution entitled, 'Other People's Wars: the Great War in a World Context.'[7]

The common fallacy of all doctrinaire history is that it always serves a current political agenda. It is not as though the historical roots of a current political movement are being conscientiously investigated; rather the accent is on mining the past for any data at all which can be pressed into service to bolster current political goals. The Reverend Dr Davis McCaughey, the former Irish-born governor of Victoria, has pointed to this phenomenon with regard to the way Irish nationalists write their history. Their concern is not scientific or detached scholarship but the winning of current political conflict.[8]

It would be appropriate here to recall how the Great War broke out as a consequence of the great international crisis that erupted after the assassination of the Austrian Archduke at Sarajevo 28 June which escalated until 4 August. For example, the German refusal to give guarantees about the future of Belgium's or France's overseas territories in the event of their defeat at German hands was tantamount to a self-unmasking of what Germany would do with British colonies should she succeed in defeating Britain.[9] Germany certainly did not regard the British Dominions as any more than dependencies and prizes to be fought over. But even before the outbreak of hostilities, the Australian government had been concerned about the long-term effect of the German naval build-up on Britain's future ability to maintain adequate defence of the exposed Dominions.

It was surely a demand of the utmost prudence for the Commonwealth leadership to be observant about the European balance of power. The notion that distance from Europe, the source of conflict, gave an assurance of security was illusory. If Germany succeeded in destroying the Royal Navy as she had intended (Tirpitz Plan) then the overseas Dominions would have been without effective protection.[10] Any Great Power with the naval capability would have posed a threat. For example, there was the perennial worry about Japanese intentions. So, it was hardly a matter of indifference to the Australian government if Britain had succumbed in a struggle with Prussia-Germany.

Indeed, the contributions from the Left in general are an example of what Davis McCaughey identified as 'applied history'; you leave out that knowledge of the past that does not fit into your current political agenda.[11] There was, indeed, a threat to Australia's continued existence mounted by the Prusso-German Empire in 1914. A German victory over the Allies at that time would have left Australasia virtually defenceless. At the very least there would have been an increase in German naval strength in the Pacific that would have been the pre-condition for any future intervention in Australian affairs that the Germans cared to make. A Pacific region dominated by Germany was a prospect too unbearable for any Australasian politician to contemplate whether Labor or Conservative. The perennial Left play down Australian anxiety concerning German naval intelligence operations in the Pacific as unwarranted. This they could only do by refusing to take cognisance of the detailed research of Dr Peter Overlack on this subject.[12]

As well, it would be important for Left-wing critics of Australia's entry into the Great War to try to grasp the significance of recent research on the so-called German *Sonderweg,* that is 'separate path', meaning Germany's failure to develop into a modern parliamentary democracy similar to France, Britain and the United States. The work of the two English erstwhile Marxian historians, David Blackbourn and Geoff Eley that argued some time ago that there was no appreciable difference between Wilhelmine Germany and the Western powers of the time is fundamentally flawed despite some structural parallels.[13] This has been seductive in leading many people into underestimating the real and crucial differences in political culture between Prussia-Germany and the Western parliamentary states. Certainly, Wilhelmine Germany evinced many modern traits that were admired by Western observers such as the system of social services, the training of apprentices and the excellence of all phases of education, primary, secondary and tertiary. None of these undoubted advances, however, could make up for the fact that Wilhelmine Germany was essentially a modernised military state governed by an elite that held the Western political system in the greatest contempt and was especially hostile to the labour movement. In short, it was implacably hostile to modernisation where it really counted, namely in the sphere of political culture. And it was this factor that caused anxiety to all neighbouring states.

CHAPTER 4

Recounting the Rise of the Prussian Menace and German War Aims 1914–1918

Sir Christopher Clark has argued in his study, *The Sleepwalkers*, that the Powers stumbled into the Great War in a state of somnambulist confusion, that is, quite unintentionally. As all the other members of the 'Fischer School' of historians this writer also sees a clear intentionality in German war policy.[1] Going to war in Europe had always been a realistic possibility from Bismarck's earliest years as Reich Chancellor. For example in April 1875 it was seriously considered in Berlin to threaten France with preventive war should the French begin cultivating ideas of a war of *revanche* for the loss in 1871 of Alsace-Lorraine to Germany. In short, *Kriegsbereitschaft* (war preparedness) was an essential feature of Prusso-German diplomacy, sometimes called 'sabre rattling.'

But here the initial purpose is briefly to review the 'intentionalist school'. The afore-mentioned work of the Anglo-German scholar, Professor John Röhl on Kaiser Wilhelm II is arguably the most advanced example. From him we may learn a great deal about the power structure in a country that was essentially a military State despite its parliamentary façade. It is not surprising that Professor Röhl has made this very clear because he found it necessary to instruct English students about how different the German ruling classes were in contrast to their British cousins.

As indicated in the Preface and Introduction, historiography is inevitably ideologically driven, despite the heroic attempts of historians to be as objective in their accounts as humanly possible. Obviously we must always bear in mind that historians in open societies may espouse any ideology they prefer so long as they do not advocate sedition. They may also market their ideas, however bizarre or under-researched they might be or however prejudiced.

Having discussed these issues with many German and trans-Atlantic historians as well as Australasian colleagues over many years one learns to prize open-mindedness and even-handedness. This was stressed by my mentors, both as an undergraduate in Queensland and later as a post-graduate student in Germany. They were invariably men of liberal mind who admired decency and abhorred injustice. That means they were obviously neither nationalist nor Marxist in their convictions. None of them would have said anything as dogmatic as the late R. S. Neale used to assert, namely that if one were not a Marxist then one was practising serendipity. On reflection I would suggest now that the scholars under whose direction I studied were all to some degree 'Whig' historians.

This is meant in the restricted sense that they simply endorsed the notion that history traces a political-pedagogic process that leads to freedom and human equality. From where they derived these convictions was, of course, not entirely apparent. In the case of Professor Gordon Greenwood of Queensland (see the photo between pp. 200–1), Whig ideas were clearly uppermost in his table of values and these were infused into what and how he taught. Indeed, he made no secret of the fact that he admired the evolution of the English constitution and the doctrines of parliamentary control of the executive. Further, in respect of the pedagogic purpose of history, Greenwood was in no doubt that it was the storehouse of experience for what he called men of affairs; historical study was necessary especially for those aspiring to a career in politics. Certainly Professor Greenwood belonged to the age when political bullies whether of fascist or communist provenance were constantly in the news and presaged great difficulties for what was then known as the 'free world'.

The Prussianisation of German History

I encountered a similar situation in Germany 1961–65 when I studied under the above mentioned Professor Franz Schnabel, who clearly attributed the disastrous course of German history from Bismarck to Hitler to the failure of Germans to develop a Whig tradition. In short, that meant the encouragement of the principles of self-government such as had been advocated in Germany by Baron vom Stein during the Prussian reform movement after the Napoleonic Wars. These, however, were never adopted by the Prussian kings although throughout the period 1815 to 1848 known as the *Vormärz* (literally 'pre-March', meaning the era leading up to the 1848 revolutions), an increasing number of German professors all over the country in the various principalities had been advocating German unity on the basis of a liberal parliamentary constitution. By 'liberal' in those days they meant something very revolutionary, namely the demand that princes abandon their divine right sovereignty and allow elections for a legislative assembly along the principles already in place elsewhere such as in England. In short they wanted to introduce a new concept of sovereignty.

These professors were, of course, not revolutionaries in the Marxian sense, but basically radical liberals who hoped to modernise German domestic politics rationally without violence. Contrary to their high hopes the outcome of the 1848 revolutions in Germany and Austria was a humiliating defeat for all liberals and social democrats. The King of Prussia, Friedrich Wilhelm IV had been offered the throne of a united Germany without Austria under the condition that he accept a liberal constitution. This he flatly refused to do by saying that such a constitution would be like a dog-collar chaining him to the revolution. He was still irrevocably committed to the notion that he was a monarch by divine right and firmly rejected the doctrine of the sovereignty of the people. One needs to recall that the memory of the Terror that followed the French Revolution was still present, having been refreshed by the failed revolutionary attempt of 1830 in Paris. None of the German princes was inclined to make any concessions to the spirit of the times and demonstrated this forcefully by using their armies under the leadership of Prussia to put down all attempts to keep the Frankfurt National Assembly alive, even in its rump form.

During the year 1849–50 a violent counter revolution led by Prussian arms triumphed throughout the Germanic lands. This left the German liberals with nowhere to go. Everywhere the Germans were ruled by military force although some monarchs allowed elections to legislative assemblies that did not have any control over the executive. What happened next was an interesting example of the reciprocal relationship (*Wechselwirkung*) between politics and historiography. This means simply that historians who had arrogated to themselves the role of prophet by virtue of their knowledge of the past, had acquired the right to point the way to the future. As the leading historian Johann Gustav Droysen (1808–84) observed at the time, the State needed historical studies for its instruction and leadership, in short to provide a roadmap for the future to the political decision-makers.[2] The collapse of the liberal movement of 1848 indicated to some of the intellectual leaders at the time that they should abandon the idea of importing foreign political traditions into Germany such as parliamentary democracy because these were clearly not going to work, given the historic hold on power which the princes had. So they developed the idea that one had to recognise the real existing situation and try to work within it, that is, to submit to realities.

Readers with some knowledge of German intellectual history will be aware of the political philosophy of Georg Wilhelm Friedrich Hegel (1770–1831) who was known in his life time with the semi ironic appellation of the 'Royal Prussian State Philosopher'.[3] This was a reference to the role Hegel played behind the scenes as a professor of philosophy in Berlin (1818–31) from where he exerted considerable influence on German thinking about the role of the State in history. As an indication of his importance Hegel was made *Rektor* of the University of Berlin in 1828. He taught among other things that the State was the agency of almighty God on earth and in doing so anchored in the German mind the teachings of Martin Luther (1483–1546) that the 'powers-that-be' are ordained by

God.[4] This was a most effective confirmation for the doctrine of the divine right of kings.

This, we should recall, had been overthrown in England in 1641 followed by France in 1789. In Germany, as we have seen, the doctrine was unsuccessfully challenged in the 1848 revolutions. By 1850, the princes and the monarchical principle had prevailed over the forces of political and social change. As a consequence in Germany the old Lutheran principle of obedience to the divinely sanctioned authorities, 'the-powers-that-be' (*Obrigkeit*) was reinforced and this was a major factor in delaying the political modernisation of a country that in all other respects, that is industrially, commercially and scientifically, was becoming a leader in the civilised world. Indeed, Germans were being educated in the conviction that subservience to the 'powers-that-be' was the supreme virtue. Dissent was, in that case, tantamount to a mortal sin because it opposed the will of the monarch who was God's anointed authority on earth. That is why the German Lutheran churches in particular functioned as the most effective bulwark against political modernisation right up to the time of Adolf Hitler.[5] They were confirmed in their political conservatism most powerfully by Hegelianism. And this posthumous triumph of Hegel was due largely to the above mentioned Johann Gustav Droysen who had produced between 1855 and 1886 a 14 volume study of Prussian history. It is certainly not insignificant that Droysen was the son of a Prussian army chaplain and had begun his academic career by focussing on ancient Greece. He had already written a history of Alexander the Great in 1833 followed by a history of Hellenism in 1836–43. Here he had developed a great admiration for Sparta and the military tradition of that political entity. For Droysen the parallel between Sparta and the Prussia of his day had become highly instructive. Both were military monarchies with a vocation to unite the surrounding states under their peculiar political culture, that is by military force. This idea became an obsession with Droysen and it shaped his subsequent historiography.

Historiography as Political Ideology

The evolution of the profession of history at German universities from the period of reaction post 1850 until the virtually unchallenged triumph of the Prussian School that reached its peak under Heinrich von Treitschke (1834–96) is an object lesson in the power of ideas in the shaping of human affairs. During the heyday of Marxism, one often heard that the controlling agency of human action was economic relationships. Those who controlled the production, distribution and exchange of goods dictated the course of history. If one wanted to be a loyal Marxist-Leninist, one had to accept this dogma. For the historian this meant that one studied and taught the nature of class relationships from antiquity to the present as Marx prescribed. What happened in the past was to be explained by understanding who had control of the means of production, distribution and exchange. It was an attractive blanket explanation for all human relationships at the base of which was the doctrine that labour power was the source of all value. This kind of historiography prevailed in the entire Soviet bloc and especially in East Germany (the German Democratic Republic) from 1945 until 1989 when the infamous wall was broken down. It was a time when historians in the Soviet bloc laid claim to having the absolute truth (*der absolute Wahrheitsanspruch*). The march of time was to prove them wrong.

Once this had been demonstrated to have been a manifest absurdity with the implosion of the Soviet bloc in 1989 there appeared a remarkable study entitled *The End of History* by the Japanese-American Francis Fukuyama who envisaged that the nations of the world were moving toward the establishment of 'universal and homogeneous state' with a liberal or social democratic government and where a modified capitalism would prevail. It was an optimistic but premature augury. Fukuyama's earlier confident prediction underestimated the rise of terroristic religion such as is manifested in many Islamic countries which have declared war on the liberal democratic West. The point here is that such phenomena illustrate that fanaticism or extreme religiously motivated ideologies can and do alter the course of history. Ideologies and religions can and do inspire people to follow what they perceive to be great and noble goals either in the name of their God or some other driving force, and by rigorously following these imagined injunctions may perpetrate all manner of mayhem and atrocity because the attainment of their goal justifies it. Any human beings who get in the way are therefore expendable. Such systems of rule are often called 'murderous Utopias'. Even considered more noble is the phenomenon of the suicide bomber, namely the one who willingly sacrifices him or herself for the great cause. In one version of Moslem teaching, soldiers who die in the cause of Islam (martyrs) are received in Paradise by seventy virgins.[6]

It is sobering to recall that the willingness to self-sacrifice in the service of one's country is as old as recorded history. *Dulce et decorum est pro patria mori* (It is a sweet and noble thing to die for one's country) was a saying frequently used in the aftermath of the Great War but it had been formulated initially by the Roman poet Horace (Quintus Horatius Flaccus, 63 BC–8 BC). In the famous anti-war novel by Erich Maria Remarque, *Im Westen Nichts Neues* 1928 (*All Quiet on the Western Front*) it is cited by a fervently patriotic schoolmaster in a German town from whose 6th form (*Arbitur Klasse*) earlier in the war his senior pupils had enlisted and of whom many had already fallen for the fatherland. The scene evokes the actual horrific events of trench warfare in which the author as a German soldier himself had participated. The disturbing reality is that in Germany still to this day the battle in the Belgian town of Langemarck, 21–24 October 1914, is remembered because in the cemetery there are circa 10,000 graves of German soldiers who fell in that campaign and many of those were very young unblooded volunteers, just out of school. The myth recalls that they went into battle singing *Deutschland über Alles*! In some ways Langemarck compares to those battles or campaigns which Australians remember, namely Gallipoli, Fromelles, Pozières and Villers-Bretonneux during the Great War. In the interwar period pacifists in Germany who abhorred the glorification of war found life extremely difficult and in the Nazi era were openly discriminated against. The ultra-patriots regarded any such anti-war sentiment as virtual sedition.

Focussing now on the political-pedagogic role of history helps us to understand the rise of such a mentality in Germany. If we are aware of the dominance of the profession of history at the universities and secondary schools we grasp that history was indeed taught as the school of patriotism or nationalism. As indicated, the so-called Prussian school came to exert an intellectual hegemony over education throughout the country. It was a phenomenon of particular concern to Germans of socialist and liberal persuasion because the Prussian school of history was committed to a class structure that ensured the dominance of conservatism and monarchism. Indeed, the professors of history in Germany with few exceptions functioned rather like a chorus, such as in a Greek play, eloquently proclaiming the glories of the militaristic Hohenzollern dynasty of Prussia. The dire consequences of this systematic indoctrination were at last recognised by the German professors after the destruction of German militarism in 1945 by the combined efforts of the Soviet Union and the Western Allies. It was acknowledged, at least by some leading German history professors, that the legacy of the Prussian school had been deleterious. It had functioned, apart from exalting militarism and sanctifying a brutal racism, to inculcate anti-democratic values, indeed to spread the idea that to embrace liberal or social democratic ideas was incompatible with being a good German. This was a problem that had to be confronted by profession post 1945. Leading academics from among the historians, political scientists, philosophers, theologians, jurists and sociologists were all challenged to revise their paradigm of political conviction.

This kind of revisionism or need to re-assess the significance of ultra-patriotic historiography might have occurred after the Great War but except for a handful of genuine pacifists who suffered ostracism most German historians remained obstinately unwilling to re-assess Prusso-German militaristic culture. Indeed, the majority of German social scientists refused to endorse the accusation of sole German war guilt or even consider it. They affirmed, instead, their pre-war conviction, namely that militaristic Bismarckian constitution was the most appropriate for Germany. The liberal-democratic parliamentary constitution of Weimar that had been virtually smuggled in via the shameful November 1918 revolution by the social democratic-liberal coalition at the Constituent National Assembly in June 1919 was a totally unworthy political instrument for the German people. The parties of the right regarded it at best as a despised foreign import from the West or at worst a Marxist-Jewish subterfuge. Under these conditions the Weimar constitution was crippled from birth. Historians certainly played a significant role in hastening the demise of the democratic parliamentary Weimar Republic. For example, one of the most high-profile historians of the time, namely Professor Hans Delbrück (1848–1929) was bold enough after the defeat of 1918 to write a spirited defence of the Bismarckian constitution indicating strongly that he did not approve of the adaptation of parliamentary principles derived from England, France or America. In contrast to his Anglo-Saxon interlocutors, Delbrück saw no continuity between the militarism of Bismarckian-Wilhelmine Germany and decision for war in August 1914.[7] Neither did the rambunctious Professor Gerhard Ritter (1888–1967) after the Second World War who became the implacable enemy of Fritz Fischer and his school.

It is this kind of defiant, truculent imperviousness to new ideas among those Germans who were in a position to advocate liberal and humane political change that weakened their ability to resist the palpable evil of National Socialism when it finally seized power in 1933. Tragically, these men acted as an unconscious conduit between the militarist, anti-Semitic Bismarckian-Wilhelmine Empire and the unquestionably rogue state of Adolf Hitler that was hell-bent on revising the settlement of Versailles and re-constituting Germany not with a restoration of the Hohenzollern dynasty, but as a ruthlessly racist and terrorist regime, the polar opposite of a benign, liberal, humanitarian state which with the passage of time contemporary Germany has become, and, as one hopes, will remain. The regrettable fact is, however, that there was an undeniable continuity between the militaristic Empire that Bismarck founded in 1871 and the militaristic and racist Third Reich of Adolf Hitler. The undoubtedly major link between the two eras of modern German history was the foreign policy and war aims of Imperial Germany which as the Swiss historian, the late Adolf Gasser emphasised, were driven by the German generals.[8] With the allegedly punitive Treaty of Versailles in 1919 the ambitions of the German power elite to pursue the war aims of 1914–18 had by no means been crushed or forgotten They crackled beneath the crisis-ridden surface of the ill-fated Weimar Republic for a further fourteen years until the seizure of power by the Nazi Party enabled the war-lord, Adolf Hitler to re-mobilise them. Most generals of the *Reichswehr* were only too eager to fall in behind the *Führer*, aided and abetted by the captains of German industry. They all wanted to realise the frustrated 'Ideas of 1914' thus re-enforcing the continuity in modern German history.

CHAPTER 5

Historicism: The Forgotten Ideology Behind *Weltpolitik**

Understanding Prusso-German *peculiarity* is the essential pre-condition for any explanation of *Pan-Germanism* and its world-historical consequences. Indeed, what might be called the formation of the nineteenth century 'German mind' constitutes an intellectual challenge for the uninitiated. This is very evident when trying to understand the war-guilt debate unleashed by the publication of Sir Christopher Clark's *The Sleepwalkers* in 2012. This has given rise to some concerns. A major one is Clark's apparent unwillingness to evaluate the deep-seated cultural differences between Germany and the West. As indicated above, these issues became pre-eminent for German historians post 1945 in their strenuous efforts to ascertain the root causes of the antagonism between Wilhelmine and then Nazi Germany on the one hand and her European neighbours, both in the East and in the West, on the other. Indeed, the intellectual-historical dimension in Clark's work seems at best attenuated. Hence this chapter seeks to add to our understanding of German intellectual peculiarity, dominated as it was by the phenomenon of *Historismus* or historicism.

It is an exercise essential for comprehending the Prusso-German mind and the way in which it comprehended the world. It is argued here that the German way of thinking about the nature of States contributed significantly to the discrediting of liberal-democratic ideas and to the

---

* I wish to acknowledge the constructive commentary made by the late Professor Georg G. Iggers on an earlier draft of this chapter.

acceleration of first cultural and then political nationalism thus deepening the gulf between Germany and the West. The fateful consequence of this alienation cannot be overestimated as the savagery of the Great War attests.

It is precisely here, that is in the divergence of the German mind from Western political values, where more strenuous efforts of understanding need to be made. Bismarckian-Wilhelmine Germany was a very much more ominous entity than the *gemütlich* (easy going, good natured) 'land of poets and thinkers'. It was indeed ominous due to the incorrigible nature of the Prusso-German power elite who were implacably opposed to any ideas of political reform advanced by the people of liberal or social-democratic persuasion. The latter comprised in fact the majority of the German population as the above mentioned election results of 1912 had emphatically demonstrated when the desire for democratic change was clearly expressed.[1] The ruling elite had been put on notice that their political dominance was unacceptable. German domestic politics exhibited more and more all the hall marks of irreconcilable class struggle which resulted in a 'stampede into war.'[2]

As will be seen, the German ruling classes were so reluctant to make democratic concessions to accommodate the social democrats and liberals that they preferred the option of war in the expectation that a great victory over the French, Russians and the British would shore up the autocratic monarchical system for imaginable time.

The American scholar-diplomat George Kennan once perceptively commented, the Great War of 1914–18 was 'the seminal catastrophe of the 20th century.'[3] Not surprisingly, interest in that war and Australia's part in it has been re-awakened at this time of the centenary. In Europe the urgent question of who was really responsible for that conflict in the first place is being posed yet again. And this has led to a drama on the broader European stage in which the afore-mentioned Sir Christopher Clark of St Catherine's College, Cambridge, played the key role. Apart from *The Sleepwalkers: How Europe went to war in 1914* (2012),[4] Clark had distinguished himself with an even larger work on Prussia entitled *The Iron Kingdom: the Rise and Downfall of Prussia 1660–1947* (2006). Previous to that again he had produced a biography of the third and last German Emperor, *Kaiser Wilhelm, A Life in Power*. Christopher Clark's historiographical achievements have been so remarkable that the Queen has bestowed a knighthood upon him for services to Anglo-German relations.[5]

Numerous other accolades have been reaped by Clark that honour the sheer expanse of his scholarly achievement but as well there is an undoubted political dimension. By attempting to show that imperial Germany was no more guilty for the outbreak of the Great War in 1914 than any other of the belligerents Clark has won widespread acclaim especially in conservative circles in Germany where the sales of the translation of *The Sleepwalkers* had reached astronomical figures. [6] Despite such worldly success, however, Clark has had to endure severe criticism, especially from the democratic Left in Germany for failing to consult sources that negate his argument. In short, Clark is challenged on the grounds of *strategic selectivity* of documents. This is grave criticism for a professional historian who is supposed to remain as clinically objective as possible. For example, serious criticism has been levelled by Professor Klaus Wernecke and others for only selecting those documents that support his argument while omitting others that would counter it. In this regard, Clark would seem to be weaving a story he wants to narrate for purposes known only to himself.[7]

That is one thing; the other is that Clark has presented in *The Sleepwalkers* a narrative that claims only to explain *how* the Great War broke out. The deeper and essential question of *why* is studiously avoided, and so there are many colleagues who are wondering why this crucial question was not posed. We have the history of the superstructure with the substructure left out as one German critic has noted.[8] It is as though the profound cultural differences among the belligerent Powers played no part in influencing political decisions. The purpose of this chapter is to draw attention to what might arguably be considered the key factor in German political culture, namely historicism (*Historismus*), the peculiar 19th century German way of understanding the character of nations. There has, of course, been much written about German 'peculiarity'. For example, the German intellectual community with few exceptions were well known for their endorsement of war as not only endemic to the human condition but also for regarding it as culturally necessary. The following excursus provides a succinct explanation for this and answers the deeper question why the Germans saw no alternative to declaring war in August 1914.

It was a question that had been exercising the mind of leading German historians ever since 1945. Particularly since Professor Fritz Fischer (1906–97) threw down the gauntlet to his conservative colleagues at the first post-war Historians' Congress which was held in Munich in 1949 there has been a highly politicised debate about this subject. Fischer's pioneering work signalled the outbreak of a controversy that is ongoing. [9] One wonders why Clark felt no need to draw attention to this. Is not the historian in particular obliged to highlight cultural differences between nations, specifically to show how different Germany was from the West and how the German intellectuals and the ruling classes celebrated their putative uniqueness.[10] This demands careful explanation.

***

In the 1950s the German historian Ludwig Dehio (1888–1963) published, in a spirit of honest self-examination, a pioneering paper entitled, 'Ranke and German Imperialism'.[11] In this he sketched out how an entire generation of German historians from the 1890s onwards had become the most fervent advocates of Germany's mission to become the greatest world power, to exercise, in short, hegemony over the entire world. These historians functioned like a self-appointed propaganda agency for *Weltpolitik*, that is the German version of imperialism. In fact they behaved more like a chorus in an unfolding Greek tragedy. Calling themselves Neo-Rankeans, they saw themselves as the spiritual heirs of the founder of the German historical discipline, Leopold von Ranke (1795–1886) because they projected his doctrine of the balance of power as the controlling mechanism of European politics from the time of Napoleon I to around 1900, to the age of the new imperialism which was playing out on the wider world stage. In doing so they claimed to discern a special role for the German Empire, namely to prevent the various nations of the world from being stifled by a culturally inferior power, namely England, which in the then German usage meant the entire British Empire.

It is well known that particularly from 1890 onwards Anglo-German relations were becoming very strained and there was much journalistic as well as academic comment about the possibility of war.[12] Foremost among the political commentators on the German side were the historians, – most of the Neo-Rankeans. It would, however, be wrong to attribute their anti-British attitudes solely to an emotionally based chauvinism; they were, on the contrary, the logical expression of the particular brand of historicism which became for them nothing more or less than the ideology of imperialism. For them that was the result of what they called *wissenschaftliche Erkenntnisse*, meaning rigorous scholarly observations and insights.

Since Dehio's pioneering paper of sixty-five years ago there has emerged, initially from West German universities, a variety of studies which reflect the crisis in German historical and hence political thinking. These frankly expose the historicist assumptions on which it was based. What follows is derived from the work of mostly West German scholars on historicism and its significance for what they call the formation of political will (*politische Willensbildung*).[13] When a survey is made of the close connection between German historicism and politics the question must be posed that if a theory of national history is not a political program then it is at least political ideology. In short, the historicist ideas of Johann Gottfried von Herder (1744–1803) which were developed by G. W. F. Hegel (1770–1831) and Leopold von Ranke (1794–1875) ultimately became through their disciples a virtually incontrovertible ideology of imperialism. And this ideology was translated into catastrophic reality.

The procedure now will be first to outline the evolution of historicism of which von Ranke became the supreme exponent; secondly, to explain how this was developed into an ideology of so-called *Realpolitik*, and thirdly to demonstrate how, after the foundation of the Reich by Bismarck in 1871, it became transformed into a highly persuasive ideology of *Weltpolitik*, that is, the rationale for Prusso-German expansion into the world.

Although there are a variety of definitions for Historicism, that provided by one of the most influential of the Neo-Rankeans, namely Friedrich Meinecke (1862–1954) is the most helpful. In 1936 he published his third work on central problems of German intellectual history, *Die Entstehung des Historismus*.[14] Here Meinecke observed that historicism was the product of movements in German thought from Leibniz (1646–1716) to Goethe (1749–1832). It was the continuation of a general European movement in which German thinkers took the lead. It was, however, in one sense a revolt against the mainstream of European thought and in this regard, said Meinecke, the German spirit had performed *the second of its great historical achievements after the Reformation*. (Emphasis added.) Meinecke's language and that of his contemporaries is often distinguished by such rapturous exuberance, celebrating German uniqueness.

What one discerns here is not only the highlighting of German difference from the West, but also especially of their advanced cultural achievements. Obviously, Meinecke struggled with this during the Third Reich as his immediate post-war essay, *The German Catastrophe* reflects. He remained, however, despite the outrages against humanity perpetrated by the Hitler regime, unambiguously committed to the uniqueness of German *Kultur*. This, above all else, was precious to him and his class because it imparted to them their identity as Germans, the intellectual mentors of a superior European race. This derived from their awareness of the insights made in the period from Leibniz to Goethe, mentioned above. But as Meinecke was quick to point out, although historicism involved the application of new principles, it was more than a mere ideology; it was the break through of a crucially significant new method. By replacing the generalising approach to historical movements by the individualising approach, entirely new insights into reality could be gained. This did not mean the abandonment of the search for general laws and types in history. Indeed, the true historicist required this but in combination with a sensitivity for the unique and individual phenomena of historical life. Admittedly, said Meinecke, there had been some attention to this but the most essential dynamic forces in history, namely the soul and spirit of men had been neglected – due to an emphasis on the generalisng approach to history.[15]

Meinecke explained it this way: Hitherto historians had taken the view that man with his reason, passions, vices and virtues remained essentially the same in all periods of known history. This generalising view, however, barred the way to recognising the profound changes and varieties of experience which the spiritual and intellectual life of the individuals and peoples went through in spite of the permanence of basic human characteristics. The predominant belief in the uniformity of human nature and reason which permeated Western thought from antiquity asserted that human reason, when liberated from passion and ignorance expressed essentially the same things and cultivated the same values and therefore was capable of establishing transcendent, absolute and universally valid truths.

Historicism represented a revolt against this belief in absolutes. Indeed, it was seen and welcomed as a liberation of the human spirit from the strictures imposed by natural law and rationalism. Here, however, Meinecke qualified this by saying that the revolt was not against natural law and the absolutes of religion as such, but against that stage in the development of natural law which, as he put it, immediately preceded historicism,[16] and this was clearly the Enlightenment with its doctrine of linear progress and the perfectibility of man.[17]

Historicism with its concentration on individual phenomena allegedly overcame the sterile pragmatism imposed by the concepts of natural law. The latter, by prioritising the concept of the uniformity of human nature merely used history as a pedagogically useful set of examples of human action.[18] Such a pragmatic approach to the chequered variety of human experience was clearly inadequate; it was necessary not only to extract from history the general trends, but to grasp it as a living totality composed of unique individualities consisting of human beings, communities and of generations – each possessing unique and inimitable characteristics. Historicism set out to do justice to this aggregate of individualities and to make up for what was neglected as a consequence of the Enlightenment.[19] The founders of the movement in their creative optimism could not have suspected that they were paving the way for an irrationally nationalistic ideology that justified what was to become the most barbaric era in recorded history.

***

In order to trace how this happened it is necessary to go back to the thinker who was acclaimed as the great pioneer of historicism, chiefly for his concept of the *Volksgeist* (national spirit), Johan Gottfried von Herder (1744–1803). The importance of this for the growth of cultural nationalism cannot be overstressed. It is a clear repudiation of the Enlightenment concept of linear progress which regarded the past as *ipso facto* inferior to the present. During his sojourn in Riga (1764–69) Herder had the opportunity to observe the unique individuality of the two main ethnic groups living there and explained it as the result of the separate genetic, organic development of each group, namely the Baltic Germans and the Slavic Latvians. Each responded differently to their common environment; each group constituted a distinctly separate spiritual unity. As well, Herder perceived not only the different peoples of the world as discret spiritual entities, but also the distinct epochs in history. Human beings in their manifold diversity Herder regarded no longer as passive creatures of God but as active subjects of history, the bearers and originators of differing cultures each with an individual personality.

With such a clearly defined concept of individuality, history, for Herder was hardly an upward and uniform path of linear progress leading to the perfection of humanity. This being so it had profound implications for the investigation and writing of history. It meant that the historian now had to be concerned with the unique individuality of each epoch and of each people. The deductive approach to history prioritised by the Enlightenment had been clearly rejected by Herder in favour of an empiricism to enable a sympathetic comprehension of all historical phenomena. In this way the fallacy of over evaluating the present would be overcome by a historicising and relativising of both the temporal and geographical conditioning of each object of enquiry.

History thus conceived can scarcely discern a linear development from the beginning of recorded time to the present; it was rather an unceasing ebb and flow of divinely driven forces in constant change, in short, 'the path of God in nature.'[20] Pre-eminently, these forces can be seen in action in the various *Volk*-entities, that is, nations, which develop according to their own divinely implanted unique characteristics. Peoples, according to Herder, experience stages of growth, flourishing and decline. No *Volk* remains frozen in time; there is no absolute standard that once perfection has been reached a shut down occurs so that everything for ever remains the same. Obviously, human perfection is a relative thing, that is, relative to the particular *Volk* and its period of growth.

None of this should be surprising at the beginning of the 21st century in a world sorely afflicted by religious-ethnic violence. Some religious-ethnic groups certainly believe that what they presume to be God is calling them to launch crusades to impose their peculiar set of values on the world for its own good. The concept of a plurality of nations each representing different cultures living harmoniously along side of each other is a Utopian nonsense to them. The true God, essentially a 'warrior God', demands submission of all others to his will. But Herder in his time did not advocate any such thing. His idea of God was very much that of a loving father of a variety of nations. The point is, however, that the concept 'God' is the key element in Herder's historicism. It also reappears in that of Hegel and after him in von Ranke and all the subsequent German historicists. The Creator was the lord of the historical process which logically recognised human passions and violence as necessary concomitants to the creative aspects within the process. So there was a unity of all dynamic forces, indeed, a unity that could be grasped by recognising the principle of growth in history. There is growth in individuality, in the souls of human beings, of nations, cultures and epochs. And in this growth all dynamic forces whether good or evil played a part. It was all proceeding according to unique incomprehensible laws, the process of the manifestation of the Creator God in His universe.[21]

As indicated above, the political relevance of all this was not systematically worked out by Herder. Nevertheless, by identifying the *Volk* as an organism, as genetic individuality (*genetisches Individuum*) consisting of body, spirit and social unity simultaneously Herder paved the way for Hegel to forge his doctrine of the *Machtstaat* (power state) the idea of which was to prove so fateful for Germany. From Herder, Hegel appreciated that humanity was divided up into nations, each with its own *Volksgeist*; as a consequence, historical progress resulted from the interaction of all the above elements. And each nation perceived itself as having a unique commission from God to fulfil in the course of history. This was expressed in its peculiar culture. However, since they were all at different stages of growth, the most advanced nation was at the forefront, leading civilisation, bearing the genius of humanity. But, as history taught, when that nation reached its ceiling the signs of decay began to appear; decline was inevitable and that nation's historic task would be inherited by a younger more vigorous nation.

Note that Herder's historical theology remained a torso. It was obviously also a theology of history because the prime mover in his edifice was almighty God. The unique *Volksgeist* which Herder clearly identified remained for him essentially a cultural concept as opposed to political. Furthermore, his position remained essentially cosmopolitan. For him nations were not yet implacable antagonists locked in a social-darwinistic struggle for survival. In short, Herder's concept of nationality or *Volkstum* remained unpolitical.[22] And this points to the unresolved tension in Herder's doctrine of humanity on the one hand and his doctrine of nationality on the other. He spoke of 'restricted nationalism'.[23] Understandably as a Lutheran theologian of his time Herder perceived the real purpose of existence was the bringing of the peoples of the earth to the fullness of their humanity as the process which linked this world to the next.[24] Certainly, in order to grasp Herder's significance for the rise of German historicism it needs to be emphasised that he did regard the most natural kind of State as one peopled by the one discret *Volk* who formed a unique political community. Indeed, a State was a well organised, efficiently governed peaceful ethnic group. He could not envisage a State based on the conquest of other peoples, that is, an imperialistic power.[25] So Herder has gone down in history as the father of *cultural* as opposed to *political* nationalism.

***

From what has been said it should be reasonably clear that Herder's insight was the precursor of the ideas formulated by Hegel and then von Ranke both of whom effectively discarded the remnants of cosmopolitan thought of the Enlightenment. Hegel, however, pioneered the final breakthrough to identifying the State as the concrete and total expression of the *Volksgeist*. The ultimate goal of the developing *Volksgeist* is the formation of a State.[26] And it is right here that Hegel established the foundation for Prusso-German nationalism. In his schema, a *Volk* that fails to reach the stage of forming a viable State had no history; it has in fact not realised its 'rationality' in the dialectical process of the unfolding word spirit, to use Hegel's language. That which gave a *Volk* its life as a State is what Meinecke called the 'nationality principle.' And this is a very conservative concept, not to be confused with that which emerged in the French Revolution. There, the *Volk* of the democratic ideal was considered a mere aggregate of private individuals, *vulgus* and not *populous*, and as such only a blind, amorphous force. However, the nationality principle in the evolved historical and not revolutionary sense of 1789 contained the spiritual heritage of the entire past of a *Volk* which confronted both the present and future challenges to survival with reference to this principle.

This notion was vigorously opposed by none other than Karl Popper (1902–94) who observed that Hegel's dialectics were largely designed to pervert the democratic ideas of 1789. Popper was concerned to highlight the fateful consequences of the triumph of historicism over the rationalism and humanism of the Enlightenment. And looking back this is what we see: the State in its cultural entirety is the manifestation of the *Volksgeist*. Indeed, for Hegel the State is the embodiment of the matured *Volksgeist*. Furthermore, so that the State may maintain and develop itself in this world, Hegel concedes to it the right of unconditional autonomy to pursue the realisation of its interests. 'As an individual entity it is exclusively opposed to all other such entities.'[27] So, in the relations between States there can be no arbitrator who can decide what is right or what is wrong; there are only autonomous bodies ranged against other such bodies. This insight regarding the irreconcilable rivalry and hostility among States Hegel made into the cornerstone of his influential philosophy of history, his so-called *monism,* which claimed to impart a rational meaning to the reality of life on earth and thereby gave war an unconditional and definite place in the scheme of things. How, he asked, could there be eternal peace or permanent agreement between States when in each one resides a sovereign will?[28] The significance of this is identified by Meinecke when he wrote of Hegel:

> What his empiricism recognised his idealism had to sanction. In which case the soul of the state, the *raison d'état* and the core of Machiavelli's doctrine had to be sanctioned and so there occurred the novel and the monstrous, namely, that Machiavellism was incorporated into the context of an idealistic system which encompassed and supported all moral values; whereas previously it had existed only outside the moral order [...] What happened here was almost like the legitimising of a bastard.
>
> So Machiavelli had been restored to honour in Germany from the beginning of the 19th century. A specifically German attitude to the problem of Machiavellism began to develop ...[29]

Here is formulated what is arguably the essential difference between Germany and the West. The quasi official incorporation of Machiavellism as the basis for international relations into the mind of German decision makers was a problem that would haunt Western statesmen for decades to come. Few really understood it. One notable exception was the English foreign office official Sir Eyre Crowe who spelled it out in his famous 1907 Memorandum.[30]

As well, one should not forget in this context, Karl Popper's observation that Hegel's philosophy was essentially an apologia for Prussianism.[31] That is to say it was designed to justify the political status quo in the Prussia of his day. Virtually the same thing can be said of von Ranke's historicism. Although he differed from Hegel in one important issue, namely his doctrine of God (to be explored more fully below), he certainly did function as a political publicist with essentially conservative pro-Prussian royalist values.[32]

As Ranke expressed it, States were unique concentrations of moral energy, individual forces operating according to their own peculiar, divinely implanted logic, and to this extent Ranke was indeed following Hegel, clearly endorsing the doctrine of Machiavellism. This is clear when Ranke affirmed that nations were by their very nature programmed to act in order to preserve their identity, and that driven by their own impulses, must try to expand until they met with the resistance of other nation states. So the national egoism of each *Volk* leads inevitably to its insistence upon the unconditional right to survive, and here *raison d'état* was in the final analysis nothing more or less than the individuality idea of the State that was expressed in the mind of the leading statesmen.[33]

Ranke was, of course, fully aware that there were instances where a State pursuing its interests would transgress the moral law, but often, *necessity* allowed the statesman very little choice: *Nicht freie Wahl, sondern die Notwendigkeit der Dinge,* that is, it was not 'not a free choice but rather the compulsion of necessity' which dominated the relations between States.[34] This was the reality; the Powers were seen to be moving in permanent rivalry, constantly re-arranging alliance patterns to maintain a delicate balance. No one State was allowed to overwhelm all the rest because in cases where one mounted an expansionist challenge, the others would coalesce to redress the balance. Indeed, 'In their interaction and succession, in their life, in their decline or rejuvenation, which then encompassed an even greater fullness, higher importance and wider extent, *lies the secret of world history*.[35] [emphasis added]

It is essential to grasp that with Ranke, as with Hegel, the essence of the life of States was the drive for power. But whereas with Hegel one Power must emerge as dominant, with Ranke all power relationships were controlled by an invisible regulator that prevented exactly what Hegel prescribed. Ranke was clearly more tolerant but he still saw war as an essential and necessary factor in international life and thus for the evolution of human society. And here Ranke invoked the authority of the ancient Greek historian Heraclitus who wrote that war was the father of all things, that out of the clash of opposing forces in the great times of danger, catastrophe and salvation come the new developments most decisively to effect.[36] So, commented Theodore von Laue, 'even war contributed to the fundamental harmony which Ranke observed in all human phenomena'.[37]

***

One needs to appreciate that the historiographical tradition derived from Herder, Hegel and Ranke, was the dominant paradigm for the discipline until the revolution initiated by Fritz Fischer in 1949. The school which he probably unintentionally founded especially with the pioneering research provided by Imanuel Geiss and associates initiated a paradigm change that effectively democratised the discipline.[38] It is instructive to look back to the era when the reception of Herder, Hegel and Ranke occurred, namely from 1815 to 1866 because out of it developed the ideology known as *Realpolitik*. At that time historians and political scientists were really becoming politically active, both in the party-political sense and as political propagandists. It was a period when the interest in the national past had been stimulated by the burning political issues of the present and more particularly how a particular view of the past might be used to influence future national-political goals. In short, German historians ceased to be mere contemplators of the past but the authors of a political program for future realisation.

It is well known that the failure of the Frankfurt National Assembly (1848–50) to achieve national unity with a federal parliamentary constitution resulted in a disillusionment with liberal ideals. One witnessed then the acceptance by former liberal intellectuals of Bismarck's conservative monarchist Prussian solution to the German question. This was without doubt due to the preparation of the German bourgeoisie by the nationalist publicists from the time of the Prussian reforms but chiefly by the political philosophy of Hegel.

What now became very evident, particularly since the failure of the movement of 1848, was the conscious recourse to national history for inspiration for future political goals. There occurred a departure from Ranke's intention merely to show how the past essentially was to how the future should be. And the forerunner of an historically orientated *Realpolitik* was the Prussian historian, F. C. Dahlmann (1785–1860) although he did not coin the term. For him history was the school of political activism where one learned the principles for the formulation of current policy, both domestic and foreign. It was no accident that such a vigorous Prussian patriot as Dahlmann was a convinced Hegelian. Above all Dahlmann who had been most active in the Frankfurt National Assembly and had even drafted the constitution for a future unified Germany had immersed himself in the history of Prussia and had come to the conclusion that since the parliamentary failure by 1850 to get the constitution adopted, any unification of Germany could only take place by the exertion of Prussian political power. Consequently he set out to show that Prussia had a vocation from almighty God to establish German unity on the basis of its national tradition, that is, princely absolutism and militarism. It was very successful as history was to show, at least until the First World War.

The political-pedagogic outcome then of the failed 1848 revolution was the emergence of a school of historians who championed the Prussian solution to the German question, namely the ideology of *Borussismus*. This was neatly defined with unconcealed abhorrence in 1867 by one of its bitterest opponents, namely the Bishop of Mainz, Wilhelm Emanuel von Ketteler (1811–77) as follows:

By Borussianism we understand a fixed idea about the vocation of Prussia – a vague idea of a world task bound up with the conviction that this vocation and this task is absolutely necessary and must be fulfilled with the same necessity as a loosened rock rolls down hill and that it is not permissible to oppose it in the name of justice or of history.[39]

When Prussia had expelled Austria from the German Confederation in 1866, it appeared to the Prussian historians and *Realpolitker* that what they had predicted since the 1850s had literally come true. The term *Realpolitik* had been coined by Ludwig August von Rochau (1810–73) in 1853 and signified a reaction against the so-called politics of idealism which had so manifestly proved ineffectual after 1850. Following the disillusionment of 1848–50, prominent historians began to advocate the replacing the 'fantastic idealism of philosophy' with the 'real idealism of history'. The choice of language was significant. Hegel's influence is very apparent. In 1853 von Rochau had published his *Grundsätze der Realpolitik* (Principles of *Realpolitik*) which advocated that to rule meant to wield power and that neither a principle nor an idea nor a treaty would unite the German nation but only the superior force of one State which would overwhelm the rest.[40] Obviously, the Prussian historians were convinced that this would be Prussia, and when Bismarck 'set the points'[41] for the final stage of the journey to unity, many intellectuals who had moral reservations about Prussian policy were finally convinced of the validity of the Hegelian logic. The Prussian victory was clearly a 'necessary postulate of history'.[42]

So widespread was the effect of the Prussian victory over Austria in 1866 that von Rochau published a second volume of his *Realpolitik* in 1869. Therein he commented that Prussia's re-organisation of Germany was a necessary law of nature which could not be subjected to the canons of private morality. He went on to affirm that *success* was the judgment of history. And writing in the *Wochenblatt des National-Vereins*, 4 October 1866, von Rochau added,

With this success [the defeat of Austria] Prussia will have won incalculable merit in the service of the national cause and will have created an unshakable base for the public law of Europe; with out success Prussia would have been guilty of a grave sin against the present and posterity. [...] *because success is the judgment of history, of the tribunal of the world, of the highest authority from which there is no appeal in human affairs.*[43] [emphasis added]

The appeal to Hegel is unmistakable. And if the success of 1866 could evoke such enthusiasm for the Hegelian idea of state, the actual culmination of Bismarck's policy of unification in 1871 with the foundation of the second German Reich was to set the seal of incontestable validity upon it. In short, it was essentially the consequence of God's will being implemented on earth.

All this was a powerful vindication of *Realpolitik* and the ideology of Borussianism. In the commentary of sceptics such as Franz Schnabel it was called the *Hohenzollern legend*, and more particularly, the Hegelian idea of the State. [44] This was energetically propagated into the Second Reich by Dahlmann's more famous pupil, Heinrich von Treitschke (1834–96) as the most celebrated/notorious prophet of the Prussian school of history. While professor in Berlin from 1874 until his death von Treitschke indoctrinated generations of students with his fulminations drilling them with the Hegelian idea of the Power State. His propaganda impact resonated long after his passing through his ability to inspire future statesmen and bureaucrats not to mention history teachers.[45]

Considered as political pedagogy it is arguable that von Treitschke's teaching did more than any other German professor to sow the seeds of an albeit vulgarised Hegelianism into the mind of the German educated middle classes. It was, however, ultimately disastrous since it went hand in hand with a virulent anti-Semitism and racial hostility towards the surrounding peoples be they of Slavic, Romance or Anglo-Saxon derivation. So von Treitschke became the archetypal political professor who had spawned many imitators in the German university system. His basic mantra was that *if a nation was not expanding it was dying.*[46]

After von Treitschke's death, however, a somewhat more subtle school of German history professors assumed his mantle calling themselves the *Neo-Rankeans.* The pioneer was one Max Lenz (1850–1932). What they admired about Ranke was his insistence that the power struggle among states enjoyed the sanction of a moral God. Indeed they wanted to replace the brutal Hegelian monism of von Treitschke with a more sensitive dualism that took moral law into account. In short, the spirit of Ranke was invoked with the aim of infusing morality into the power struggle. There was an undeniable theological-mystical element operating here. This was done by re-emphasising Ranke's individuality doctrine, namely that each State was the unique expression of the divine idea, the familiar concentration of specific moral energies and the cultural heritage of the *Volk* that Herder had formulated, and these were undoubtedly planted there by the will of the Almighty himself. In this way, the essence of power, far from being corrupting as Lord Acton famously said, was idealised.[47] Power had a spiritual content as the course of Prussian history, particularly in the 19th century had shown. The moral, spiritual and cultural strength of Prussia had prevailed.[48] It was a rather fanciful way of arguing that the forces for good always will win in the end. But who decides what is 'good'?

From today's standpoint it is difficult to discern any essential difference between the Neo-Rankeans and their predecessors of the Prussian school. The formers' theological modifications to the general schema of Prusso-German imperialism were of no consequence for the end result. Here is what Max Lenz observed on the matter in 1896:

> The ideals of 1789 had released for the first time the forces which led the German nation to unprecedented power. And following its indwelling drive to expansion the German nation succeeded through its accumulated power in carrying European culture throughout the world.[49]

Here Ranke's concept of the indwelling moral energies of the *Volk* is central, but expressed as well is the conviction in the superiority of European civilisation as a justification for imperialism. Only in Europe had the concept of the power state, read: *imperialistic nation* developed. It is, of course, no accident that Professor Lenz formulated his ideas by 1900 in a seminal essay with an obvious allusion to von Ranke, entitled: *Die Grossen Mächte: Ein Rückblick auf unser Jahrhundert* (The Great Powers: A Review of our Century) when European imperial rivalries had reached a peak. Lenz and his colleagues had been educated to see the world through Rankean spectacles; it was in the nature of each Power to expand until it met with resistance. This explained the existence of super-states such as the British Empire, the United States of America, China and Russia.

But Germany, too, possessed superior moral energies and had indeed as in the medieval past expanded ruthlessly at the expense of weaker states. The then, that is in the 1890s, apparently quiescent attitude of Germany could only be explained by the pressure of containment exerted by the surrounding Powers. Consequently there was a necessity to counter this pressure by increased armament. And it was at this time that Germany had embarked on an extensive naval building program. In Lenz' view this turned power politics into a struggle for national survival which subordinated all norms of morality and international law to itself. And here, the supposed difference between the Neo-Rankean analysis and that of the late Heinrich von Treitschke becomes very hard to discern. Lenz, indeed, openly declared that Germany would once again grasp around her as soon as there was a State in such decline that it should be divided up as was the case with Poland one hundred years previously.

In such situations it was irrelevant for historians to identify aggressors; all great powers by their very nature were aggressive.[50] International politics were essentially a struggle for existence and the *extension of power*. As a consequence there was permanent tension, virtually 'cold war' in which there are no friends, only rivals and antagonists.[51] This was, indeed, the basic assumption of international politics but Lenz and his associates elevated it to the norm of world politics, as had previously Max Weber in 1895 in his famous inaugural lecture at Freiburg.[52] This, one can observe with hindsight, blocked the German view for alternative solutions to international rivalries. Scholars tended to regard their supposed scientifically derived view as absolute. Once a thing was *wissenschaftlich* (scientifically) established, there was no gainsaying it. It was a mindset that was petulantly impatient with Western pragmatism which the Germans considered, particularly as far as the British were concerned, characterised their *cant*, that is their in-bred, unctuous hypocrisy.

The Germans, understandably at that time, considered Europe the playing field where the greatest concentrations of 'moral energy' had developed due to the constant pressures exerted by the Powers on each other. And as Max Lenz and his fellow Neo-Rankeans observed, each Power responded to their implanted drives by trying to expand into the world, that is into regions where the populations had not yet developed into modern power states, namely the colonial world which was peopled by primitive or as yet politically disunited tribes. The Germans made a distinction between what they called *Kulturvölker* on the one hand (that is advanced European countries) and *Naturvölker*, which consisted of native peoples still living in an early stage of civilisation. It is of interest to note that in post-war West Germany where an economic 'miracle' of re-construction had been achieved during the chancellorship of Konrad Adenauer, it was fashionable to refer to the decolonised countries of Africa and Asia as *Entwicklungsländer*, meaning 'developing countries.' The old condescending expression *Naturvölker* had been consigned to the dustbin of history.

In the pre-1914 historicism of Max Lenz and his colleagues there was concealed a prophetic dimension. He had observed that geographically relatively small countries such as Germany, as with Prussia previously, had nothing to fear from the presence of surrounding super powers because 'the political energy of those world powers was in no relation to their geographic extent.'[53] And this concept was based on Ranke's theory of the *Primat der Aussenpolitik* (primacy of foreign policy), meaning that a State in order to preserve its integrity mobilised its entire domestic resources to meet the demands of its foreign policy, namely the challenges from abroad. Lenz interpreted this to mean that the greater the external pressure on a country, the greater was the counter-pressure from within to resist it; external pressure was thus a positively creative challenge to be met. It is not difficult to discern the implications this had for international rivalries in the Age of Imperialism. Not only did the Powers exert pressure on each other but also on the subject colonial peoples. In short, because of this direct foreign pressure the subject nationalities in Africa, Asia and the Pacific region generated their own moral energies which would eventually be expressed in movements for independence.

In the fullness of time, these movements would be accompanied by armed resistance which would test the ability of the European occupiers to maintain their dominance. Clearly, uppermost in the mind of the Neo-Rankeans at that time was the wish to see British power diminished by the rebellions of subject peoples in the Empire who were trying to win their independence. What was happening in Ireland, Africa and India, for example, led the Neo-Rankeans to conclude that the British Empire was entering a phase of national fragmentation and hence decline. The notion that the monolithic Empire could transform itself peacefully into a Commonwealth of self-governing Dominions seems to have escaped the Germans although Lenz was close to the truth when he predicted that the fragmentation came as the result of a series of crises within the Empire.

It was indeed a significant insight attributable to Lenz's neo-Rankean historicism that enabled him to foresee the transformation of the world by the emergence of new nationalities at a time when the Powers were the dominant political and cultural centres of civilisation. The conclusion drawn by the Neo-Rankeans, however, was that the many struggles for independence would stretch the capacity of the metropolitan Power to sustain control. It was argued that because of this the Powers would try to avoid friction among themselves over the colonies. A collision of European Powers would not only destroy the basis of civilisation but would jeopardise the European colonial possessions by accelerating the desire for independence among the colonial peoples. The balance of power depended on the diplomatic restraint of the Powers. Nevertheless, a war that threw everything out of balance was always a possibility. And this caused the Neo-Rankeans to reflect how best peace could be maintained, and it is here that their schema took on its prophetic aspect.

It was reasoned that the Powers, pursuing as usual a policy based on *raison d'état*, would under these circumstances shrink back from war. Furthermore, the possibilities for colonial activity were still great enough to absorb the energies of the Great Powers so long as they did not turn against each other. And even friction between Great Powers did not have to result in war; border incidents did not necessarily ignite major conflagrations, 'otherwise Europe would be constantly in flames'. Where there were disputes there was always the possibility of conferences and diplomatic negotiations which could reduce tensions. Frequently two disputants could find agreement at the expense of a third rival such as had occurred historically in the divisions of Poland among the Russians, Prussians and Austrians. And this is precisely what Lenz recommended in 1900 for the conduct of *Weltpolitik*.[54]

The great issue of the time was how to prevent a major European disaster, and here the Neo-Rankeans appeared as a volunteer propaganda agency. It was argued that world peace could only be maintained by the possession of superior armaments which functioned as a deterrent, the best guarantee for peace. This reasoning was echoed with considerable resonance at the highest levels of government. The German Chancellor, Theobald von Bethmann Hollweg had, as we have seen, employed a brilliant young man named Kurt Riezler (1882–1955), with encyclopaedic learning, as his personal assistant. Riezler was without doubt a convinced Neo-Rankean as evidenced by the book he published in 1913 under the pseudonym J. J. Ruedorffer entitled *Die Grundzüge der Weltpolitk der Gegewart* (Basic trends in world politics at the present). The work went into many editions selling thousands of copies. In it Riezler rehearsed the way that Germany should conduct her international relations. His recommendations reflected exactly the schema proffered by the Neo-Rankeans. With superior armaments, read: ability to intimidate any potential alliance of enemies, it was possible to expand overseas without firing a shot in anger. To characterise his position he formulated this evocative sentence: *Die Kanonen sprechen nicht aber sie haben eine Stimme in den Verhandlungen* (The cannon do not speak but they have a voice in the negotiations).[55] It was an apposite recommendation of the Neo-Rankean advice, namely that Germany should be strong enough to 'command the peace', *den Frieden zu befehlen.* And as a late comer to the imperialist division of the earth, Germany needed peace in order to gain control of territory that was left under the motto, 'He who is strong enough to demand something has not come too late after all.'[56]

Both the Neo-Rankeans and Kurt Riezler were, of course, well aware that this mode of power politics was by no means risk free. There was always the possibility that a European war could result from friction arising from colonial rivalries. For this reason, the neo-Rankeans, as did Kurt Riezler, advocated in particular increased naval construction. In an age of far flung overseas possessions a strong navy was an obvious necessity. The reciprocal relationship between the ideas of the professional historians and actual national policy is most apparent. The British hegemony of the world's oceans had to be matched by the construction of the German 'risk fleet'.[57]

The question posed here is a critical one for the historical discipline: *Who actually initiates policy or 'political will'?* Were the historians merely adapting their schema to explain official policy? Or did official policy grow out of the political conceptions formulated by the political pedagogy of the historians who acted rather like Old Testament prophets for whom the cause of God was identical with the cause of the nation? Were, indeed, the Neo-Rankeans conceptualising a political program in a manner comparable to their teachers of the Prussian school? The personal relationships between the eminent academics and the leading statesmen would suggest that there is much in this conjecture. There was certainly widespread academic approval of *Weltpolitik* as Fritz Fischer has reminded us. However, the important thing is that the Neo-Rankeans who formulated the ideological explanation for *Weltpolitik,* if not its ideological stimulus, emphasised, as did Kurt Riezler, that German policy was: *Weltpolitik und kein Krieg*, that is imperialism without war. So Germany's aggressive policies were meant to be essentially peaceful!

What could possibly go wrong? Ludwig Dehio, anticipating Fritz Fischer, conceded as far back as 1950 that it was German policy that had made the First World War possible. This meant that while *Weltpolitik* was to be conducted peacefully, it could fall apart during crises. It should be remembered that the concept actually functioned by provoking crises, and that could prove problematic. The pre-1914 era was fraught with crises; there was an atmosphere of permanent tension as Anglo-German relations exemplified. This led the German elites, academic, financial, industrial and political, to weave world-political plans which Fritz Stern has designated 'dreams and delusions.'[58]

In the event it was humanly impossible to sustain the apparent rationality of the Neo-Rankean schema. Instead, irrationality in the form of grandiose schemes in *Mittelafrika, Mitteleuropa* and not least the Berlin-Baghdad railway project designed ultimately to the enable the German annexation of India, drove German policy. The ultimate goal was eventually to win territory from Russia, France and the British Empire and in this can be discerned the twin ambitions first to escape the pressure of 'Encirclement' by resorting to the threat of war, that is by applying the Neo-Rankean schema, and secondly, thereby to win the long-desired pre-eminence in the world.

The July–August crisis of 1914 encouraged the German policy makers to make a 'break out to the front'[59] If Germany had not urged Austria-Hungary to march into Serbia no world war would have occurred. The German government was bent on exploiting the Sarajevo incident as a heaven-sent opportunity to unleash a war that would enable the realisation of plans that were being forged over a long period. It was hoped these could be realised if in the event world opinion would blame Russia for intervening to defend the criminal Serbians. A recent publication (see Appendix 2) by the independent scholar Dr Bernd Schulte has shown through his diligent archival researches that Berlin had secretly been urging Vienna to exploit the Sarajevo assassination of the Archduke and his consort as sufficient pretext to risk a European war.[60]

What is new in Schulte's revelations is the explanation it gives for German policy towards Austria-Hungary. Germany needed unconditional support from the Dual Monarchy for the execution of her long-term plans in Asia Minor and Middle East. Austria-Hungary was, however, economically too weak and politically internally too divided to assume the pro-active role of Germany's junior partner. The Danube Monarchy after the second Balkan war was facing economic ruin. Germany, herself was strapped for finance. Any grand foreign policy adventures under these circumstances were illusory. Of this both governments in Vienna and Berlin were well aware. Then came the Sarajevo assassination. In the light of the avenues for action it opened up, Schulte has been able to make a dramatic re-assessment in contrast to Clark who had not consulted the same documents. According to these, Schulte sees Germany calculatedly manoeuvring to localise the crisis while being ready to deal with any military intervention either from Russia or France.

If one takes a second look at the situation bearing in mind the economic circumstances which had been a major factor hitherto in restraining Austria-Hungary from acting precipitously, then Germany certainly has a case to answer. While trying to project herself as a disinterested bystander, Germany was secretly urging Austria-Hungary to invade Serbia which when conquered would be forced to pay indemnities. One could ruin a neighbour in order to redeem one's own dire situation. The murder of the crown-prince seemed to justify this course of action. It was, however, a plan fraught with risk because of the inevitable pro-Serbian reaction of the Russians. But for that the German military were prepared with their Austro-Hungarian allies.[61]

How this plan evolved was discovered by Dr Schulte in the correspondence between the German Legation Counsellor (*Legationsrat*) in Vienna who happened to be a cousin of the German Chancellor, Bethmann Hollweg named Dietrich von Bethmann Hollweg.[62] He had made it clear to Berlin that the Dual Monarchy was in a parlous state. This information in Berlin led to the conclusion that all German plans for expansion would be frustrated if Austria-Hungary were to collapse from within, and for that there was ample evidence as Dietrich von Bethmann Hollweg had explained in his memorandum of 24 June 1914. The German ambassador in Vienna, von Tschirschky, had already referred to Austro-Hungarian impecuniosity on 22 May 1914. This caused Berlin re-assess the situation and decided to venture the risk, *Jetzt oder nie*, now or never.[63]

With regard to the economic concerns it had been a long-established Prussian practice to exact indemnities from the defeated enemy to meet the costs of war. While this was almost certainly a consideration, it did not remove the strong component of risk of the domino effect of urging Austria-Hungary to invade Serbia. But it was a risk considered worth venturing.

The Neo-Rankean inspired judgements in the afore-mentioned Kurt Riezler book, made perfect sense of what happened in July-August 1914. He had pointed out that the policy of bluff could be derailed when a Great Power had bluffed too much causing an opposing power or constellation of powers to bridle and refuse to back down in a given situation. By issuing Austria-Hungary a blank cheque to go to war against Serbia risking the intervention of Russia and France, Germany had certainly over bluffed (*hat sich festgeblufft*) and this is where, as Bethmann Hollweg phrased it, the only course of action was to take a 'leap into the dark'.[64] The Neo-Rankean idea of *Weltpolitik but no war* proved to be a formula for disaster. Indeed, it operated on a principle of provoking crises and on this occasion in the tense climate of permanent crisis an explosion occurred.

When the 'cold war' that the Neo-Rankeans had been analysing especially since 1900 eventually turned into a shooting war in 1914–18 they began a frenzy of publication justifying the national cause.[65] This literature is characterised by an indignation and emotion, perhaps very understandable, which reveals that essentially they had failed to digest the intellectual-political conceptions, and above all, the moral norms embedded in von Ranke's historicism. Instead, the ever present spirit of the Hegelian *Machtstaat* materialised to mobilise the vast majority of German academics to interpret the war with values derived from a one-sided nationalistic historicism. Von Treitschke had triumphed over von Ranke.[66]

A classic example is provided by the appeal written just after the outbreak of war by German theologians and directed to the Archbishop of Canterbury giving their version of how the war started:

> With deepest conviction we must attribute it to those who have so long secretly and cunningly been spinning a web of conspiracy against Germany, which they have now flung over us in order to strangle us therein.[67]

Precisely the same idea was expressed by Max Lenz, when he wrote:

> This Narcissus-like concern of the Neo-Rankeans for their nation's power and culture as expressed in their doctrinaire historicism paradoxically crippled their striving for objectivity and led to their tragic inability to assess the world as it really was. Dreams and delusions triumphed tragically. The tool of historicism had been once a dazzling analytical instrument but it became a snare for earnest, indeed naive patriotic prophets. Perhaps we can apply what Nietzsche had said about the advantages and disadvantages of this kind of history for political life. On the one hand it sharpened the view of the historian in a particular direction with fruitful results but it also blinded him to other vital insights into historical life.[68]

The historicism of the Neo-Rankeans which was shared by the vast majority of German scholars across disciplines, including especially Protestant theologians and pastors, had produced a transfigured image of their Wilhelmine Fatherland which had been accepted largely uncritically by the educated middle classes, the *Bildungsbürgertum*. It is the one thing that made Germans so significantly different from other Europeans towards whom they cultivated an attitude of innate superiority.[69] It needs to be comprehended that these people had been exposed to a very different education from that experienced in the West. Professors and teachers could wax lyrical about the German synthesis of *Power* and *Spirit*; Prussianism and militarism had supposedly been ennobled by the infusion of ethical values. Indeed, the spirit of Goethe's Weimar had been merged with that of Fredrician Potsdam, the very heart of militarism, to produce men of honour pledged to unconditional obedience. *Macht und Geist*, power and spirit were in essential harmony, the fruit of which was the formidable Wilhelmine Empire. *Weltpolitik*, thus spiritually and ethically underpinned took on the aura of a divinely inspired cultural mission to the world; resistance to it was perceived as not only wrong-headed but as wicked opposition to the advancement of humanity.

Finally, it is well to remember that as the late Professor Manfred Schlenke (1927–97) observed, the National Socialism of Adolf Hitler grew out of the febrile militaristic culture of Potsdam.[70] Admittedly, it was a vulgarised form of that culture but at its core with its ruthless authoritarianism it was the same. And the political consequences were the greatest tragedy in the history of humankind. It is the duty of the historian to highlight this continuity. There is an undoubted co-relation between education and politics, between the comprehension of national history and the formation of political will. The self-perception of the German historical profession was that they were the unchallenged political mentors of the nation. In any effort to establish the essential cause of conflict the question concerning the educational and cultural formation of decision-makers is a crucial one and may not be side-stepped by 'honest historians.'

CHAPTER 6

Kulturkrieg 1914–18: British and Australian Professors Confront their German Counterparts about the War

That academics can exert an influence on the political education of the nation, is not an exclusively Teutonic phenomenon. Professors in all countries, by virtue of their learning, felt called upon in times of national crises to interpret the situation to their citizens. Indeed, they mobilised themselves to engage in a war of the minds between themselves and their enemy counterparts. It was, in fact virtually another theatre of operations which was conducted on a purely intellectual/spiritual level, *ein Krieg der Geister* or also often called in German *ein Kulturkrieg*. This is not to be confused with propaganda in the usual sense; rather it was a conflict of world views, *Weltanschauungen*, of interpretations of the very nature of the world, and hence a dispute about the essential meaning of the war. In a word, it was a war of ideas and philosophies which, arguably, contributed not insignificantly to the formation of political will on both sides.[1] In fact, the images projected of the enemy by many an academic commentator had every chance of becoming efficacious at the level of policy-making, since the scholars concerned had direct access to the corridors of power. This was true of Australia no less than for Germany.

If one is made aware of the origins of the war of intellects between British and German scholars, then the subsequent participation of

Antipodean professors is readily understandable, especially in view of Dominion concern that Britain not only survive the conflict but also maintain her naval superiority in the Pacific and Far East. It was not simply cheering from the sidelines out of an emotional attachment to the Mother Land. Rather, the intellectual war waged against Prussian-German militarism by these professors was fuelled by the overwhelming desire to see that the British Empire and what they believed it stood for, not only in terms of defence guarantees for the future but also for ideological reasons, should at all costs prevail against the essentially diabolical forces of what they came to designate *Kultur*.

This chapter will first explain the origins of the *Kulturkrieg*, and elaborate the so-called 'two Germanys thesis' as essential background to understanding the mental stance of the small but obviously influential academic elite in Australia who had been able to project a specific image of Prusso-German militarism. Finally, in seeking to make a general statement about their beliefs and values, the ideas of arguably their most perceptive representative, Australia's very first appointee to a discrete chair in history, George Arnold Wood of Sydney, will be summarised.

The Origins of the *Kulturkrieg*

Interestingly, but by no means surprisingly, if one is familiar with the background, the first exchanges in the *Kulturkrieg* came from theologians. The reason is simply that for the half decade prior to the outbreak of war, British and German Churchmen of all denominations had been engaged in what they thought was a serious peace dialogue. They had wanted to promote friendship between the British and German empires based on a presumed common understanding of the Gospel, and had even formed an association for that purpose. It had arisen out of the concern of the leading theological brains of the day that the kindred Teutonic and Anglo-Saxon peoples should avoid at all costs an armed struggle which would doubtless assume apocalyptic dimensions. Spectacular exchange visits, which enjoyed royal patronage on both sides, of groups of well over a hundred theologians on a completely ecumenical basis had been arranged first for the Germans to Britain in 1908 and then in 1909 for the British to tour Germany. Out of these emerged what was to become a genuine Christian peace endeavour, virtually a Christian Internationale to parallel the Socialist Internationale of the day. Negotiations had developed to the stage that by August 1914 two great peace conferences had been arranged, one Evangelical, that is non-RC or Protestant, and the other exclusively Roman Catholic. The dates and places are not without a certain ironic historical interest.[2]

The non-Roman Catholics were to meet on 3–4 August in Konstanz (at the site of the famous Reform Council of 1414 when John Hus had been burned at the stake), and some eighty delegates representing twelve churches had actually gathered there. The international Roman Catholic delegations were to meet in Liège, Belgium, a week later! Count von Schlieffen's fateful war plan – an example of *Kultur* in practice – frustrated the would-be peacemakers' good intentions rather abruptly. The declaration of war on 4 August created dismay and confusion. For example, the British and American delegations which included high-ranking Anglican clergy, were forced to catch the next available train to the French border, standing in corridors, minus luggage, shoulder-to-shoulder with German troops, travelling with passes authorised by the *Summus Episcopus* of the State Church of Prussia, Kaiser Wilhelm II himself.[3]

On arrival home – their luggage having been duly forwarded – the next thing many of them would have heard from their German Evangelical brethren was an open letter in *The Times* (30 September 1914) – the famous address 'To Evangelical Christians Abroad' – in which the outbreak of war was attributed to the threat of French and Russian invasion. It was this that had compelled Germany to take preventive action by marching into Belgium. 'Then', addressing the British Church leaders, the German Evangelical theologians declared,

> our adversaries [meaning the French and the Russians] were joined by those who by blood and history and faith are our

brothers, with whom we felt ourselves in the common world-task more closely bound than with almost any other nation. Over against a world in arms, we recognise clearly that we have to defend our existence, our individuality, our culture, and our honour.

The British theologians thus challenged were quick to respond, stating that they had to disagree with this version of the causes of the war, insisting that a dispassionate analysis of events leading to hostilities would indicate that Germany was indeed solely responsible.

The facts thus related [claimed the British theologians] are in our belief incontestable. We can only suppose, incredible as it seems, that these honourable and gifted men who signed the German appeal were aware of the obligations by which we were bound, and also of the story of the negotiations. A violation of such promises [i.e. the British guarantee to Belgium] on our part would have been an act of the basest perfidy.[4]

What the British theologians said next in their public reply is crucial in trying to comprehend the ensuing *Kulturkrieg*. They expressed astonishment that the views of their supposedly 'honourable and gifted' German colleagues coincided with those of the widely read Prussian-German nationalist historian Heinrich von Treitschke and those of the Pan-German publicist, Friedrich von Bernhardi. Academics in Britain had been aware of the cult of Prussian militarism for some time, but until then it had always been supposed that the 'honourable and gifted' scholars with whom they had studied as students, conducted research, exchanged visits and attended international conferences, were immune to these barbarous ideas. In fact the British academic world had always supposed that there existed two Germanys: one of culture and learning, and the other of a militaristic cult practised among the Prussian nobility. The British theologians could not initially comprehend how, for instance, a theological colossus like Adolf von Harnack could identify with the militaristic-imperialistic views of a Heinrich von Treitschke. How could the world's leading authority on the life, ministry and historical impact of Jesus of Nazareth, the Prince of Peace, share the same nationalist values as the latter-day apostle of Machiavelli?[5]

What then served to intensify the *Kulturkrieg* was the news of how German troops had behaved during the invasion and occupation of Belgium. This had resulted in the summary execution of some six thousand civilians as well as the destruction of the famous university library at Louvain. These atrocities unleashed a wave of revulsion throughout the Western world, especially among academics. In fact, institutes of higher learning throughout the world were sent a circular letter, originating in Dublin (31 August 1914), concerning German action in Louvain. It pointed out that the destruction was,

> not only a violence against defenceless non-combatants unparalleled in European history since the Thirty Years War, but as an injury to learning, science and education, to history and art, to religion and citizenship which was wholly without precedent, and which no military exigencies or expediencies could extenuate much less justify.

The authors of the circular concluded: 'We regard this act as one of the gravest injury to the whole fabric of life of European and general civilisation, since it destroys guarantees hitherto respected by combatants.'[6]

On the basis of this notice the recipients were urged to lodge a protest through the nearest available channels to the Imperial German Government and to the Hague Court. In the meantime, the British press published a series of manifestos by British academics condemning the actions of the German army and government, but implying that their German counterparts, the scholars and scientists, would certainly distance themselves from the excesses of the military.[7] But this only provoked the famous response of the ninety-three German intellectuals known as *An die*

Kulturwelt (To the Civilised World), on 4 October 1914, in which all the charges of German lawlessness, aggression and atrocities in Belgium were indignantly repudiated in six apodictic assertions each beginning with the words, *Es ist nicht wahr* (It is not true). The final one stated:

> It is not true that the struggle against our so-called militarism is not a struggle against our culture, as our enemies hypocritically affect to believe. Without German militarism German culture would have long since been swept away. It arose for its protection in a country which had been for centuries subjected to periodic depredations as no other. The German army and the German people are one. This awareness unites 70,000,000 Germans into a brotherhood regardless of differences in education, estate or party-political allegiance.[8]

Then, in order to proclaim the solidarity of virtually the entire German professoriate, the following declaration composed by the internationally renowned classicist at Berlin University, Ulrich von Wilamowitz-Moellendorf, was issued on 16 October:

> We teachers at the universities and institutes of higher learning in Germany serve scholarship and pursue a work of peace. However, it fills us with indignation that the enemies of Germany, chiefly England, wish to draw a distinction, allegedly in our favour, between the spirit of German scholarship and what they call Prussian militarism. But in the German army there is no other spirit than in the German people because both are one, and we also are part of it. (*Wir gehören dazu*) Our army also cultivates science and learning and its achievements are not least attributable to that. Service in the army makes our youth efficient as well for peaceful pursuits as for scientific. Indeed, army service inculcates into

our youth a self-denying sense of duty and loyalty, and lends them the confidence and sense of personal honour of the truly free man who voluntarily subordinates himself to the whole [community]. This spirit is alive not only in Prussia but is the same in all provinces of the German Empire. It is the same in war and peace. Our army is now fighting for Germany's freedom and at the same time for all the benefits of peace and civilisation (*Gesittung*) not only in Germany. Our belief is that the salvation of the entire European civilisation (*Kultur*) depends upon the victory which will be wrought by German 'militarism', the manly discipline, the loyalty, the sacrificial spirit of the united and free German people.[9]

This declaration was endorsed by over 3,000 German academics; only a handful distanced themselves from it, among whom were such pacifists as Georg Nicolai, Albert Einstein and Friedrich Wilhelm Foerster.[10]

The impact of these two manifestos on Western academics was particularly alienating because they destroyed the previously comforting illusion which Western admirers of German scholarship had cultivated, namely that there were in fact two Germanys – that of the poets and thinkers and that of the Prussian officer class.

The Two Germanys Thesis

The idea that there were two Germanys was repeatedly expressed at the beginning of the war. In fact a mere month after the outbreak: of hostilities on 14 September 1914, the British Foreign Secretary, Sir Edward Grey, addressing his constituents in Berwick on the reasons for declaring war on Germany stated:

The progress of the war has revealed what a terrible and immoral thing German militarism is. It is against German militarism that we must fight. The whole of Western Europe would fall under it if Germany was successful in this war ... It is not the German people but Prussian militarism which has driven Germany and Europe into this war. If that militarism can be overcome, there will be a brighter day for Europe, which will compensate us for the awful sacrifices that war entails.[11]

Here for the first time the thesis of the two Germanys was invoked by a British statesman to justify the necessity of waging a war à *outrance* against a power which had incidentally mounted the greatest existential threat to the island kingdom since Napoleon.[12]

Prussianism presented itself as a barbarous ideology which demanded the subjugation of Europe (and possibly the world) to its autocratic system. The danger was perceived in Britain as especially acute because of the well-known and undoubted efficiency of the German army and the state-of-the-art technology employed by the rapidly expanding German battle fleet. These factors exposed, at least for the Admiralty, the Army and the Foreign Office, the critical state of Britain's imperial overstretch.[13]

It was not, therefore, against the German people, but against Prussian militarism, that the bitter struggle was to be waged. And from that time onwards a spate of publications began to appear in the form of pamphlets and books by academics and journalists claiming to speak authoritatively on *Kultur*. Besides these, numerous works by German writers were simply translated and published, all with the object of explaining just what it was that could inspire a great cultural nation to embark on the brutal conquest of Europe with the goal of establishing a Teutonic hegemony that extended beyond Europe to the entire world.

On reading this material today, that is literature which reflected the immediate Anglo-Saxon response to German aggression in 1914–15, one is confronted with an interpretation of German imperialism, and especially the mentality of the power elite which coincides in all major respects with that advanced by the Hamburg Professor Fritz Fischer and his school since the early 1960s. This group of scholars had very much unsettled the more conservative elements within the German historical profession by frankly exposing the illiberal, anti-democratic, racist and quasi-Social Darwinist values of the German power elite, which while it was ideologically convinced of the historical rightness of Germany's cause, was extremely nervous. Certainly, in 1914 they were worried about the imagined socialist threat to their monarchical system and the shrinking possibilities of imperialist expansion to which they believed they were being called by Providence. This entire value system was subsumed under the concept *Kultur* which, of course, was rejected by most German Social Democrats as a highly questionable educational device for maintaining the existing oppressive class structure. Further, the illiberal implications of *Kultur* also evoked most negative reactions from Anglo-Saxon intellectuals.

The content of *Kultur* as they understood it was neatly summed up by the British scientist, William Ramsay, in the April 1915 issue of the *Quarterly Review* (which was devoted to the subject of *Kultur*) as follows:

> One form of collectivism is Socialism ... The other form is *'Kultur'*. The leaders of the German nation, having learned that much can be done by organisation, have made it a fetish. Theirs is a kind of socialism inculcated from above by their self-elected rulers. They have spent more than a century organising their army and their education; they have more recently organised their trade; and they now believe that the world is to be reformed only by having this system thrust upon it by German methods and German bayonets.[14]

And he could have added, German battleships! So the belief was propagated by British scholars that this was the German intention, which German scholars obligingly confirmed in their numerous manifestos throughout the war. And *Kultur* in action had been witnessed by the entire world in Belgium. Were there still two Germanys now? Had not the successors of Goethe, Schiller and Beethoven declared their solidarity with Friedrich II (the Great), Blücher, Clausewitz and von Moltke? Had not now the Germans of international scholarship, those superlative intellects in both the sciences and humanities, by their own admission identified themselves with the creed of militarism – a doctrine which might reasonably be called 'world revolutionary *attentisme*',[15] that is a belief that world history was unfolding inexorably along a path which would eventually see a great reckoning between the German and British Empires for world hegemony. In short, superior Teutonic power was ready and waiting to revolutionise the order of the world. A confirmation of this came barely a month after the 'Declaration of the 93', in the following statement by the notable chemist, Professor Wilhelm Ostwald (1853–1932) of Leipzig:

> Germany ... has attained a stage of civilisation far higher than that of all other peoples. This war will in the future compel those other peoples to participate under the form of German social efficiency, in a civilisation higher than their own ... The French and English have attained only the degree of cultural development which we ourselves left behind 50 years ago. You ask me what it is that Germany wants. Well, Germany wants to organise Europe, for up to now Europe has never been organised.[16]

This may be regarded as a relatively moderate statement of German self-estimation. The combined effect on the international community of scholars of all such manifestos was, understandably, disquieting. If the 'honourable and gifted men' of learning whom the outside world had formerly venerated were now functioning as the harbingers of Prussianism, there was, regrettably, no alternative but to resist. The so-called *Gelehrtenrepublik,* or 'commonwealth of scholars', which had been presumed to exist across national boundaries before August 1914 had now collapsed as ignominiously as the Second Internationale of Socialists. Hostilities saw the academics, like the workers of all countries, rally around their respective flags to place their talents at the disposal of their governments. Australian professors were not slow to do the same.

Australia's Academic Garrison

It is clear from the available evidence that Australian professors were just as well informed as their British counterparts concerning the threat of *Kultur*. This is explained by the fact that not a few, such as George Arnold Wood of Sydney, were English by birth and training, or were English-trained such as George Cockburn Henderson of Adelaide.[17] And a common feature of their European experience had been the almost obligatory semester or two at a German university. Some had spent much longer and acquired doctorates. What these men did after hostilities broke out was to form what amounted to an academic garrison, almost literally. They not only offered their expertise directly for the war effort, they even set up rifle clubs, established military training units within universities, and spent time – health and age permitting – drilling themselves for home defence. In fact, the establishment of War Committees in each university was fostered, a move in which Melbourne appears to have taken the initiative.[18] Indeed, there emerged there a veritable think-tank which, with great concern for the security of the Empire, analysed for the benefit of the general public the origins of the war, its implications for Australia, and formulated the principles upon which Australia should contribute to the imperial war effort.[19]

There are indications that this activity played some part in influencing the shaping of national policy because not only was Melbourne then the seat of the Federal Government, but the think-tank centred on Melbourne University actually included such high-ranking public servants as Robert Garran and Frederic Eggleston. At any rate, the nature of Prussian-German militarism and the assessment of the Imperial German threat were analysed and presented to the community by men possessing the right credentials. And it is with this aspect of the academic war effort that we are concerned rather than with the technological contribution made by certain professors who were actually seconded to England to assist in munitions production or who busied themselves with the development of such items as submarine detection equipment.[20]

The Image of Prusso-German Imperialism

The record shows that some Australian intellectuals had taken account of German policy prior to 1914. Frederic Eggleston, for example, had in 1912 published an article in the *Round Table* in response to the second Morocco crisis, giving an Australian perspective. He was clearly aware of Germany's forceful diplomacy and the challenge which her spectacular naval build-up presented to Great Britain. However, he still believed that Anglo-German naval rivalry could be defused through astute diplomacy and an increased naval build-up by the Empire. Indeed Eggleston appeared to believe that it would be more prudent for Britain to ally herself with Germany and drop the French and the Russians. He was certainly aware of the explosiveness of the world situation but seemed to cultivate the faith widely preached by the pacifist, Norman Angell, at that time.

The effect of this was to dull Western liberal perception of the true nature of German political will. One preferred to believe that no Great Power would be so misguided as to risk a war that would inevitably result in the destruction of the entire European economic system including its own.[21] There was, it appears, a reluctance to take on board the writings of the Pan-Germanist Friedrich von Bernhardi, for example, who was disarmingly frank about the necessity of an armed conflict between Britain and Germany.[22] Such reflections could be easily dismissed as the outpourings of a fevered brain with no relevance to real decision-making. This comforting thought was, however, soon discredited after the invasion of Belgium when men with the appropriate qualifications began to examine what it was that made the German Empire behave like a bull elephant run amok.

One of the very first such scholars was Archibald T. Strong, who by 1914 had become acting head of the Department of English at Melbourne University. By October 1914, he had begun to publish a series of articles in the *Melbourne Herald* which a year later appeared in book form. The foreword to that volume sums up Strong's motivation which clearly came to be shared by most academics throughout the country:

It seems to me as certain today [August 1915] as it seemed twelve months ago that Australia has more at stake in this war than has Britain; that her very existence depends on it being carried through to a clean finish; that an inconclusive peace jeopardising British naval supremacy, and giving Germany a chance of beginning again, might easily mean our eventual subjugation; that the worker has more at stake in the war than any other class in the community; that even while we are in the throes of the present struggle we must look ahead to the effect our action or inaction will have on the coming generation; and that no sacrifice is too great which will rid the Empire, to which we owe everything, of the hideous Teutonic menace.[23]

The War Committees in all universities functioned precisely in this spirit. They perceived themselves as fulfilling a crucial national role, contributing to the eradication of the 'hideous Teutonic menace'. They were without doubt convinced to a man that the defeat of Britain and France in Western Europe would have the direst consequences for Australia. And in order to make this plain to the community at large they organised patriotic meetings, and staged lecture programmes in the cities. Individuals toured country centres, first to explain why Australia was at war and then to advocate conscription.[24]

Central to this activity was the need to portray the character of the enemy, to present a rational analysis of the problem of how the great German cultural nation could be the same as the one which perpetrated the Belgian atrocities. In short, they had to explain the triumph of Prussian militarism over liberalism in Germany. And this was not easy because the intellectual left and other elements in the Australian labour movement resisted the academics' arguments.[25] The problem was exacerbated by the persistence of anti-British attitudes of sections among the Irish-Australian community which characterised the conflict as a trade war.

But none of the advocates of all-out resistance to Prussian militarism was as persuasive and perceptive as George Arnold Wood, the first incumbent of the Challis Chair in History at the University of Sydney (1891–1928). Certainly Archibald T. Strong in Melbourne, and George. C. Henderson in Adelaide may have been more prolific and peripatetic in their campaign of words against the 'hideous Teutonic menace', but without doubt it was Wood who both investigated the roots of Prussianism more perceptively and portrayed it most objectively. And he was doubly qualified to do so. First, he had more than a nodding acquaintance with Germany, having twice spent time there as a student. This had been initially to strengthen his grasp of the language and then to read theology at Marburg.

It had been Wood's intention to equip himself for a clerical career in the Congregational Church, so after his history training at Balliol he entered Mansfield College, Oxford, to devote himself to theological studies. Part of this training was the preparation of a minor thesis dealing with the Wallenstein Problem during the Thirty Years War. It was an excellent study of the complex interrelation of theology and power politics in seventeenth century Germany. Significantly, the work concluded with a comparison between Wallenstein and Bismarck, the former having striven valiantly but in vain to unite Germany in the name of the Habsburg dynasty and the Church of Rome, the latter having succeeded in doing so for the Hohenzollern dynasty and its allies, namely the barbarous feudal aristocracy of Prussia and the Evangelical State Church of Prussia.[26]

Wood's second qualification was his radical liberalism, which during the Boer War he had applied rigorously and with disconcerting effect to critique British policy. Indeed Wood was the intellectual spearhead of the Anti-War League in Australia, something which earned him a censure from the Senate of the University of Sydney for alleged disloyal utterances.[27] So when the war of 1914 came Wood was fully immunised against infection by vulgar anti-German hysteria.

It is significant that Wood ventured no public statement on the war until he had consulted the available documents. These included *The British White Paper*, and the *Collected Diplomatic Documents Relating to the Outbreak of the European War.* On reading these, as well as the most informed British and American commentators (and clearly having in mind the manifestos of the German Professors of whom he said it was not their wickedness but their ignorance of the facts which appalled him), he concluded emphatically that Germany had, after all, willed the war. But until he had carried out that exercise he remained suspicious that the British Government had been influenced by those old imperialists who regarded 'war as a good thing', and that the government had not exhausted every possibility to resolve the crisis diplomatically.[28]

Wood's deeply religious, critical, radical liberal attitude to the State caused him to write:

> If the British Government enters upon an unjust war, it is the duty of British citizens not to fight in that war, but to fight against that war until it is ended. Therefore, I say, the first duty is to understand the war; to understand sufficiently to be able to form a reasoned opinion on the question, is it a just war or is it an unjust war, a war we fight for God, or a war in which we fight for the Devil? In the case of this war not much study was necessary in order to obtain this degree of understanding. Never has the British government waged a war so evidently just. From the first we understood the war sufficiently well to know that the duty of the day was to fight.[29]

That, however, was one thing for Wood. His meticulous examination of the July-August crisis led to the overwhelmingly clear conclusion that German diplomacy had been the most transparent cover-up of the underlying intention to provoke a reckoning with Russia and France. But what he really wanted to know was, why? In a previously unpublished lecture, 'German History and the War', held 14 August 1915, he stated the problem:

I had a conception of German culture that was well founded on facts. It seemed to me one of the noblest and most humane and most spiritual that have existed. The accusation that Germany had willed this war and was waging it on a deliberately thought-out scheme of frightfulness was so contrary to my conception of German culture that I found it well-nigh incredible.[30]

Wood then went on to develop what is arguably the most refined version of the 'Two Germanys Thesis' in spite of the fact that the inheritors of the tradition of Goethe and Schiller had declared their solidarity with the 'policy of frightfulness'. This Wood put down to their political naivety. The German academics and clergy, he wrote, were 'political asses', employing a quotation from the book, *Imperial Germany* by the former Reich Chancellor, Prince Bernhard von Bulow. Wood reiterated:

We are at war with them not because their mind is the Prussian mind but because the will to obey has caused them to deceive themselves. They do not approve the immoral use of force. They are not aware that force has been used immorally. They believe with sincerity and with fervency the Hohenzollern story. And the Hohenzollern story itself pays this tribute to German virtue: it tells, and in a way that may easily convince the ignorant that the Hohenzollern cause is just, that Germany fights for her life against a conspiracy to destroy her. 'We have our faith', say the German scholars, 'firm as a rock upon our righteous cause'.[31]

That faith Professor Wood saw as most tragically misplaced. He clearly deeply regretted the failure of a Whig tradition to take root in Germany, and rightly recognised from his study of Bismarck and von Treitschke that liberalism had been intentionally stamped out by Hohenzollern *Realpolitik*.

Certainly, after he had informed himself about Bismarck's political style, Wood came to regard him as a 'gigantic ruffian'.[32]

Indeed, it was basic to Wood's understanding of Germany that what he called a 'barbarous feudal aristocracy' had for purely selfish class reasons, and by ruthless use of force, captured the political leadership of Germany at the expense of the well-meaning but politically inexperienced liberal movement and social democrats. In his major statement on this process, Wood most fervently revealed his own Christian radicalism and Whig consistency. Discussing the unification of Germany under Bismarck, Wood observed:

> If German union was achieved by parliamentary methods, then German union would mean democracy and peace; would mean in other words the end of Prussianism. But if German union was achieved by war, by war under the king of Prussia, then German union would mean the absolute rule of the Prussian War Lord, not only in Prussia, but also in Germany. War could be used as an instrument that would at the same time unite Germany and exalt the greatness of the Prussian monarch. The rule of united Germany might be placed in the hands not of a specific democracy but of a divine-right Hohenzollern War Lord at the head of a 'state of soldiers and officials.'[33]

Wood's image of Bismarckian-Wilhelmine Germany was that of a State forged in a series of unjust wars, and one thoroughly committed ideologically to the use of force as an instrument of both domestic as well as foreign policy. Prussianism was simply the German form of a doctrine of political violence as opposed to reason. It was sustained by the successful Prussian military caste, of whom Wood observed again:

> [This] caste, so far as I know, had never for a moment swerved from their fidelity to their God. Everywhere and at all times

they have 'preached the gospel' of the Kaiser's 'sacred person'. The Kaiser is indeed prophet of the one God: but that one God is Force.[34]

It was this devotion to Force as the exclusive means of resolving political differences which appalled Wood. In 1914, peaceful methods of achieving international justice had been cynically rejected and the German sword thrown into the scales. This led him to conclude that,

> It was the result of a habit of mind; the habit of mind that regards the use of force as a thing natural and good, that thinks only of Power, and that the endeavour to increase Power is regardless of morality and humanity. I say it is the Prussian government acting, as I believe, often under severe and long continued pressure from the Prussian military nobility, that is guilty of this war, and that especially is guilty of the perpetration [of the atrocities] with which this war has been waged.[35]

George Arnold Wood portrayed an image of Prusso-Germany which was shared by the intellectual elite of Australia and New Zealand. Kaiserism was seen to stand for everything anti-liberal, anti-democratic and inhumane that could be imagined. It was not mindless barbarism; it was barbarism backed by intellect, both philosophical – the doctrine of the *Machtstaat* (the Power State) – and technological: the renowned achievements of German science. This made *Kultur* an insidious evil to be eradicated at all costs, and that certainly became not only the rhetoric but also the unswerving policy objective of the Australian government from 1914 to 1918.

Finally, for those Antipodians with an educational background sufficient to make a rational analysis of the underlying causes of the great Anglo-German antagonism in which they were irrevocably involved, it could be reduced to a collision of two incompatible political cultures: the

British shaped, but not always guided, by the Whig tradition; the *German* dominated by a rigorously authoritarian, feudal, aristocratic tradition that maintained itself by suppressing all forms of internal as well as external opposition. Moreover, it was a tradition that had been systematised into an intellectual edifice which was defended and propagated with all the scientific power of the German universities.

Wood was acutely aware of the internal German opposition to the Hohenzollern system, especially among the Social Democrats, and this made the war doubly tragic because it required that Australians fight against the common German people. He formulated the dilemma, thereby giving expression again to his thesis of the two Germanys, as follows:

> My conclusion is that though the German people now fight for the Hohenzollerns, they fight for objects which are different from those for which the Hohenzollerns fight. The Hohenzollerns fight for Dynastic power, and the gospel of the Kaiser's sacred person. The German people fight for hearth and home, for national existence, for those rights to which all the world admits the German people are entitled. For the innocent the distinction between the mind of the Prussian government and the mind of the German people seems of little practical importance. We cannot negotiate with the German people. We can only strive to smash the Dynasty. But, in view of the future, the distinction seems to me to be of very great importance. For it gives grounds for hope: for hope that means may be found to convince the German people that they may fight for the fatherland not by fighting for the Kaiser, but by destroying the Kaiser and Kaiserism.[36]

With this formulation, then, George Arnold Wood encapsulated the ideology of Australia's academic garrison during the Great War. The tragedy was that it had to be reapplied when Prussianism re-emerged in the even more brutal guise of National Socialism. But Wood, and those like him, who had expressed great hopes for the cultivation of a liberal democracy in Germany after the adoption of the Weimar Constitution in 1919, was spared the obligation of having to comment upon that new form of Prussianism, though how he would have done so is perfectly clear.

Conclusions

The Australian educated elite 1914–18 was a small but highly articulate, well connected and influential pressure group which formed itself spontaneously out of the various War Committees of the then six state universities. As has been seen, such behaviour was not unique because the academic elites of all belligerent nations at the time acted in a similar way. They not only functioned as well-informed analysts of international relations, but also as scientific advisers who made available their training, inventiveness and administrative skills to the authorities for the more efficient prosecution of the war effort.

There was a broad distinction, of course, as to how the representatives of the different disciplines actually served. Those with historical, philosophical and/or linguistic expertise would have been more active as publicists and propagandists, though some (and further research is expected to document this) such as J. J. Stable of the Department of English at Queensland University, worked on behalf of the Commonwealth bureaucracy as a censor. A scientist such as the Queensland chemistry professor B. D. Steele, mentioned above, was a prominent public speaker on the nature of the war to the people of Brisbane before he was seconded in 1915 to Britain to manage the production of munitions. Indeed, Steele was an excellent example of an English student of chemistry at a German university (Leipzig) who had on the one hand profited from the scientific brilliance of his German mentors, but having become familiar with the implications of *Kultur* emphatically rejected its toxic anti-liberalism. Certainly Professor Steele was unbending in his determination to help smash Prusso-German militarism, and his voice was clearly heard in the corridors of power since his plan for naval defence of the Empire was reportedly considered at the highest level in the imperial government.

The point is that the academics' assessment of the imperial German menace was both authoritative and accurate. Current West German research in particular confirms this. The Wilhelmine Empire was a highly volatile political entity, polarised between the social democratic labour movement on the one hand and the various groups on the other which considered Social Democracy as subversive to the monarchical system and therefore a danger to be eradicated. Given that the *Kaiserreich* was such an internally unstable structure it is unsurprising that the power elite resorted to an aggressive foreign policy in an attempt to contain and reduce the rising democratic challenge. There was as well, of course, essential to any understanding of the *Kaiserreich,* the factor of the self-appointed ideological praetorian guard of the Prusso-German constitution: the university professors. As has been pointed out, they functioned over many decades to educate the nation to its imperial calling, enjoying a virtual monopoly of such ideas. The German professors said in effect that to be a good, patriotic German, one had to be an unquestioningly loyal monarchist and understand the mission which Providence had imposed on the new Reich, namely to change the power relationships in the world and to infuse it with *Kultur.*

It was in analysing and responding to this German sense of mission that the Australian academics for their part saw themselves rendering a crucial national service in a time of great danger. They recognised better than anyone else that if Germany succeeded in carrying out her mission, liberal Anglo-Saxon political culture would be obliterated. This recognition imposed the iron necessity to fight the German empire to a 'clean finish'. It was, as Professor Wood acknowledged, a tragic necessity because it meant fighting the ordinary German people who basically wanted no part of militarism, but who were forced in a sense to fight for Hohenzollern dynastic goals because these coincided with the population's need to defend hearth and home.

Clearly for the 'Australian Academic Garrison', as it became for President Woodrow Wilson of the USA, a world under Prusso-German hegemony was intolerable to contemplate. It would have meant in their estimation a return to the political values of feudal times. Anyone remotely familiar with the British parliamentary heritage would have had to resist such a possibility. This, in the circumstances, required a pro-Empire, pro-war and hence pro-conscription stance. To the 'Academic Garrison' this was self-evident. For Australasians to have any future worth contemplating it had no alternative but to make the necessary sacrifices. So, in a sense, the experience of the 'German War' was a process of national maturation in a world threatened by a Great Power run amok.

Indeed, for thoughtful citizens, the determination to fight against Prusso-German militarism was the Australasian calling above all others. It meant one was aware of the need to defend the democratic heritage of these new countries which was fortunate since they were not hampered in their growth by the existence of a hereditary nobility. Australia and New Zealand, in short, had the potential to become a genuinely free and egalitarian democracies. This was certainly the view held and propagated by Professor G. A. Wood of Sydney who was arguably the most whiggish of his contemporaries. It was not, for example, Wood's view that the war experience should make Australians more dependent upon Britain, but rather it was an experience which should enable them to develop an even more radical and humane democracy out of the tradition inherited from Britain.

With this in mind it would be a mistake to classify members of the 'Academic Garrison' as a group of jingoistic Empire loyalists. Certainly most would have been loyal out of sentiment and conviction, but this loyalty in no way conflicted with their commitment to Australia. They had a view of Australia in relation to the wider world which foresaw the development of a unique form of Anglo-Saxon democracy. A German victory in 1914–18 would have frustrated that vision.

Finally, because of their unique status and qualifications, the 'Academic Garrison' functioned if not as de facto policy-makers, but as political pedagogues. Their rhetoric filtered into national policy. The Commonwealth's chief war aim had been to contribute to the destruction of Prusso-German militarism with all available resources, human and material. This had, of course, some less than edifying side-effects such as the aim to break up the German-Australian community through a policy of internment. However, this episode can only be understood in the light of the analysis of the true nature of Prussian-German militarism and its long-term objectives. If the latter's major goal had been the destruction of the British Empire, then the victimisation of the German-Australian community was at base a precautionary policy enforced for straight-forward security reasons. Previous analyses of the implementation of the policy of internment, most recently that by Dr Gerhard Fischer, as having been based on xenophobia, racial prejudice, ignorance, cultural immaturity or primitive revenge motives will be difficult to sustain.[37] The explanation is certainly far more complex than hitherto assumed.

CHAPTER 7

German and Australian Perceptions of the War in 1914

It is a curious but no less striking fact that for both Germany and Australia the experience of the Great War meant a fundamental change of direction. In both countries the conflict brought with it massive socio-economic as well as national-psychological crises of identity, or self-perception, with long-term consequences.[1] Admittedly, many other countries, too, were affected in similar ways. As Bill Gammage had also pointed out, Turkey also 'changed direction' in her political culture as a direct consequence of the traumatic Dardanelles campaign.[2] And, of course, the most dramatic example of 'direction change' was Russia which experienced ultimately the Bolshevik revolution, which made the most radical attempt of all to make a clean break with the past.

However, in the cases of Australia and Germany the problem was how to maintain *continuity* with the past national heritage and at the same time take account of the inescapable readjustments to such basic questions as what now constituted the 'nation.' In Germany, in the light of the essential contribution of the working class to the war effort, a class which had hitherto been intentionally excluded from the so-called 'nation', there had to arise a debate concerning the extent to which the proletariat could be recognised constitutionally and accepted. Up to 1914, the 'nation' comprised only the nobility, the upper middle classes, the *Bildungsbürgertum* and the *Mittelstand,* all of whom revered the monarchy and were generally comfortable with the dominant but quite illiberal political culture. Voters of social democratic and trade union affiliation formed at best a 'negatively integrated' opposition. Indeed, the Wilhelmine Reich was very much a polarised state, and the war appeared to not a few leaders on both sides of the political spectrum to be an opportunity to fuse together the mutually suspicious blocs into one cohesive nation.[3]

For Australia, the crisis of identity engendered by the war, namely Australia's pivotal historical experience, as Ernest Scott observed,[4] arose over the question of why the remote self-governing Dominions should become so sacrificially involved in an imperial conflict which apparently did not concern them? But having become so involved, did the sacrifice win the credentials of nationhood? The national rhetoric of past decades, certainly of the inter-war years and immediately after the Second World War was strongly infused with the idea that Australians won their identity as a people through their sacrifices in the Great War. However, there is still a question as to what the inner content of a unique Australian identity was, and this question in the age of multi-culturalism is now more acute than ever before. In the era after 1918–19, though, there was no doubt in the mind of Australia's intellectual elite, the group whose task it had been to clarify the issues of the *Kaiser's War*, just what Australia stood for and where her future lay. For this elite in particular, both the realities of world politics and the heritage of British political culture rendered any thought of a radical loosening of the imperial connection not only disloyal but imprudent. It is instructive to recall why they thought so, and this recollection may serve as a contribution to understanding an important segment of the debate over identity.

This chapter demonstrates through a juxtaposition of the so-called 'Ideas of 1914' in both Germany and Australia that Australia and New Zealand were locked into a *Schicksalsgemeinschaft*, a community of fate, with Great Britain because, if her capacity to maintain the security of the Empire had been undermined by Germany's world political ambitions, the future of the Dominions would have been at the very least problematic, if not disastrous, as the late John Robertson had pointed out.[5] In a world dominated by *Kultur*, the expressed antithesis of Anglo-Saxon civilisation,

Australian democratic aspirations would almost certainly have been suppressed and all the Dominions subjected to unwelcome Teutonic pressure.

By taking the foregoing into account, this chapter has the additional aim of underlining the very ideological nature of the Great War. From a portrayal of the German self-perception it will be seen that their peculiar sense of cultural mission in the world, which gained its frankest expression in the 'Ideas of 1914', revealed the Germans as a nation bent on the uncompromising realisation of hegemony, not only in Europe but also overseas. This hegemony was not conceived of in commercial terms only but, more importantly, in political-cultural values. The German power-elite, whose ideas derived from the universities, especially since the 1870s, really wanted to infuse the world with 'German ideas' by means of German commercial, military and naval power. Indeed, power and culture were mutually reinforcing terms: the one was the expression of the other. It is also very important to note that in focussing on what the German intellectual elite in 1914 had to say about the nature of the war, as they perceived it, we are only commenting on a phenomenon which received wide publicity in the West at the time. Rightly or wrongly Anglo-Saxon observers took German academic pronouncements to reflect the mind of the German political leadership. Failure to comprehend this will inevitably result in confusion about the reasons why Australia and the other Dominions believed they had to fight alongside Britain, France, Russia and finally the United States, against the Prusso-German Empire.

Given, then, the importance of this 'pivotal experience' in Australia's history, it would appear essential to document as reliably as possible the mind of Australian opinion-makers concerning the precise nature of the conflict in which the young Dominion had become so deeply involved. The point of such an exercise would be to clarify the issues, to comprehend something of the self-perception of the generation who sent so many men to perish on battle fields in countries so remote that in ordinary circumstance they would have had little or no relevance to Australia's past, present or future. Such a task, it would seem, ought not to be avoided because it would assist in achieving some answers to the apparent dichotomy between Dominion nationalism on the one hand, and Empire loyalty on the other. And central to this is the perception of Imperial Germany's role in the world at the time because without clarity on that score there can be no progress in understanding this alleged dichotomy.

In justifying the methodology adopted here it is taken as given that there is such a thing as a reciprocal relationship between national policy and what the educated elite say about it. The fact that the educated elites in all countries engage in a dialogue with the public known as civic discourse is well enough appreciated, but beyond that there is a documented dialogue between the educational and power elites, groups which while not precisely co-terminus, certainly overlap.[6] That is to say, scholarly experts frequent the 'corridors of power' either as advocates for certain causes or as invited expert advisers/commentators. This was an established tradition in Germany, and in Australia we witness the same phenomenon. It was the staffs of the then six state universities who, by virtue of their overseas experience and education, their special expertise in history, philosophy or the physical sciences, became political analysts and scientific and military advisers. However, before investigating the Australian educated elite, German political will in 1914 has to be assessed because it was against this that the Australian academics were reacting, and their assessment in turn had arguably a considerable impact on the formation of political will in Australia.

Prusso-German Anglophobia

It is crucial to grasp the German self-perception in 1914 because it instructs us why the Germans (who were regarded until the invasion of Belgium as a great cultural nation) were so radically different from other Europeans and Anglo-Saxons generally. This will make clear their essentially toxic attitude to Britain and her Empire, as well as towards the French and the Slavs; the nature of German Christianity and anti-pacifism as opposed to Western Christianity; German cultural and racial self-perception; German hostility to democracy; German war-aims; finally, how the world would have looked if German war aims had been realised.

Information about national-self-perceptions must be sought from the foremost intellects, from those who taught the nation's history, the nation's religion, wrote the nation's literature: in short, those who articulated the nation's culture. In the two decades before the Great War in Germany it was the historians and the theologians who were universally regarded as the political mentors. They interpreted the nation's past and were thus qualified to pronounce on its future political direction. The historical profession was the collective custodian of the national heritage and was looked to in order to lay down the principles of national policy.

In the German context this combination of the disciplines of history and theology together shaping the nation's political culture is hardly surprising when it is recalled that the 'nation', the Prusso-German Empire, was really the end result of the Reformation experience. Luther was the major pre-condition for the fragmentation of the medieval constitution of the Holy Roman Empire of the German Nation, and thus was the celebrated harbinger of the rise of a strong protestant state-tradition which inevitably had to rival and confront the champion of the papal cause in the Holy Roman Empire of the German Nation, the House of Habsburg.[7] But it was not only modern historians and theologians who were prophets of Germany's national resurgence; the medieval and ancient historians, not to mention the Germanists themselves, were not less prophetic in their respective disciplines, as a study of the 'Ideas of 1914' indicates.[8] In short, all disciplines in the humanities were inspired by a uniquely German spirit and evinced in all their writings a peculiarly Teutonic quality, a characteristic which fascinated and attracted humanistic scholars from the entire world. German scientists also were held in the highest esteem by foreign colleagues. When, however, the war broke out these learned men also revealed themselves to be essentially nationalistic, although their disciplines were ostensibly not subjects which were limited by the borders of nation states. It is curious, but no less true, that even chemists and physicists in Germany believed that there was a specific German way of doing science, and foreign students improved in quality to the degree to which they appropriated the German way. Indeed, it is interesting to note that the outbreak of war unleashed a barrage of polemical literature from both sides in which the natural scientists took a prominent part. The British, for example, asserted that the famous German professors had not really measured up to their grossly inflated reputations because, in the end, they had almost to a man endorsed Germany's 'barbaric' militarism.

For their part, German scientists replied by dismissing most foreign scientists as pale imitators of their great pioneering work, and so on. These polemics, too, belong to the 'Ideas of 1914'. However, it was the humanities professors who with great fervour and eloquence articulated the ideas, formulated the German self-perception most accurately and, incidentally, revealed the mind of the German power elite.[9]

The German 'Ideas of 1914' had a long ancestry central to which was the conviction that the dissolution of the British Empire was historically determined. So the question of German Anglophobia must be posed at the outset. The once forgotten German historian, Eckart Kehr (1902–33), began to unravel the problem in a paper in 1928, *Englandhass und Weltpolitik* (Anglophobia and World Politics).[10] For the period, his method was revolutionary. Instead of explaining imperial rivalries in terms of struggles for overseas markets or as the consequences of the peculiar thinking of the Prussian general staff, Kehr sought and found the underlying sociological and domestic political causes. He observed:

> The problem of history is not the wilfulness of human beings who appear to be directing these institutions [meaning government departments and so on] but the fact that they are captives of the laws that govern their institutions and their class and are subordinate to their interests without even being aware of their dependence.[11]

The first 'law' to bear in mind is that of the founding of the Bismarckian Empire, or the nature of the 'Prussian solution to the German question'. The last of the wars of unification, the Franco-Prussian war of 1870, determined that the new Teutonic power would have to be virtually an armed fortress, always ready to engage in a pre-emptive war against France and her allies, should they appear to threaten the new Reich. The nature of German unification was a permanent affront to France, and for that very reason German unity made the militarisation of Europe inevitable. So there was always a German Francophobia, and with the Franco-Russian rapprochement of the mid-1890s, Russophobia increased. Anglophobia, which came to overshadow everything else, derived, paradoxically, from British attempts to befriend Prusso-Germany. Kehr observed in 1928:

> The major turning point in the foreign policy of the imperialist powers is the outcome of negotiations for an Anglo-German alliance at the turn of the century.[12]

Since these talks failed, and had to fail because of internal German conflicts, two rival power blocs arose which found by 1914 that they could only resolve their difficulties in all out war. The roots of the Great War are deeply imbedded in the domestic social-political conflicts of the 1890s within the *Kaiserreich*.

It is important to dwell upon this in order to comprehend what was in retrospect the suicidal foreign policy of the Wilhelmine Empire, the policy to which France, Russia, Britain and the Dominions had to respond. And here we must be aware of the internal power structure of the Reich. Bismarck had devised the constitution to secure first his own class, the conservative, East-Elbian Junker, the land-owning class, and then the so-called *schaffende Stände*, the productive classes, that is those who controlled the means of 'production, distribution and exchange' to use the Marxist designation. Herein lay the core of the problem, and the answer why the Reich ultimately self-destructed.

Again, as Kehr observed:

At the turn of the century, the principle problem of foreign policy for conservatism was the relation between agrarian and industrial states on the one hand, that is Germany and England, and between the agrarian states of Germany and Russia, on the other. This view of foreign policy originated in the internal political and social sphere, in Germany's industrialisation and the concomitant development of large cities ... [and] German conservatism carried its detestation of cities and industry over into foreign policy.[13]

So, for the German conservatives, Britain, a near neighbour, a close relation even, and the world's most advanced industrial and commercial power, was a most dangerous example.

As the detestable nation of shop-keepers, Britain was utterly materialistic and her liberal and democratic institutions, despite the continued existence of a monarchy, were essentially the outgrowth of the shop-keeper mentality. Above all, the German conservative power-elite esteemed aristocratic, patriarchal values which they saw threatened by the advance of industrialisation. Certainly, it was they who nurtured 'the warrior class', having been the traditional source of officers for Prussia's armies. But now, in the age of industrialisation, they still wanted to maintain the highest level of military preparedness. Indeed, 'these agrarian conservatives were the most determined spokesmen of the modern power state' (*Machtstaat*).[14] The fact that it now had to rely on the existence of a large industrial and urban proletariat seemed to elude them. They never asked themselves, according to Kehr, how a predominantly agrarian state could ever afford the upkeep of such an army.

This curious failure to think things through characterized the German conservatives' attitude towards foreign policy and is sufficient proof that the Anglo-German antagonism was ignited not only by their manifestly incompatible philosophies, but also by the rivalry between 'traders and heroes' as Werner Sombart proclaimed. It reflected the attempt by the

Junker class to preserve at all costs its own position in the face of capitalist-industrial growth.[15]

Kehr's general analysis of the mainsprings of German foreign policy was, of course, heresy to his conservative mentors when he presented it. In time it became the orthodoxy not only of the left-wing liberal historians of the so-called Kehrite school in West Germany but also of the Marxist East Germans. In particular, Kehr explained how, after initial resistance, the agrarian conservatives came to advocate the construction of an unnecessarily large battle fleet, the key issue which alienated the British. Admiral von Tirpitz' new High Seas Fleet of capital ships, as opposed to long range cruisers for colonial and trade route protection, was pre-eminently a weapon of industry and aggressive enterprises abroad, namely *Weltpolitik*, and for that reason had been regarded with suspicion by the conservatives. As Kehr made clear, and he possessed a sharp vision for the more hidden causal connections, the British victory over the Boers in South Africa, whom the German agrarians admired for their patriarchal values, convinced them once and for all that the British model had to be opposed. That is to say, a great industrial power with a bourgeois, liberal constitution, appeared to them to be ultimately an existential threat. It did not need to wage war on Germany; it simply had to continue successfully going about its business.

Consequently, the German power-elite was in a dilemma. Industrialisation was a repugnant development, as was also the accompanying revolutionary potential of the rising labour movement. Indeed, the increasing strength of both political and industrial labour in Germany during the 1890s began to drive together all anti-democratic elements, regardless of religious or socio-economic background (*Sammlungspolitik*). And this posed a dilemma for the agrarian conservatives. If they wanted now to preserve their position in the new German Empire, they had to be prepared to make concessions to German capital and to let it pursue its *Weltpolitik,* for which it needed the 'fat' ships (*dicke Schiffe*). In the end this was palatable because firstly it promised to check British world supremacy and secondly it united all parties against organised labour which, if it was not openly revolutionary, was at least demanding unacceptable, system-changing parliamentary reforms. So *Weltpolitik* and naval expansion became for the politically all-important German conservatives the means of preserving their own class rule. It determined that Anglophobia was to be a permanent feature of German political life.[16] Anglophobia was not, however, the sole prerogative of the conservatives.

The German bourgeoisie had its own reasons for hating England. These derived from the values of the pre-industrial education system, and were sustained well after industrialisation. How this came to be so is explained by the late Fritz Ringer, who established that the highly educated class in economically backward Prussia conceived of themselves as an intellectual and cultural elite, distinct from the burgher world on the one hand (from which they came) and the hereditary aristocracy. This group which controlled the universities evolved the ideology of *Bildung,* meaning *not* just the pursuit of knowledge, but spiritual-intellectual formation within the context of the exclusively German cultural experience. This emphasis on spiritual-cultural formation contrasted strongly with nineteenth century Britain's bourgeois ideology of economic individualism. There the emphasis was on utilitarianism, on the individual conceived as a rational economic and political agent functioning within both the market and the political process, an arena in which conflicting individual choices are balanced and aggregated into collective trends and policies.[17]

Bildung, by contrast, connoted a paradigm of values and beliefs which were appropriated by the German middle classes. They were values which had social and historical, as well as purely intellectual, roots. As Fritz Ringer observed, it is an important historical task to link the German ideology of *Bildung* to certain peculiarities of German historical development. For our understanding, then, of Imperial Germany, it is essential to know something of the self-perception of the *Bildungsbürgertum* because Anglophobia was a key component of its paradigm, which of course overlapped with and reinforced that of the Junker class.

So, why did Anglophobia become paradigmatic for the *Bildungs-bürgertum*? It was not always so because many leading German liberals at the time of the 1848 revolution and the Frankfurt National Assembly saw in Britain the political model to emulate: a constitutional monarchy within a sovereign national parliament. However, with the crushing of the 1848 movement, the intellectual leaders began to turn to Prussia to unite Germany, regardless of whether Prussia adopted a liberal constitution. And because the Hohenzollern dynasty proved so tenaciously hostile to liberalisation, the *Bildungsbürgertum* persuaded themselves that the philosophy of liberalism was a luxury Germans could not afford if national unity was the supreme goal, and so developed the counter-philosophy of the power-state for which the groundwork had been adequately laid by such thinkers as Luther, Hegel and Fichte. In short, the post-1848 reaction in Germany was ideologically justified by the newly discovered principles of *Realpolitik* explained in chapter five and these had been elevated to the level of dogma by the increasingly influential Prussian school of historians.

In practice this allowed the removal of national policy from any form of moral scrutiny. In fact, Friedrich Meinecke, as we have seen, justified it most eloquently. Indeed, the will of the power-state, Prussia, became co-terminous with the will of God.[18] The Machiavellism, or *Realpolitik,* of Bismarck was interpreted as the working out and ultimate triumph of the Prussian *Volksgeist* with obviously divine sanction. The Prussian state tradition of militarism, authoritarianism and bureaucratism, the very antithesis of liberalism, had behaved simply in accordance with the divine laws of history when it imposed its will by force over those states which ultimately formed the German Empire.[19] From then on, there could be no more admiration for liberal, parliamentary Britain even though the English were of Teutonic stock. Anglophobia became virtually obligatory for all patriotic Germans.

Given this mind-set it will be clear that the Bismarckian-Wilhelmine Reich was scarcely fertile ground for cosmopolitan or pacifist thought. So Germany became a State in which the highest virtues were always military ones, and this held true not only for historians but particularly also for theologians. Paradigmatic here was Luther's exegesis of St Paul's Epistle to the Romans, chapter 13, in which 'the powers that be are ordained of God' and where obedience to the sovereign was the first duty of the Christian man. This meant that the Lutheran churches in Germany saw their chief task as inculcating into the faithful loyalty and obedience to the princes who were the supreme bishops of their respective states. So German Christianity, in contrast to Western Christianity, served as a bulwark against liberalism and even pacifism.[20]

All this contributed to a unique and pugnaciously anti-Western political culture in Germany. By the crucial period of the 1890s, when the rise of Social Democracy was perceived with increasing suspicion, the power elite and the *Bildungsbürgertum* endorsed *Weltpolitik* and the associated battle fleet as fulfilling the dual functions of confirming Prussia's vocation to expand and of uniting all elements loyal to the monarchy against the growing revolutionary threat of Social Democracy. The *Kaiserreich* became and perceived itself as a fearsome political entity called by God to ensure that the world did not succumb to the inferior Anglo-Saxon civilisation, which was regarded as essentially decadent and moribund. This is not to deny, however, the existence of a degree of cultural pessimism but, as Fritz Stern has shown, this only contributed to the political volatility and to crippling further the growth of an essentially optimistic Whig tradition in Germany. So the Prusso-German self-perception distinguished itself from the West with this essentially anti-British ideology. And this is why the creation of the High Seas fleet received the virtually universal endorsement of the *Bildungsbürgertum* as the instrument by which the Prusso-German will would be exerted throughout the world.[21]

Not surprisingly, the consequence of German policy was to alienate Britain, causing her to feel her 'imperial overstretch' ever more acutely and generating great antagonism in Britain. But the Germans saw this as virtual proof that the policy was right. That is why all British attempts, first at alliance negotiations and then at arms limitation, were brusquely rejected as non-negotiable, without any visible sign of misgiving or self-doubt. While the British after 1900 came to see the *Kaiserreich* increasingly as posing the greatest existential threat since Napoleon I, the German power-elite comforted itself in the belief that God was unquestionably on their side. Virtually no German commentator of the time apart from Social Democratic intellectuals could assess the real effect that the construction of the High Seas Fleet was having.[22] That it was the prime reason for the so-called encirclement of the Reich seemed never to have been grasped. Instead, the series of alliances and ententes formed around Germany were attributed to British envy, French revanchism and pan-Slavic delusions of grandeur. Britain, France and Russia had merely put aside their rivalries in order to frustrate Germany's legitimate aspirations in the world.[23]

Before rehearsing the 'Ideas of 1914', the role of the German professoriate as the acknowledged spokesmen of the *Bildungsbürgertum* has to be understood. They seemed to experience a sudden change of character in August 1914, becoming extremely bellicose. Their numerous public statements in defence of *Kultur* and in denunciation of the enemy, especially Britain, are a matter of record. And in the light of the tradition of which they felt themselves to be such a central part, indeed, the spokespersons, it is not tenable to describe their assessment of the war as a mere knee-jerk reaction to a potential national calamity. Some German authorities pose the question of whether there really was a 'war mentality' among academics before 1914, and seek to weaken contemporary Anglo-Saxon assertions that the professors were really advocates of militarism, by suggesting that the research necessary to verify this has yet to be done.

Be that as it may, what is known already is the paradigm of imperialism which the *Bildungsbürgertum* assumed to be *scientifically* valid. It was termed neo-Rankeanism as explained above in chapter 4 and it meant that they believed states and empires to be expanding organisms. If they were not expanding they were dying. They had life-cycles. And from their assessment of the world situation prior to 1914, the dying empire was Britain's; the ascendant one was that of Germany.

The German 'Ideas of 1914'

When Europe was plunged into the 'murderous anarchy' of August 1914, the mind of Germany was made known to the world by her professors, chiefly in response to British academic denunciations of the violation of Belgian neutrality in which, be it noted, British scholars initially refused to believe that their German counterparts could have possibly endorsed such action by the German army. However, that was precisely what the German professors did in numerous declarations. They proclaimed themselves in complete solidarity with the military because the German military and academic/scientific tradition formed integral parts of one organic whole called *Kultur*.[24]

In the ensuing *Kulturkrieg*, or war of values, between the Anglo-Saxon and the Germanic academic worlds, the irreconcilable 'Ideas of 1914' were expressed. Various German authorities have recently made the point that in the 'Ideas of 1914', formulated in the heat of battle, so to speak, were the truest expressions of the German mind. All their beliefs about the Reich and their aspirations for the future were most frankly and honestly ventilated at that time. The late Professor Wolfgang J. Mommsen commented on the Hegelian mind-set as follows:

> The efficacy of this ideological mental schema in the political culture of the *Kaiserreich* is simply impossible to estimate. And nowhere did it gain clearer and sharper expression than in the debate over the spirit of 1914 which among the German leadership elite in general was understood as the expression of a specifically German political mentality which was different in principle from that of the Western democracies.[25]

Indeed, all attempts to define the nature of the war were made in this sense. And it was given even sharper intensity when Protestant theologians and pastors analysed the war. They had been used to projecting the Prussian solution to the German question as an act of divine providence, and so attacks upon it by inferior civilisations lent the German stance a quality of righteous anger. For them at least the Great War was a *holy war*, the *Weltgericht*, the tribunal of the world, in which the Power which had been selected by Providence to lead the world would mete out direst retribution to those frivolous enough to oppose Germany's world-historical calling.[26] And if the Prusso-German Empire had been founded upon unique principles utterly distinct from the Western democracies, now in 1914 was a God-given opportunity to re-assert those principles. For the professors and pastors, this was a time for the moral and spiritual regeneration of the German people, a time which provided the impulse for the development of an ideological edifice which was designated by such thinkers as the Munster pedagogue Johann Plenge, the theologian/historian Ernst Troeltsch, and the Swedish political scientist Rudolf Kjellen as 'The Ideas of 1914'.[27]

Central to these ideas was not only the unchallengeable superiority of German culture, but the sense of mission, encouraged by the war, to impose this culture by force on the enemy. Consequently, right from the outset there was no pre-disposition on behalf of the intellectual elite of Germany, some notable exceptions notwithstanding, to sheathe the sword and negotiate a peace. For them the war could only be concluded with a *Siegfrieden*, a victorious peace, preferably a dictated peace such as was realised in the victory over Russia and the concluding Peace of Brest-Litovsk (3 March 1918). Indeed, the war-aims in the East having been achieved successfully for a time at the defeat of Russia were essentially those which had been tabled by the German government in September 1914, the September Program. The accomplishment of the war aims in the West would prove, of course, incomparably more difficult, not least because of the combined resistance of the French, British and Imperial forces and ultimately the Americans. But the effect of the success in the East with such éclat encouraged the German leadership to persist with the aims of the September Program and to go all out for total victory over the Western allies. And this aim was never abandoned until the German armies had been forced to retreat between August and October 1918.[28]

At the very least the Reich had hoped still to maintain occupation of Belgium, such was the persistence of the *Siegfrieden* mentality.[29] The war was not only a struggle for the extension of German military power but, as emphasised, for the establishment of the Prusso-German political culture both at home and abroad, particularly at the expense of Anglo-Saxon civilisation. The reciprocal relationship between official war-aims and their ideological justification was virtually complete. In the German view, the West had been upholding the banner of liberty, equality and fraternity since 1789 but these were hypocritical values since they were but the fig leaf to hide the nakedness of the crass materialistic commercialism that was leading the world to a state of superficial non-*Kultur*, that is mere *civilisation*.

The time was now ripe for a new revolution, a *German* revolution, which like the French one of 125 years earlier, would usher in a new epoch of world history, the exact opposite in spirit and content of its predecessor.[30] Instead of the dissolution of society into atomistic individuality, the German revolution would bring about a creative concentration of all elements behind the State, and in practice that meant the idealisation of the semi-authoritarian political system of the *Kaiserreich*.

It was argued that a modified Bismarckian constitution would be far better placed to solve the world's problems in future. What was needed was some form of corporatism or 'national socialism' which would exploit the German genius for organisation, an essential component of *Kultur*. A world left in the hands of mere traders like the English would be a sorry place indeed. This was, in fact, the central message of one of the most eloquent expressions of the 'Ideas of 1914', Professor Werner Sombart's 1915 book, *Händler und Helden* (Traders and Heroes). Therein the famous German economist averred:

> The war which constitutes the fulfilment of this heroic state
> of mind itself does not fall victim to the powers of evil, the
> crawling commercial spirit. The war, a product of this spirit,
> enables its re-birth out of its loins. And this view of war is
> not just a recent thing as often asserted, that is, the result of
> our modern German development. It was not the Germany

of Bismarck and Moltke which first pronounced war sacred.[31]

Sombart then invoked a much earlier authority, namely Friedrich von Schiller (1759–1805): 'War is fruitful like the plagues of heaven. It is good, it is a gift like them'. In the very next breath Sombart dismissed Immanuel Kant's philosophy of eternal peace as a sad and less than honourable exception in the German intellectual tradition.[32] Indeed, he discredited all cosmopolitan, liberal and pacifist ideology, and there were numerous such pronouncements. The Freiburg historian, Georg von Below made the point:

> The experience of the World War has exposed the collapse of the ideals of the French Revolution. The ideas of liberty, equality and fraternity have been replaced by the German ideas of duty, order and justice.[33]

The range of German intellectuals who endorsed these views encompassed virtually the entire university community as well as leading figures in the world of literature and the theatre, perhaps the most celebrated having been Thomas Mann in his *Reflections of a Nonpolitical Man* (1918). Essentially this was not a sudden upsurge of academic patriotism but the intellectual elite's frank self-perception of a culture which had been consciously setting itself apart from the Western Enlightenment heritage, at least since the era of Herder, Hegel, Fichte and Goethe. Their heirs on the outbreak of war in 1914 had merely behaved in accordance with the established notions about the State and culture, which notions had assumed paradigmatic status by the time of the foundation of the Reich. If that Reich was under siege from alien and inferior civilisations, it had no alternative but to assert itself in accordance with its culture, and God would ensure the victory over the combined Slavic, Romance and Anglo-Saxon non-cultures. Hence the spate of self-justifying pronouncements relating to the invasion of Belgium and the allegedly treacherous role played by the putatively Teutonic England.

Finally, it is essential to grasp that the ideology of the German spirit in 1914 was not satisfied merely with asserting the German way of thinking and being against a temporary enemy; rather it was totally convinced that in the German spirit was contained the *truth per se*. Indeed, only in German thought and action was the spirit reified, indeed the divine spirit of the universe made flesh. But the German spirit was not merely *idea*, not just another way of looking at the world, it was also *will*. And this combination of idealism and realism enabled Germans in 1914 at last to venture, in full awareness of the higher value of their culture, to confront a world of enemies, namely to confront the will to resist them with an even greater determination to assert their uniqueness, until the final victory had been wrought. And the object of that final triumph had to be above all Britain: the hatred of Britain and her Empire had become a principle of national life.[34]

The Australian Ideas of 1914

Not surprisingly, the British, and Australians too, had made rather heavy weather of trying to comprehend the Germanic enemy, possibly because of a traditional Anglo-Saxon reluctance to grapple with the undoubted mystical and philosophical dimensions of German policy. Consequently, there was never uniform understanding of the decision-making process in Germany, and various groups, such as the *Union for Democratic Control* in Britain and other critics of British policy, advanced interpretations of the war which totally ignored the ideological component, preferring to regard it as a gigantic struggle for world markets between equally rapacious capitalist power blocs.[35] But current German scholarship in this area, as has been indicated, confirms that the *Kaiserreich* with its unique cultural self-perception and sense of mission made it an extremely aggressive power in 1914–18. Indeed, all the current intra-German debate about 'war-guilt' 1914–18 and the nature of the Third Reich, the Second World War and the Holocaust is ultimately an exercise in trying to come to grips with Prusso-German political culture and the peculiar ideology behind it.[36]

These current German debates on the nature of the *Kaiserreich* and the 'Ideas of 1914' certainly relate to a country as remote as Australia since

Australia's pivotal historical experience was gained in a struggle against the *Kultur* of which the *Kaiserreich* was the incarnation. This struggle was extremely costly and divided the nation. Consequently, it is of central political-historical importance that Australians, like Germans, finally comprehend that the First World War was a collision of political cultures, a contest between what was essentially a sophisticated form of tribalism on the one hand and an evolving cosmopolitan-liberal political culture on the other.

In essence, then, the 'Ideas of 1914' which the Prusso-German Empire seemed bent on realising, can be summed up as a repudiation of everything for which the British Empire stood. That is to say, German ideas and actions denied the basic principles of liberalism, of individual rights, of national self-determination and of international law. But in the German self-perception, these denials were rather affirmations that the individualism and cosmopolitanism of Anglo-Saxon political culture themselves were moribund and needed to be supplanted by an incomparably more vital culture. What Anglo-Saxon liberals regarded as progress was, in the German view, decay. The real progress of humanity depended upon the triumph of the German 'Ideas of 1914': that liberty in the Western sense was a nonsense; that equality in the tradition of Anglo-Saxon law was a patent absurdity; that fraternity was a relic from the Enlightenment of decadent cosmopolitan sentimentalism. In their place there would come the Prusso-German concepts of duty to the State, submission of the individual to the collective ideal of the community and, above all the assertion of the obviously superior culture over all others. Clearly, for the German 'Ideas of 1914' to be realised, it was necessary to defeat decisively the coalition of powers ranged against the Central Powers in 1914, and the key to ultimate triumph was the intimidation of Britain and her Empire. This was the logical consequence of both the conservative and bourgeois German Anglophobia.

Australian professors and senior public servants, having 'read, marked, learned and inwardly digested.' the published manifestos of the German professoriate, were quick to grasp the implications, as the setting up of War Committees in all universities indicates.[37] These bodies existed to mobilise the resources of the universities, both intellectual and technical, in the service of the national war effort. One of their chief functions was to identify for the benefit of the general public, and the politicians, what the key issues of the conflict were. It is clear from the range of professorial statements that the authors had taken pains to inform themselves about the German 'Ideas of 1914' and were well able to counter them, rooted as they were in the Anglo-Saxon liberal tradition. It is not surprising, then, that once the Australian academics had understood the ideas of their German counterparts, they drew the only conclusion possible, namely to fight until the *Kaiserreich* had been utterly defeated and was unable ever again to mount another threat to the international community.

The value of an investigation of Australian professorial comment on the Great War lies in revealing how well-informed and rational it was. There can be no doubt either that their assessments were made known in the corridors of power. Indeed, they constituted self-convened think tanks some of which, like Melbourne's, included senior public servants. At the very least the professors engaged in a high level of 'civic discourse' on the war which contributed significantly to public debate and to the formation of political will. The reciprocal relationship between university and government became very apparent. In a word, the Australian 'Ideas of 1914/15' became as efficacious in their way as those of their German counterparts.

The overwhelming impact on Australian professors of the German invasion of Belgium, the violation of the treaty guarantees on the one hand and the outrages perpetrated on the civilian population and cultural property on the other, was one of incredulity. How could a great cultural nation commit these crimes? This compelled the professors to take a systematic look at Prusso-German political culture, something so obviously necessary in view of the declarations of solidarity of the intellectual leadership with the military and their simultaneous bitter attacks on Britain.

The outcome of these investigations was that German political culture had been determined by the militaristic aristocracy of Prussia which scorned the principles of international law. As Dr McKellar Stewart of Melbourne phrased it:

> Government is of the people, by the Prussian State, for the Prussian State; and for this State, and, therefore, indirectly for the German people, whom it has exploited, the cult of forcible expansion is the central and dominating ideal.[38]

If they had not begun to do so before, Australian academics began now to appreciate the implications of Bismarck's constitution. Not a few had lived and studied in Germany and had the greatest respect for German scholarship and an abiding affection for the country and its people. What the war forced them to do was to account for the apparent dualism: the undoubted existence of a barbarous militarism which could perpetrate the Belgian atrocities on the one hand, and the intellectual-spiritual achievements of the German mind on the other. In schooling themselves for this task, the professors consulted, among others, the publications of General Friedrich von Bernhardi, the historian Heinrich von Treitschke and the ex-Chancellor Bernhard von Bülow. These apologists of Prussianism puzzled the liberal-minded professors initially. It was not unprecedented for a large country to produce a lunatic fringe of authors who advocated policies based on a radical revision of accepted norms of civilised human behaviour. However, when it emerged that such authors, including Nietzsche and the cult of the amoral 'superman', were either directly or indirectly endorsed by the mainstream of scholars, it was realised that a new assessment had to be made.

Once it was recognised that the German professors of their own volition not only supported Prussian-German policy but heralded its success as the working out of the supposed laws of history, the Australian professors began to reflect on their own ideological position.[39] This is very evident in all their public utterances on the war. To begin with they uniformly condemned 'Kaiserism', the virtually autocratic powers of the German emperor based on the long-since discredited doctrine of divine right. But this had to be accompanied by an affirmation of the constitutional heritage in which Australia, as a British Dominion, participated.[40]

Having read the various coloured books of diplomatic documents, the professors became convinced that Britain had made every effort to avert war and had declared it finally only as a matter of honour and self-defence. First of all, it was not considered possible for Britain not to have taken Belgium's part. To have stood aside, as the German government had obviously hoped, and allowed the occupation of Belgium followed by the defeat of France, would have been abandoning Europe to the law of the jungle, of which the Kaiser and his Grand Admiral von Tirpitz were regarded as the chief exponents. As Professor Mungo MacCallum of Sydney University formulated it, when reflecting on the possible outcome of the war:

> Whoever wins, Germany must in the long run fail. The mills of God grind exceeding small, even if they grind too slowly for our personal hopes; and it would be blasphemy to suppose that such a power could permanently obtain the control of the world. For the typical Prussian or Prussianised German, though among his own people he is doubtless a man as other men are, has, in his dealings with non-Germans, quite lost his moral sense, and of human nature retains only the most brutal passions which it has inherited, with the most unscrupulous intelligence which it has evolved. And we cannot believe that in God's universe the nation that shows itself a Caliban-Iago to all save its own members, will in the end be allowed to wield the sceptre or to escape its reward. A Thug Empire and a Thug Emperor is not the final goal for the aspirations of mankind.[41]

Quite plainly, Prusso-Germany stood for a criminal principle of brute force which it had elevated to the level of a dogma through the philosophy of Hegel and such disciples as Treitschke and Bernhardi. For all peoples of decency, then, there was an obligation to resist such immorality, regardless of personal cost. Conscience had demanded that Britain should take up arms, but this obligation rested no less upon Australians. Beyond this, though, because Britain was unprepared, it was vital for Australians to render all the support they could. And an added reason for declaring solidarity with the mother country was that her defeat would lead, almost certainly, to unwelcome German pressure on Australia, if not invasion.

The grounds for taking such a view derived from the British *White Paper,* particularly the section where the German Chancellor would give no guarantee to the British ambassador as to the future of France's colonies should France be defeated.[42] It was deduced therefore that, if Germany defeated Britain, her colonies and Dominions would get no guarantee of freedom in the future. The Australian understanding of Prussian-German Machiavellism caused the academics to place total credence in this assumption. Therefore, the duty of the Dominions was perfectly clear.

Supporting such a pro-Empire stance, too, was the analysis of the mass of statistical, industrial and scientific medical data which Australian professors of economics, physics, chemistry and medicine were able to produce. Many of these men had studied in Germany and were aware of German industrial-scientific capacity and what it would take to match it. They were adamant that Australia not only had to produce fit, trained men, but also men properly armed and equipped for a long and costly struggle. Frederic Eggleston, for example, in emphasising the significance of the Imperial connection pointed out: 'We cannot wage this war on a limited liability principle.' He had in mind, of course, spiritual rather than material resources which would have to be called upon to produce the qualities of leadership and citizenship necessary to prevent national disaster.[43] But this implied the urgency of improving and augmenting the slender material and human resources available.

In many ways the intellectual leaders of Australia were very similar to their German counterparts. They all saw the war as a testing time for the national character. There had been much slackness in all sections of the community, within capital as well as labour; citizens had not appreciated sufficiently the benefits of the political system under which they lived; the war was a great challenge to spiritual renewal, a time when divisions should be done away with and a spirit of great common purpose generated. This says something, perhaps, of the prophetic role which academics as well as Church leaders seem automatically to assume in times of national crisis. But above all the Australian professors emphasised the need for solidarity with the Empire. Again, as Frederic Eggleston defined it: 'The empire is not a mechanical device for protecting the British race against the competition of its neighbours, but a political principle which can only survive through a maximum effort and sacrifice'.[44]

It is well enough known that these sentiments were not universally shared within the Australian community. Indeed the issue of the war proved to be bitterly divisive. However, as has been shown, the Australian academics' analysis of Imperial Germany's political culture and war aims had been based on first hand experience of Germany and on the statements of her 'statesmen, historians, essayists and philosophers whom they assumed to be expressing the avowed ideals of their nation'.[45]

Consequently, as the Melbourne professor of history, Ernest Scott, urged at the time:

> Our people need thoroughly to grasp these factors, to realise how more than foolish, how wicked and suicidal, would be any peace with Germany which did not completely shatter her hopes, and compel her to realise in the bitterness of utter defeat that not only has she been wrong, but that wrongness such as hers does not pay in the modern world. The prolongation of this war will indeed entail great suffering: but consider how much more, and what a prolonged agony, a premature peace would entail.[46]

As we have seen, the professor of history in Sydney, George Arnold Wood, who had made numerous statements about the Prusso-German menace during the war and the imperative need to resist it, ventured a reflection immediately after the German defeat and revolution entitled 'The

Place of the War in History.[47] This would have been presented to students at the beginning of first term in 1919, while the newly elected Constituent National Assembly was deliberating the new parliamentary constitution at Weimar. The content of Wood's lecture reveals that he had understood from the beginning of the war that the Prusso-German power elite had intended to destroy the liberating heritage in the West of the 'Ideas of 1789' and to replace them with the enslaving German 'Ideas of 1914.'

Wood had been cautiously optimistic that the defeat of Prussianism and the apparently successful revolution had established the pre-conditions for the Ideas of 1789 to flourish in Germany. Such a hope had been clearly representative of all the Australian academics. As has been seen, their notions of what constituted a humane and decent political culture had been diametrically opposed to the German 'Ideas of 1914'. They had understood particularly well both what was in the mind of the German academic elite and the German government, because they possessed the tools to investigate the latter's political culture. However, making this clear to the Australian public proved to be extraordinarily difficult. Many thousands of workers suffered prolonged privations because of the war, while profiteers rendered all the rhetoric about the need for everyone to make equal sacrifices cynically hollow. Also, other Australians of Irish ancestry resented intensely Britain's apparently ruthless suppression of all agitation for Home Rule. How could plain, blunt men and women comprehend that a major industrial nation such as Prussia-Germany could be waging war so ferociously for such a nebulous ideal as *Kultur?* Surely all wars were trade wars in the end, motivated by greed? Something as intangible as *Kultur* could scarcely have had anything to do with it. Behind the great conscription debates in Australia lay this understandable incredulity. Ironically, though, the professors' assessment proved correct, especially when it was prophesied that if the spirit of Prusso-German lawlessness were not completely crushed it would rise again.[48]

CHAPTER 8

Did Australia Face an Existential Threat in 1914? German War Planning and the Realities of Australia's Position

by Peter Overlack

One of the most ill-considered myths surrounding Australia's Great War involvement suggests that it was a war of choice. Yet, no matter how distant from European affairs we may have seemed, Britain's enemies had no inclination to view the self-governing dominions as anything but legitimate targets; if not critical in their own right, then useful for applying pressure on the motherland.

– David Stevens, In All Respects Ready

Perhaps the greatest failing of some historians writing on the theme in the current climate of war remembrance enthusiasm is to reject or trivialise the concept of an existential threat faced by a geographically isolated Australia on the eve of World War I. That this is denied by some Australian historians despite the overwhelming archival evidence highlights the importance of the ongoing debate.[1] Rather, the idea is presented that Australia reflected a narrow, pro-British mindset resulting from cultural isolation, and that participation in the War was an automatic imperialistic reflex action explained by residual 'cultural cringe'. On the contrary, from their experiences at German universities a number of Australia's eminent political figures had a clear view of exactly what Germany's war aims were and the implications for this country if the existing balance were overturned by a German victory. (See above chapters 5 and 6.)

It is first necessary to define the threat. It was not one of 'conquer and occupy' but rather economic and strategic, which affected Australia's function as a key supplier of raw materials to Britain. This is clear from the German documents which present undeniable evidence and which has too often been conveniently ignored or brushed aside because they contradict the desired anti-imperialist paradigm. The later British Prime Minister Arthur J. Balfour commented wryly in 1899 that whenever there was trouble in some part of the world, the Germans would sit down and work out an action plan.[2] It is this predilection for order and preparedness in the form of records and numerous drafts and revisions that now provides a comprehensive picture of the intent and extent of cruiser warfare operations. The minutely detailed preparation of operational plans according to the changing international situation and tensions that waxed and waned among the Powers provides a clear insight into German intentions and methods.

The exercise of German naval power was acknowledged as the most likely threat to Australian security. The navy was seen not only as an instrument in support of overseas economic expansion, but also as a tool of diplomacy and strategy in German aspirations to world power.[3] Australia was considered a vital link in the chain of supply of essential resources for the British war effort and so had to be neutralised. Was this a real or imagined threat? What so many Australasian historians fail to grasp is the ideological imperative of Wilhelmine Germany. In the words of Gustav Schmoller, professor of political science at Berlin,

> We wish ... to expand our trade and industry so that we can live and support a growing population ... we want to oppose the extended robber-mercantilism of the three world powers which excludes all other states and seeks to destroy their trade. It is only to achieve this modest goal that a large fleet is necessary.[4]

Germany had to strengthen itself so that it could match, even supplant, the British world-empire. Already in 1898 Colmar von der Goltz wrote in *Das Volk in Waffen* (The Nation under Arms) that naval power guaranteed greater strength for a nation, even when its navy was not in a position to influence land operations directly. He used the striking example of the American Navy in the Spanish-American War to show how crushing victories could win valuable prizes for the nation's useful strategic and economic colonial possessions. Between relatively equal opponents, final victory would go to the one which could maintain control of the seas. Germany, too, had to be in a position to determine such an outcome.[5]

It is in this crucial underlying psychological sentiment as expressed by Schmoller and others that one of the basic imperatives of German expansion is to be found. Britain's 'world domination' had to be challenged in order for Germany to thrive:

> The war, which can follow from this conflict situation, and how many believe must follow, has for us the [...] goal of breaking England's world domination, and thereby the freeing of necessary colonial possessions for the necessary expansion of European states.[6]

Many believed that it was economic rivalry which would bring the inevitable confrontation. For Schmoller, international rivalries were economic ones which impinged on national sovereignty in a climate where mercantilism increasingly prevailed. With its imperialism, Britain was aiming to create from its scattered possessions an enormous, self-sufficient world empire closed to economic rivals. It was the infusion of the naval idea into existing policy which gave the latter a new and aggressive dimension, and transformed it into *Weltpolitik*. The old Eurocentric vision was replaced by a new creed in which the Navy was an instrument of the growing economic interests that were pushing Germany out into the world, and this would inevitably result in a clash with Britain – and consequently also its Dominions.[7]

With the focus on the battleship program under the State Secretary of the Navy Office (*Reichs-Marineamt*) Alfred von Tirpitz, it has been often overlooked that in his early career, he had had the opportunity to travel widely, including to South America and, finally in 1896, as Chief of the then East Asia Cruiser Division, to the Far East. It was the latter which gave him first-hand experience of Anglo-German economic rivalry in a rapidly expanding market which influenced his subsequent views.[8] Historical thought played a large part in his thinking. The legacy of Leopold von Ranke, political realism and deification of the state in Heinrich von Treitschke with whom Tirpitz had a close personal relationship, merged with and reinforced the Social-Darwinist basis of navalism espoused by the American Alfred Thayer Mahan, whose writing Tirpitz had translated and distributed by the Navy Office.[9]

The editor of the influential *Preußische Jahrbücher*, Hans Delbrück, wrote in 1912 that it was an obvious truth that the German Navy was the clear instrument of a divinely ordained cultural mission: a stage had been reached where German economic development and inherent cultural values compelled it to aim higher, to 'give us that share of the control of the world which is due to nations with high cultures by virtue of their character and the fact that they are destined for greater things'.[10] It was the infusion of the naval idea into existing policy which created a new and aggressive dimension manifested in *Weltpolitik*, and which was to be directly relevant for Australia by 1914. The German historian Peter Winzen has clearly presented the alternatives with which foreign policy gambled: either international decline or the opportunity to expand Germany's world-power position.[11]

Given that Australia was of interest to Germany as evidenced in the mass of naval planning records still extant, how was detailed information obtained? It was necessary to know the level of naval and military support the Dominions could offer Britain. The reports of the German Naval Intelligence Service (*Marine-Nachrichtenwesen*) operatives in Australia cover a wide range of economic, strategic and political topics. When put together over a period of time all this provided a clear enough picture of Australia's defence capability. The new Commonwealth was doubly concerned, first with British concentration in the North Sea and secondly with the effective implementation of cruiser warfare plans against Anglo-Australasian commerce and communications in the Asian-Pacific region in tandem with similar plans against the South American Atlantic trade routes. There were numerous reports on the progress towards an Australian Fleet and the internal political debate which could affect this. Consul-General Paul von Buri commented in October 1901 about the suggestions by Rear-Admiral Sir Lewis Beaumont for improved naval defence (a squadron of fast cruisers); acting Foreign Minister Oswald von Richthofen forwarded this to both Naval Secretary Alfred von Tirpitz and Chief of Admiralty Staff Otto von Diederichs.[12] The information had clear practical implications for proposed German naval action in the Asia Pacific region.

How did the Germans assess the naval situation in terms of Australia? By 1909 it had become clear to the British that without the effective participation of the Dominions it would be impossible to maintain the 'Two-Power Standard'.[13] Australia's possible contribution to a conflict had real implications. Germany took Australia's participation in the War very seriously – hence the foresight of the many years of observation and information gathering that preceded it. One Admiralty study in 1914 stated that it was only with Dominion assistance that British naval supremacy on other oceans could be maintained.

Some of the most far-ranging operational plans were composed in the period 1902–10 when, as Holger Herwig observes, there was 'a return to Admiral von Tirpitz' *Stützpunktpolitik* – the policy of acquiring a system of naval bases circling the globe – which ... found its most distinct expression in the work of Vice-Admiral Wilhelm Büchsel.'[14] It is where German acquisitions in the Near and Far East fit into this 'globe-encircling' system that needs to be considered broadly. Germany felt the lack of bases which would enable it to operate on the world scale that the Royal Navy could; only in this way could *Weltpolitik* be implemented. Strategic points were sought wherever they might enable pressure to be exerted on the British Empire from Constantinople to Tsingtao (Qingdao).[15] Ernst Jäckh, confidant of Foreign Secretary Alfred von Kiderlen-Wächter, wrote that 'Baghdad and the railway can threaten England at its most vulnerable point, on the Indian and Egyptian borders ...'[16] Kiderlen was described in the *Sydney Morning Herald* as 'an original member of the notorious *Camarilla* which for several years composed the inner circle of Court favourites.'[17] With German influence and military-naval power operating in tandem from east and west, the richest part of the British Empire would be caught in a vice. From an Australian perspective, there a was a kind of domino-theory in operation. If such a crucial part of the Empire were threatened, how safe would Australia be? And the threat was real. In 1905 the head of the Naval Cabinet, Admiral Georg von Müller, asked Tirpitz rhetorically what should be done if Germany's naval armaments policy led to a war with Britain. The answer: 'I feel we ought to be clear about this question even before it is asked ... a world war which will lead our armies into India and Egypt.'[18]

Germany's war aims included clear intentions of expanding its foreign bases with the view to consolidating its post-war world-power position. Holger Herwig observed that if Tirpitz' pre-war *Stützpunktpolitik* (overseas bases policy) had been 'quite modest and even reticent', the naval leadership formulated extensive war aims between 1914 and 1916 which were intended as 'a *minimum* requirement which would make possible the Reich's future leap to an actual world power position.'[19] Colonial questions were not a large part of war aims as specifically formulated, mainly because it was assumed that these would be realised in the re-division that would occur after a German victory. The value of British possessions such as Burma, Ceylon, Malaya and Hong Kong to Germany was well recognised. Chief of Admiralty Staff Admiral Henning von Holtzendorff wanted major sea lanes controlled and used as steps to the central African colonial empire (*Mittelafrika*) which would be established. The importance of *Mittelafrika* as a part of overseas-Germany stretching from the East African coast to East Asia, and the control of the Indian Ocean it was hoped it would bring, thus cutting Australia's connections, must be keep in mind.[20] New Guinea with its cobalt and nickel deposits would increase in importance. Further into the Pacific, possession of Tahiti would provide control of American trade between the Panama Canal and the Far East in any future conflict.[21]

It is generally accepted that Tirpitz did not want war in 1914 because the battle fleet was incomplete and the War was to secure Continental hegemony, not the *Weltherrschaft* (world hegemony) in whose achievement the Navy was to have the leading part.[22] It saw an opportunity to obtain those naval bases around the world which were essential for future expansion after the Continent and *Mitteleuropa* had been secured. One memorandum pointed out that Germany would need to control the entire Indian Ocean coast of Africa to hold the British in the Suez and Red Sea areas. With Turkey dominant in Arabia, Germany could control the eastern trade routes.[23] With a German victory, not only would Britain have been defeated militarily, but its economic survival – and that of the Dominions – would have been completely dependent on German goodwill. It is within this larger picture of overall intentions that the function of proposed commerce warfare in general, and the task of the East Asia Cruiser Squadron in particular, receive their real significance. German naval policy overseas as distinct from the North Sea was clearly an essential piece on the chess board struggle for hegemony.

CHAPTER 9

German Surveillance Activity in Australia and Local Defence Concerns – Growing Fears

by Peter Overlack

The inability or unwillingness to investigate the German naval records has hampered some historians of Australian defence issues prior to World War from being able to form a realistic assessment of the Imperial German naval threat. A result of this has been that the purpose of the German East Asia Cruiser Squadron, based at Tsingtao in northern China, has never been fully taken into account. Knowledge of the war plans of this naval force illuminates not only Germany's intentions as an imperial power generally, but also its assessment of the resource-rich Australasian Dominions in particular. An examination of Germany's interest in Australasian defence issues, and the rationale for this deep interest, has too often been overlooked. The fate of the Dominions would undoubtedly have been negotiable had German ambitions to negate the world-encircling reach of British naval hegemony as expressed in their overall military and naval planning been realised. That is to say, a military and naval defeat of British Empire forces would have exposed the relatively defenceless Dominions of Australia, New

Zealand and South Africa to the possibility of political and commercial pressure from a victorious Germany which they would not have been able to withstand.

An examination of the German naval records for the Pacific region reveals the extent of the threat posed to Australia and New Zealand by the East Asia Squadron. This is highlighted by the cruiser warfare plans of that naval force which were continually updated from 1902. Documents in the German Federal Military Archive (*Bundesarchiv-Militärarchiv*) in Freiburg[1] show that Germany was preparing to implement cruiser warfare against Australasian shipping in the event of a war with Britain, with the aim of cutting supplies of raw materials and food, thereby weakening Britain's capacity to wage a European war. Details and emphases varied from time to time, but the main aim remained constant. The information required for this planning was obtained both from open observation by Imperial German consulate personnel, and through the naval intelligence gathering network coordinated from within the Consulate-General in Sydney.

Australians were well aware of a danger from Germany. Indeed, press and politicians had warned about German expansion in the Pacific since the first encounter between Queensland and Germany over New Guinea in 1884. By the early years of the 20th century, strategic commentators in Britain and Australasia pointed to an arc of German influence stretching from the Netherlands Indies through New Guinea and Micronesia as far as Samoa. In the Germans' own words, their naval program was intended for the purpose of 'annexing the British colonies within ten years', the Kaiser himself having declared that Britain was the rival against whom a strong fleet was required.[2]

There were two clear threads of antiGerman feeling: the hostility which followed developments in Anglo-German relations, and a feeling of threat which reached back into the 1880s and had its roots in the fear of German intrusion into the near north and south Pacific from where a possible strategic threat to Australian maritime trade and coastal cities was seen to come from naval bases in German colonies. That the latter was not only possible, but indeed planned for, is shown in the wartime role of the East Asia Squadron. It was expected that Australasian trade would be paralysed. When it was known that German cruisers were near to ports, no ship would leave harbour, and no insurance company would cover them if they did. 'This blockup will quickly follow through as far as the Suez Canal and the Cape ...' As neutral shipping would be in great demand, there was little likelihood that much would be redirected to Australasian ports until considerable time had elapsed.[3]

By 1914, the semicircle of German Protectorates encompassing New Guinea, the Melanesian archipelago, the Micronesian islands and the Samoan group was seen as a hindrance to British trade and communication with Asia and North America, and, as was frequently highlighted in Federal Parliamentary debates, providing bases for attack on Australian coastal trade. Debates in Parliament also pointed out the potential threat of German influence in, and assumed designs on, the Dutch Indies. Given the reality of German pressure on the Dutch, particularly regarding port facilities and telegraph communications, this was far-sighted. The Germans did not mix their words. In 1909 Cruiser Squadron chief Friedrich von Ingenohl stated bluntly what was required: 'Holland clearly will align its position in an Anglo-German war according to its own interests, and it will more easily close an eye to that Power from which it has more to fear.' To ensure the appropriate Dutch attitude, he bluntly recommended that Admiralty Chief of Staff Max von Fischel consider 'whether stronger measures are to be employed'.[4] Either way, the Dutch would feel the full weight of German expectations. The relevance of the Netherlands Indies to Australian security was to be a recurring concern in Australian parliamentary debates.

This chapter proceeds by first outlining the organisation of the German intelligence network in Australia; secondly, it analyses the observations made by consular staff and by visiting German naval personnel, and thirdly, it examines the Australian perception of threat from Imperial Germany.

Gathering the Facts:
What Were the Germans Doing?

It needs to be stated clearly and emphatically that there was a well-established German intelligence gathering system operating in Australia. The Naval War Intelligence System (*Marine-Kriegsnachrichtenwesen*) which operated throughout the East Asian region was, despite frequently issued specific guidelines and instructions, at ground level a fairly loose organisation, dependent upon individuals operating with varying degrees of flexibility. It was based upon a group of 'Reporters' (*Berichterstatter*) and 'Confidants' (*Vertrauensmänner*), whose functions were often combined. They were responsible to a 'Chief Reporter' who in turn acted in close cooperation with the Consul-General in Sydney and the Senior naval officer of the Australian Station. The Reporters were responsible for gathering a range of material of general military use. The methods of intelligence gathering were basic and consisted of personal observations of incoming and outgoing ships, inconspicuous conversations with persons in the shipping trade and in docks and through a regular perusal of the local press. The material assembled by the Chief Reporter was assessed by the Senior Officer and reports prepared for the Chief of the Admiralty Staff. In places where Chief Intelligence Agents (*Hauptberichterstätter*) were located the Consulates kept a sealed envelope containing the cover addresses in Berlin for the Admiralty, separate for despatches and letters, a list of the Reporters with location, name, function and allocated number, telegram and postal address and codename.

Under these conditions it is not surprising that security was a constant concern for the Sydney Consulate-General, particularly as anti-German feeling increased. Where possible, the actual wording of messages was composed in commercial language. This example was in use in 1902, the sender purporting to be a wine merchant:

German wine	German forces
foreign wine	enemy forces
large quantity	battleship
small quantity	cruiser
bottles	torpedo boats
transport	sail

The first letter of the wine name was used to indicate the name of a ship. Other cover businesses used similarly compatible language, trade names and designations serving to indicate barriers, fort armaments, placing of maritime signs, departures of troop transports and so on. It was left to each Reporter to work out a suitable system. In peacetime, all instructions and materials were kept either on board the Station warship, or at the local Consulate. This included the 'Blue Book' containing addresses and codenames, code keys and instructions for use, a copy of the trans-shipment points for the outfitting of steamers as auxiliary cruisers, lists of German naval shipping movements, a copy of the arrangement concluded between the Admiralty and the Consul, and contracts with local firms.[5]

When put together over a period of time in conjunction with the regular and detailed military-political reports of the warship captains, a clear enough picture of Australia's defence capability was provided. And the Germans paid particular attention to expressions of Australian concern about the withdrawal of Royal Navy units from the Far East and Pacific in order to strengthen the British presence in the North Sea. Australian worries about what the German Cruiser Squadron could effectively achieve in the Pacific in the event of war were carefully noted, and naturally there were numerous reports on the establishment of the Australian Fleet Unit and the domestic political debate between the supporting and opposing factions of this concept within Australia, all forwarded to Berlin.

The sources of information used by the German observers were often the most obvious. Indeed, in 1913 one Australian politician warned that with the establishment of the Fleet Unit, it would become the target of espionage, and much less information should be revealed in the press.[6] This was one of the easiest sources of information, as the many clippings with annotations in the German archives show. The German need for naval intelligence concerning Australia, however, dates from at least a decade prior to the establishment of an Australian Fleet Unit. Already in April 1901 it was arranged for the Senior Officer of the Australian Station (*Korvettenkapitän* Max Grapow) to discuss the bases of 'War Case D' – war between Germany and Britain – with Acting Consul-General H. Grunow. 'There is need', Grapow minuted, 'for another conversation with the Consul-General, the General Representative of the North German Lloyd, and with the Confidential Agents before the arrangements can be implemented'.[7] Cooperation between the German Government and shipping lines was particularly necessary and valuable, dependent as the cruisers were on designated merchant vessels acting as auxiliaries to relay intelligence and deliver supplies.

One of the earliest documents illustrating the role of the German consular officials is a report from Consul-General Paul von Buri to Chancellor Bernhard von Bülow in September 1901. This concerned the acquisition of military maps from the Defence Department 'through the mediation of resident Germans who have business connections with the Ministry.' Clearly there was a network of locally domiciled Germans working for Naval Intelligence. Buri gave instructions to his agents to obtain the plans of individual fortifications, but, with the delicate nature of the business, it was difficult to say when this would be possible, 'one or other of the officials concerned being recruited by my middlemen'. The material was taken by Consulate Secretary Baehrecke who was conveniently departing on leave, and was to be personally delivered to the Foreign Office.[8]

A document in the Foreign Office Archives listing prospective Confidants throws some light on the kind of persons required for what would be a crucial function in a period of war preparation. In Perth, Richard Strelitz was the agent for the German-Australian Steamship Company (DADG) as well as acting as Consul for Denmark and Sweden, 'a very trustworthy person of considerable commercial success.' He was considered most suitable, as the Honorary German Consul (Carl Ratazzi) did not have much social influence. The maritime connections of Strelitz Brothers as one of the leading Perth firms would be of obvious advantage. Adelaide was a post of considerable importance due to the German settlements in the interior. Honorary Consul Hugo Muecke was regarded as being too much under 'English' influence (through his wife) to be suited for such a delicate post, but Herr Rischbieth, owner of the old established firm of George Hills & Co., which also had the German-Australian Steamship Company Agency, was deemed most suitable. In Melbourne, Honorary Consul Wilhelm Adena was approved, and had a trustworthy back-up in Herr Pfaff 'who is regarded as quite talented'. Adena's firm of Ostenneyer & von Rompey managed the North German Lloyd Agency and 'some success can be expected from this representation'. In Sydney, Dr Pupke of the DADG provided appropriate support for the Consulate-General.[9]

The need for secrecy in all aspects of information gathering and reporting was emphasized. In 1906, the Admiralty Staff commended the commander of *Condor* for his 'important service' with his recent reports on potential assembly and supply sites during the voyage between Yap and Sydney: 'The results have made valuable contributions to our Intelligence Service in the Pacific.'[10] This is reinforced by an insistence on all information being coded for written transmission, and in one instance in 1910 Oberleutnant z.S. Emsmann was reprimanded for his uncoded report.[11]

In a political climate dominated by the 'Dreadnought scare' which peaked in 1909, Consul-General Dr Georg Irmer expressed considerable reservations about the involvement in the Intelligence network of Consuls and the Consulate-General in particular. A major problem was the safekeeping of secret material on Consulate premises, as following British Colonial Office practice, foreign consuls in British possessions lacked the privileges accorded them by other nations. Thus the Consulate-General was regarded as a private dwelling without any diplomatic immunity. Given that even in peacetime the private apartments of the Consul-General as well as the Consulate offices were open to any police intrusion, how much more so would this be in the event of threatening war or on the outbreak of hostilities? Irmer wrote to Berlin that 'it can be assumed with some certainty that these quite unscrupulous Colonial authorities will use any pretext to subject the archive of the Imperial Consulate to a thorough inspection as soon as war with Germany appears unavoidable.'[12]

The German Foreign Office itself, which oversaw the consular service, was concerned about the use of its officials for military intelligence purposes, but for different reasons. In March 1910, it wrote to the Admiralty reiterating the serious reservations it had about the use of the Honorary Consuls in Fremantle, Adelaide, Brisbane and Auckland, as these men were all British subjects. Only those in Brisbane (Hirschfeld) and Fremantle (Ratazzi) possessed dual nationality. Under these circumstances, some Admiralty officials advocated the prudence of withdrawing all secret codes from these Consuls, but 'only insofar as our war preparations permit' and another suitable person could be found. Irmer commented that individuals of dual citizenship holding secret documents 'contains within it the great danger that ... this material can fall into undesirable hands before I can intervene.'[13]

All the information gathered was collated by the Chief Reporter for the Australian Station. This function was performed from 1910 by the Commercial Attaché, Walter de Haas, and he managed agent '640', Oscar Plate, the manager of the North German Lloyd Agency, and '6401', businessman Otto Bauer. De Haas had been appointed on the direct recommendation of Irmer as he had 'extensive commercial contacts through the whole Commonwealth' and was unobtrusive and judicious.[14] However, de Haas had already come to the notice of the authorities in 1911 when Major Cox-Taylor, the Commanding Officer on Thursday Island advised that de Haas had arrived ostensibly to enquire into pearl fishing, 'but this is believed to be a blind', Cox-Taylor minuted, 'real object attack and defence.' Consequently, Cox-Taylor was directed to take all steps to prevent information being obtained, and to keep de Haas under day and night surveillance. After leaving Thursday Island, de Haas continued on to Darwin where he was described as displaying 'more than a passing interest in the railway and ... the cable company's station.'[15]

It was on news of 'imminent war' (*drohende Kriegsgefahr* – one of the formal process stages) at the latest, that the whole Intelligence System in East Asia would be activated for the support of the Cruiser Squadron, and in October 1912, the Senior Officer of the Australian Station emphasised the importance of organizing the postal steamers as auxiliary cruisers by the Reporter/Confidant in Sydney.[16] Early in 1913, in consultation with Consul-General Richard Kiliani, some adjustments were made to the Reporter/Confidant system. In March, *Korvettenkapitän* Paul Ebert (SMS *Cormoran*) carried out an inspection of the role and confidential papers of de Haas, Plate and Bauer, and found everything in order. Some alterations to the codes were advised, and de Haas was provided with the latest details on the operation of radio telegraphy stations in the Pacific.[17] Their most important function was to be performed in the period of tension prior to any conflict, to ensure that supplies of coal and provisions were obtained for the steamers designated as auxiliary cruisers before any embargoes or impounding of vessels could take place. This was crucial, as these steamers were to bring the news of conflict to the warships at sea (the small ships on the Australian Station not having radio) and then to attack merchant shipping.

Ironically, the outbreak of a war involving Britain would see the use of the Reporters and Confidants come to an abrupt end. It was planned to de-activate them since as aliens they would be placed under observation and be in personal jeopardy. This accounts for the lack of hard evidence as to the activities of a 'spy ring' after the outbreak of war, which is used by some Australian writers to deny the very existence of German intelligence gathering. Plate and Bauer successfully concealed any proof of their activities from the Australian authorities, although the Defence Department view was that as an agent of the North German Lloyd, 'which is closely associated with the German Navy', Plate was 'a dangerous enemy alien.' He was interned and finally deported in October 1919.[18] The final clause of an appendix to the report on de Haas' induction as Chief Reporter makes it clear why there was no evidence of his activity, or that of any other Reporters or Confidants, so assiduously searched for by Australian authorities. In the event of a war with Britain, 'the complete secret material including all related papers of any kind are to be destroyed, and activity as Chief Reporter will cease.'[19]

Consequently, the myth purveyed by some Australian historians that there was no German spy activity in Australia prior to the War has no basis in fact. It is a curious assumption that the German-Australian business and professional people who were interned early in the war were essentially all reliable stalwarts of the British-Australian community.

German Observations and Assessments of Australia's Capacities

An investigation of general German attitudes towards Australia in the early part of this century reveals an interesting mixture of assessments ranging from the contemptuous to the adulatory. Both in newspapers and in the reports of the warship commanders visiting Australian ports, there was grudging admiration for the new Commonwealth's determination to stand on its own feet and to provide for its own defence – even if the latter's effectiveness was regarded with some disdain. In January 1903, the *Kölnische Zeitung* discussed at length Prime Minister Edmund Barton's efforts to convince the populace of the worth of the government's recently concluded naval agreement with London.[20] Three years later, the *Frankfurter Zeitung* commented that Australians regarded the existing naval protection provided by Britain as insufficient, and it was improbable they would long remain satisfied with London's rejection of their proposals for increases to the existing squadron.[21] Yet the Germans did not misjudge the mood in Australia. Strong differences of opinion did not imply a growing trend for a political break with Britain. While there were strong pro-American feelings in the population which were used to good effect by Deakin to pressure Britain during the enthusiastic reception accorded to the 1908 visit of the American 'Great White Fleet', and, as *Korvettenkapitän* Alfred Begas (SMS *Condor*) noted that while 'the population is in general very democratic and republican', it fully realised that in reality the defence of Australia was impossible without the support of the Royal Navy.[22]

Korvettenkapitän Georg Ahlert (SMS *Condor*, 1908), in an assessment of the Australian fleet, commented on the pessimism of its chief architect, then Vice-Admiral William Creswell, who gave the impression that 'he did not set any great hope on realising his plans for the creation of an Australian Navy.' This was partly due to the fact that naval circles in Britain took scant heed of his efforts, and to the limited prospects which came from the Imperial Conference held earlier in the year. As frequent visitors to Australian ports, officers of the German warships were in a good position to make assessments. Ahlert's opinion of the crews of the Australian Squadron was dismissive: the British officers 'commented on the large amount of training time required by the frequent changing of personnel'.[23]

A report from the Naval Attaché Erich von Müller in London to the Navy Office head Alfred von Tirpitz in September 1908 throws light on the German view of Deakin's persistent campaigning for an independent Australian fleet unit. After looking at the proposal in detail, he concluded that the most noteworthy aspect was that this force would be under Commonwealth control in time of war, even when a British commander was on the Station. Müller wrote optimistically that 'This point above all ... would break with the principle 'one Navy, one control', and would mean a concession by the Imperial Government to the Commonwealth, which might be the first step synonymous with a break of this rising colony in questions of self-defence.'[24]

Irmer commented on the Parliamentary debate on the 1908 defence proposals that it was conducted with a 'maximum of oratory and a minimum of knowledge, and the general opinion was that it would not pass in its existing form. The German Navy was seen as 'primarily serving aggressive purposes', and Australia should look with more concern toward Germany than Japan.[25] This mood anticipated the outbreak of anti-German feeling in the 'Dreadnought scare' of 1909, when the British realised that in a few years the German battleship construction program would give that country an effective advantage. Opposition Leader George Reid was not alone in his reference to Germany being 'in the first place among the enemies of England.' A supporter of the Australian 'Dreadnought gift' idea for Britain, in April he stated that Germany would thank Australians to build ships and keep them here in wartime. If Germany sent a fleet across the Channel 'they would say to Australia ... Keep your Dreadnoughts until we smash up England, and then we will deal with you afterwards'.[26] *Korvettenkapitän* Otto Kranzbühlcr (SMS *Condor*, 1909) commented that the anxiety about aggressive German intentions was nothing short of astonishing, the most ridiculous things being believed.[27] The assessment of Adolf von Trotha (SMS *Planet*) was that while the majority was for the creation of an Australian fleet, this would not be realised in the foreseeable future due to the lack of personnel: the very thing that the Motherland needed more urgently than Dreadnoughts, namely men for the manning of ships, would not be found here. 'English officers only shrug their shoulders at the mention of an Australian Navy.'[28]

In December 1909, Irmer reported to Chancellor Theobald von Bethmann Hollweg on the construction of an Australian Squadron. Australia received the entire naval depot at Garden Island as a gift, but its maintenance and ongoing extension would cost the Commonwealth so much money that it 'would soon recognise the true character of this Greek gift.' He also made some pithy comments about the 'fairly warlike statements of the temperamental Prime Minister Deakin', who held the world situation to be too critical to believe in a lasting peace. This pessimistic view rested chiefly on the cables received from London, 'which ...have been expressly fabricated by Australian journalists in London with the cooperation of Deakin's imperialistic Party for the purpose of naval agitation.' To illustrate the mood existing in Australia's 'imperialist' circles against Germany as a naval Power, Irmer enclosed a 'typically characteristic' leading article from the *Sydney Morning Herald*. As far as he could ascertain, this was composed by the Chief Editor himself, whose anti-German sentiments had been recognised for years. He wanted to know nothing of the Chancellor's assurances in the *Reichstag* about peaceful relations between Germany and Britain:

> ... between the lines one reads clearly enough that the imperialist circles in Australia, to whom this writing belongs, hold the conflict between Germany and Great Britain for naval supremacy as practically inevitable. Deakin's statements in the Commonwealth Parliament are not too far from this view. [29]

The whole naval debate had been characterised by an attempt to make a connection between Germany and the British-Australian naval plans, so much so that it 'appeared like a parliamentary arrangement ... which has proceeded on London's directions.'[30] It was not surprising that London wanted to keep a guiding hand on proceedings. In the event, the Government fell before the matter could be fully debated and decided. The new Deakin-Cook ministry introduced a revised Bill which Irmer condemned it as 'a really mediocre and superficial effort' and in no way could it be designated a defence measure. With a disregard for its populist approach, he noted that

> What is proposed here is little more than a series of decisions about principles in the selection, training, discipline, mobilisation and payment of Australian service personnel. It cannot appear doubtful to anybody that a defence law which must serve the iron necessity of war, and where it deals with the very existence of a young nation, cannot be concerned with humane feelings and moral points of view, and even less with voting masses ...[31]

While Joseph Cook's speech introducing the Bill provided interesting insights, Irmer could discover no new positions in defence matters. In the final analysis nobody would succeed in doing that, he added, as new ideas in the area of defence were even less frequent here than in Europe. The essence of what Cook had to say had for months been the topic of conversation in English clubs. While most reports on Australian defence arrangements were dismissive, here Irmer stated that while the manner in which Australia came to terms with its defence was a question of little interest for most other countries, the matter was hardly one of indifference for Germany. Given that a major re-organisation of British-Australian land and naval forces was being carried out 'before the gates of our militarily and navally unprotected colonial areas in the Pacific', the implications needed to be carefully considered.[32]

In December 1909, Field Marshal Lord Kitchener, who was to retire from the position of Commander-in-Chief of British forces in India, began an extensive tour of Australia, at the conclusion of which he advised on land defence planning. His sojourn in Australia was followed with great interest and reported on in detail by German officials, not least because it provided them with an opportunity to observe Australian land defence preparations at first hand. They probably already knew what his verdict would be: one that 'gave few grounds for rejoicing ... in Brisbane they were pleased when he was gone.'[33] The previous June, the commander of SMS *Planet* had reported on the difficulties experienced with a citizen army. The exercise for the land defence of Sydney had suffered considerably because of the availability of men only on weekends, and even then participation 'very much depended on the goodwill of the individual'.[34]

A year later the situation had not improved, and the troops' unprofessional turnout and the statements of supposed experts evoked sarcastic assessment. While the local press reported in glowing terms on the troop turnout, Irmer noted that there was considerable absenteeism at Liverpool where they were to assemble. Nearly forty per cent of the 5th Light Horse remained on their farms as good rain had just fallen, and the 4th Infantry Regiment, composed mostly of Newcastle miners, when ordered to carry out earthworks promptly downed tools until their daily pay of 8 shillings was assured. In Melbourne things did not fare much better: of the 6,476 men expected to appear, fewer than half turned up, and then declared that they had no intention of remaining the full eight days. [35] In conversation with the commander of SMS *Planet,* the commandant of naval forces in Queensland, Captain Richardson, commented that in so young a nation the people possessed no real understanding of what was necessary for national defence, and believed they would come out alright with half-measures and a little money.[36]

The Admiralty Staff strategic study by Kapitänleutnant (later Admiral) Paul Wuelfing von Ditten written in the winter of 1909–10 (The Planned Defence of the Australian Commonwealth and its Participation in the National Defence of Great Britain) shows that there was real and practical interest in any naval and military opposition on the part of Australia which might interfere with a planned attack on Australian shipping in the event of war with Britain.[37] The most important section was entitled 'Australia's reasons for the creation of its own Navy', and while acknowledging the fears of Japan, Germany, 'whose colonial possessions in the Pacific lie disquietingly close to Australia, is seen as a possible and dangerous enemy.' Australians were united in the view that there had to be a change in current defence arrangements, but there were considerable differences of opinion as to how this could be achieved. However, it was stressed that all such efforts were undertaken in loyalty to the Empire, and the voices of anti-imperialism had been silent for some time.

The existing Naval Militia was considered to have 'very little military value' and could not be seen as a basis on which to draw for a new active fleet. British officers had frequently expressed the opinion that they were less than thrilled at the prospect of training and commanding Australian crews. It remained to be seen to what extent the country's financial means made implementation of the naval plan possible. Given the small land-based population, there was absolutely no chance of manning the new Australian fleet with volunteers. Any further expansion of the Australian Navy was 'a highly uncertain problem of the future.' The final consideration was how Australia was to pay for its new Navy. The naval plan coincided with a time when the economy was on a downturn and the picture worsened when one considered that expenditure for the Army and Navy would rise to an estimated £2,500,000 annually due to the re-organisation. In addition came the massive development projects such as railways and the opening of land for settlement. 'Prophecies are an uncertain thing...but I would say that a further expansion of the Australian fleet is not to be expected in the next ten years.'[38] These views had been confirmed by Irmer in November 1909. He reported that the Defence Bill had passed through Parliament without noteworthy alterations, although there had been much heated debate, from which he gained the conviction that 'the Federal Parliament does not have the most basic grasp of military matters.'[39]

In June 1911, *Korvettenkapitän* Paul Ebert, the new commander of SMS *Cormoran,* reported on a meeting with the Commander-in-Chief of the Australian Station, Vice-Admiral Sir George King-Hall, an 'outspoken friend of Germany' who had visited the country on several occasions and was a friend of Admiral Georg von Müller, Chief of the Naval Cabinet. The significance of this meeting was that in the course of conversation, King-Hall intimated that steps for an Australian fleet had progressed to the stage where it was probable the Commonwealth would assume responsibility for its own naval defence within two years.[40] However, the commander of SMS *Planet* (Siemens) noted:

> Apparently the Admiral views the coming drastic changes with very mixed feelings, and even if he did not specifically say so, I nevertheless had the distinct impression that he places only limited trust in the new system. The Australian people desperately needed some good 'discipline' and he hoped for an improvement with the introduction of universal military service. The badly suppressed sigh he emitted with these words clearly indicated how small his hopes in this direction are.[41]

British defence policies in these years were a practical consequence of changed circumstances. The 'naval race' required a reallocation of defence resources, the most dramatic of which was the 'calling home of the legions', as the *Standard* put it.[42] Thus from 1911 the role that the Australian

Fleet Unit was to play in the overall scheme of Imperial Defence was a source of ongoing interest for the Germans. It was obviously to Germany's advantage that the British Home Fleet be weakened as much as possible by the demands of Dominion defence. The Germans were constantly looking for chinks in the armour of Imperial unity, and to foster these when discovered. *Kapitänleutnant* Rehder's 1914 memorandum, *The Development of the English Colonial Navies,* specifically considered the implications of their formation from the standpoint of Germany's strategy in a war with Britain.[43] Imperial defence had been discussed only in an academic way at the Colonial Conferences from 1897, and as a result, the relationship of the Navy to the colonies and their position in Imperial defence was, in the British view, not understood by them. While the Colonial Office's view was that there was a 'parochial inability to see any problem either in its imperial perspective, or within the realities of the international context', there was equally little perception of or sympathy for the Dominions' local interests.[44] How this political relationship would develop was of interest to German observers because of its strategic corollaries both in the North Sea and to their own plans in the Pacific.

According to Rehder, by 1909 it had become clear to the British that their hope of securing an enduring preponderance through the construction of large battleships would not only fail, but that without the effective participation of the Dominions it would be impossible to maintain the Two-Power Standard. To this end, financial rather than personnel contributions were preferred – which was not at all what the Dominions had in mind. Rehder wrote that Australia believed the naval concentration in the North Sea would lead to the loss of British dominance in the Pacific, and 'this dominance could become a question of survival for the colonies.'[45] At least in the Pacific, Germany would not have much to fear for some time, the commander of the *Cormoran* commented in August 1913. There were no prospects of agreement for the unification of Australian, New Zealand and Canadian forces into a Pacific Fleet. Jealousy, particularly between Australia and New Zealand, and the striving for independence of action would certainly not permit this union for the present.[46]

Nevertheless, there was little doubt that support for Britain would be forthcoming, for 'in all colonies there is the lively desire to assist the Motherland, and this will remain so'. Directly addressing the local issue, Rehder commented prophetically:

> In a war our Cruiser Squadron would only have to deal with the Australian ships inside the Australian Station. However, we would perhaps have to deal with a separate Australian fleet later on, in view of the strong Australian aspirations towards our Pacific possessions.[47]

Problems within the Australian construction program, however, reduced German anxiety about the level of any immediate threat to their position in the Pacific. In the coming five years it would be necessary to man the Australian ships with British personnel, with the possibility that on the outbreak of a war, within five weeks all the British sailors would be withdrawn by the Admiralty leaving the Australian ships high and dry.[48]

Perhaps the most clear understanding and important assessment of the defence relationship between Britain and the Dominions was that written for Tirpitz by Erich Müller, the Naval Attaché in London in November 1913. Combined with its social legislation obligations, the financial burden which naval expenditure would impose on the population of Britain would be such that a continued undefined increase in defence spending, which the requirements of Britain's world role demanded, could only be met with the assistance of the Dominions. It was an unlucky coincidence for Britain that this was occurring at a time when 'a unified naval policy was sadly lacking.' Müller further observed that, 'the constitutional-theoretical problem underlying the military question, namely the participation of the Dominions in the political leadership of Imperial matters, has not been grasped and today still requires a solution.' It was quite obvious that under present conditions, that was, as long as the Navy was directed by a Cabinet that represented only the population of Britain, 'the tendency of the Dominions, in the absence of a voice in the Government, would be directed toward local navies which they could control themselves.' Despite outward signs of progress, British Imperial defence policy was seen as wracked by internal problems and had become weakened.[49]

What was the German view of the strategic implications of the Dominion fleets? As seen in Irmer's colourful 1909 analysis, the concern was primarily local, indeed specifically for the German Pacific possessions, not for any effect on the European naval balance. Even when placed under the control of the Admiralty in wartime, they could not provide the same service as a unified fleet. The implications lay in another direction: specifically with their small fleet units, the Dominions could not withstand serious attack from Japan, which Germany was working assiduously to woo out of the Anglo-Japanese Alliance, and their defence would be reliant on the Royal Navy, with its proportionate weakening in European waters.[50]

On the whole, while the Dominion fleets at this point were not seen to be of 'any serious military importance' in themselves for Germany, these would be in fact to Germany's advantage, when the 'divisive endeavours which they probably help to further took more acute forms in the course of time, particularly as the Dominions became more preoccupied with their respective Stations as their own areas of power.[51] Similar sentiments were expressed in 1912 by Müller in London: it was in Germany's interests that the British Admiralty did not succeed in its desire to abolish the independent fleet units. The British naval structure would be a much less cohesive one if it involved local Dominion fleets.[52] If the Dominion navies' planned formation into special flying squadrons came about, however, Germany would then have to concentrate on the protection of its own and the destruction of British trade with similarly formed groups, which would 'necessitate considerable changes in cruiser warfare planning and warship deployment throughout Asia and the Pacific.' [53] Clearly, what Australia planned had direct implications for German naval operations, with interest intensifying in the immediate pre-war years.

Australian Reactions

While the Germans noted the grounds for Australasian concerns about their presences in the Pacific region, they were at a loss how to allay the suspicions they aroused among antipodean Britons. It also seemed to bode ill that the Vice-President of the Executive Council, Dr Maclaurin, was a man who 'must be counted among the most bitter opponents of Germany.'[54] As far as the *New Zealand Herald* was concerned, it was entirely the fault of Germany that there had been any change in relations at all. The 'overweening pretensions of the Kaiser and the bombast of the German people' had given rise to bitter feeling. But then New Zealand had a long-term axe to grind after futile attempts to pre-empt German expansion in the Pacific, particularly in Samoa, and was not likely to forget quickly Germany's 'presumptuous insolence with which she thought to dictate…to free British colonies.'[55]

An article in the *Sydney Morning Herald* in January 1905 pointed out the possible danger to Australia from a German presence in Timor, which Germany was attempting to purchase from Portugal. If this succeeded, German warships would be within a day's steaming of the Australian coast, and such a foothold could not be permitted to fall to a Power whose naval ambitions were growing into direct rivalry with British interests.[56] Similarly, the *Globe* in March observed there was a feeling of unease in the Commonwealth which looked with grave suspicion on the steadily increasing development of German interests in the Pacific. Germany would soon be 'occupying a position highly favourable for offensive operations against Australia.'[57] That same year Senator Staniforth Smith wrote a series of articles for the *Daily Telegraph*. One of his concerns was that Simpsonhafen in New Guinea could 'simultaneously accommodate two of the largest warships', and was an excellent anchorage capable of being turned into a naval base which would command all Australian sea routes to eastern Asia, and a large portion of the Australian coast. If this came about, the East Asia Squadron could operate anywhere in the western

Pacific with impunity. German harbours might be used for coaling stations and strategic bases from which cruisers could issue forth in time of war and prey upon commerce or shell coastal towns.[58]

In April 1907, the commander of SMS *Condor* was in no doubt that in the event of a war between Britain and Germany, Australia would take a hostile attitude towards Germany. The Australian, he observed, was from the ground up of democratic sentiments:

> His view of a politically reactionary Germany is a thorn in his eye; in particular he perceives our possessions in the Pacific as an infringement on his rights ... In any war in which Germany is involved ... the hope would be great that we would forfeit our Pacific possessions to Australia.[59]

The year 1909 brought the sudden realisation that Germany's naval construction program would provide it with a fleet capable of challenging Britain's supremacy.[60] The *Sydney Morning Herald* pointed out that two things could be taken as certain. First, the Kaiser would not hesitate to strike at any European Power which stood in the way of pan German expansion, and secondly, in the decisive hour the German nation would be solidly behind him. 'Our rivalry with Germany cannot be avoided. We have to meet it.'[61] And further, given that on 24 May that year 8,000–10,000 city workers had collected in Martin Place in Sydney and applauded every reference in the speakers' addresses to the unity of the Empire, there can be no doubt that in the view of the majority, Australia's security concerns were identical with those of Britain.[62] In June 1909 the *Age* mounted one of its strongest attacks on German policy and presumed intentions. Germany perceived Australia to be a rich continent, sparsely populated, situated too distant from Britain to be held secure if its naval power were broken. Germany was 'being worked up into a frenzy by the Kaiser's policy.' It was a dynamic power whose interests were best served by war, and the conquest of Britain would mean that Australia 'would become a German possession'.[63]

It was during this 1909–10 period of strained Anglo-German relations that the German warships noted in detail the nature and strength of harbour defences during their stays in Australian ports. One interesting example of this is a 1910 report with sketches of the modernisation of batteries in Melbourne and Hobart.[64] Already in 1901 German naval observers had stated that 'aggressive implementation of cruiser warfare', particularly against Australian harbours, would cause public panic and force the Australian Squadron to remain close to the coast and thus not pose a threat to wider German operations.[65]

Creswell wrote in his 1907 memorandum for Prime Minister Alfred Deakin that German activity in Morocco was designed to gain a position as a counterpoise to Gibraltar, 'the desire to acquire a good point of observation ... and overlook the Cape route.' The Mecca railway could place a Turkish army in Egypt, 'rendering quite conceivable the closing of the Canal, and severance of our line of communication ...' More specifically, the Baghdad Railway, attempts to establish a foothold in Persia, and various schemes in Asia Minor 'are all directed to effect a through line to the East as a direct communication with Germany's Eastern possessions.'[66]

There was a sustained concern over the whole period about German designs on the Netherlands Indies and implications for Australia. Creswell's 1907 memorandum on naval defence stated clearly that if the Indies came into German possession, creating an arc in one unbroken line from Sumatra to New Guinea and overlapping hundreds of miles of ocean on either side, the defence problem for Australia needed no elaboration. With Germany excluded from the Americas by the Monroe Doctrine, the proximity to Australia provided a temptation which 'would in any case be irresistible'. In the event of war, cession of territory would be the price for peace: 'Neutrality would ask for its "compensation".'[67] It was stated in the Senate in 1910 that it was quite possible the Indies would become German, 'and we shall then have a German ring around the northern and north-eastern portion of Australia.' Australia needed to beware of the great European military Power which was fast becoming a great naval Power as well.[68]

Portuguese Timor, in which Germany had expressed interest, was also a particular concern. Negotiations between Britain and Germany on the future of the Portuguese colonies were fraught with some danger for the former, since rumours which came to the ears of the Dominions might 'induce them to ask awkward questions...the indignation in that quarter will undoubtedly be exceedingly vociferous.' The Dutch also looked with the 'greatest apprehension ... and with good reason' at a German acquisition of Timor.[69] When it was rumoured in 1911 that compensation might be found for Germany in the Pacific as a trade-off for concessions to Britain elsewhere, the *Sydney Morning Herald* made it clear that any intrusion would not be tolerated, 'an ever-threatening menace right at our door.' Why did Germany want a *quid pro quo* in the Pacific, if not to provide 'the point of departure for a much more far-reaching attempt at aggression...it is open to Germany to construct a naval base at our backdoor whenever she feels inclined.'[70] In 1914 these appeared to come true: 'Quietly, under the guise of mercantile expansion, Germany ... built up this naval base, right within striking distance of Torres Strait, where all lines between Australia and the East converge'.[71]

From the German perspective, it was firmly believed that the Squadron's operations against Australian trade 'will affect a vulnerable area of English interests, and cause great disruption...A penetrating attack against Australian trade can thus be recommended.'[72]

A taste of what might have occurred on a much larger scale is provided by the success of SMS *Emden* which, between August and November 1914, eliminated over twenty Allied vessels. Only the quick action of interning German postal steamers in Australian ports on the immediate declaration of war, a number of which were designated for conversion to auxiliary cruisers, and the subsequent occupation of New Guinea and Samoa, prevented a potential major loss of shipping. Australia's exports of grain, wool, minerals and other raw materials and foodstuffs, were totally dependent on continued British naval supremacy for their protection.

It must be counted among the more untenable distortions in nationalist Australian historiography that its champions believe that Germany constituted no threat to Australia during the era of Anglo-German rivalry. The German documentation shows clearly enough that over the entire period from Federation, Germany was preparing to implement cruiser warfare plans against Australasian shipping, which if successful, would have had a seriously detrimental effect on Britain's war effort. Australia, too, was sustained from the sea, and in the view of the *Sydney Morning Herald,* it was vital for the very existence of the Empire 'that the roads for our commerce and communications should be kept clear.'[73]

The problem that recent commentators have lies in their failure to understand that in the mind of Australian policy makers at that time, there was nothing inconsistent or subservient in the relationship to the Mother Country. Close defence cooperation on the one hand did not diminish the Australasian aspirations to increased independence in self-government. That was a matter of plain common sense. Both politicians and the academic community were acutely aware of this. It was perfectly clear to them that the defeat of Britain in Europe and the consequent loss of the Royal Navy's protective umbrella Australia would have been isolated both physically and psychologically. The Commonwealth would have sustained as well extensive commercial/economic damage and become exposed sooner or later to Pan-German expansionist political demands. In the light of the detailed German planning for naval operations against Australasian shipping and port facilities, as well as the intelligence gathering activity, the fledgling Commonwealth and New Zealand were in a precarious position in August 1914. The survival of the Empire was a real-political pre-condition for the continued existence of Britain's Pacific Dominions as self-governing egalitarian democracies in the Antipodes. The following chapter documents both the extent and depth of German naval operational planning in the Pacific.

CHAPTER 10

German Naval War Planning Against Australia, 1900–1914

by Peter Overlack

Since Australia as an English colony is also an enemy ... there is enough evidence that there is no lack of opportunity for our Cruiser Squadron to inflict damage in Australian waters.[1]

New Guinea and the Bismarck Archipelago are the necessary strategic footholds for the conduct of our naval war against Australian maritime traffic.[2]

As Paul Kennedy indicated some thirty years ago, studies of operational planning before 1914 are of particular importance because it was the first time that war plans were formulated in a systematic manner in peacetime.[3] Why was so much time and effort invested in yearly 'War Case' (*Kriegsfall*) planning on what many would consider the periphery of world events? The increasing complexity of modern warfare made it essential to have definite directions, and the German documents state expressly that the merchant trade of Britain, its Empire and allies would be a prime target. Germany regarded itself as justified in adopting all measures 'by which we can affect the general economic life of England'

and thus 'considerably influence its capacity to continue.'[4] The twofold aim was to damage the British economy and cause disruption to war supplies and social unrest, which would force Britain to negotiate both a European and colonial peace on terms advantageous to Germany. This German activity in the Asian-Pacific-Indian Ocean region is placed in a worldwide political context.

Australian trade with Britain was a major target for German commerce warfare planning from its first inception. Although commerce warfare had a limited function in the scheme of Tirpitz' battleship program for the 'deciding battle' in the North Sea, it was a very specific one which targeted high value commodities, and was supported by him. Preparations over many years would not have been undertaken if it were not believed that considerable damage could be inflicted on the import of raw materials and foodstuffs upon which Britain depended to fight a war. It must be remembered that not only was commerce warfare planned in the Asian-Pacific region, but also for the Atlantic and South America (particularly against Argentinean exports).

The detailed plans formulated for the East Asia Squadron and its support infrastructure in the region show that it was intended to make an appreciable contribution to Germany's war effort. The American naval writer Arthur J. Marder observed that, deprived of her trade, 'Britain could not possibly have maintained her industries, fed her rapidly growing population, or equipped her armies.'[5] There are also wider implications of Germany's intentions in the Asia-Pacific region. If the threat to Australasian, Asian and Atlantic trade could be affected by small forces, it was believed that the insecurity created on the overall British economy would reach a level leading to panic. It was hoped that this would achieve a key strategic aim, to lure British forces from European waters. Vice-Admiral Günther von Krosigk stated in 1911:

> In every place the English must appear in superiority and strengthen their foreign service forces ... in a considerably larger measure than we do ... certainly [this] would create a measurable relief for our conduct of the domestic war.[6]

The threat came from the major German naval force outside Europe, the East Asia Cruiser Squadron, based at Tsingtao in the Kiauchau 'leased territory' in northern China.[7] The administration of the colony, the defence of Tsingtao, and arrangements for the coaling and provisioning of the Squadron and any other ships, such as auxiliary cruisers, were the responsibility of the Imperial Naval Office (*Reichs Marine-Amt*). On the other hand, operational planning was handled by the Admiralty Staff (*Admiralstab*). Despite rivalry in Berlin, the two offices cooperated reasonably well outside Europe. As early as 1900 Admiral Felix von Bendemann (Chief of Admiralty Staff, 1899), and in 1901–2 Admiral Otto von Diederichs (Chief of Admiralty Staff, 1899–1902), saw the function of the Cruiser Squadron to relieve pressure on the main North Sea theatre of war and cause maximum damage to the enemy on the periphery. One Professor Schliemann, writing in the *Kreuz-Zeitung* in 1908, stated that 'England will not be able to avoid sending back a part of her fleet to Far Eastern stations', and it would certainly be in Germany's interests to hasten the necessity if it could.[8] In an article in the *Deutsche Rundschau* in March 1900, General Colmar von der Goltz wrote:

> Great Britain is forced to distribute her fleet over many seas... and her home squadron is surprisingly weak in comparison with her fleets in the Mediterranean, India, the Far East, Australia ... and the Pacific. In that necessary distribution of her strength lies her weakness. Germany is in a better position: her Navy is small, but it can be kept together in Europe ... If India, Australia or Canada should be lost ... they would remain lost forever.[9]

The German aim was to withdraw the Cruiser Squadron upon outbreak of war to a yet unspecified position with the intention of keeping Anglo-Australian forces in the dark as to its whereabouts. The latter would be forced to divide to conduct a search. Merchant traffic would be greatly reduced if not compelled to cease in the climate of uncertainty and threat, and the divided naval force would offer suitable targets for attack. The situation might even be so favourable as to enable the Squadron to achieve regional superiority long enough to ensure the crippling of all commerce. In a response to my original research, the German-Australian writer Dr Gerhard Fischer dismissed the seriousness of any threat to Australia, so this chapter discusses the operational plans and their rationale in considerable detail.[10] The German documents are consistent and emphatic in their assessments. There was absolutely no doubt in the minds of German strategic planners that an attack on Australasian merchant shipping, and even port facilities, was not only feasible but necessary, and would be successful.

Developing a Strategy, 1900–1909

The broad thrust of operational directives remained basically unchanged in the period 1900–14. The aim of commerce warfare, which the Squadron was to implement in all the planned war cases, involved damaging Anglo-Australasian trade, protection of German trade, and battle with local naval forces.[11] Plans formulated in 1899 were speedily in place by early 1900 with the comment that the specific support arrangements from Sydney 'could be implemented due to the great skill of agent No. 35' (who was unnamed). The 'Implementation Instructions on the Australian Station' of 1900 set out in detail by the Senior Officer on the Australian Station, *Korvettenkapitän* Hugo Emsmann, outlined what was a simple but effective attack plan. Copies were held by the Consul-General in Sydney, and the Governors in Herbertshöhe and Apia.[12] As political tension developed, they were to hand over the instructions to arriving warship commanders who would discuss any changes to their own standing orders. Sydney was to be kept informed telegraphically of the positions of all warships, and in turn was to inform German commanders of the movements of foreign warships. The same applied to the German consul in Auckland, and colonial governors in Apia (Samoa), Herbertshöhe (New Guinea), Ponape and Yap (Caroline Islands), and Jaluit (Marshall Islands) concerning their respective regions.

In each port the Consul or Intelligence Confidant (*Vertrauensmann*) was to dispatch a steamer for this purpose. Sydney and Auckland, were to despatch one steamer each, so that each warship had two support vessels.[13] From Sydney and Auckland the auxiliaries were to sail direct to Henry Reed Bay in New Ireland (Neu-Mecklenburg).[14] If a cruiser was in telegraphic contact with the Confidential Agents, it could specify its own additional requirements and arrange to meet its auxiliary earlier. This would assist the speedy implementation of attack on commerce, which was emphasised. Depot and reserve ships to supply warships travelling between America and East Asia were to be anchored at Likieb in the Marshalls and Suvarov Island near Fiji, and Uriei in the Admiralty Islands.[15] As soon as the warships received news of war they were to proceed to Henry Reed Bay, and once supplies had been transferred would begin operations. The Consul-General in Sydney was also responsible for the dispatch of a fast Norddeutsche Lloyd (NDL) postal steamer, which after transferring the crew of the survey vessel (*Planet*) would proceed to Henry Reed Bay for its orders as an auxiliary cruiser.

Already by November 1901 the Station Senior Officer, *Korvettenkapitän* Max Grapow, had worked out detailed plans for inclusion in the Operations Orders. It was assumed that war between Germany and Britain would be preceded by a fairly long period of political tension which would provide time for Germany to prepare as comprehensively as possible. Although according to international law neutral vessels in belligerent ports were allowed a short period of grace to leave after a declaration of war, Grapow did not expect Britain to observe this.[16] The short time had to be used to implement those measures enabling the cruisers to be in a position to perform their tasks. In an assessment which was a major misjudgement, having catastrophic results for later German operations in the Pacific, Grapow commented:

> One can assume that there will be enough time available
> on the Australian Station for this. The Commonwealth of

Australia, already almost independent of England, will certainly *not* comply with directives against international law from the Motherland. Such a directive would be one requiring the impounding of postal and freight steamers in Australian harbours immediately on declaration of war.

In any case, the Germans had the advantage that the steamers of the NDL and the Hamburg-America Line (HAL) in Sydney and Melbourne had large holdings of coal and provisions which would be available to the Navy, and the NDL steamers had the speed to outrun the British warships on the Station, with the exception of *Royal Arthur* and *Phoebe*.[17]

For commerce warfare to be implemented on the Station, Grapow's view was that a joint operation of cruisers and auxiliaries was necessary. He designated Likieb Atoll in the Ratak Chain of the Marshall Islands as an assembly point after a stop for provisioning at Jaluit, the administrative capital. From there, the British coal depots at Butaritari in the Gilbert Islands, Gavutu in the Solomon Islands, and Port Moresby could be raided. Then 'the threatening and neutralisation of Australian and New Zealand coastal areas might be considered after the occupation of Thursday Island.' The implications for the country's limited naval defences of the successful establishment of a German operational base on Australian territory and the ensuing threat to shipping must not be underestimated. Grapow was confident that such a plan would be successful, as

> the English have relatively few and very inferior ships at their disposal for the defence of the Pacific possessions. The so-called [Australian Squadron] is bound to the coast. Of the English Squadron the two Station vessels in New Zealand … and the two old survey ships … can be dismissed.

Given this, if the cruisers and their auxiliaries kept together, 'the prospects for success in cruiser warfare are reasonable'. There was another important aspect to German planning. Attacks on Australasian harbours would cause a panic in public opinion which would force the Australian Squadron to remain close to the coast and not pose a threat to wider German operations.[18] This was to remain a significant consideration in subsequent planning. If both Station cruisers found themselves in Australian waters at the outbreak of war, another meeting point could be arranged at Saumarez Reef off the Queensland coast, 330 km north east of Gladstone, which had a major coal depot.[19]

Squadron Chief Vice-Admiral Richard Geissler's October 1902 directives for the Station cruisers in wartime began with a consideration of the Intelligence System whose observations were to be provided regularly to the Squadron Command in peacetime. These would then be distributed to individual captains, the Chief Intelligence Reporters and Staging Support Zone (*Etappen*) Officers.[20] The importance of properly formulating the materiel requirements for the Station ships, particularly coal, was emphasised. Geissler wanted to ensure a tighter organisation of the preparations to enable speedy and effective implementation of operational plans when the time came.

The clearest statement of the aims and methods of commerce warfare was outlined in the 1902 proposal of *Kapitanleutnant* Max Freiherr von Bülow. Its depth of detail and well-thought-out concepts, as well as the extensive Admiralty marginal comments it bears, show how seriously the idea was entertained. Indeed, subsequent operational plans by various Chiefs of the Cruiser Squadron reflect the same approach. The study was entitled, 'The attack on trade at the sources of enemy import, outlined in an attack of the Cruiser Squadron on English wool imports from Australasia.'[21] Strategically, the four most important regions were:

(1) from Sydney to Adelaide through Bass Strait which contained the greatest volume of shipping traffic. Around 50 British steamers a month passed through this region, converging at Cape Leeuwin on the way to Suez and offering an ideal target. There were three major harbours which were also the major wool export ports. The most valuable steamers

of the regular British lines passed here.

(2) The Cape Leeuwin region via Colombo or Aden to Suez, and to the Cape, which included the major harbours of Fremantle, Perth and Albany; third, Torres Strait via Batavia or Singapore to Suez, which had mainly transit traffic to and from Queensland which exported much less wool;

(3) and the New Zealand region-the major harbours of Auckland and Wellington with heavy traffic concentrating in the Cook Strait.

The advantage of surprise gave the German cruisers a considerable superiority over those of the Australian Squadron. It was expected this would enable them to achieve supremacy or at least a blockade of the Australian forces in one of the defended harbours. Either eventuality provided the prerequisite for a successful attack on trade. This meant that Australian forces had to be brought to battle as soon as possible in order for the Germans to achieve control of coastal waters.

There was a small operational time frame between defeat of the defending Squadron and the arrival of British reinforcements from East. Asia, which would outgun the German force. However, British interests were so important that it was believed the commander would not detach ships to another Station unless he remained convinced that his own Station was no longer threatened by the German Squadron's main body. A German pincer operation now would threaten shipping in the region. The German Squadron had to maintain the impression for as long as possible that it would threaten East Asia or India, and this would be provided by the careful choice of route to Australia which would be obvious to Anglo-Australasian forces only at the last minute.

From the starting point of Tsingtao, the proposal worked within a hypothetical time-frame beginning with a departure date of '1 January'. On '24 January' the Squadron would stand before Melbourne. The following possibilities existed: first, Australian ships were engaged. The extent of

German success would determine the degree of control of Bass Strait and progress to Sydney. Second, if Australian ships declined battle in expectation of the arrival of reinforcements from Asia, the port would be blockaded, thus cutting off Australia's prime trading and second wool export harbour. If the blockade included the warships in port, the un-armoured cruisers could be ordered on to blockade Sydney. If the Australian armoured cruisers stood outside Melbourne, it would depend on circumstances how many ships could be spared for Sydney. Third, if they were at Sydney, they would be blockaded there by the German armoured cruisers.

Bülow emphasised that the German Squadron had to increase pressure to draw in the Australian ships which would make it easier to deal with them in one undertaking, and free the Squadron to concentrate on its main task of attacking trade. Given the successful implementation of these scenarios, 'in all circumstances our attack on trade would make economic blockade a means of warfare and succeed in cutting off one if not both of Australia's chief wool export ports for all maritime trade'. Neutral ships would be turned back from the blockaded ports. Coal could be obtained from captured warships, or from coal freighters for which the blockade could be extended from Sydney north to include Newcastle and south to include Bulli and Wollongong.

These operations would have to be concluded by '31 January', by which time British reinforcements would have arrived. The Squadron now would change its operational field to New Zealand where the defending naval force was far inferior. The four heavy cruisers would suffice for the complete blockade of Wellington and Cook Strait. The expected results were:

- five days attack on trade on the Fremantle-Melbourne route;
- two days attack on trade between Sydney and Wellington;
- disruption of trade for an unspecified time on the sailing vessel route to Cape Horn;
- seven days blockade of Melbourne;
- five days blockade of Sydney;

- four days blockade of Wellington.

There was the conviction that no other activity for the Squadron promised such a lengthy and productive use of its fighting strength:

> One might be of another view of the suitability of use of the Cruiser Squadron – and the coal question could lead to this – but from what can be achieved in absolute terms, it must be concluded that in the light of our concrete example, with the correct choice of object, time, and place, an attack on trade at the sources of enemy import can be an effective means of warfare.[22]

That this could be practically implemented was not doubted in Berlin. The Squadron's 'Mobilisation Overview' submitted by Geissler and approved by the Kaiser in November 1903 specified that in war with Britain, those ships not accompanying the flagship would undertake commerce attacks while under way to the assembly point at Palawan (U-534). Cables to British possessions were to be cut in preparation for further activity.[23] Copies of necessary requisitions and directives were deposited with the Consul-General in Sydney, and with the Governors in Herbertshöhe and Apia.[24]

There was also provision for more awkward situations. The dock facilities at Sydney were used for regular repairs and overhauls by the German cruisers on the Australian Station. Should one find itself in an Australian harbour on the outbreak of hostilities, it had to escape and reach Herbertshöhe or one of the supply points scattered through the Pacific and Dutch Indies. Coal and provisions could be obtained from undefended Australian harbours – the central Queensland coal ports such as Gladstone were recommended – or in Noumea, or from captured steamers. If it were impossible to escape or continue the voyage, then the cruiser 'should inflict damage on the enemy according to opportunity and act as best befits the honour of the flag'.[25] The deleterious effect of a trapped German warship firing on Australian harbour installations and shipping can scarcely be imagined given the existing nervous state of the political and public mind.

In 1906 Squadron Chief Vice-Admiral Alfred Breusing oversaw a major reassessment.[26] The British China Squadron had to protect the extensive Chinese coastal region, the Malayan archipelago and the trans-Pacific connections. The weak East Indian Squadron oversaw the Gulf of Bengal, the Arabian Sea and their trade routes. These promised a rich cruising ground.[27] The Australian Squadron had to protect the Colombo-Fremantle, Fremantle-Melbourne, and Melbourne-Sydney routes, and it would be difficult to protect important Australian coastal traffic because of its dispersal. Additional Australasian trade routes were to South Africa, North America, Chile, Japan and New Caledonia. An important factor in Australian shipping was that 85% was under the British flag, which meant that in wartime a quick substitution by neutrals would not be possible. The Australian wool trade which made up 22% of total exports, with a value in 1905 of £34,727,797, continued to be of particular interest as a target of interdiction: 'The Australian Squadron cannot adequately protect this valuable trade spread over such broad distances', noted Breusing.

The Squadron's strike against Anglo-Australian trade now was planned against trade routes from New Guinea southwards and coastal harbours were to be harassed as far as Tasmania. It was considered possible to take coal from coastal towns, particularly in Queensland. Then the Melbourne-Fremantle route would be harried, before attacking trade on the Fremantle-Ceylon route. Coal would be replenished at a trans-shipment site near Sumatra, opportunity being taken to cut the telegraph cable on Cocos Island. The final leg would take the Squadron to East Africa. There was an optimistic assessment of the weakness of any resistance which might be encountered: 'The poor defence of Australia makes the accessing of open harbours there for the replenishing of supplies appear quite possible. For example Gladstone, recently recommended as a coaling harbour'. The broad area of operations would make the despatch of sufficient forces for pursuit more difficult. If it came to a battle with the Australian Squadron, the superior armoured cruiser *Fürst Bismarck* would inflict considerable damage. It was anticipated that the lengthy uncertainty concerning the

Squadron's exact whereabouts would cause widespread panic: shipping companies would keep their vessels in port; trade would back up; scarce neutral ships would need to be chartered; and freight costs would rise. Breusing emphasised that this,

> would be felt particularly by the enormous wool trade where a lengthy blockage can produce severe economic results. If the Cruiser Squadron succeeds in evading its pursuers for several weeks, then even without the direct capture of prizes, the economic damage would be a very considerable success for our small group.

The possibility of continuing to East Africa, attacking Indian Ocean trade routes under way, gave the undertaking an additional significance.[28]

In June 1906, following consideration of the recommendation of Admiralty Chief of Staff Wilhelm Büchsel that the Australian wool trade be the main object of attack, Breusing determined to operate primarily off the West Australian coast where shipping converged. His reasons were that the Fremantle-Colombo traffic was the most frequent; the steamers on this lengthy route would not be noticed missing for some time; approaching from the west towards the ships, more could be taken than if in pursuit from the east; and entering coastal ports for re-coaling on the eastern route would reveal the Squadron's presence and strength. This would tempt the combined Australian and British, China and East Indian Squadrons to engage. It would be more secure to position supply depots at suitable remote Western Australian coastal points, then head west for further depredations in the Indian Ocean via Ceylon to East Africa.[29] Two steamers of the North German Lloyd in Sydney were to be requisitioned to bring news of war and supplies to the cruisers stationed in the Pacific. Orders were to be conveyed to the captains personally by a *Vertrauensmann* of the naval intelligence service, or by a trustworthy official of the Lloyd. These orders and, if possible, information on the movements of Australian warships and their intentions were to be composed by the Consul-General in Sydney. If a German cruiser found itself in an Australian harbour at the time of the declaration of war, instructions were to attempt to reach Herbertshöhe as quickly as possible. With obvious foresight, Büchsel observed that,

> since ships of the Australian squadron superior to our cruisers will be sent ... to our main stations Herbertshöhe and Apia, in order to capture our cruisers and neutralise the coaling stations. The English will also easily receive information about the latest movements of our cruisers through their agents among their many nationals in our colonies.

It was left to each commander's judgement as to whether he replenished his coal and provisions in Noumea or from 'undefended English harbours, or from ... captured steamers'.[30]

The standing orders of the Senior Officer of the Australian station for 1909 elaborate the action to be taken in the various stages of escalating hostility.[31] The practicalities of implementation received detailed attention. In December 1909, Squadron Chief Vice-Admiral Friedrich von Ingenohl reviewed the Squadron's operational plans for war against Britain and the United States combined (Case C). The planned first operation, ending in Exmouth Gulf in northwestern Australia, envisaged an extension into the Indian Ocean for further operational possibilities. In particular, he favoured swinging back to the rich East Asian routes after action in the eastern waters of Australia. In order to be able to proceed as quickly as possible, he recommended that more colliers be allocated for Exmouth Gulf.[32]

The details were continually refined. In any conflict with Britain, it was essential to ensure the timely departure of vessels from harbours so that they could be neither interned nor shadowed. There was ample opportunity to practise both the organisation of vessels and the secrecy which this demanded. Early in 1909, Consul-General Georg Irmer was occupied for several weeks with the arrangements for the Squadron's voyage to Samoa. Before being relieved, Vice-Admiral Carl Coerper had cabled from

Manila requesting a steamer with large quantities of coal and provisions to be dispatched from Sydney to Suva. Despite the legal requirement that destination and cargo had to be declared to the Australian port authorities, these were successfully concealed so that it was only on the day of *Leipzig's* arrival in Suva that the Sydney press learned of the matter. The services of Lohmann & Co. which represented the NDL in Sydney and its manager, the Intelligence Confidant Oscar Plate, had proved indispensable in the success of the operation.[33]

Seeking the Richest Hunting Ground: Targeting the Attack 1910–1912

The European situation from 1909 brought a marked deterioration in Anglo-German relations with the commencement of the 'Dreadnought race' in battleship construction. Parallel to this was a detailed examination of the function of commerce warfare, and a sharpening of focus on the most effective form of attack on merchant shipping. This section examines three specific and crucial operational plans which targeted export trade. They clearly show the threat to both the British war effort and the economy of the Dominions if essential raw materials and foodstuffs were interdicted and foreshadows the real prospect of naval engagements before main Australian ports.

Attacks on merchant vessels in Australasian waters were made more attractive by the fact that the Squadron would have to leave Chinese waters in any case to avoid its British counterpart whose prime aim would be to search out and destroy the Squadron before it had a chance to damage British trade in East Asia. It was stated clearly that,

> The aim of cruiser warfare ... is damaging enemy trade, protection of our own trade, combat with enemy forces insofar as these tasks permit ... it is recognised how much the Australian government fears an attack on its coasts and

trade, and that it does not consider the present English naval forces in Australian waters sufficient. It can be assumed that operations by the Cruiser Squadron against Australian trade will affect a vulnerable area of English interests, and cause great disruption ... A penetrating attack against Australian trade thus can be recommended.[34]

At the beginning of 1910, *Oberleutnant z. See* Hermann produced a major study called 'At which points do the main English trade routes in Australian waters offer cruiser warfare the greatest prospects of success, and on what basis is this to be implemented?' The prime considerations were the value of merchant trade in Australian waters and the commodities it transported for the British economy and the points at which the greatest number of ships converged as well as the strength of opposition which could be expected.[35] What was important was the British reliance on specific items coming from Australia. From the table of exports provided, it was clear that wool was to be the main object of attack, since the economic consequences of an interdiction of supplies would be severe:

> If one considers that in London ... in 1900, 49 per cent of imported wool was exported again, then it is clear what sort of damage the English merchant has to expect if the import of this article is cut off ... the damage of a branch of industry which employs 800,000 people in England can cause horrific waves in economic life ... through the ensuing increase in wool prices· and clothing ... the whole population will be affected ... These observations lead to the conclusion that Australian trade is a suitable object for our attack.[36]

It also had to be borne in mind that not just the cargo but also the merchant ship itself was a desirable and valuable target of attack. In 1906, 1,095 British ships had left Australian harbours carrying 2,557,061 tons of cargo, and 368 Australian ships carrying 319,610 tons. 'Since Australia as an English colony is also an enemy ... there is enough evidence that there is no lack of opportunity for our Cruiser Squadron to inflict damage in Australian waters.' Based on a graph of the value of exports from the Australian states and New Zealand, the region from Adelaide through the Bass Strait to Brisbane was the mercantile heartland, and 'the given target of our operations'. Based on a comparison of relative strength, it was considered that the Cruiser Squadron, given a surprise appearance in Australian waters, would 'be able to gain by force the control of the seas which is...a prerequisite for the successful exercise of cruiser warfare'.

It was assumed that the British commander, to whom the Australian Fleet was subordinate in war-time would attempt to seek out the main Squadron body and destroy it in a decisive battle. The Germans thus would need to pass the routes Amoy-Formosa-Philippines and the Sunda Strait, if possible unseen, and 'to leave the opponent unaware as long as possible of our own operation and to surprise him with our appearance in Australian waters'. The broad expanse of ocean would make it difficult for the British to concentrate forces and the tightly formed Squadron could easily shake off any pursuer. The task of the auxiliary cruisers was to distract attention from the main body through their own operations, for example, by disrupting trade in the Indian Ocean or South China Sea. The smaller *Cormoran* and *Condor* would select as targets sailing vessels moving from the southern Australian coast to the Cape Horn route, whose cargo value was still considerable.[37]

The route was as follows: the Squadron would proceed from Tsingtao with the view of implementing commerce warfare on arrival in the operational area without an intervening engagement. The flagship *Scharnhorst* and the three un-armoured cruisers would put to sea on the evening of the first day, sailing due east to clear the coast as quickly as possible. The Germans would be favoured by the element of the unexpected. Subterfuge was essential: other steamers would confuse the direction headed with diversionary movements, while the warships headed past the Philippines to Sumatra and southwards to Australia. This would hopefully indicate any proposed attack on shipping in the Indian Ocean, more probable to the Anglo-Australian forces than actually attacking in Australian waters.

The Squadron then would proceed along the west coast of Australia and around Cape Leeuwin to Bass Strait, 'inflicting constant and effective damage on enemy trade until reaching its source in the southeast of Australia.' Given that by this time southern Australian waters would be well on alert and have an increased naval presence, a re-coaling depot in the Campbell Islands south of the Auckland Islands was chosen. It had no cable connection, and was only 300 miles from the southernmost point of New Zealand, whose Cook Strait was a, target area in any case. Attacks on merchant vessels would be carried out on the entire voyage. After re-coaling, a second return thrust northward into the major shipping lanes was planned. The degree of success depended on how far Anglo-Australasian forces had converged at this stage. The 1,000-mile head-start from Batavia to Exmouth Gulf which the German Squadron should have ahead of the British China Squadron would extend into the whole undertaking. 'The 16 days of the first stage of our cruiser warfare (from Cape Leeuwin to the Campbell Islands) ... suffice to show that the whole undertaking is an effective means of warfare against England.'[38]

It is somewhat ironic that while *Condor* was in Sydney in March 1910, its commander composed a revision of the operational steps to be implemented on the Australian Station against his hosts.[39] *Condor* would outfit the auxiliary cruisers at Daja-Hafen in the Solomons and then attack along the east coast of Australia to New Zealand. *Cormoran* would outfit its auxiliaries at Möwe-Hafen (Neu Pommern/New Britain) and attack between Fiji, New Zealand and the Australian east coast. The auxiliaries of these two would be arranged by the Confidant in Sydney, and were to bring as much coal (minimum 3,000 tons) and supplies as possible, that for the *Condor* also bringing steel to reinforce gun mountings on converted auxiliaries. Arrangements had been made with Governor Albert Hahl for the immediate dispatch of coal and supplies from Rabaul to Daja-Hafen upon request.[40]

In November 1910 Kranzbühler also recommended the upgrading of the type of cruiser on the Station.[41] The dispatch of a second cruiser had been mooted first in 1908 at the request of the Colonial Office. Naval Secretary Admiral Alfred von Tirpitz informed the Admiralty that it was not possible due to the constrictions of the naval budget, and could not be reconsidered until 1910. Nevertheless, he agreed that an improved presence was 'thoroughly desirable for various reasons and [I] shall do the most to satisfy the needs of the overseas Stations.' On the basis of this somewhat thin prospect, the Chief of Admiralty Staff, Friedrich Graf von Baudissin, assured the Colonial Office that something would be done 'as soon as the means are at hand.'[42]

Of equal importance, the appearance of modern cruisers in Australian and New Zealand ports would be of value not to be underestimated for raising German prestige and to strengthen the self-awareness of the local communities. Germans of every class had repeatedly asked to be visited by a modern warship, 'an understandable wish by those who also follow the growth of the Navy without ever sighting anything of it.'[43] It was clearly stated in various reports that, despite the speedy integration of German immigrants into English-speaking society and the unwelcome presence of individuals of social-democratic persuasion among many, the German community was to be fostered as a valuable political pressure group.[44]

German planning was based on assessments of the ineffectiveness of an Australasian military response. During the 1909 'Dreadnought scare', Consul-General Dr Georg Irmer reported to Chancellor Bernhard von Bülow on the creation of an Australian Fleet, and as to the effectiveness of such an Australian force, 'English officers only shrug their shoulders at the mention of an Australian Navy.'[45] In 1911 the commander of the *Cormoran* reported on a meeting with the Commander-in-Chief of the Australia Station, Vice-Admiral George King-Hall, whose negative assessment of the naval future further reinforced German confidence. Problems within the Australian construction program reduced any German anxiety about the level of an immediate threat to their position in the Pacific.[46]

In 1910 a detailed proposal for widespread action on the East Asian and Australian Stations in the event of war with Britain was formulated. *Scharnhorst, Gneisnau, Nürnberg, Emden* and *Leipzig* would operate in the South China Sea on the Manila-Hongkong and Shanghai-Singapore trade routes. Koror-Hafen at Palau in the Caroline Islands was designated a central coaling base. All cruisers were to proceed via Vlaming Head in Exmouth Gulf to the Indian Ocean. An aggressive operation was planned. As only inferior warships from the British China and Australia Stations were anticipated, 'surprise attack on individual posts at dawn or at night offers success, the more so when the Cruiser Squadron is operating as a unified body.' During this time *Condor* and *Cormoran* would be conducting commerce attacks in Australian waters.[47]

By the end of 1910, more aggressive action was countenanced: the Squadron was to attack shipping lanes and, while battle with superior forces was to be avoided as far as possible, it was not to be so in principle. It was in this year that a detailed study of the aims of cruiser warfare in the Pacific was prepared. The main object was to cause maximum economic damage by an attack on trade at the sources of enemy exports. Where were these attacks to take place? The area specified was 'the section from Adelaide through the Bass Strait to Brisbane, concentrating on the-three most productive provinces of Victoria, New South Wales and Queensland'. Cape Leeuwin to Adelaide was secondary, the stretch from Brisbane to Torres Strait was not considered as it carried only local coastal traffic. Based on a comparison of ship numbers and armament, it was considered that a surprise appearance in Australian waters would ensure success. Speed and surprise were the keywords. It was assumed that the British/Australian forces would seek out the Germans and attempt to dispose of them in one hit. Therefore 'The goal is to break through to the south, if possible unseen, to leave the opponent as long as possible unaware of our own operation and to surprise him with our appearance in Australian waters.' The task of the auxiliary cruisers – the converted Lloyd steamers – was to distract attention from the main body by disrupting trade in the Indian Ocean and South China Sea while the Squadron steamed southward on the extreme east.

'The view of attacking the trade routes in the South China Sea or in the Indian Ocean must appear more probable to the English [than] carrying out cruiser warfare in Australia.'[48]

Further considerations were dealt with in a detailed examination of theory and practical application in a memorandum by Squadron Chief Vice-Admiral Günther von Krosigk in April 1911.[49] This may be taken as the definitive statement of what the German Navy hoped to achieve in the region, and highlights its important correlation with naval considerations in Europe. Commerce warfare in close proximity to the British homeland where all trade routes converged had to be rejected as unfeasible because of the superiority of the Royal Navy. However, it was certainly possible to cause mass panic by means of cruiser warfare on foreign Stations, which would lead to considerable forces being dispatched to distant parts of the world and thus provide relief for German naval actions in the North Sea. To achieve this, attacks on trade had to be primarily against the import of bulk commodities and commence immediately upon outbreak of war.

Attacks on shipping travelling to the Suez Canal offered the greatest prospects of success. In the narrow straits of the Indies, the long tracks off the Australian coast, and at the entrance to the Red Sea, shipping was compelled into restricted patterns while the Atlantic trade was on open seas. The effectiveness of this secondary naval activity was not to be underestimated, and could tip the scales to Germany's benefit because Britain could not afford to ignore disruptions to its shipping in distant regions. The effect would be twofold: loss of British imports, and the dispatch of forces from Europe which would weaken the British position there. Considerable disruption of British economic life could be achieved by attacking shipping in East Asian and Malayan waters. A cruiser force operating boldly would inflict severe damage on the Australasian export trade to Britain. Numerous successes in the one region also would make the danger appear greater and lead to temporary cessation of shipping services. In conjunction with attacks on south Atlantic commerce, the insecurity created in British trade would reach a level producing the desired domestic panic which would pressure the government to negotiate. That the British had to appear in superiority and strengthen their foreign service forces In various parts of the world, in a considerably larger measure than was necessary for Germany, 'certainly would create a measurable relief for our conduct of the war in home waters.'[50]

In June 1911 Krosigk elaborated on the strategic exercises the *Nürnberg* had carried out between July and September the previous year, when the conditions were planned to replicate as closely as possible what might occur on the Australian Station in time of war.[51] The question posed was: 'How must we proceed in the prescribed operation: cruiser warfare against English trade in Australia?' Firstly, the Squadron had to show itself on the most frequented Australian sea lanes, and 'The more undetermined our presence, the greater and more productive the disruption of trade.' The first German activity envisaged leaving Apia then heading directly to Möwe-Hafen in New Guinea where *Condor* and *Cormoran* would be met. *Scharnhorst*, *Nürnberg*, and *Emden* with the collier *Titania* would proceed via the New Hebrides to the Australian coast near Brisbane. Because coal had to be obtained in the vicinity of the operational area, it was assumed that this would come from captured ships, or from local harbours particularly north of Brisbane. Ideally Sydney should be reached with a four-fifths bunker capacity. Krosigk stated that in order to 'spread further agitation, I would sail around Australia, move against Melbourne, Adelaide and Perth, and then to the NW coast where coal sources lie closer to re-coal from waiting steamers.'

What was the expected damage to Australian trade? When it was known that German cruisers were near Australian ports, no ship would leave harbour. If they did, no insurance company would risk covering them. 'This blockup will quickly follow through as far as the Suez Canal and the Cape.' As neutral ships would be in demand everywhere, there was little likelihood of many being redirected quickly to Australian harbours. Krosigk's critique of events as played out in the *Nürnberg's* exercise emphasised that the 'precise and careful execution of a great strategic problem … a quite complicated undertaking' deserved special recognition. Crucially, it also proved and reinforced the value of the whole idea of commerce warfare which had existed since the turn of the century: 'an attack on Australian trade by the Cruiser Squadron always will remain an undertaking to be given serious consideration.'[52]

In April 1912, the new Senior Officer (*Korvettenkapitän* Ebert) wrote to the Admiralty emphasizing the importance of New Zealand ports to be visited regularly, as done in Australia. On the basis of wartime operations plans affecting the ships of the Australian Station, he regarded it as essential for the commander and officers to have a personal familiarity with the harbours, steamer routes and climatic conditions in the region. During a period of 'political tension' the previous year, he had the opportunity to consider in detail the implementation of operations plans, and suggested that Auckland, Port Lyttleton, Wellington, Westport and Milford Sound be ports of call, as well as the frequently travelled Cook Strait which was a specific target area.[53]

Establishing Priorities: 1912–14

In late 1913 Squadron Chief Vice-Admiral Maximilian Reichsgraf von Spee emphasised the strategic importance of the Pacific region. This shows the flexibility in his thinking and his ability to construct alternatives to ensure the Cruiser Squadron functioned as effectively as possible in a Pacific war. 'We have to appear in tight formation where the traffic comes together, before important harbours or in unavoidable passages.'[54] Following a review of the situation with the Station Senior Officer and personal observations during the Squadron's recent Pacific voyage, Spee advised the Admiralty that it should also be possible to contact German postal steamers then at sea by radio. This had every prospect of success with the approaching expansion of the major transmitter station at Yap. *Condor* would operate in the region Solomon Islands-Australian east coast-New Zealand; *Cormoran* would operate in the region Fiji-New Zealand-Australian east coast, both using Daja-Hafen (Solomons) and/ or Graciosa Bay (Santa Cruz) as bases.

Spee anticipated direct engagement of Australian naval forces by the Squadron. Apart from attacking commerce, he stated that, 'under specific circumstances the prospects for success in direct battle with the opponent are not to be excluded.' It would appear that he was thinking in terms of preventing a combination of the British China Squadron and the Australian Fleet Unit, which would give his Squadron superiority on both the East Asian and Australian Stations. He did not believe that Australian warships would leave their own waters, and any chance of this would lessen 'when the ships are being paid for and crewed by Australians.'[55] The Squadron's position being unknown, attacks on trade and even on port facilities would be effective, given the effects on enemy morale which would ensue. This in fact was what did occur, if for a brief time, in the first two months of the War.

The actual potential of German attacks was clearly acknowledged by the British. From the time Vice-Admiral Sir Thomas Jerram assumed command of British forces in East Asia in March 1913, he pressed the Admiralty for reinforcements in order to match the capabilities of the German Squadron: '... English mercantile trade in the whole operational area will be continually disrupted and damaged.'[56] As the political situation in August 1914 deteriorated, the crucial question which occupied Spee in determining his course of action was assessing Japanese intentions. Although the Squadron was approximately equal to its British counterpart, the two factors which could change this quickly were the appearance of the 'Dreadnought' *Australia* and Japan's entry into the war.[57]

However, in terms of tangible results, the disruptive effect nevertheless was considerable. The *Emden* in particular, and to a lesser extent *Karlsruhe*, *Möwe* and *Wolf*, achieved successes which indicate what could have eventuated on a larger scale. The *Emden* struck where the maximum political and commercial effects would be obtained. With the British Admiralty having little information as to its whereabouts from the time it left Tsingtao until it appeared in the Bay of Bengal, similarly about the Cruiser Squadron until it reached Tahiti, Spee used the 'fleet in being' to considerable effect. Had it not been for the disarray into which his plans were thrown by the entry of Japan into the war, and the quick occupation of the German colonies resulting in the loss of coaling depots, the whole Squadron would have attacked merchant trade on a widespread scale according to its operational plans in East Asian, Pacific and Indian Ocean waters, causing considerable economic damage.

Conclusions

The aim of German planning against Australian shipping and trade may not be seen in isolation. The key factor for understanding the validity of this is the interconnection with overall war planning for outcomes in Europe. Germany's aggressive activity in the Asian-Pacific region was particularly important because attacks on trade with the aim of forcing Britain to its knees would be effective in the sense that,

> it lies completely within the realm of possibility to create popular panic by means of commerce warfare, which will lead to the detachment of considerable forces to distant parts of the world. This will greatly contribute to the relief of our domestic war situation and in conjunction with other operations perhaps make the English government inclined to accept a peace suitable to us.[58]

To achieve this goal, bulk commodities (foodstuffs and raw materials) had to be the prime target, and operations had to be implemented immediately on the outbreak of war. While it was accepted that overall commerce warfare was secondary, an Anglo-German conflict being determined by the battleship fleet in the North Sea, 'the effect of this secondary warfare should not be underestimated and can suffice ... to tip the scales to our advantage'. To ensure this, as many ships as possible had to be made available for commerce warfare. Britain could not simply look on while its trade was attacked in distant parts of the world, and would have to detach forces from the European front to deal with the threat. This would be the opportune moment for the battleship fleet to strike. Successful attacks on merchant shipping in Asian and Australasian waters would cause,

> a considerable disruption of English economic life. It can be accepted that a Cruiser Squadron operating boldly and offensively, interdicting Australian exports to England, will achieve the desired effect indirectly on the routes Australia-India, Colombo-Aden, or the blockade of Australian ports can be considered.[59]

The Royal Navy would be forced to appear at numerous remote points in considerable strength, which would relieve pressure on German naval operations in European waters. The planned depredations of the Cruiser Squadron provided a unique opportunity to force Britain to reduce its forces in home waters, thus limiting its strategic flexibility already under pressure by Dominion demands for protection. This would force it to come to an agreement on terms which would guarantee and consolidate Germany's world-power position. This was well understood as the respected navalist writer John C. R. Colomb stated that failure to provide adequate maintenance for Britain's position in this part of the world, if it were threatened, 'probably would affect the British position as a whole.'[60]

What needs to be kept in mind is what was *intended* to be achieved. The German naval operational plans speak for themselves, clearly spelling out the intention to attack Australasian shipping, blockade and in some cases shell Australian port facilities, and if necessary engage Australian warships in their own coastal waters. Yet the optimistic scenario was fatally flawed with the underestimation of the capability of Australasian forces. The use of ports and anchorages in German Pacific colonies to support operations shows the wisdom of the immediate occupation of New Guinea by Australia and Samoa by New Zealand in 1914 which considerably disrupted the Cruiser Squadron's planning, quite apart from considerations of the impact of Japan's entry into the war.

The Squadron had real prospects of success despite the enormous distances to be traversed and the problems of coal supply. The climate of uncertainty and fear which was created in the Dominions, the slowing of export and coastal trade, the tying-up of naval forces in search and pursuit, and the delay of troop transports were still considerable hindrances to the Australasian war effort.

In considering this whole matter, as A. W. Jose wrote perceptively in the official history, the reader who wishes to understand it has to reconstruct the situation as it appeared to those who were in it. It was inconceivable that the Germans would not use their armoured cruisers to the greatest effect, and 'there were many known reasons why [Germany] should attack Australia.'[61]

Given the successes of the *Emden,* and that the Squadron main body remained unlocated, the climate of apprehension, 'a very deadly influence on Australian opinion', could have delayed the dispatch of the Australian Imperial Force to Egypt for months, rather than weeks as occurred. Jose's projections ring true in view of the Germans' documented intentions to create a climate of fear and panic. The sinking of Australian troop transports might have destroyed faith in the Admiralty and made cooperation difficult for the remainder of the war. Andrew Fisher, only recently Prime Minister, 'conjured up a picture of thirty thousand young untried men afloat, of enemy cruisers dashing in to sink them'.[62] Such an eventuality would have been a success beyond Spee's imagining, had he not been preoccupied with evading his Japanese pursuers in the western Pacific, and could well have reduced Australia's contribution to the war effort to insignificance for months.

Ongoing German interest in the region is also indicative not only of a pre-war, but also of a future threat. This is something that is completely overlooked by commentators on the issue who have not accessed the German archives. German planning, seen in the broadest context, had two clear aims. The most obvious was to preserve the nation's status as a world power in the face of what was believed to be a deliberate policy of containment by Britain. The second was one often forgotten in the preoccupation with the events leading up to and in the first year of the War. This was to gain a position which would enable a peace settlement on terms which could provide Germany – at a minimum – with a basis for increasing its world-political influence, and in this scenario, Australia had much to lose.

In November 1916, Chancellor Theobald von Bethmann Hollweg requested from Admiralty Chief of Staff Henning von Holtzendorff an indication of the strategic points the Navy required. Holtzendorff specified that in the Indian Ocean the 'objects of attack ... are the traffic along the African coast as well as on the routes via India to East Asia and Australia', and in the Pacific 'New Guinea and the Bismarck Archipelago are the necessary strategic footholds for the conduct of our naval war against Australian maritime traffic.' He believed that if the return of this area could not be achieved, 'then Portuguese Timor must be obtained.'[63]

Wilhelm Solf, former Governor of Samoa and now State Secretary in the Colonial Office, was quite specific: New Caledonia should be obtained for its nickel deposits, the phosphate islands, and the British Solomons as a labour source.[64] These documents, along with those detailing operational plans prior to 1914, must be seen as part of the long-term attempt to destroy British naval hegemony, a political reality which was accepted by most contemporaries as a precondition for Australasian security, totally separate from any grass roots movement to independent policy on other issues.

As Vice-Admiral Sir George King-Hall stated on Empire Day in 1911, international politics in both West and East had undergone a great change, and now and in the future the nation could not but be affected by what occurred elsewhere, and by the influence which international political shifts must have on the Empire. He also spoke of Australian nationalism, and made the point that this did not mean the loosening of Empire bonds. Indeed, these were essential for Australian defence: 'We must have a large horizon ... if the command of the sea is lost to the Empire, Australia would be prey to the strongest maritime power ...'[65] by which he meant Germany, if indeed not a German-Japanese alliance. The strong national spirit which had arisen in previous decades was no less imperialistic because it was Australian. Politicians and defence personnel of this period were eminently practical men who read the international spirit of the times soberly and accurately.

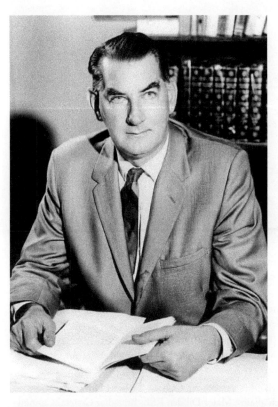

Left

Gordon Greenwood
(1913–86)

Below

Paul Michael Kennedy
(b. 1945)

The Brisbane Anzac Day Commemoration Committee, 1921. *The Week*, 17/2/1922, Library of University of Queensland.

Fourth Row: Messrs. A. Watson (Chamber of Manufacturers); Charles Gibbon (Fathers' Association); Colonel McKenzie (Salvation Army); Stanley Wilmott (Overseas Club); Arthur Exley (St George's Society).

Third Row: P.J. McDermott (Irish Association); J.F. Maxwell, MLA; E.R.B. Pike (joint secretary ADCC); W. Meyers King (Chamber of Commerce); Rev. A.G. Weller (chaplain); Ald. Faulkner (Mayor of South Brisbane).

Second Row: Canon D. J. Garland (Secretary ADCC); Lt. Colonel Durant; Rev. Dr E. N. Merrington (chaplain); Major Dibden RSL; Brigadier General Cannan RSL; Major General Bruche; Captain Maddock.

Front Row: T.A. Ryan; Archbishop G. Sharp (C. of E); Jon. J. Harry Coyne (chairman ADCC); Archbishop J. Duhig (R.C.); Alderman Down; Hon. A. J. Thynne

Troops in Fremantle prior to Embarkation to South Africa. Padre D. J. Garland standing front second from left. Public Library, Perth, WA

Appendices

1. ESSENTIAL KNOWLEDGE FOR UNDERSTANDING DOMINION INVOLVEMENT IN THE GREAT WAR

Imperial German War Aims

Given that the war of 1914–18 was a response to German belligerence/aggression one needs to understand what German objectives were and how and why they were developed and became official policy from August 1914 until November 1918. These questions were only able to be posed by German historians in both parts of the divided nation after 1945. That is to say, only then did historians in East and West Germany have the opportunity to investigate the available archives without hindrance for the very first time. During the Weimar Republic 1919–33, for example, there had been many books written and documents published on the lead up to and the course of the war but archival access was restricted to politically acceptable historians.[1] It was an example of political control being exerted over the freedom of enquiry. In short, the German governments after 1920 were preoccupied with the need to show that Germany had not been solely guilty for the outbreak and duration of the war as it stipulated in the Treaty of Versailles paragraph 231. Their motivation was that if it could be historically demonstrated that Germany was not solely guilty then the justification for the imposition of reparations would be rendered untenable. Consequently the work of German historians and those Anglo-Saxon colleagues who had been awarded German grants to produce studies that contested sole German war-guilt, were all basically flawed and their findings thus untenable.

The situation post-1945 was very different. Particularly after the first German *Historiker Kongress* after the war, namely at Munich's Ludwig Maximillian University in 1949 and the early publications of Fritz Fischer's articles in the *Historische Zeitschrift* (1951, 1959, 1960, 1964) the war-guilt debate 1914 was re-opened and led to the production of numerous studies by leading German scholars and their students which investigated both official policy-making and the biographies of leading statesmen of the time. However, again the 'politicization of research' was very evident especially in the publications of pro-Prussian conservative scholars such as Gerhard Ritter, Karl-Dietrich Erdmann and others.[2] Further, that of East German historians was also heavily influenced by their Marxist-Leninist masters to demonstrate that the Great War was also the consequence of the 'crisis in capitalism.' Ideology could not be kept out of what should have been strictly objective scholarly investigation and narrative. So the decade between the late 1950s and the late 1960s saw the emergence of what has become known as the *Fischer Controversy*. It was so named because Fischer's work and particularly that of his chief research assistant at that time, Dr Imanuel Geiss (1931–2012), argued that the archival record showed unequivocally that what they called the *Machtelite* (Power Elite) of Germany had long been cultivating annexationist ambitions in East-Central Europe (*Mitteleuropa*) and also overseas, especially in central Africa (*Mittelafrika*)

Behind these ambitions were various imperial German pressure groups such as the Pan German League, the Navy League, the Army League and a variety of commercial and industrial interest groups. On top of that the Army had inherited an ancient culture of embarking on so-called preventive wars in order to annex border regions, actions deemed necessary for German security. This had been especially evident in the exceptionally long reign of Frederick the Great of Prussia from 1740–1786. The Prussian premier, Otto von Bismarck exploited this tradition in his three famous wars of German unification or rather of Prussification of Germany: 1864 (Denmark), 1866 (Austria) and 1870 (France).

Thereafter, using the threat of war became an obvious means of solving foreign policy problems for Prusso-Germany when Bismarck had united all the Germanic states except Austria and Switzerland into one extensive federation, *das deutsche Reich*. In short Bismarck's mode of conducting foreign policy using the *schimmende Wehr*, literally the 'shining weapon', that is the always combat ready army, became accepted practice of German statesmen ever since. As Fischer and Geiss have shown the war-aims of imperial Germany envisaged the complete domination of Central Europe from the Belgian coast to the Ural mountains and much more besides. The documentary evidence for this was discovered by Imanuel Geiss in the imperial German archives housed in Potsdam during a research visit in 1959. It was a memorandum composed for Cabinet and tabled in September 1914 on the eve of the first battle of the Marne 7–12 September 1914. Up to that point the German army had been enjoying spectacular successes against both the British and the French forces in executing its famous Schlieffen Plan. However, at the Marne in the proximity of Paris the German army met with dogged resistance from both allies and so the German expectation of victory in the West within a matter of weeks ('Home before Christmas') was totally frustrated. The conduct of the war from then on took the form of dogged trench warfare with each side trying desperately to devise ways and means of breaking the stalemate.

The historiographical significance of the 'September Programme' is that it reveals the ambition of the German government to establish its domination of Europe and the colonial empires of the vanquished European powers, especially Belgium and France in Africa and Asia. What the September Programme says about Holland is especially interesting for Australia. The Dutch were a people of clearly Germanic origins so Holland was to be associated with Germany in a 'special relationship'. The Dutch colonies would not be occupied but, for example, the Dutch East Indies would be made available to the Reich for the establishment of naval bases.[3] The implications for Australasian defence are manifest.

The Persistence of German War-Aims

As a consequence of the lost Battle of the Marne the German supreme army command was so despondent that the chief of staff, General von Falkenhayn referred to the army as a 'shattered instrument' (*ein zertrümmertes Instrument*) in conversation with the Reich Chancellor Bethmann Hollweg in December 1914. Earlier he had confided to Matthias Erzberger (1875–1921) a *Zentrum Party* (Roman Catholic) member of the Reichstag, that he thought then that the war had effectively been lost at that battle.[4] This, however, did not deter the German government. The Chancellor's hands were effectively tied by those leading personalities who led the push for a war with annexations. He felt constrained to down play the significance of the Marne defeat in the hope of sustaining the nation's morale and will to win. In short, with some inner reservations Bethmann Hollweg opted to conform to the will of the annexationist lobby and decided to not negotiate for peace until Germany had won an unassailable position of power. In effect the Chancellor became the hesitant if not nervous agent for the most extravagant Pan German ambitions. These were, in sum, the final removal of the old system of 'balance of power' which would be replaced by the establishment of a German predominance (*Vormachtstellung*) in Europe. The Chancellor elaborated on this objective then on 2 November 1914 in the Reichstag.[5]

Remarkable is the fact that the Chancellor seriously expected that Britain would voluntarily stand aside and abandon her position in the world in favour of Germany. And in this regard he was in total accord with the Kaiser and vast majority of the German bourgeoisie. Why did they believe that it was absolutely necessary to embark on such a reckless, rash and foolhardy enterprise? Why, indeed, could the Chancellor labour under the delusion that England (meaning the entire British Empire) would submit peacefully to German demands? Was he mesmerised by the ever growing capacity of the German high seas fleet to intimidate the Royal Navy? Was he encouraged by the prospect of total victory over France and Russia to intimidate Britain to acquiesce to the new German *Machtstellung* (position of power)? Indeed, the entire German bourgeoisie ever since the 1870 victory over France had become enthralled by the vision that from then on Germany could and should expand at will throughout the entire world. For this reason Germans with apparent boundless enthusiasm marched to war in August 1914, except, of course, the working class. Their parliamentary representatives, the Social Democrats had been persuaded to vote for war credits in the Reichstag by the Chancellor in the belief that the war was one of national defence against Tsarist Russia, though even some socialist deputies came later to endorse annexations. It was this that caused the famous split in the SPD which led later to the formation of the German Communist Party (KPD). It was certainly the well-known propensity of German philosophers, historians and theologians for self-delusion which encouraged an unjustifiable confidence in such vacuous Hegelian-inspired concepts such as 'the necessity of world development', meaning German military and naval predominance in the entire world conceived of as the great German cultural task (*Kulturaufgabe*) imposed on Germany by the 'God of history'. The following example of this mentality is provided in a speech by the luckless General Helmut von Moltke which he delivered to the *Deutsche Gesellschaft* (German Society) in Berlin. He proclaimed as follows:

> The Romance peoples [*meaning the French*] have already past the pinnacle of their development; they are no longer able to contribute anything fruitful to the overall development of the world. – The Slavic peoples, chiefly Russia, are still so culturally backward that they cannot aspire to the leadership of humanity. Indeed, under the dominance of the Russian knout Europe would be condemned to a condition of spiritual barbarism. – England pursues exclusively materialistic goals. Only through Germany is the further cultural development of mankind possible. And for that reason Germany cannot go under in this war. She is the only nation at the present time that can assume the leadership of humanity and guide

the peoples of the earth towards higher goals ... The war will lead to new developments in world history and its outcome will be that the entire world will be set on a new path on which to advance in the centuries to come.[6]

These thoughts of von Moltke breathe genuine Neo-Rankeanism, which, as explained in chapter five was the doctrine taught by leading German historians to argue that the time had come in the course of world history for Germany to expand throughout the world especially at the expense of Russia, France and Britain. This ideology that advanced an imperative for German aggression had struck deeps roots within the *Bildungsbürgertum* as Kurt Riezler's summing up of the purpose of the war shows. He wrote that the threefold purpose of the war was *first* defence against France, *second,* preventive war against Russia and *finally* struggle with England for the dominance of the world.[7]

The evidence, then, is overwhelming that German power elite had been awaiting the opportunity to unleash a war to establish German hegemony in the world for imaginable time as spelled out in the September Program. This grand objective, however, had really been frustrated at the latest by 18 November 1914 with the loss of the Battle of the Marne. The puzzling question, then, is why did not the German power elite draw the rational conclusion not to continue the war against three world powers to which another two, namely Japan and the United States would be added? The answer is that they were mentally imprisoned in an ideology that was essentially a wish-dream, a delusion which convinced them that only a victorious war could ensure the social and political status in the Reich to which they aspired. Kurt Riezler had already spelt out this ideology in his remarkable pre-war 1914 best seller, *Grundzüge der Weltpolitik in der Gegenwart.*[8] As already mentioned, this book had gone through some dozen editions before the war's end. In it the Neo-Rankean ideology served to justify German expansionism. This did not absolutely necessitate war but simply the threat of war. For this reason Germany had to be so massively armed both at land and sea as to be able to command the peace (*den Frieden zu befehlen*). State of the art armaments were necessary to force any power foolish enough to stand up to Germany to back down and submit to Germany's demands rather than to risk a fight. Of course, Riezler was aware that a coalition of determined opposing powers who refused to back down could pose a problem for German *Weltpolitik* in which case one had to accept the risk involved. And this is what in fact actually happened.

The personage of Kurt Riezler has again become very newsworthy in documenting the German determination to manipulate the July-August crisis in 1914 to force a war against both Russia and France in August 1914. In doing so it was essential to manoeuvre the diplomacy so as to let Russia appear as the aggressor and Austria-Hungary, Germany's ally, as the victim. If that could be made to appear credible within the diplomatic community, then Germany could never be accused of initiating the crisis; she was simply acting to fulfil her treaty obligations towards Austria-Hungary. In a word, Germany was most concerned to avoid being branded guilty of unprovoked aggression. This point had been made emphatically by Fritz Fischer and Imanuel Geiss already over fifty years ago. More recently the former Fischer doctoral student, Bernd Schulte has through his independent research confirmed in detail that Germany had urged Austria to invade Serbia knowing that it would provoke the Russians to make an armed response.[9] None of this research has been evaluated by Sir Christopher Clark in his strenuous efforts to relativise German guilt. Obviously Clark knows about this research but has chosen not to use it because it would negate his argument that Germany was no more to blame for the catastrophe than the other Great Powers.

Below follows a translation of a document that confirms what the German government was thinking when they believed that Germany stood at the cusp of an enormous military success against France and Britain. It is the so-called September Program and it deserves particularly close study because it gives an accurate picture of how the world should look had the Schlieffen Plan succeeded. In short, it was the Pan-German wish-dream.

The Text of the September Program [composed by the Reich Chancellor's personal assistant, Dr Kurt Riezler]

The general aim of the war is security for the German Reich in west and east for all imaginable time. For this purpose France must be so weakened as to make her revival as a great power impossible for all time. Russia must be thrust back as far as possible from Germany's eastern frontier and her domination over the non-Russian vassal peoples broken.

France. The military to decide whether we should demand cession of Belfort and western slopes of the Vosges, razing of fortresses and cession of coastal strip from Dunkirk to Boulogne. The ore-field of Briey, which is necessary for the supply of ore for our industry, to be ceded in any case. Further, a war indemnity, to be paid in instalments; it must be high enough to prevent France from spending any considerable sums on armaments in the next 15–20 years.

Furthermore: a commercial treaty which makes France economically dependent on Germany, secures the French market for our exports and makes it possible to exclude British commerce from France. This treaty must secure for us financial and industrial freedom of movement in France in such fashion that German enterprises can no longer receive different treatment from French.

Belgium: Liège and Verviers to be attached to Prussia, a frontier strip of the province of Luxemburg to Luxemburg. Question whether Antwerp, with a corridor to Liège, should also be annexed remains open.

At any rate Belgium, even if allowed to continue to exist as a state, must be reduced to a vassal state, must allow us to occupy any militarily important ports, must place her coast at our disposal in military respects, must become economically a German province. Given such a solution, which offers the advantages of annexation without its inescapable domestic political disadvantages, French Flanders with Dunkirk, Calais and Boulogne, where most of the population is Flemish, can without danger be attached to this unaltered Belgium. The competent quarters will have to judge the military value of this position against England.

Luxemburg: Will become a German federal state and will receive a strip of the present Belgian province of Luxemburg and perhaps the corner of Longwy.

We must create a central European economic association through common customs treaties, to include France, Belgium, Holland, Denmark, Austria-Hungary, Poland [*sic*], and perhaps Italy, Sweden and Norway. This association will not have any common constitutional supreme authority and all its members will be normally equal, but in practice will be under German leadership and must stabilise Germany's economic dominance over *Mitteleuropa*.

The question of colonial acquisitions, where the first aim is the creation of a continuous Central African colonial empire, will be considered later, as will that of the aims to be realised vis-à-vis Russia.

A short provisional formula suitable for a possible preliminary peace to be found for a basis for the economic agreements to be concluded with France and Belgium.

Holland: It will have to be considered by what means and methods Holland can be brought into closer relationship with the German Empire.

In view of the Dutch character, this closer relationship must leave them free of any feeling of compulsion, must alter nothing in the Dutch way of life, and must also subject them to no new military obligations. Holland, then, must be left independent in externals, but be made internally dependent on us. Possibly one might consider an offensive and defensive alliance, to cover the colonies; in any case a close customs association, perhaps the cession of Antwerp to Holland in return for the right to keep a German garrison in the fortress of Antwerp and at the mouth of the Scheldt.

(Fritz Fischer, *Germany's Aims in the First World War*, W.W. Norton & Company, Inc., 1967. Reprinted by permission.)

It will be appreciated that in Germany the revelation of this document, discovered by Fritz Fischer's then Assistant, Dr Imanuel Geiss, in the Potsdam Archives, at the time in East German hands was sensational. It came as a shock to those conservative patriotic German historians who wished to argue that Germany had no such war aims. Rather, they would have preferred to argue that Germany was only fighting to protect her national security. The fact is, of course, she wanted to change the map of the world in her favour for 'imaginable time' as it says above.

Students need to grasp that historiography is an on-going argument; at least it is so in all *open societies*. In dictatorships there is no freedom of information, no 'public sphere' in which contrary ideas might be openly discussed. Dictatorships only allow the ideology of the ruling clique to prevail in education. In short, as we have seen under such regimes as Nazi Germany and those under Soviet domination that only one ideology is permitted, namely that of the party in power. What happens in open societies is that rival parties espouse different views for specific political-ideological reasons but the main thing is that in the market place of ideas everyone is entitled without fear or favour to express his or her views and engage in non-violent debate.

In present day Germany we have such an 'ideal speech situation' (Jürgen Habermas). This, of course, is broadly true on the surface of things. However, it so happens that influential cliques are formed consisting of academics of a particular ideological persuasion and these work against the toleration of contrary opinions, especially in explaining the peculiarities of German policy leading up to the Great War of 1914–18. Dissenting voices are marginalised as in the case of Dr Bernd Schulte, a former doctoral student of Professor Fritz Fischer. He has, despite the many obstacles placed in his way, managed through the courage of his convictions and his independence of means to publish findings which not a few more conservative colleagues find disconcerting or unpalatable. So far none of his numerous books have been published in English. For this reason I have translated a concise summary of his findings about exactly how the Great War started. As the Germans often say, 'The Devil is in the detail'; you have to burrow deeply into the archives and ask pertinent questions in order find the rational answers.

2. THE EVENTS LEADING TO THE GERMAN DECISION TO URGE AUSTRIA TO WAR AGAINST SERBIA

Translation of the introduction to Bernd F. Schulte, *Das Deutsche Reich von 1914: Europäische Konföderation und Weltreich* (Hamburger Studien zu Geschichte und Zeitgeschehen Reihe II Band 2) 2012, pp. 9–18.

The historical value of this text lies in the fact that for the first time confirmation of Germany's dependence on Austria for the realisation of its aims is documented so graphically. The record of personal link between the Chancellor, Theobald von Bethman Hollweg and his cousin, Dietrich von Bethmann Hollweg in his role as Legation Councillor in Vienna has proved to be a revealing source which confirms both Germany's anxiety and desperation to implement her expansionist ambitions for which Austro-Hungarian cooperation was essential.

Translator's note: In my rendering of Dr Schulte's text into English I have used italics for place names of locations in Germany and Austria that are less likely to be known to readers. These are either country estates or localities in the countryside. Names of individual personages refer to high ranking civil servants or statesmen.

It is a foregone conclusion that the decisions of the Berlin politicians presumed the assurance in the military superiority of German armed forces. Even the Chancellor's critics, such as the von Bülows and Schoens and the German ambassador in Paris 1914, assumed that it would be a short war and in any case they had complete confidence in the Chief of General Staff, Helmut von Moltke. Nevertheless, such confidence concealed certain errors of judgement which occurred already at the beginning of the century with regard to precisely this nomination of the Chief of General Staff. The younger von Moltke could not really be compared to his more famous uncle. Indeed, already in the course of the war when it became clear that the situation had become hopeless the Chancellor himself in private conversations expressed doubts about the pre-war planning especially that of the military. Such expressions of doubt had been confirmed by older civil servants such as especially Botho von Wedel. These related to the doubtful assumptions of the military leadership and the Foreign Office which were recognised as the flawed points of departure of a misguided policy. The over-optimistic assessment of the German army and the exaggerated confidence in its fighting capacity, the 'sacred cow' of German self-estimation as Wedel recognised, and which was shared by Bethmann Hollweg, Jagow, Zimmermann and other diplomats, led them to pursue an inflexible 'policy of pretention'. Certainly, the political administration of those years, later called the 'Bethmann circle' could not be regarded as representative of pacifist policy. Even Bernhard von Bülow himself belonged to this circle.

As one would expect the archives contain but few documents of the Reich Chancellor which relate to these question as seen by him personally. There is, for example, the memorandum for the Reichstag committee of enquiry of 1919 which in its central concern stressed the importance of maintaining Austro-Hungarian power. The former Reich Chancellor in his total commitment to the Austrian alliance, tied the maintenance of German standing in the world to the independence of Austria, thereby seeking to justify his actions for the initial stages of the First World War.

The problem confronting the German leadership in June 1914 was the 'allegedly dying Austria' as Bethmann Hollweg wrote. And this automatically led to the 'isolation of the German Reich'. Indeed, as the former Reich Chancellor emphasised the world situation had 'become rigidified' and, he went on,

> since the two previous Balkan wars the only thing that had changed was the anti-German coalition that came about with the linking up of England to the Russian-French dual alliance, the arrangements of which acquired both a diplomatic and military significance.

What emerges in the following at all turns is how aggressively both the Eastern and Western Powers exploited the situation for the coming war. For example, the key intention of Serbia had been to break off parts of Austria and thereby initiate the splitting up of the Danube monarchy. In addition the interplay between Petersburg, Belgrade and London becomes particularly evident. Bethmann Hollweg, a reputed Anglophile, stands out in view of the deep rooted suspicion in London towards Berlin, a factor that diminished the prospects of an Anglo-German rapprochement.

Petersburg's war aims appeared clearly to be the elimination of Austrian influence in the Balkans. And contrary to the findings of recent research Bethmann Hollweg saw the ominous significance of the reshuffling of the previous alliances in Europe which had emerged in the wake of the Balkan wars. In contrast to the judgement which will be explained here, Bethmann Hollweg had dilated in 1919 that Austria had in her *Promemoria* of 5 July 1914 drafted the aim at the general diplomatic restoration of Austrian influence in the Balkans, 'a program for the long term'. Thereby the previous Reich Chancellor had sought obviously to foist the burden of responsibility on to Vienna for everything that followed.

Indeed, according to Bethmann Hollweg the decisive factor that unleashed everything that followed was the assassination of the Archduke, Franz Ferdinand. The rapid decision in Berlin that was the basis for the events of early July 1914 becomes clear in what Bethmann wrote:

> This was the last possible minute for the Austria to reassert her authority in the southern Slav region. If this opportunity were not to be irrevocably lost one had to act firmly and quickly. Consequently a war with Serbia was both possible and probable. We [Germans] had not ignored the possibility in our instructions but neither demanded it or in any way urged it upon Austria. We advised, however, rapid action as the best possible way to avoid world complications (*Weltkomplikationen*).

This was the so-called 'localisation policy'. Today we know that the German policy did not allow Austria a free hand in the way that Bethmann

Hollweg here would have us believe. The aim was to make Russia alone to appear responsible in connection with various mistakes made in Vienna. The key issue was the concern of Austria-Hungary in June 1914 about her future economic and military capacity to stay viable (*Leistungsfähigkeit*). That was confirmed by Bethmann when he wrote:

> The force of the circumstances in which we found ourselves became more and more evident. The decision facing us was whether an attempt should be made to strengthen the position of the Central Powers by resisting a possibly initial attack that could have been sustained or whether is was already too late and we had to accept the break up of Austria and thereby the diminution of our own position.

The Legation Councillor [*Legationsrat*] in the Vienna Embassy of the German Reich, namely Dietrich von Bethmann Hollweg, cousin of Willibald von Bethmann Hollweg, the Reich Chancellor, forwarded to his eminent relative on 24 June 1914 a confidential economic report compiled by him. The German ambassador in Vienna, von Tschirsky, had noted upon the report as follows: 'Considering the subject matter herein ... to be treated in confidence' [*vertaulich behandeln lassen zu wollen*].

The question is whether this communication was about state secrets or whether the questions raised therein were intended for a wider circle. The Legation Councillor had discussed the peculiar economic, financial and domestic-demographic circumstances of the Danube monarchy and on this basis took into consideration its value to the German Reich as an ally at the time, that is in June 1914, and for years into the future.

Above all the expenditure on the army and navy which made up 20% of the entire national budget of the Danube monarchy was emphasised. As a consequence investments had been reduced. As well the government in Vienna was attempting through new taxation legislation to raise via loans 222 million *Kronen*. However, because neither the population was growing to the required extent or was expanding in either its purchasing or taxation capacity it meant that raising loans on the international market could only be arranged under humiliating conditions. Only if military expenditure could be reduced would it be possible to attain the desired budgetary objectives. Dietrich von Bethmann Hollweg emphasised to his cousin that the delayed military credits had been responsible for the great expenditure of the annexation crisis and the Balkan crisis and had led to a disturbance of the entire economic life of the monarchy. Further, he confirmed that for the military leadership the Russian trial mobilisation had resulted in the need for Austria to maintain such a high state of military preparedness that she would not be able to sustain it. The situation had developed to the extent that the monarchy felt compelled to hold itself permanently *en vedette* [that is, in the spotlight] which would gradually exhaust it and lead to economic ruin. The key problem according to the counsellor was:

> ... In view of the foreign policy situation of Austria-Hungary based on the premises that a reduction of military expenditure is not advisable and rather that an expansion of the defence forces is required, the question remains how the necessary funding can be made available.

Dietrich von Bethmann Hollmann went on to observe that neither an economic improvement nor a parallel increase in taxation could be expected. He proffered a realistic consideration of the prevailing situation between a donor and a supplicant state as follows:

> If we consider the second path [i.e. seeking loans] it has to be to be kept in mind that it is only a temporary measure because the monarchy would still be deeply in debt and the root cause of the problem remains as before without having been tackled. Obviously by repeatedly seeking ever larger loans Austria Hungary will fall into greater dependence upon the donor state. On the other hand the donor Power will find itself in a politically embarrassing situation such as is

the case between France and Russia. The embarrassment of the creditor with regard to the debtor will only become worse when the economic development of the debtor appears slight and that state is compelled repeatedly to request new loans.

In this situation, the donor state, Germany, was financially at the end of her capacity to act. 'Cheap money', as Hugo Stinnes demanded, was just not available from Berlin. German export statistics in May 1914 had not been as low as they had been two years previously. Indeed, the recession had begun to affect both the banks and the shipping sector. Dietrich von Bethmann observed further that an economic up-turn in Austria Hungary in the foreseeable future could not be expected. The opportunity,

to raise the necessary taxes needed to improve the armed forces had been missed due to the geographical situation and many political mistakes that had caused a difficult foreign policy situation.

In his report to the Reich Chancellor, Dietrich von Bethmann Hollweg by no means tried to hide the fact that one should be very sceptical of the deteriorating situation in Austria-Hungary. The chief factor was the 'nationalities question' that crippled everything. This hindered any possible economic improvement. Further, the effectivity of the public service was being reduced because the entire system into which each nationality demanded to have its representative was being unnecessarily expanded and consequently there was permanent pressure on the 'total interests of the state' caused by the contrary interests of the various nationalities. This became acutely apparent in the extreme financial developments in Bohemia where 'Austria-Hungary' was virtually bankrupt. Again, the very future of the Monarchy depended on whether a Czech-German settlement could be achieved. Certainly here there seemed to be no grounds for a favourable prognosis. As well, the parliament was not functioning; the Minister President Count Stürgkh had not even ventured to convene the upper house (*Reichsrat*) in order to debate the budget.

Finally the Legations Councillor judged that any economic up turn would be hindered by the diminished enthusiasm for work in the population. There appeared to be a general atmosphere of hopeless resignation which had a crippling effect. What would be decisive in spite of all attempts to gild the situation was,

> that between the population's capacity for work and the development of the monarchy on the one hand and demands being made on Austria-Hungary on the other caused by developments in the outside world an unbridgeable gulf existed.

The consequence was that the Danube monarchy had expectations of her place and role in the world that she in reality could not fulfil. But with regard to the German policies towards both Turkey and England that had to do with the Baghdad rail project Austria-Hungary's leading statesman Count Leopold Berchtold [joint Foreign Minister 1912–15] had his reservations. According to Dietrich von Bethmann Hollweg this was well known in Vienna. He certainly made this patently clear to his cousin in Berlin in the following words:

> Austria-Hungary, in spite of the internal fragmentation and the increasing tendency since the Balkan wars towards decentralisation caused by strengthening of neighbouring states and despite her economic weakness which makes any expansion of the armed forces difficult, still wishes her position to be made clear with the same emphasis as before. However, she feels that if there is no significant economic improvement soon *time will have run out*. [Emphasis in the original.]

Consequently, in the most recent meetings of delegates [of the Empire] more than previously, these two factors have been recognised. During the Balkan crisis of 1912/13, the view was wide spread that Austria-Hungary had to have a war to clear the air. The confirmation for this was:

> That it would be perhaps possible by means of a *joint action* abroad to weld together the divergent sections of the monarchy *and if the war could be brought to a victorious conclusion*, it would serve to revitalise the economy. [emphasis in original, p. 12]

The crucial encounter between the German and Austrian decision-makers took place in the hunting lodge at *Springe*. On 23–24 November 1912 on the occasion of a state hunt on the Deister, the Austro-Hungarian eagerness for war had to be bridled because of plans in Berlin to make decisive expansions in the German army. The fact that Bethmann Hollweg was not opposed in principle to a belligerent solution becomes clear in the following:

> Dispassionate observers of the overall situation might say that the advantages of a victorious war may not in the long term outweigh the significant price that would have to be paid. *Indeed it cannot be denied,* that the economic depression that occurred during the course of the Balkan crisis and its consequences for the monarchy were very serious and that here the view has been expressed that it is not cool calculation that retrains Austria-Hungary from war but that also weakness and indecisiveness play a part. [emphasis in original]

This was exactly the content of the discussion during the above-mentioned crisis conference in the hunting lodge at *Springe.* When the Germans resisted following the Austro-Hungarian plans for war exactly that situation arose which Bethmann Hollweg detailed in the following:

In order to cover this up Germany accepts gladly the reproach that she restrained the monarchy from war. If we had declared war at that time, *so it is argued, we would have had peace (Ruhe)* whereas we are now in a worse position and are economically less able to sustain the pressure. [emphasis in original]

Clearly there was no talk of German–Austro-Hungarian alliance in *Nibelungentreue*, that is in blind, unconditional loyalty. This is explained by Bethmann Hollweg as follows:

The fact of German competition in the Balkans is often raised and pointed out that in its relationship to Austria-Hungary she does not adequately involve herself in the economic sphere.

Indeed, this relationship was fraught with considerable competition whereby the Austrians and the Germans hindered each other in the struggle to conclude favourable business deals. In this regard Dietrich von Bethmann Hollweg in the most recent negotiations between delegations had with the utmost clarity pointed out to his Austro-Hungarian partner Dr Baerenreither that the Austro-Hungarians had expanded their commercial activities and occupied those areas which the monarchy had left having accumulated considerable debts. Vienna should rather try to imitate the Germans and operate with the profits which they have made there. On the one hand the Reich has outstripped the alliance partner but thereby destroyed the promising initiatives of Austrian economic policy which this situation is trying to sustain.

Dietrich von Bethmann Hollweg was an important link between his cousin the Reich Chancellor Theobald von Bethmann Hollweg and the embassy in Vienna. The frequent trips of the Legation Councillor between Vienna and Berlin are a good indication. These trips took place not only for official vacations. For example Dietrich von Bethmann Hollweg arrives in Vienna at the end of January 1910 and on 2 February 1911 is already on vacation in Berlin. Then on 13 September 1911 he is again discharging official duties in Berlin though ostensibly on leave. For the same reason on 11 November he is there again with official approval granted after the event which suggests strongly that there was an urgent cause.

In those weeks and months since 11 July there was the threat of war breaking out with France and England over the Morocco question. In February 1912 the Legations Councillor is again in Germany for a family gathering and recreation. On 1 October 1912 he is on leave on his estate Runow (near Wirsitz in the province of Posen) having been promoted to Legation Councillor. He is back in Berlin on 5 December 1912. He carries with him an 'open letter' to/from the *Zentralbüro* of the foreign Office. Again he is on leave in Berlin between Thursday 12 and Sunday 15 December 1912 discharging official and family affairs as confirmed by the ambassador von Tschirschky. His presence there concerned the decisions arrived at in Springe and Berlin. The fact that the situation had become more critical, correspondingly requiring more urgent consultation is reflected in the frequent travelling made by Dietrich von Bethmann Hollweg in the following months of 1913 which was undeniably a time of much preparation in many areas. Between 1, 4, 5 and 21 February 1912 in Berlin the official purpose was 'private business.' At that time there was a visit to the regional command of the army. Indeed, a military exercise took place during a period of leave between 28 March and 27 May 1913. Besides that he received permission to take annual leave in Switzerland between 13. August and 15 September 1913. The Reich Chancellor spent between 2 and 17 September in Graubünden. Then from 3 September Bethmann Hollweg assumed the function of envoy in Belgrade (officially appointed on 30 August). On 2 September he left Vienna and arrived in Belgrade the next day as ordered. Between 18 October and 9 November he was able to add leave in Berlin at the hotel 'Zum Reichstag'. The Chancellor went on 7 November to a hunt (*Hofjagd*) in Königs-Wusterhausen. Between 4 and 7 December there followed a hastily taken leave there, and that was followed by a further period of 'leave in Germany' for 'private matters'.

On 22 April 1914 Dietrich von Bethmann Hollweg was again relieved of having to submit an economic report. He then continues his leave to attend to 'family affairs' on the estate at Runowo near Bromberg. The Reich Chancellor returns on 22 April from his trip to Korfu (Achillaion) having arrived on 23 in Brindisi. On 1 May Dietrich again is on leave to attend the funeral of the Reich Chancellor's wife in Hohnfinow. During the July crisis – after his economic report of 24 June (why now?) – the Legation Councillor applies for 8 days leave to travel to Berlin (Dietrich von Bethmann Hollweg to Goldbach, 16 July 1914). In this connection he considers 'as things were at that time' offering to go on leave to Berlin for a short time (8 days) and in particular to see his mother in Runowo … *because circumstances suggest in the event that authorities in Berlin are so inclined to grant me this short absence which in the context of the possible events appears convenient* [emphasis added]. That meant he wanted to see his mother before he joined his regiment that had already been mobilised. In that case Dietrich was aware on 16 July 1914 that there was going to be a war. Theobald von Bethmann Hollweg had been since 4 July in Hohenfinow ('I am here for the time being').

On 20 until 23 July Dietrich had taken leave ('Address while on leave Runowo-Mühle District of Bromberg, and then to Berlin, Hotel Excelsior'). The Chancellor had arrived in Berlin on 25 July while on 27 July Legations Councillor Bethmann Hollweg arrived again in Vienna back from his leave to await his marching orders after the outbreak of war in Vienna. He confirmed to Count Mirbach in the Berlin Central Office (of the army) as follows:

I understand the order addressed to me is that I have to await the order to report for duty. I hope that it comes soon.

Let me again indicate why Dietrich Bethmann Hollweg at this particular time was required to supply for the Chancellor an economic evaluation of Austria-Hungary after the ambassador had delegated this task to him in April. Obviously there was a particular interest in this document at a higher level.

At this point in time, a few days prior to the assassination of the Archduke Franz Ferdinand in Sarajewo the Legations Councillor had emphasised that the situation was hopeless – in spite of the loans which Germany had made to Austria Hungary in the first half of the year 1914 the situation had become serious as Bethmann Hollweg emphasised:

> A possibility for a stronger and quicker economic development of Austria-Hungary lies perhaps in the raising of larger loans whereby capital could become available to crank up economic activity. – *But even here the problem again arises in the disjunction between the ability and the will.* As was illustrated in the question of the Bosnian loan the Austrians certainly want to have the money but then declare that it is beneath the dignity of the monarchy if the loan contains conditions attaching to the transfers or concessions. *Austria – Hungary was not exactly Turkey.* [emphasis by B.S.]

As far as Austria is concerned the alliance with Germany takes on considerable significance because Vienna's relationship to Berlin excludes any possible French association with the loans market. Consequently financial isolation is a big factor. Indeed, French capital was withdrawn from Austria at the time of the Morocco crisis in 1911. As a result the Danube monarchy became financially dependent on Berlin. That is the background for the considerable loans made during the first half of 1914.

Indeed the concerns raised in the light of the 1,000,000,000 Reichsmark which had been invested in Bosnia were considerably intensified and unleashed discussion Berlin at the highest level. Dietrich von Bethmann Hollweg compared this experience with those of the *Norddetusche Lloyd* and the difficulties which arose in Germany on the question of the eastern network of the Orient Railway. Any further German investment would only be forthcoming in the event that German nationals who would be working in the Monarchy did not encounter any difficulties.

Jagow had already in April 1914 pointed out that Austria would withdraw from the Triple Alliance if loans had been refused. Overall, the Legation Councillor Bethmann Hollweg predicted that Vienna in the years to come because of further financial weakness would repeatedly turn to Berlin in order there to secure the funds necessary. There was no other likelihood of achieving this. Jagow insisted that it was not his task to decide to what extent German political interest and the alliance relationship to Austria – Hungary imposed an obligation on Berlin to strengthen the economic and thereby also the political relationship by support in securing the necessary funding. Obviously, though, the Reich as Dietrich Bethmann Hollweg had mentioned, would have to reckon with such approaches.

The image that Dietrich von Bethmann Hollweg projected on 2 August to Frau Scharffenorth, the daughter of Albert von Mutius, to the author [B.S.], although she had seen him when she was still a child, is nevertheless of considerable significance:

> He was furious, highly irritable. I can only say that he saw everything very differently from Theobald von Bethmann Hollweg. Quick to judge and particularly hard. Bold in asserting his opinion.

Even this representative of a more forceful, more modern German foreign policy expressed a serious warning against further extended financial involvement in Austria-Hungary. And these reservations were further expressed by the personal go-between of the Chancellor in Vienna. He was, after all, his cousin, indeed, an important cornerstone in the leadership system of Chancellor Bethmann Hollweg. All together in view of the depressing financial and domestic situation in the Danube monarchy it was nothing less than a warning that Vienna in the short or long term was facing bankruptcy if the German Reich did not continually support it. But was the German Reich in a position to keep doing that? The situation presented virtually no prospects of any improvement in the capacity of Vienna to fulfil its part of the conditions of the alliance. Jagow already by the end of May 1914 in immediate proximity to his discussion with the Chief of General Staff von Moltke expressed the concern that with a collapse of Austria-Hungary and its division there would arise in its place a Slavic confederation and the German component would be marginalised. The German ambassador in Vienna von Tschirschky referred in this regard on 22 May in conference with the foreign minister as follows:

> But I see no other political constellation which in spite of everything could replace the advantage which the alliance with the central European power provides. Indeed, without this alliance our policy would be perforce compelled to aim at a partition of the monarchy. Whether we would receive *carte blanche* for that from England, even if we could achieve a really firm relationship with her is doubtful ... The fruit, it seems to me, will have to ripen further. Time will tell whether someone will succeed in welding together again more strongly the disparate forces within the nations of the monarchy. *Should this attempt fail then surely the decomposition will occur very quickly and then we would have to revise our policy accordingly.* [Emphasis by B.S.]

Of course, all of that collapsed, at the latest by 26 June 1914 with the memorandum by Dietrich Bethmann Hollweg discussed above. Then, with the murder of the Archduke Franz Ferdinand in Sarajevo two days later his thesis, namely that Austria-Hungary would scarcely be able to remain a useful ally takes on a totally new quality. Tschirschky's admonition to wait was in the end ignored; in the worst case scenario any prospect that the Austro-Hungarian army would be able remain effective for only a few be months. Despite this, however, the Reich Chancellor may have felt constrained due to the development of the situation to have advised Austria to declare war on Serbia in order to test the *Entente* between Russia and France. Indeed, this appears to have been the case particularly in view of the fact that the Chancellor had already on 8 March advised Jagow as follows:

> We urgently need to clear the air with Vienna. In fact Vienna is beginning with her overall policy strongly to emancipate herself from us and needs to be *meo voto* promptly reined in. If you agree[,] I would request that you advise me before communicating with Vienna.

The course of the 'policy of pretention', which immediately prior to the July crisis was repeatedly tested, namely the diplomatic method of the Reich Chancellor, was strictly followed. It was a variation of the so-called 'risk policy' (*Risikopolitik*) as illustrated by the 'blank check' to Austria on 5 July. This is confirmed by the formulation of the hard ultimatum to Serbia of 25 of July and the attempts subsequently in the course of the month to localise the conflict. This political line was pursued with the rejection of any idea of mediation after the Serbian reply to the Austrian ultimatum on 25 July and continued with Bethmann's policy in the 11th hour between 29 and 31 July and finally extended with the persistent attempts to secure British neutrality. Gradually these attempts to win England over evolved as a *deus ex machina*. This option acquired central significance particularly after the failure of the localisation of the conflict on the Balkans. In like manner were the tactics immediately prior to the German declaration of war on Russia on 1 August which declared Russia as the aggressor. It was an example of a well conceived crisis management which was willing to accept the highest risks. It was the Chancellor's concept to strengthen Austrian will to crush Serbia as quickly as possible. Chancellor von Bethmann Hollweg understood full well the possible consequences:

> [Bethmann Hollweg] A future war will be a world war (*Weltkrieg*) and Germany will have to reckon simultaneously with the hostility of both Russia and France. That cannot be helped.

These prospects cancelled out Petersburg in any possible English and French efforts to localise the conflict. The Reich Chancellor had to take that into account; indeed, already in the 1913 crisis the German ambassador in Petersburg, Albert von Pourtales had warned against an attack by Austria against Serbia because it would certainly lead to strengthening of the war party at the Tsar's court.

Comment

Under Theobald von Bethmann Hollweg's Chancellorship, Germany would obviously have preferred not to have to use the 'shining weapon' in battle if by means of bluff the objective could have been accomplished. However, as Kurt Riezler argued, there could come a time while one is practising this kind of policy which Schulte calls, *Policy of Pretension* (using these English words), when the opponents actually call one's bluff and then one has to be ready to fight; indeed gamble in the expectation that one's belief in the superiority of one's forces and generalship is totally justified. For Prussia-Germany, though, the 'dreams and delusion' of hegemony over the entire earth were so persuasive in the mind of the Kaiser, power elite and the *Bildungsbürgertum* that even after the disaster at the Marne mid-September 1914 they determined to carry on and try to implement the original objectivess of the Schlieffen Plan. History has thus pronounced an indictment on the naivety of the *Bildungsbürgertum* as manifested in their wide-eyed confidence in what they perceived to be the German mission to the world. The two German wars of the 20th century were not just explicable by nationalism gone berserk; they were rather the consequences of the German belief in their ideology. Behind all nationalisms there is an ideology at work; a belief in the mission of the nation to fulfil self-nominated goals in the world. But for Germany the evidence is that many of her subjects from the Kaiser down to the lower middle classes and even to some among the working class lived in a kind of 'parallel universe', that is an alien world of ideas totally different from nations anywhere else, and this unique universe had been constructed in the period from the post Napoleonic era after 1815 to around 1895 by which time the Pan German ideology was endorsed by virtually all classes, except the vast majority of the working class.[10] So from then on for at least one hundred years a perception of Germandom (*Deutschtum*) developed the chief characteristics of which were admiration of Prussianism, especially after the Bismarckian successes in uniting Germany in 1871, an associated admiration of militarism, and anti-liberalism and fierce anti-socialism plus, finally, a remarkably virulent anti-Semitism.

These were the core components of what became known as the afore-mentioned 'Wilhelminism'. Social Democrats were regarded as the 'vagabonds without a fatherland' (*vaterlandslosen Gesellen*). So, as pointed out above, by the beginning of the 20th century, Germany had only been 'negatively integrated' to use the designation of Dieter Groh. The Social Democrats, who although increasing their electoral appeal dramatically by 1912 were known in upper circles (*höheren Kreisen*) of society as the internal enemy (*den inneren Feind*). Consequently, as the late Wolfgang Mommsen had observed German society had become increasingly volatile. Karl Kautsky, after the war in 1919, as the chief ideologue of the Social Democratic Party, described Germany as a powder keg waiting to be ignited. How this happened and then set virtually the entire world in flames has been graphically documented in the work of Dr Bernd Schulte.

Dr Schulte's painstaking research serves to reinforce the earlier findings of Professor Fritz Fischer and his school at the University of Hamburg. Indeed, Herr Schulte was a student of Professor Fischer before he became an officer in the West German army, the *Bundeswehr*. After completing his period of service Herr Schulte devoted himself to researching and writing history becoming a distinguished private scholar with many publications to his credit. It is in these that he has published so many hitherto un-accessed documents of key significance. He found that not being a member of staff in any university history department proved to be a distinct advantage. Freed from the obligation to teach undergraduates, and disposing over private means, Dr Schulte could spend more time than most of his contemporaries investigating the private archives of the old military families and deceased politicians. It is precisely in those repositories that he was able to find some of the most valuable source material that provided sharper insight into the imperial German decision-making process than was possible through being restricted to the official state-managed archives. The foregoing has been a most illuminating example. He has shown how desperate the rulers of the German empire were to pursue, despite the huge risks involved, their cherished dream of attaining world predominance for which they needed to sustain Austria-Hungary's viability as a first-class power, albeit as junior partner.

Corroboration

It has subsequently been corroborated by the appearance in 2014 of the second edition of Professor Helmut Bley's book, *Bebel und die Strategie der Kriegsverhütung 1904–1913* that has evaluated the efforts of the long-time leader of the quasi German loyal opposition in the Reichstag, namely the Social Democratic Party, August Bebel (1840–1913), to head off the looming war. Bebel had hoped to accomplish this by urging the British government to intensify efforts to curb the expansionist policies of the German government. He had to do this secretly by making contact with the British Consul General in Zurich, Switzerland Heinrich Angst (1847–1922) who then communicated Bebel's concerns to the British Foreign Office throughout the period 1907 to 1913. Angst seems to have had an English mother (Margaret Jennings) and so grew up both bi-lingual and bi-cultural. His links to the British establishment could not have been stronger as he was knighted in 1903 (Honorary Knight Commander of St Michael and St George) and proposed for admission to the most exclusive Athenaeum Club at that time by none other than Lord Salisbury. Consequently through these associations Angst had the ear of the Foreign Office. He was also in close contact with the British emissaries in Vienna, Copenhagen and Darmstadt and as such well informed about German affairs. So Bebel could not have found a better situated British official with whom to communicate in confidence his anxieties about the belligerent tendencies of the Berlin 'Junker' regime. These in turn via Heinrich Angst found their way to London and are accessible mainly in the papers of Earl Grey in the Public Record Office. Bebel's correspondence with Angst and the latter's diaries are located among Angst's papers in the *Zentralbibliothek* of Zurich.

The value of Bebel's correspondence with Angst lies in the accuracy of the German socialist leader's analysis of the essential objectives of German policy and his observations about the ideological mainsprings of that policy. His analysis of the power relationships and class struggle within *Kaiserreich* highlights its dangerous *peculiarity*.

3. ROUND TABLE MEMBER, WILLIAM ST CLAIR GEORGE ALFRED DONALDSON (1863–1935): THE KEY IMPORTANCE OF KNOWING ONE'S ENEMY

It is the responsibility of the historian to try to comprehend the past through the eyes of the people who have bequeathed their observations of life in their time to the present. It is most fortunate when the past observer was a person of considerable education, especially one who had studied history and was also acutely aware of the complexities of international relations. Such a keen observer was William St Clair George Alfred Donaldson (1863–1935). He was the first C. of E. Archbishop of Brisbane having occupied the See from 1904 until 1921. It proved to be a lively episcopate mainly because of Donaldson's pre-occupation with asserting the Church's witness in a remote British colony where educated and cultivated subjects were not overly represented.[11] Despite his patrician background being the third son of Sir Stuart Donaldson and having been educated at Eton and Cambridge where he gained a First in Classics, the new scholarly prelate strove to build bridges to the Labour movement while at the same time he worked hard to promote missionary activity both within the Australian continent and in the wider Pacific region. He was in the full sense of the term an enlightened imperialist in the Gladstonian mould.

With regard to the Church specifically he is remembered for having supervised the building of the first phase of St John's Cathedral which was dedicated by 1910. Its final completion and consecration took place decades later in 2009. Overall Donaldson became known as an extremely energetic and far-sighted Archbishop who saw in the British Empire an agency of Almighty God for the extension of His Kingdom on earth. This was a widespread notion at the time, shared indeed by most Anglican bishops.[12] In this endeavour, of course, he was bound to ruffle the feathers of the Irish Roman Catholic hierarchy although he really did try to maintain cordial relations with his RC counterpart, Archbishop James Duhig. Rome, of course, brooked no rivals, especially the Church of England. The

Anglican leaders of the Oxford Movement during the 19th and at the turn of the 19th to the 20th century had tried rather optimistically to at least build bridges between Canterbury and Rome, but the Papacy was at that time determined to deny the Church of England any Christian validity at all. Pope Leo XIII (r. 1878–1903) had, indeed, declared Anglican Orders 'absolutely null and utterly void' in 1898 with the Bull *Apostolicae Curae* thus effectively declaring the English Church a sham institution.[13]

This massive rebuff by Rome had effectively poisoned Anglican-Roman Catholic relations for some considerable time although with the lapse of time and the witness of such prelates as St Clair Donaldson who insisted firmly upon the essential Catholicity of the Church of England, ecumenical relations between Canterbury and Rome have now become remarkably cordial with the founding of an Anglican Centre in Rome in 1966. The 1898 repudiation of Anglican orders has been allowed to drift into oblivion in typical Roman fashion, that is without ever being officially repudiated. Why? *Apostolicae Curae* was an official Papal declaration and thus had the force of infallibility, but that is no longer referred to except in ultra conservative Roman Catholic circles. Instead Papal attitudes towards the Anglican Communion have been cordial for some time and may be described as even filial whereby the search for ever closer ties and collaboration has been intensified.[14] Time and scholarly reassessments of past debates have served to heal old wounds. However, at the time of the Great War of 1914–18, sectarian rivalries crackled ominously beneath the outwardly civilised surface. After all, Archbishops of rival Christian churches have to preserve decorum especially when they are together in public. But the situation in Brisbane during the Great War while potentially volatile was not nearly as much as it became in Melbourne where the R. C. Archbishop Daniel Mannix behaved in such a way as to make it totally impossible for any ecumenical dialogue with his Anglican counterpart Lowther Clark (r. 1903–20) to take place at all.[15] In Brisbane, the aristocratic English prelate, Donaldson treated his Irish RC counterpart from Limerick at all times with Christian charity which was for the most part reciprocated. Nevertheless, there was one occasion when the sectarian dragon reared its fire-breathing head and the two prelates felt obliged to engage in some public jousting over allegations that the R. C. Premier and leader of the Labor Party the honourable T. J. Ryan was stacking his cabinet with 'Catholics'.[16]

Indeed, Australia was a Dominion of the British crown that was plagued by the spirit of sectarianism for some considerable time to come. The Irish troubles had repercussions that were felt in the four corners of the earth wherever the sons and daughters of Eire had either been transported in convict times or later arrived and settled as free but mostly poor immigrants, always and understandably an aggrieved minority.[17] The outposts of empire for them they determined should never replicate the blatant injustices that characterised Ireland's relationship with England. Hence the Australasian Irish developed a feistiness that at times exacerbated inter-church resentments. Anglican prelates in the mould like the normally amicable and ecumenically minded Donaldson stood, of course, for reconciliation but were equally adamant that British political culture should prevail. This became most apparent when war with Germany broke out.[18]

Of all the pro-war commentators in Australia Donaldson would have to be considered arguably among the very best formally educated and informed through his establishment family connections in England, as we shall now see. Not only had he won Firsts in Classics at Cambridge, his brother was a very high-ranking civil servant who had been placed in charge of the critical wartime department of munitions production. In short, Donaldson was well connected to the British Establishment. So his commitment to the Empire was a given. That, however, did not prevent him from becoming an advocate of Australian nationhood and for an independent Church in Australia. But as well, Donaldson, as were most of his brother Bishops in Australia, was acutely aware of the tense relations that had been building up between Britain and Germany primarily over the building of Dreadnought class battleships.

In spite of this the German ambassador in London especially from 1907, Count von Lichnowsky, really worked hard to make clear to the Kaiser's government that it was a mistake to alienate the British.[19] Of course, as Paul Michael Kennedy has shown, the deeper causes of the rivalry between Britain and Germany went beyond colonial or commercial ambitions. Rather the hostility was at base ideological. As Bismarck himself believed, close relations with a parliamentary state were bound to be unstable because with the inevitable changes in government that characterise parliamentary states treaty arrangements entered into by one regime could easily be repudiated by a subsequent regime of contrary ideological commitment. As earlier indicated Bismarck preferred alliances with essentially autocratic, monarchical regimes.

Consequently, the Prusso-German political mentality was schooled to be suspicious of all parliamentary regimes. Educated Britons came only gradually to comprehend the underlying reasons for this as the *Eyre Crowe Memorandum* of 1907 illustrated.[20] But as well as politicians, British Churchmen of most denominations also came to be concerned about relations with their German cousins as the remarkable tour of Germany by British Churchmen of all denominations in 1908 had illustrated.[21] At the base of the mistrust, as was eventually revealed, was the German-Lutheran/ Hegelian comprehension of the nature of the State as an entity which functioned as the agency of almighty God on earth and which was not subject to any moral restraints imposed by the Church. In short, the State was *sui generis*, and as such a completely autonomous entity with the power to pursue any policies it deemed necessary for its continued existence. The Church, for German Protestants at least, was only relevant in the private sphere and had no brief to interfere in the business of politics. Indeed, the Protestant Church perceived itself as the handmaid of the State. Although ostensibly autonomous in the spiritual sphere it was very much subordinated to the all-powerful State. This is very different from the self-perception of the Church of England precisely because it was/is the Established Church of the realm which perceived itself as essentially the *conscience of the State* and did not shrink from admonishing the State if its political leaders acted in contradiction to the ethics of the Gospel.[22] Consequently, in order to understand the Church of England at the time of the Great War one needs to comprehend this principle. It certainly was dominant in the mind of

Archbishop Donaldson when he wrote and published his addresses on Christian Patriotism, in Brisbane during Lent (the weeks between Ash Wednesday and Easter) 1915.

In a remote and obscure corner of the Empire a prelate of considerable intellectual stature was able to compose a uniquely Anglican theological rationale for the Christian duty to resist Prusso-German expansionism. *Christian Patriotism* is a document of Australian, indeed imperial intellectual history that has been overlooked by the secular historical profession. This needs to be rectified because as an analysis of Anglo-German relations at that time it is uniquely perceptive. Donaldson had only returned from leave in England just after the outbreak of war. While there, through his intimate Establishment connections in the person of his high-ranking civil service brother, Donaldson learned of the seriousness of the breakdown of relations between London and Berlin. Two great world Powers of indeed kindred racial roots were about to engage in a life and death struggle to re-constitute the world in their own image. [23] So, apart from being as well informed as it was possible to be about British perceptions of German designs, Donaldson was by education and commitment able to bring to bear his unique insights into the seriousness of the situation.

What these carefully crafted addresses indicate was that Donaldson had a sharpened perception of what the enemy intended and from where their political will derived. He wished to demonstrate to his flock who consisted of 'all sorts and conditions of men', many of whom were educationally disadvantaged, that they were up against an enemy of an especially peculiar kind. Donaldson knew about Prusso-German peculiarity and was at pains to inform his listeners what the implications of this were. Hence the addresses are a series of admonitions to *know the enemy*. The highly educated Archbishop felt compelled to enlighten first the people of Brisbane and then the wider Australian population what they were up against in the unfolding struggle between Britain and Prusso-Germany, and he had the training to do just that.

The addresses are structured in such a way as first to make clear to the Brisbane audience the danger with which the entire Empire was confronted. Donaldson appreciated full well that the people of the Antipodes experienced some difficulty in comprehending this. The vast distances separating the people of Australia from the centre of conflict in Europe, especially those living in the outback, impaired their capacity to see that they were in any danger at all from the consequences of that conflict. This clearly exercised Donaldson's mind as it did many academics at the time. There was a great need to inform the citizens of the country about the war in all its aspects.[24]

Secondly, Donaldson was in the unique position, as were most of the Anglican bishops, for being able to understand German war theology. For their German counterparts, especially in the Lutheran Church, war had a totally different purpose. God for them was essentially a warrior God as was frequently the case in the Old Testament for the Hebrew tribes. The extent to which this theological concept has influenced German thinking about politics, especially, international relations, is immeasurable. As was shown in chapter 3, Prusso-German political culture from the time of Martin Luther's struggle against the Papacy in the 16th century had developed a vastly different comprehension of Church–State relations in contrast to that which came to distinguish English political culture. Some people, even today, tend to think that if a statesman was pious and believed in God and the Church then his policies would be benign and life-affirming. This was never the case in Prussia-Germany because the Prince was always *summus episcopus* as well as being an absolute monarch who had at times to take decisions that appeared to contradict the ethics of the Gospel. Nevertheless, the monarch's will was in effect God's will, and subjects should never venture to question the will of God. On the eve of the Great War, as already indicated, strenuous efforts were made, especially by British churchmen to inform themselves about Church-State relations in Germany. Archbishop Donaldson had been clearly aware of this as is illustrated in his addresses reproduced here.[25]

So Donaldson's purpose in his lecture series *Christian Patriotism* had been to explain to his people who obviously did not have the same educational advantages as a Cambridge Don what a German victory over England would mean for the overseas Dominions. His approach, admittedly, may have been far too theologically subtle. For example, Donaldson was at pains to show that the point of prayer to the Almighty was not to be guided to victory but to recognize God's will: 'Thy will be done!' And there was a distinct possibility that God's will could favour the enemy. If this were so one had to accept it and live with the consequences because nothing is outside the sovereignty of God.

It will be seen, however, that Donaldson's informed views about the nature of German political culture re-enforced his belief that the British ideal of Empire was closer to the mind of the God as revealed in the New Testament.

These lectures are included here because they provide insight into the mind of thoughtful people at the time, and in their judgements about the mind of the enemy they are acutely perceptive. Finally, though, the reader will see that Archbishop Donaldson was highly conscious of the unique gifts bestowed on each nation which contributed to the greater good of humanity. Each nation including especially the German, had its particular strengths and in Donaldson's conviction these derived from the Creator. But in his estimation of God's plan these should work in harmony with the Powers, not in conflict. In short, Donaldson's views stood in starkest opposition to those embraced by most German theologians and intellectuals as indicated in chapter 5 where the historicism of the Neo-Rankeans is discussed. For some, no doubt the difference between that and Donaldson's 'Christian Imperialism' may be too subtle to comprehend. But we are encouraged to try.

What follows is a statement by Archbishop Donaldson in the form of a series of short Lenten address held at St John's Cathedral in early 1915, that is at a time before the Gallipoli campaign when people had not yet fully grasped the implications of the great European war. As he wrote:

> I should not have thought it worth while to print these addresses – I am doubtful about it even now were it not that

they embody certain ideas which seem to me important but have not yet found a lodgement in the public mind.

Our object in these days should be to create an enlightened public opinion which may direct the policy of our leaders when peace comes in sight: and that public opinion depends upon the earnest prayers and calm thinking of citizens who are not only patriots but also Christians.

St Clair Brisbane.

Christian Patriotism

I

The Fundamental Assumption

I must begin this course of addresses with a few words as to their scope. The object of our gatherings will not be directly the worship of God: for that ample opportunities are provided in this place at other times. Nor will my aim be to lead you to think of those great things which Lent more especially brings to our minds. Of these I hope to speak more directly on the next six Sunday evenings.

My object on these Thursdays is in some sense a special one. The times are abnormal, and while undoubtedly they cannot fail to affect every single one of us in one way or another, the danger is lest we miss the greatness, the epoch-making greatness of the crisis we are passing through, lest now that the hour of trial is upon us we should fail in the test.

In what sense are we under trial? On the outward political, military side of things it is easy enough to describe it. We are at war, and the war will tax the resources of our Empire to the very uttermost, both in wealth and in human life; and we are on our trial in that it will now be shewn whether we are prepared to endure right to the end the suffering and struggle which must inevitably be the price of our Empire's freedom. Assuredly our first duty is to school ourselves in a way we have hardly begun to do as yet to make sacrifices for the common weal.

But the trial which has come upon us on the unseen and spiritual side of life is very much more difficult to describe, very much more complex in its character and infinitely harder to confront worthily. I cannot state it better than in some recently uttered words of Bishop Gore of Oxford. 'The duty has come upon us,' he says, 'of seeking to interpret the purpose of God in this tremendous crisis of the world's history, and to organise in the Nation a common mind among those who above all things are anxious to know our Lord's will, and so to prepare that the issue of the war may serve the purposes of the Kingdom of God.'

The war is testing our Christianity. It will now be known whether the crisis has caught us unprepared, unwatchful, unable to feel rightly about so great a thing. It has come to try our Faith in God's Purpose: it will search out our readiness to sink self and all personal desires in the paramount desire that His will may be done. And the test comes in another way; our practical effectiveness as Christians is to be tried in the face of a great crisis of evil. We hold a faith which is capable of lighting up and explaining the most perplexed passages of human life. We believe that we share a life which has a dynamic force upon all evil everywhere, and we find ourselves today like a break-down gang on the railway that has just arrived at the scene of a ghastly railway accident. It is our duty to understand what has happened, to work unceasingly at the grim task of delivering the crushed and quivering human frames of the victims out of the savage confusion of the broken machinery. It is our business to clear up that same machinery, to renew it, to piece it together for the beneficent use of man. In a word, we are called today in the power of Christ to get to work upon the broken debris of civilised society, to turn evil into good, to stop the present mischief as soon as may be and to make it serve the purpose of the Kingdom of God.

This is the searching trial which is now before God's people. It is a trial of a moral and spiritual kind, and so is far more difficult to meet than any mere call to arms. And we can only hope to come worthily through the ordeal if we are prepared earnestly and patiently to enquire of God, to endeavour to understand His general purpose and to test our own preconceived notions, by the teachings of our faith. It is my object in these lectures to confront this task. It is a complex task: for not only our mind, but our heart and will is concerned. Not only must we discern the facts before us: we must think rightly, and feel rightly about it. And to begin with, we must use our imagination to estimate the gravity of the crisis. This is an elementary duty and would not be so necessary if we Australians were living nearer to the grim realities. But it seems that, do what we will, we cannot stir ourselves to measure the issues at stake. We must try, then, to realise the greatness of the crisis, and we must view it as it concerns ourselves. 'What is required of me, how can I help, what can I give?' But there awaits us a far more difficult duty than that. We must face the crisis in a right spirit. The Christian conquers the world not so much by his actions as by the spirit in which he acts. 'This is the victory which overcometh the world,' says St John, 'even our faith.' And our faith means more than a mere belief that God will help us. It reveals to us God's purpose and the spiritual side of political events, and so brings home to us our own duty in view of these spiritual facts. And then, conscious of the spiritual issues at stake, we must try to think out our relations as an Empire with the nations of the earth. We must clear our mind as to the principle for which we are fighting and which we seek to leave established in the peace which is to follow. For indeed it is not too early to be thinking of peace. If we wait until peace is in sight, our chance will be gone. It will be too late to learn our duty. It is now, while the awfulness of struggle and suffering is upon us, that we shall most truly and completely ascertain the will of God.

You will see then that a difficult task is before us; and for my part, I have been reluctant to speak on so great a thing; but the call was imperative, and I knew that if only a few of us are earnestly trying to view the crisis aright, God will enlighten us, and others perchance by our means. Accordingly I have undertaken to speak upon Christian patriotism. In my second address I hope to speak of our obligation to our Country viewed from a Christian standpoint, and then we will examine the religious meaning of our Empire, and in the last address we will endeavour to probe the future and recognise the price we have to pay for our Empire's progress and the particular duties which will be involved in our efforts to secure a lasting peace.

But today I must pause over the fundamental assumptions upon which all our duties and all our aspirations are built up, for everything depends upon this. Our outlook upon the work, our judgment of it, our conduct in it all depend ultimately on our creed, and human creeds are really the basis of all human actions. It is true that often in modern Christian society a man may act upon Christian principles although his real beliefs are quite materialistic; he is carried with the stream and appreciates the conclusions, even though he cannot accept the premises of the Christian argument. But ultimately the Christian is able to pitch his ideals higher than the materialist simply because he forms them on the assumption that spiritual help is available for the realising of them while the other does not. It is natural that a man who has no hope of help from anywhere outside himself will be less bold in his spiritual adventure than a man who says, 'I can do all things through Christ which strengtheneth me.' Thus in considering our obligations as Christian patriots everything depends upon our grasp upon the Christian assumptions with regard to the conduct of the world and the trend of human history; and you must bear with me if I seem in what follows to digress far from the subject in hand. Indeed it is not a digression, but vital to our whole view of the subject. All that I shall have to say in future addresses depends upon what I am going to say now.

The Fundamental Assumption

The one great fundamental assumption upon which all Christian thinking must be based is that, behind the visible order of things, inspiring, permeating, directing all is the will of a Personal Being. We believe that the whole universe is just the expression of His mind, and that His mind and will is in every particle and detail of it. We assume that He gave existence to this great order of things with a definite purpose, a purpose of love, and that this purpose of love is as a matter of fact being worked out on a scale infinitely beyond our ken, yet including all that we see and know and experience. We believe that in the prosecution of this purpose of love the human race bears a part; that in the slow evolution of the world the human race was to appear on earth according to the counsel of God, to play some glorious and wonderful part in the drama.

A God of Love

This is the fundamental assumption. We believe that there is a God of Joy and that in spite of all the confusions and perplexities we see, He is working out in the universe His great beneficent purpose. Without this assumption the world would be a chaos; it lies at the base of the Christian creed.

The Fall

But the Christian believes that the purpose of God is passing through a particular stage, an episode, as we may call it, in the Drama of the universe. He believes that the purpose of God has suffered hindrance through the sin and wilfulness of man, and that whereas the Divine counsel contemplated a steady upward course in the development of creation from the lower to the higher, from the beast to the man and from man material to man spiritual – a check has occurred; material man has not gone on to the higher spiritual status; he has remained stationary, endowed indeed with spiritual capacity but enslaved also to the material. This is the ancient doctrine of the 'Fall,' and although in modern days we have been led greatly to modify the drapery in which human thought has clothed that far-off and mysterious event, yet nevertheless it remains true that fallen greatness – a spiritual career corrupted – is the best explanation of the contradictions and confusions which we all know are characteristic of human nature. If you want to see this thesis magnificently stated, I would commend to your notice the *Thoughts* of Blaise Pascal, from whom I can only quote a brief extract.

What a chimera, then, is man! what novelty, what monster, what chaos, what a contradiction, what prodigy! – judge of all things, imbecile worm of the dust, depository of the truth, sink of uncertainty and error, the glory and refuse of the universe. Who shall unravel such a tangle?... We have an idea of happiness and cannot attain to it; we have a conception of an image of truth, and only are in possession of falsehood; capable of absolute ignorance and certain knowledge, thus much is manifest, that we were once in some degree of perfection from which we have unhappily fallen.

Since Pascal's time the theory of evolution has arisen, but while that theory has modified our thinking it has in no way excluded Pascal's postulate of the Fallen Greatness of Man. The Christian evolutionist looks back to the dim past and sees man gradually emerging from the lower creation, developing, not further capacities of the body, but instincts for the higher life, a new and undreamed of consciousness of himself, the impulse to rise to the divine. But all the while he feels the pull of the lower nature too, and he uses his nascent freedom to choose the lower and reject the higher and so begins to oppose his will and purpose to the will and purpose of God. This is the beginning of the trouble and this is the fundamental truth about human nature which is taught us in the allegory of the Garden of Eden.

The Great Process of Recuperation

But that is not all. The Christian holds that man has not been forsaken in his collapse. A great recuperative process is at work. Since the Incarnation, the spirit of Christ is operating in the world, bringing men back to the original purpose of God. We contemplate the Fall of man without despair, because we believe in his redemption. It is as though a great rebellion had taken place in a well-ordered State. An official is appointed to restore order, but the task is long and arduous. It is only by steady perseverance, by the slow development of the spirit of loyalty permeating the population that order can be restored. One by one the citizens must learn obedience, but meantime the official remains in office. That is St Paul's view of the world in its present stage. The confusion is being unravelled; there are many sets back; but in the whole there is progress. Meanwhile the power of Christianity is undiminished though not yet finally victorious. 'He must reign,' he says of Jesus, 'until He hath put all His enemies under His feet.' But in another place we read, 'We see not yet all things put under Him.'

A State of Transition

Here then is the fundamental assumption with which we Christians look out upon the world today. It is in a state of transition. It is gradually passing out of the wild state of lawless rebellion into conformity with the original purpose and Will of God. The process will be a long one, and we are not taught to expect that all enemies will be put under His feet at any period within the ken of living man; but our faith teaches us to believe that sin will at last be conquered here on earth and that then (if I read St Paul aright), man being at one with God, will gain the Spiritual nature originally intended for him and so will rise superior to death, 'For as by man came death, by man came also the resurrection from the dead. For as in Adam all die, even so in Christ shall all be made alive.'

We have travelled far away from the main subject. But I think you will have marked the connection. We must see clearly the Purpose behind human affairs before we can rightly play our part in those human affairs; and my point is that races and nations are called to co-operate in the furtherance of the great purpose of God for the world. That is what they exist for; and their prosperity and greatness, as well as the happiness of the world, is involved in the faithful obedience with which they fulfil their destiny. But of this I shall have more to say in my next address.

Meanwhile our duty is plain as the followers of Christ whether corporately or individually, whether as citizens of a nation, and members of a Church, or as individual souls working out our personal destiny, we know that the duty of duties is to seek the Will of God and make it the purpose of our life to conform to that. The one priceless possession given to us here on earth is the power to choose; and so the real battle in every life (a battle which is only won through constant conflicts and many failures) is to choose the thing in life which is really worth doing, to surrender our own personal will in loving obedience and unfaltering trust to Him who made us. It is not merely that we must accept things which happen to us in that spirit; we must dedicate our energies, we must consecrate the creative power which is ours in the same direction. In His great struggle for the conquest of evil today, Christ calls for the co-operation of every one of us, and He is content with nothing less than the loyal offering of our will. 'Sacrifice and meat-offering, Thou wouldest not: but mine ears hast Thou opened. Burnt offering and sacrifice for sin, hast Thou not required: then said I, lo, I come. In the volume of the book it is written of me that I should fulfil Thy Will O my God; I am content to do it; yea Thy law is within my heart.'

II

Our Obligation to Our Country

If my object in these addresses were merely to kindle patriotic enthusiasm, I think I should spend my whole time today in telling you stories about Ancient Rome. Roman history teems with fine stories of patriotic devotion, and the example of those sturdy Roman patriots appeals perhaps in a special degree to the congenial British character. I will, however, content myself with only one.

Marcus Atilius Regulus was a Roman General and Consul in the 9th year of the first Punic war, 256 BC. After several brilliant victories Regulus was completely defeated in the year 255, and taken prisoner by the Carthaginians. After five years' captivity he was sent, in the year 250, to Rome on parole to initiate a peace, or at least an exchange of prisoners; but the fierce old soldier lent all his energies and all his eloquence to defeat the

Carthaginian proposal. 'There must be no peace,' he said, 'and no prisoners must be exchanged. The discomfort, the sufferings, even the death of a few of Rome's sons in the land of their enemies is nothing compared with Rome's present opportunity of crushing Carthage; let there be no truce, no consideration of individuals so long as the Senate can secure the peace and well-being of Rome.' Such was the spirit of Rome's life and death struggle with Carthage. The friends and relatives of Regulus pleaded with him for some compromise. But he turned a deaf ear and presently went back in fulfilment of his word to an unknown death in the land of his enemies. Later and perhaps less authentic stories relate in detail the tortures which the Carthaginians inflicted in their disappointed rage upon the obstinate Roman who had defeated their schemes. They are probably without foundation, but I begin with this story today because it throws into relief the principle upon which all great patriots act, viz., that our country has a right to everything we have; our money, energies, well-being, our health, and even our life itself. That since we have adopted the social ideal and chosen to live as members of a State, we must pay the price of our privileges. The State can only exist if we recognise this principle. It can only remain happy and peaceful in so far as the citizens readily and cheerfully accept this paramount and solemn obligation.

But we must not suppose from this that patriotism is a mere contract; merely the price we pay for certain privileges such as protection, peace and civilized life. Rather it is a fundamental instinct sown in our hearts. The love of one's country is in some ways parallel to a man's love for his mother. It is a natural instinct. The capacity for love no doubt varies with the individual; it is certainly stronger in some than in others, and for aught I know there may be some few who lack it altogether, but as a general rule the capacity is there, and we deem him something less than a man who is without it. I think I may state it as an axiom without fear of contradiction that the love of one's country is an essential element to the noblest character and that through this channel, more perhaps than through any other, there has been opened a road to heroism and self-sacrifice even to those characters whose previous moral record has been elementary or confused.

But if patriotism is capable of mending the broken wares of Society, how much more does it transfigure and glorify the average citizen? And for this cause I confess to a certain jealousy for the character of the citizens of Queensland. Of the general soundness of our patriotism I have no doubt at all; and we must, I suppose, admit that we cannot reasonably expect the same alertness of mind, the same poignancy of emotion, or the same prompt readiness to act in the inhabitants of the bush districts of Queensland that we find in parts of the Empire which are more directly threatened by the enemy. Moreover, when calculated by financial tests or by the actual numbers sent to the firing line, the share of Australia in the Empire's struggle, though obviously far below what it might be and far below what Britain itself is providing, is calculated to win the commendation of Imperial authorities. But I confess that I am not satisfied. Considering the weakness of our youth as a nation and our utterly unprotected coast-line, the present confidence of Australia suggests not self-reliance so much as childish ignorance. The fate of Australia, the fate of Queensland is now being tested upon the battle-fields of Europe and in the North Sea, and I cannot but feel it strange in such circumstances to note the apathy and self-content aye and sometimes the self-conceit of many of our people. I commented the other day upon the absence of recruiting in a certain bush district and asked the reason why no young men were forthcoming. The answer was that they 'reckoned that they might get killed'. In connection too with the proposed defence force of senior citizens, I heard of a cricketer who asked, 'Will this defence force interfere with our cricket?' These two instances are certainly not typical of the general feeling, but they do suggest that even now our people are not alive to the crisis; they do not yet see that when the national· existence is at stake it is unmanly to cling to the amenities of life. They have not yet learnt that patriotism is something more than an exhilarating emotion and means sacrifice.

But I must not linger on this subject. It is very familiar to you, and the outward and secular side of our country's demand is on all lips. If I have felt obliged to say familiar things over again, it was because I simply could not speak about our obligation to our country without delivering my soul.

But my object today is altogether different from this. Our subject is *Christian Patriotism*, and it is time I made clear what I mean by the term. Patriotism, as we all know, is not an exclusively Christian virtue. I have already spoken of it as an instinct of human nature, and I need only point to the example of Japan in its war with Russia to show how deeply this noble passion can stir a non-Christian nation. But Christian patriotism is a more spiritual thing. It appears when the natural instinct is blended with certain· presuppositions about the conduct of the world, certain convictions about man's relation to God: and when these ideas and instincts are blended together the old human quality begins to shine with a new radiance.

National Vocation

Here then I take up the thread of my theme of a fortnight ago. The Christian's fundamental assumption, I said, was that God has a purpose of love for the world, and that that purpose is working itself out, in spite of sets back and confusion in all directions, through the steadily operating force of the Spirit of Christ working among men. This purpose, we believe, is finding its fulfilment, among other ways, through the medium of *nationality* and *race.* I cannot now stop to discuss the fascinating question of the origin of these great phenomena. I dare not even attempt definitions. But my meaning is, I think, sufficiently clear when I claim that not only individuals but races and nations often develop obvious distinctive characteristics and capacities, through which they are able to contribute to the world's progress. History gives abundant instances of this. *Rome,* for instance, has left an indelible mark upon the civilization of the world, and its characteristic gifts to the world have been due to its genius for law and government. *Greece's* impress upon the world has been no less indelible, but Greece's strength has been in the direction of art and philosophy. The *Hebrew's* distinctive genius has been the capacity for knowing God and realising man's true relation to him. If we could analyse our modern civilisation, we should find how utterly different our mental equipment would have been if any of these three races had been omitted from history. To each of them we owe an incalculable debt; and we could not have achieved our present stage of progress without them. And we can extend our review into modern times. The *Teutonic* race has some plain characteristics. On the one hand its intellectual activity, and on the other hand its mysticism, has enriched the world. The *French* nation, the most vigorous of the Latin races, has an intellectual and artistic leadership of its own among modern nations, but perhaps its most characteristic contribution to the modern world has been its spirit of relentless logic, both in thought and in practical life. The impetuosity – I had almost said the violence – which characterises French history is due to this tendency to press things to their logical conclusion. And herein lies a speaking contrast between them and the Anglo-Saxon with his instinct for compromise. But I must not enlarge upon the contribution which seems to be characteristic of the *British* race for that will occupy us, I hope, next week. I am only concerned now to insist that races and nations, in so far as they are true to themselves, have each a characteristic contribution to give to the world's progress, and that this is part of the larger purpose of God. And if any doubt remains as to the teaching of our religion in this matter, I would advise you to turn again to the witness of the Old Testament. Throughout the early history of Israel, the Patriarchs, the Judges and the early Monarchy, we trace the principle of selection; the selection, that is, first of individuals and then nations not to privilege but to service, not merely to worldly greatness but to opportunities for contributing to the well-being of humanity. The call of Abraham was essentially a spiritual thing. There was indeed a promise of worldly prosperity, but the object set before him in plain language was that in him and in his seed all nations of the world should be blessed. So it is all through the history of the Old Testament. Even Gentile nations were recognised as called and used of God. 'For this cause have I raised thee up,' Jehovah is made to say to the representative of the Egyptian nation, 'to shew in thee My power.' And in the case of Israel itself the sense of vocation steadily grows. The prophets are full of it, and the whole principle is re-stated with memorable fervour by St Paul in his Epistle to the Romans.

III

Application of This Principle

If all this is true you will see that the Christianising of patriotism throws a new and transforming light upon much of our ordinary thinking. It teaches us that God calls Nations as well as individuals to His Service: thus it corrects current ideas as to what patriotic duty really is; it teaches us new things about the spirit of our prayers in war time, solving incidentally some familiar problems, and it points us with new emphasis to old and familiar duties.

It affects our prayers

(1) I would begin with our prayers. The very moment war begins men are thrown back at once, so to speak, upon their spiritual reserves. They seek to claim the highest sanction they know for the justice of their cause; they fly to prayer. And herein lies a difficulty. When Christian nations are at war, both sides are turning to God. At the present moment, days of prayer and humiliation are being held in Germany as well as among us, and I need hardly remind you that this fact is eagerly taken up by the scoffer and the cynic. In the Boer War an atheist lecturer in a London Park sneeringly said that Boer and Briton alike are appealing to their God, but it is all waste of time because victory will go to the big battalions. And I was surprised and I confess rather disgusted to read the other day an article in the *North American Review* for October last taking the same line. The writer pictures the hurry and confusion in the courts of heaven as the prayers come soaring up from belligerent nations. 'In the meantime,' he writes, 'prayers continued to accumulate in the outer courts and it became a crying question, 'What is being done about them?' Particularly as those human beings, steeped to the lips in the 'blood of their fellow men and kneeling on the festering heaps of those they had slain had all been praying to the same God, 'the God of peace, the God of truth, the God of righteousness and love and

mercy.' They came to their 'altars reeking of slaughter, their faces lurid with the smoke of powder and the flames of the peaceful cities and villages they had burned ... Yet something must be done about their prayers for victory; these prayers could not all be turned down; they could not all be granted. The most embarrassing phase of the affair was their praying, friend and foe alike, to 'the same God, and claiming Him their Champion with implicit belief in His devotion to "their interests".' All this is very unpleasant and cynical and we might well be surprised that a great periodical like the *North American Review* should descend to such cheap stuff, if it were not a fact that the current ideas among Christians about prayer do not seem to reach to a much higher level.

Undoubtedly the ordinary man's idea is that prayers in time of war are necessarily prayers for victory. He has not thought enough on the subject to take a deeper view, but the deeper souled Christians, wherever they may be, in Germany, Russia or England, are praying less for victory and more *that God's Will may be done* whatever it be. The more the Christian progresses in his Christian course, the more his prayers tend to take this form. The object of our life is to co-operate with God's purpose and for the mature Christian I suppose God's Will and his own personal happiness tend to coincide. *We* must bear this in mind in our prayers about the war. I do not for a moment suggest that we cannot conscientiously pray for victory, but I plead for a wider outlook, a truer spirit of surrender. Our object is that the Will of God may be done: 'Thy Will be done on earth as it is in heaven'; that is our daily prayer, but that Will of God might conceivably involve the defeat of our arms. It might conceivably be that the things we love and the interests which concern us are the things which must go to Calvary for the world's good. It is hard to contemplate such things, but as Christians would we not a thousand times rather have it so than win a victory against God's Will? God's Will is the essential thing; it is the key to the world's happiness and progress, our own as well as others, and after all, in the seeking of God's Will lies our national progress and well-being, even though national defeat and disaster were an incident in the process. Whichever way it be, through success or failure, through victory or defeat, the Christian must eagerly, self-forgettingly, whole-heartedly be striving after God's Will. Does this seem a high and impossible line of prayer? Surely not if we have taken hold of the truth of national vocation. If nations and races are called to a God-given career, if each has some contribution to give to the world's progress, then surely our prayers in war time are regulated by due safeguards. We pray that no nation's vocation may be frustrated by the tyranny of man, whether through the oppression of the weak nation by the strong, or through the intemperate use of victory when the war draws to a close. Again we shall pray that no nation's vocation may be frustrated through its own transgression or failure in duty. If our own British policy is selfish, though we know it not, or ambitious or prompted by avarice, we pray God to shew us our fault and to bring us to repentance and amendment. 'Faithful is He that calleth you who also will do it.'

It Affects Our Political Attitude

(2) And that leads on to another corollary of the principle of national vocation. It throws, as I said, a new and transforming light upon our current ideas of patriotic duty. It reminds us that for the Christian the love of his country cannot be a mere blind love. I compared the love of one's country to the love of one's mother, and after all a noble son's love of his mother is a discriminating thing. If he sees her falling into some degrading temptation, the very love he bears her prompts him to interfere. A tragic situation may indeed arise in consequence, but his very love nerves his will and many a noble son of a drunken mother has faced the ordeal to the end. Even so, the doctrine of 'my country right or wrong' must always be abhorrent to the Christian. It is not mere territorial expansion or increased wealth or fame and reputation which he desires; he longs to see his country take the upright line and stand always for what is noble and good. In other words, believing in his country's vocation, he desires above all things to see her walk worthily of that vocation and to come short in nothing.

And for this reason there are times when a Christian patriot may be called upon to face bitter opposition and obloquy, for the lower pagan sort of patriotism is still far too common amongst us. Much that goes by the name of patriotism among us is merely selfishness masquerading under a false name. There are commercial men whose hunger for fresh markets is the real impulse of their patriotism. There are promoters of great schemes of territorial development, promoters of great railway projects and so forth, whose patriotism is self-regarding and whose desires have never considered the well-being of neighbouring nations. Against such influences, from time to time the Christian patriot is called upon to protest. The Old Testament gives us a noble archetype upon which to model our conduct in this matter. The prophet Jeremiah represents the tragedy of the situation in its acutest form, and thank God few of us indeed are called upon to take his stand. He preached the surrender of his native city and incurred the undying obloquy of all his countrymen in consequence, though indeed his love for Jerusalem· was deeper than that of all his opponents. But he knew that in surrender lay the best hope for his country, and subsequent events proved that he was in the right. It was a terrible and tragic ordeal, and we shall all hope and trust that we may be spared such an experience. The mere possibility of it however ought to make us very tender and patient to those who, however misguided they may seem to us, feel it their duty to oppose the national policy. You remember the bitterness shewn against the pro-Boers during the Boer War and Mr Ramsay Macdonald and Mr Keir Hardie are facing a like opposition today. I do not wish in any way to associate myself with these statesmen. I am totally unable to conceive their position, and the arguments with which they have defended it seem extraordinarily weak; but I do with all my heart admire their courage. They happen to be on the wrong side as we view the case, but we must never forget that from time to time Christian patriots are called to stand up in the breach and stem the tide when the current of national opinion is setting to what is wrong.

It Affects Our Attitude Towards Religious Work

(3) But the occasions for such protests will naturally grow rare as the standard of Christian thought and feeling rises in the nation and this

leads me to the third and concluding corollary of our principle of national vocation. The surest way to secure national faithfulness is to promote national religion and this promotion of religion, if you think it out, becomes a duty of every single patriot who claims to be a Christian. We come here on to very familiar ground, but I should be untrue to my message if I did not say over again in this context, what we Christian preachers are saying times without number in all contexts and in all connections. The national life, the national strength and well-being is based upon the fear of God, and there is no question more crucially important for the statesman to consider than that of the sound encouragement of national religion. It is true that our unhappy divisions have imported new difficulties into the task, but the fact remains that the raising of the religious standard of the people is the most important of all the elements of national well-being. And this in plain language to you and me means the support of the Church. I am not ignoring the obligation felt by those of the Christian community who are not of us. The obligation is upon them as it is upon us and as we are debarred through our own sin and disputing from the inestimable benefit and strength of a single national Church, it remains for us to promote each our own expression of our Christian faith as best we can. And in this work of cleansing and raising the national life who can doubt that the Church of England is called upon to play a pre-eminent part? She is rich with the treasures of the past. In every age of our national history she has played a great and generally a faithful part. She is holy with the record of a great line of saints, whether kings, statesmen, doctors, or priests. She is strong with the sturdy strength of the race which she has molded into a nation. She is living, yes still living as we know by countless experiences, with the life of Her Lord which first called the Church into being and is ever manifested to us in the sacraments. Can we be blamed if we look to our mother Church of England as the hope of the great Australian Nation to be? Can we expect forgiveness if we cease to work and pray that that Church may grow and take root and be strong and fruitful in this new soil for the healing of the nation as it grows, for the enriching of the world, and for the glory of God?

IV

Christian Imperialism

In the year 1788, in the presence of a great company representing the flower of the nation, Edmund Burke in Westminster Hall opened his memorable impeachment of Warren Hastings. Warren Hastings had recently returned from India, having laid down his office of Governor General. He had done more perhaps than any living man to lay the foundations of an Empire in that sorrowful and stricken land. But he had been a Governor of the old Roman type. He had mingled with his supreme capacity for governing an evil strain of cruelty and extortion, and so on his return, Edmund Burke was determined that he should be brought to book, and the greatness of that long struggle in Westminster Hall lay not merely in the calibre of the men opposed to one another, but in the clash between two ideals of Empire which there came to a head. Edmund Burke's nine days speech on the impeachment of Warren Hastings may be taken as marking the dawn of modern British Imperialism.

What is Imperialism? Since Burke's day the British Empire has spread all over the world, and Britain's fame and influence and commerce have penetrated far beyond where her flag flies. But I must at the very outset distinguish between the British Empire and what it stands for: between Britain as a political organization and British Imperialism as the force behind. The former is a political combination; it is a matter of territories, peoples and government. The latter is an ideal, and it is the ideal about which I am to speak today. I hope to shew that Imperialism in the sense that I shall presently define it, is characteristic of our race; an instinct which, after lying dormant for a while is now coming out into full consciousness, the secret force to which we owe all that is best and noblest in our history. More than that, I hope to shew that this instinct implanted in our race is a sacred trust committed to us by God, a gift entrusted to us for the good of mankind, a talent for which we must give account.

Imperialism then is the formative ideal – Empire is the embodiment. And if we would study British Imperialism, we must first look at the British Empire in which it has found expression. 'By their fruits ye shall know them.' And in the story of the British Empire we have the fruits of British Imperialism, the characteristic expression of its inward nature. It is a great, moving spectacle and to understand it fully we must get behind the great panorama of noble lives and actions which have brought it to its present position; we must discern by a comprehensive view the underlying principles; and then it is, and not till then, that we shall marvel at the mighty experiment which is going on at this moment before our eyes. The British Empire as we see it today is unique in the world's history. There has been nothing like it since the dawn of time, and it was with full intention that I just now used the word 'experiment.' We cannot claim as yet that the Empire is more than an experiment, but the more we study it, the more hopeful we are of the future, the more certain we are that the experiment is worth trying.

The unique character of our Empire is seen when we compare it with those which have gone before. History tells us of many; of Babylon and Assyria, of Egypt and Persia, of Greece and Rome, of Spain under Philip II. and France under Napoleon. All these Powers, though widely different in their setting, may claim I suppose to be Imperial, but differing as they do, there is one characteristic common to them all and in sharp contrast with our Empire of today. Between them and us there is a great gulf fixed, and it goes down to the fundamental ideas upon which their Power is reared up. The old conception is passed away: a new spirit, a new idea has been behind the Empire-building of Britain. What was that old conception, the characteristic of all conquering nations of the past? It was this. *All other Empires have been based upon the extinction of Nationality.* With the Assyrians and Babylonians this, as you all know, was a settled and conscious policy. The Assyrians deliberately removed the whole population of Israel and dispersed it in Halor and in Habor and in the cities of the Medes, that the national tie might for ever be dissolved. Nebuchadnezzar in like manner transported the population of Judah and with a like intent. Imperial Rome, throughout the period of her dominance, crushed out nationality with a heavy hand, and sought to establish Roman citizenship as the one and only Imperial connection. And she succeeded so completely, she mixed the races throughout Italy, Greece, Egypt and the East so thoroughly that a chaos of races ensued through the centuries succeeding her fall which only the new nationalities surging up in modern Europe have been able to shake off. And Napoleon's policy was the same. His motive was selfish ambition, and in his schemes of conquest nationality found no place: there was no lingering sense of responsibility for the people he conquered, and wherever he applied a constructive policy, he applied it in the interests of the governing and not of the governed State. And so we might go on. The old ideal of Empire was power, wealth, and dominance, and the first step to this was always the destruction of nationality.

But the British Empire is founded upon liberty. With the British race the word 'Empire' has come to bear a new meaning. The old definition no longer applies and our Empire of today stands upon a foundation far above the Empires of the past. In that one word *Liberty* we find the secret of Britain's moral greatness, aye, and also the safeguard of her strength.

Liberty

There is indeed more than that, but liberty is the main foundation, and we must trace the influence of liberty in the history of our race before we pass on. The ideal indeed has been with us from the first, and the love of liberty has been mingled with our blood from the dawn of our existence: but we can point, I think, to a definite crisis in our history when we learned to apply our instinct in dealing with others. It was our American colonies who taught us the lesson. Up to the end of the eighteenth century we had not as yet learned the true principle of Empire. In dealing with our American colonies we were prepared, like all our predecessors in Empire, to be self-regarding, to govern them in London in London's interests and not their own. But our American Colonies rose in revolt, and in throwing off our yoke they schooled us to a new and better ideal. We did not make the same mistake twice. Colonies began to spring up in other parts of the world and England had her chance again. To these new and vigorous communities the Motherland spoke with a new and different voice. 'Realise yourselves,' she said, 'develop your resources, grow into nations and I will protect your coast line from attack. Look to me as your Mother. I will expect no return from you in the days of your weakness. My reward will be to see you nations like myself.'

England learned to substitute the policy of liberty for the policy of dominance and so laid the foundations of an Empire such as the world has never seen before. It is still, I admit, an experiment. Never before have a number of free nations attempted to act permanently in common. Never before have peoples far asunder from one another been bound together by mutual confidence in the purest spiritual bond, the bond of their common passion for freedom. We are attempting in the British Empire to reconcile two words which the world has hitherto regarded as mutually exclusive- Empire and Freedom. The experiment may fail, but I ask you in God's name, is it not worth the attempt?

Justice

But the Empire stands for more than this. Freedom is for grown men. The atmosphere of freedom is too strong for the tender spirit of children. They must be under authority during their tender years, that they may qualify for the freedom of manhood through a period in *statu pupillari*. As with children, so it is with the child races of the world, and nowhere is the Imperial instinct of our race shewn to better advantage than in shepherding the child races which have come under our care. What is the secret of this? Let me here say in parenthesis that I do not ignore the darker side of our history. All British statesmen, soldiers, and merchants, have not been true to type, and there are many dark spots in the history of our expansion which no comprehensive view could possibly ignore. But I am not here giving a comprehensive view of our history. I am seeking to emphasize the main features of British rule and in my conscience I believe that the picture I am drawing is substantially true. What then is the secret of Britain's marvellous influence upon all subject races? It would be hard to answer this question briefly and I will content myself with mentioning the main ingredient in her success. British influence is due mainly to British justice. Wherever the native races learn really to know the British governing classes, they know Britain is to be trusted. A British official keeps his word. A British official judges justly and moreover is not to be bought with money. This has been the secret of our influence. We have no doubt done a great deal of fighting in India, but the peoples of India have come under British rule not so much through conquest as through the conviction they themselves have felt that in Britain they would have an assured protector and a ruler under whom they might live in prosperity and peace. Within our own memory Egypt has afforded an example of the same process, not less eloquent than India. What is the significance of the twenty years' administration of Lord Cromer in Egypt? It is just a triumph of Britain's integrity, a triumph of her unselfish devotion to the wellbeing of the poor and backward over the injustice and oppression, the selfishness and incapacity of the Ottoman rule. But I need not multiply instances, for the facts are plain to you already. The British Empire is built upon justice as well as liberty and the policy we have pursued is assuredly vindicated before the whole world today. We seem to be reaping our reward. From the very beginning of the war we knew that one objective of our enemies would be the seduction of our subject races from their allegiance. That objective has been pursued with persistence and skill. Nothing seems to have been omitted in the attempt to foster disaffection in India, Egypt, and elsewhere, and the end of it all so far as we can see is unshaken loyalty to British rule. This is no small thing; it means that our work has not been in vain. For generations we have given them of our best; hundreds of statesmen, civil servants, officers and financiers have toiled and sacrificed their health and often their lives in the service of the millions of our coloured fellow-citizens; it is no small reward in these days of the Empire's stress and danger to find that our coloured fellow-citizens do not forget. I believe that when posterity reads the lessons of this war in their true proportion, the loyalty of our native races will stand out as a final and convincing testimony to the integrity and justice of Imperial Britain.

So then freedom and justice – for these things the British Empire stands. It is by virtue of these two shining characteristics that our race has expanded over the world, has shewn so unparalleled a permanence and cohesion and has exerted so magic a power in the development of subject races. How then shall we define Imperialism? What is the ideal, the instinct at the back of it all? It seems to me some innate, unexplained, inevitable tendency to concern ourselves in the affairs of other peoples. Not as busybodies, not from motives of self-seeking; but because of an instinctive conviction that we are able to help. You have seen a jibbing horse in Queen Street. The crowd looks on inactive, but one man comes out of the crowd and helps the driver in his distress. What makes him more active than the others? It is that he knows that he can help. Even so, there is an instinct in our race which understands the desires and aspirations of other nations. We know we can help, and so we are impelled by a sort of destiny to mix in their affairs. Imperialism has been defined *as patriotism transfigured in the light of the aspirations of humanity* (Professor Cramb). I am content to leave it at that.

V

The Empire

A God-given Responsibility

We see then that British Imperialism is an instinct implanted in our race, which marks us off from other nations, not by any superiority, for they too have their talents, but as giving us a distinctive task to perform in the progress of humanity.

Whence did it come and what is its spiritual significance for us Christians? We are in no doubt as to our answer. It is the gift of God. It is a talent bestowed upon us, not merely for our own well-being or wealth, still less to minister to our pride, but as a means of helping the world; and a great responsibility is attached to it. We cannot glance over the history of our race without growing increasingly conscious of a Divine purpose linking together the epochs and the fortunes of successive generations into a consistent whole. If we believe in the general purpose of God for the world, if we believe that God uses nations and races, as I tried to shew you last week for the fulfilment of some part of his plan, then a glance at English history will convince us beyond gainsaying that Britain is a case in point. We look back to the beginnings of the Nation in England and we know how our Anglo-Saxon and Celtic forefathers were left to consolidate their national life for generations undisturbed from outside. Once they had landed, the sea they had crossed preserved them from interference. Thus independent national characteristics could grow in ·strength and simplicity. Then we see how the nation grew through the long centuries, nourishing in its soul the thoughts of liberty and expressing itself in that direction time and again when potentates at home or abroad seemed to challenge its spirit, until through the bitter struggles of civil war the people of England in the 17th century made themselves finally masters of their own destiny. So the great turning point approached. Having won liberty to themselves it was inevitable that the people of Britain should eventually secure it for others. It is not for nothing that all through the 18th century British adventurers were swarming all over the globe, carrying with them the national love of freedom. Burke first gave formal expression to the thought of Britain's mind, and all the political combinations which have sprung up in the 19th century, the self-governing dominions in Canada, South Africa, New Zealand and Australia have but embodied the principles which he first heralded to the world.

Can we· mistake the lesson? Can we shut our eyes to the purpose which has directed this great process? Can we doubt that in the Divine counsels for the progress of the world Britain is called in the providence of God to play a great and noble part? This is the faith of the Christian Imperialist. With the historian and politician he marks and rejoices in the racial characteristics; but on his own account he recognizes that these characteristics constitute a solemn call to serve the world, a responsibility given of God.

The Larger Patriotism

If I have made myself clear today you will see that our study of Christian Imperialism has laid upon us a new obligation. With the obligations of patriotism in the narrower sense I think we are already familiar, and no one can live long in Australia without knowing that the love of his country is a living and a burning motive to the Australian citizen. I believe that the Australians are prepared to give their all for the safety of Australia. That is as it should be, and I thank God for it.

But today we are contemplating a wider patriotism. The obligation to the Empire is not so easily grasped as the obligation to our country. It is a more spiritual thing. It has its home chiefly in the world of ideas and is not like the narrower patriotism rooted in the soil we tread, in the air we breathe. Consequently I doubt whether the average Australian is as yet alive to the obligation which rests upon him as a member of an Imperial race. He does not as yet understand how he himself is involved in the fortunes of England and Canada and South Africa. Still less can he conceive that the contribution of Britain to the world's progress depends upon the moral and spiritual attitude of such as he. I believe a great deal of education is needed before we can reach this point, and my main objective in delivering these lectures has been to call attention to the subject. Our Imperial destiny is threatened by other foes than those who are fighting us in Europe. It is threatened by the ignorance, the carelessness, the narrowness of mind of so many of our citizens. Great as are the possibilities of the future, it is certain that they cannot be realized by the dreams or the labours of a few outstanding men. If the Empire is indeed to be used of God in the future for the good of man, the first essential is that the Imperial idea should permeate the national life and grip the mind and heart of the average citizen. We have to take the spiritual, the Christian view of Empire. *We must rise above the more selfish view which is so commonly taken, at all events in Queensland, that the Empire is a convenient safeguard to Australia against possible enemies.*[26] We must rise to the thought that, as a race we have a great calling from God and that that calling can only be realized by efforts on our part in two main directions. First we must promote the unity of our scattered dominions in order that, united closely together, we may keep alive the spiritual ideals which at present we hold in common. The Empire is worth maintaining, not merely because of its value as a means of defence against military attack, but far more because it is the shrine of a sacred flame which must be preserved in the interests of the world. And secondly, following from this, we should be prepared to defend it against all attacks. Men usually go to war for causes which are tangible and concrete; but wars are sometimes waged for causes which are tangible and concrete; but wars are sometimes waged for an idea, and in the strength of an idea men will fight as they cannot fight for a meaner cause. It is not altogether in self-defence that we are now at death grips with the power of Germany. Deep in the heart of the British race there is an idea, and if we are faithful to our trust now, that idea will bear fruit and multiply among our descendants in the generations to come.

VI

The Price of Imperial Progress

We have heard a good deal in the past few years about the decadence of the British race. Things have happened in the past six months which have effectually put a stop to talk of this kind. But nevertheless it is natural to wonder at times whether our Empire has passed its youth. As in the life of the individual, so in the life of a race, youth is shewn in the capacity for enthusiasm for a great ideal. 'Capacity to frame, resolution to pursue, devotion to sacrifice all to a great political end.' So also, when a race becomes incapable of unselfish enthusiasm and wedded to self-interest, when its individual members become self-centred and cynical, then the process of decadence has begun. Can we estimate in this sense the present age of our Empire? Professor J. A. Cramb, of Queen's College, London, in his book, *The Origin and Destiny of Imperial Britain*, makes a carefully drawn comparison between the rise of the Roman race and that of our own, and he sums up his enquiry as follows:

> 'If the question were asked, With what period in the history of Rome does the present age correspond?, I should say, roughly speaking, it corresponds with the period of Titus and Vespasian when Rome has still a course of three hundred years to run.' But he goes on to guard himself against prophesying about the future. 'The British Empire may be said to have reached today a stage represented by the age of Vespasian and Titus in ancient Rome, but the difference in the circumstances of the two Empires makes it impossible for us to produce the lines of parallel into the future.'

At the same time while the inscrutable darkness of the future prevents our promising ourselves another three centuries of active life, that same future may have things in store for us which may prolong and develop the Empire's career far beyond that period. Fresh blood adds new energy to effete stocks. The self-recuperative powers of the race have been strengthened in the past. They may be strengthened again and again in the future. We hope they are being strengthened by this war. At least we may believe that the Empire has not yet passed its prime and that, given certain conditions, a great and ever expanding future lies before her.

Given certain conditions. It is the price of Imperial progress to which I seek to direct your attention today. I remember when I was an undergraduate, hearing the late Mr W. E. Forster address a great meeting in Cambridge on the subject of Imperial Federation. The idea was new in those days and perhaps the vast audience of undergraduates stirred the blood of the old statesman, for I have never forgotten and I do not think I ever shall forget the emphasis and the emotion with which he directed us to the future.

'We often hear it said,' he spoke somewhat to this effect, 'that our Empire must inevitably go the way of all Empires, it must grow old and crumble and die. But what has brought past Empires to their down fall? Has it been the mere effluxion of time, or has it not rather been the luxury and self indulgence, the vice and selfishness into which they allowed themselves to fall? But these things are not beyond our control. The future of the Empire depends upon you. If you will follow Rome in her self-indulgence you will hasten your Empire's end; but set before yourselves the ideals of your fathers; follow duty and self-discipline, preserve humility and the fear of God, and the Empire may yet grow beyond our dreams in the generations to come.'

That was the substance of Mr Forster's appeal to us undergraduates, and we know that history corroborates his words. The issues at stake in the Empire's life are not physical, but moral and spiritual, they lie not in the world of politics or commerce, but in the world unseen.

And we have the corroboration of our view from a direction quite other than history. Our fundamental assumption throughout these lectures is that the world is directed by the purpose of God. We are regarding the career of nations and races from the Christian point of view as dependent upon their obedience to the Divine will, and we believe that the same penalty follows disobedience with them as with individuals. Like the individual, the race which has ceased to fulfil the Divine will is removed out of its place.

> Every branch that beareth not fruit, He taketh away, but every branch that beareth fruit He purgeth that it may bring forth more fruit.

The progress of our Empire in the future depends upon the moral and spiritual standard we achieve.

The Coming Test

If I am not greatly mistaken, the moral and spiritual standards of our race are shortly to be probed and tested to the quick. Before many months are out we may hope, the great problems of the peace settlement will be coming before us, and that period will bring with it a trial far more searching than the trial of war. In war it is the material strength of the nation which is put to the test and the human qualities which war brings out, the spirit of sacrifice, courage, endurance, patience, are all indirectly connected with material things. We are all of us thanking God that so far our race has come triumphantly through this ordeal. But after all, what a common thing courage is! Every incident reported of the war seems to include some deed of heroism. In this, all nations seem alike. There seems little to choose between German and British, Frenchman and Turk. The German troops can advance majestically to certain death singing the *Wacht am Rhein*, and German sailors as well as British can line up on board their sinking men-of-war and face death with a cheer. Heroic courage is no rare thing. But at the close of the war we shall be called to a more difficult task than the task of dying well. Whatever the peace settlement may be, a challenge will be made to the choicest and rarest gifts of the human soul. The possibility of our defeat hardly bears thinking of; but this much is sure, that if it should come the Christian element in our patriotism must be to the fore, or we shall perish indeed. In national calamities the distinction between true and false patriotism will inevitably shine forth. If you want a speaking example of the contrast between the two, read over again the story of the revolt of Ishmael the son of Nethaniah, after the destruction of Jerusalem, and compare it with the silent, passive, yet undying patriotism of Jeremiah. In his insensate revolt and the murder of the Governor Gedaliah, Ishmael believed he was playing the part of a patriot, but it was a false patriotism and only brought further disaster upon the country he claimed to love. May God deliver us from any such experience. But I pass from this contingency to the other and I plead that we should prepare ourselves to judge rightly in case victory crowns our arms. Let us assume that Britain is in a position to speak with weight with regard to the final settlement. Let us assume for the sake of argument that she is free to impose or remit burdens upon the vanquished, to take or leave for herself as she pleases. What, in this contingency, in view of our position in the world, in the light of the vocation of our race, are the principles for which we should stand?

(1) First and foremost we must bear steadily in mind the great principle which we have proclaimed to the world as the ground of our intervention. We are lovers of liberty, and when we sent our ultimatum to Germany on account of the violation of Belgium we were proclaiming the sacredness of Nationality; we were claiming the freedom of every nation and race to realise itself, to develop and preserve its full maturity, to make its appointed contribution to the world's progress. This claim for freedom has ever been conspicuous in our relations with the smaller races of Europe.

When in 1821 Greece began her long struggle for independence from the Ottoman yoke, the sympathy of Great Britain took a practical form in the operations of the British fleet.

Then in 1832 the national spirit of Belgium claimed separation from the alien rule of Holland, and again England helped and joined in guaranteeing her as a neutral State by a treaty – that scrap of paper of which we have heard a good deal in the past six months. Poland, partitioned by the Congress of Vienna, has constantly chafed at the disintegration of her national unity and again British sympathy has been with her more than once, though practical help has been impossible. And what shall we say of Italy? England thrilled with the first vibration of national unity which stirred Italy in the forties and England stood by her with staunch and cordial sympathy until in 1866 the cession of Venice to the Italian monarchy completed the establishment of Italian nationalism. Yes, we believe in a nation's right to realise itself and however much the inexorable logic of facts has at times deterred, and rightly deterred us, from embroiling ourselves, yet the sympathy has been there; the principle has been there, and it is ours today. But we must apply it all round. Germany too has her rights, and supposing the day were ever to come when the future integrity of Germany depended, however indirectly, upon British policy, we are bound by our past history and by our present convictions to respect her national integrity as a sacred duty. Her present insolent pretensions must not blind us to the truth of her Divine vocation. What we are fighting is not the true German spirit, but a monstrous perversion of it. We must indeed take no risks in our efforts to ensure the future peace of the world, and if Germany cannot be taught to renounce her dreams of world domination by force, we are bound to go on until we render these dreams impossible or perish in the attempt. But Germany also has a contribution to offer to the higher wealth of humanity and we must respect that contribution, if ever the occasion arises, as no less sacred than our own.

(2) And what then? We must not indeed allow ourselves to be too optimistic with regard to the final abolition of war. The Congress at Vienna which met in 1815 after the Napoleonic Wars, believed that it was establishing a reign of universal peace, yet the war drum was heard again in Europe within six years; and even if the menace of Germany were removed, the possibility of war would exist in a dozen other directions. But nevertheless it is impossible not to hope great things at the end of this war, and we may surely expect a far greater step forward in the direction of peace than has ever been taken before in the world's history. When the war is over the world will be in a chastened mood, and it is surely safe to predict that nations will enter the Council Chamber this time with a quite unexampled willingness to listen to reason. It is true that after other wars exhaustion and suffering have taught men reason, but this time surely there will be more than the mere exhaustion of war. In the first place for a generation now the civilised world has been growing more and more impatient of armaments. Everywhere there is a growing determination that, whatever happens, we will never return to the insane, wicked, wasteful accumulation of arms which had reached its *reductio ad absurdum* in recent days. Peace when it comes must somehow preclude for all future time the insane folly of national competition in armaments. Militarism was beginning to make life impossible.

And there will be another motive if I am not mistaken, deeper than this. The last century has seen surely a wonderful change in the general conscience of Christians on the subject of war. We have grown more tender – softer if you will – towards physical suffering; and the sufferings of war, brought home to us nowadays with all the vivid accuracy of the camera and the stop press cable have a direct effect upon us which was unknown to our fathers. The career of Florence Nightingale stands out as a landmark in the course of this development. The opposition, indeed the indignation, with which her work of mercy was at first received among soldiers of the old school is on record as an indication of the rapidity with which our feelings have developed. But it is not only on the physical side. Men are beginning to feel in their conscience that war is wrong and in this war at least the new spirit has been unmistakably shewn. We have lost the old self-confidence, the loud swashbuckling spirit, which was formerly the fashion in war time. Instead of that there are inward misgivings, conflicting emotions, regret mingled with our indignation at our enemies; we are conscious of contradictory impulses to kill them and shake them by the hand. In all our war preparations there is a noble inconsistency. We hate war, yet we are giving all we have to prosecute· it. We long for peace, yet we refuse under present conditions even to consider it. With one hand we are spending unheard of millions upon engines of destruction, while with the other we are pouring out millions to provide amenities and mitigations of the horrors of war. Our whole attitude is becoming more and more illogical. The war spirit is coming under the scrutiny of the Christian conscience; the animal ferocity in man is being challenged by human compassion; and conscience and compassion are gaining ground.

There is reason therefore to expect that the step forward toward the abolition of war will be a far greater one this time than ever before, and meanwhile it may be allowable to consider the actual measures which it may be possible to take towards the establishment of a permanent peace.

A good deal has been said already about the establishment of a reconstructed Hague Tribunal which shall be in a position to enforce its findings by the weight of civilized public opinion, backed by a definite international force. It is an attractive idea, but I fear hardly practical politics yet. International armies have not been a success in the past, and an international force placed at the disposal of the Hague Tribunal could be controlled by no real authority and would never survive the jealousies, intrigues and misunderstandings of the nations for more than twelve months. Only if the nations of Europe were grouped together in a single government could such a force be permanently organised. But meanwhile two great principles must somehow find expression in the new Europe if peace is to be stable – the principle of the sacredness of nationality and the principle of organized co-operation between nations. Perhaps our own Empire, of which I spoke last week, has the one lesson to teach which Europe most needs. This thought is cogently expressed in an article of the current number (January 1915) of the *Round Table Review*, from which I quote:

> There are two main conditions of progress towards European stability and peace. On the one hand, all Europe must abandon the doctrine that any nationality has the right to denationalize or extirpate another; in other words, every nationality must have the right to use its own language, develop its own culture, and follow its own domestic way of life. On the other hand, it must be recognized that this interpretation of national right does not, in equity or of necessity, demand expression in a separate sovereign State. Liberty is the child of law, and law has no sufficient sanction except that exercised within its own borders by a sovereign government. Even such a government, moreover, must be strong enough to maintain its right against other governments; and many National States, if sovereignty were delimited by nationality, would never have that strength. It follows, therefore, that the British method of uniting nationalities freely within a larger State, which secures their common interests without denying their individual rights, is, in fact, the only sure road of progress towards a European polity in which the rights of nationalities will be securely fixed. English and Scotch in Great Britain,

British and French in Canada, British and Dutch in South Africa, are all examples of the manner in which this may be achieved.

Be that as it may, we look, if not for the final abolition of war, at least for its removal to a far more distant background than it has ever occupied before in the history of man. We believe this not only on account of the outward indications upon which I have already touched, but because of our inward convictions as Christians. We profess to believe in prayer. We profess to believe that the spirit of the Prince of Peace is striving with the unruly souls of men. Shall we not believe that the prayers of Christ's people throughout the world are going to bear fruit? There are many unprecedented things about this war, and among them is the fact, which I think is indisputable, that Christian people everywhere are praying with a new spirit. They are praying, not in a spirit of intolerance and enmity – as the evidence shews that most of our forefathers prayed – that their own side might win, and that God would abate their enemies' pride, assuage their malice and confound their devices, but with a new spirit of charity and humility men are praying for a rightful issue, for the return of the true spirit of Christ, for a peace which shall unite the nations for ever. This I claim is a new thing, in the inner history of war and I cannot help feeling that we Christians will be false to our creed if we are timid in our anticipations. Let us realise the difficulty, let us admit that human wilfulness and selfishness will take a long time to conquer; but let us beware of the folly, the faithlessness, aye, the presumption of those who shake their heads and say 'you will never stop war.' At least the policy of Christians must be the policy of those who mean to try.

(3) And a further obligation comes upon us, born of what I am constrained to believe is the besetting temptation of our race. We must 'take heed and beware of covetousness.' It is ever the temptation of the victorious to enrich themselves unfairly at the expense of a helpless foe, and times without number in Britain's wars, both great and small, the net result has been increased territory or increased wealth. The temptation

will assuredly be with us again; may God keep us from falling. We went into this war with clean hands; let us keep them clean when the settlement comes. Of course in any case, if victorious we stand to gain. Germany's trade has had a set-back which should open wide the door to British commerce. It will be our own fault if we fail to take the opportunity. But the eager inflow of commerce to markets unexpectedly thrown open is a different thing altogether from the policy of avarice which seeks to seize new markets by political means. And moreover the question of annexation of territory will have to be faced. Have we not already at least our fair share of the surface of the globe? Can it be part of our mission to the world to be ever seizing new land to the exclusion of other expanding nations who have a colonizing instinct? I know that a very cogent reason can be urged in each separate case for our permanent occupation of German territory which we have captured. But we must not decide upon annexation until we have looked at the matter in its largest issues. Other nations besides Germany are watching us. Other nations need expansion as much as we and they see that we fail to fill the lands we have, while there is not much room left in the temperate parts of the earth outside our Empire. When peace comes in sight the nations of the world will be watching to see whether we are really fighting for principle as we allege, or whether after all it is markets and territory and power for ourselves. Let us 'take heed and beware of covetousness.' Let us lay down the sword as we have taken it up with clean hands.

[Finally] It is always interesting to anticipate the future. It may not always be profitable and our forecasts are constantly wrong. Often we are too optimistic and often, too, the storms we anxiously anticipate do not break. But such anticipations are not necessarily waste of time and at least we ought so far to forecast the future as to be able to face it with honest and conscientious resolve. This has been my object today and in this whole course of lectures upon Christian patriotism. I have been conscious of my unfitness to handle so great a subject and it is likely enough that I have expressed opinions with which many would disagree; but this is a secondary matter. The one thing that really matters is that Christian men and women should learn to apply their Christian principles to the world of practical life and I can think of nothing at this moment of more crucial importance than that the Christian conscience should make itself felt today throughout the length and breadth of Christendom. The world's future for generations, perhaps for all time, depends upon it. The future of our own Empire depends upon it and my appeal to you is that, over and above all the material things that you are doing to serve your nation and the Empire at the present time, you should add this supreme and paramount contribution *of your own soul*, fortified by prayer to God, consecrated by honest attempt at obedience to His Will and boldly bearing witness before the world for the ideal of our race. If in our generation we can set ourselves to discern the purpose of God working in the world, if we can reverently trace the signs of His plan for our nation and race, if discerning His plan we can learn with wholehearted obedience to conform ourselves, our national policy, to His Will; we shall be doing our part to safeguard the Empire and to promote the progress of the world. But the first step is the battle of surrender in our own hearts, for it is only through our obedience that our spiritual vision will be cleared to discern the Truth. This is our hope. In the sanctifying of democracy, in the individual conversion of the mass of the citizens to the obedience of Christ lies the hope of our race. 'Thy people also shall be all righteous; they shall inherit the land for ever, the branch of my planting, the work of my hands, that I may be glorified. A little one shall become a thousand, and a small one a strong nation; I the Lord will hasten it in his time.'

4. THE GERMAN AND AUSTRALIAN NAVAL SQUADRONS IN THE PACIFIC IN 1914

German Pacific Fleet 1914	HM Australian Fleet, 4 October 1913
In 1914, the East Asia Cruiser Squadron numbered six major warships under the command of Vice Admiral Maximilian Reichsgraf von Spee	Note the significance of the addition to the Australian Fleet Unit in 1913 of the **battle cruiser**, HMAS *Australia*.
Scharnhorst-class cruisers	**Battle Cruisers**
SMS *Scharnhorst*, armoured cruiser, 1906, 12,985 tons	HMAS *Australia*, 19,200 tons
SMS *Gneisenau*, armoured cruiser, 1908, 12,985 tons	**Light Cruisers**
Dresden-class light cruisers	HMAS *Melbourne*, 5,400 tons
SMS *Dresden*, 1907, 4,268 tons	HMAS *Encounter*, 5,880 tons
SMS *Emden*, 1908, 4,268 tons	HMAS *Sydney*, 5,400 tons
Bremen-class light cruisers	**Torpedo Boat Destroyers**
SMS *Leipzig*, 1905, 3,816 tons	*Warrego*, 700 tons
Königsberg-class light cruisers	*Parramatta*, 700 tons
SMS *Nürnberg*, 1906, 4,002 tons	*Yarra*, 700 tons
SMS *Königsberg*, 1907, 3,814 tons (East Africa)	**Building in Sydney**
Gunboats	**Light Cruiser**, HMAS *Brisbane*, 5,400 tons
Bussard class	**Torpedo Boat Destroyers**, 700 tons, *Torrens, Swan, and Derwent*
SMS *Condor*, 1892, 1,864 tons	**Building in Great Britain**
SMS *Geier*, 1895, 1,918 tons	**Submarines**, AE1 and AE2
Tsingtao-based	
Gunboats *Iltis, Jaguar, Tiger, Luchs*	
South Seas Station	
Survey Ship *Planet*	
Auxiliary cruisers	
SMS *Cormoran*, 1909, 7,250 tons	

5. GERMAN POLITICIANS AND HISTORIANS WHO HAVE BOTH CRITICISED GERMAN MILITARISM AND THE DECISION FOR WAR IN 1914

Fritz Fischer (1908–99), was the first notable post-1945 historian to revise the received German version for the causes of the Great War and must be counted among the most influential historical-political pedagogues of the 20th century. His publications that exposed the aggressive militarism and expansionism of the Reich leadership of the time unleashed the so-called 'war-guilt debate' that has continued from 1964 at the latest until the present day. See John A. Moses, 'The Fischer Controversy Re-Visited' in the Bibliography.

Imanuel Geiss (1931–2012) was first educated as an interpreter for English and French and then studied history under Franz Schnabel in Munich. Afterwards he became an assistant for Fritz Fischer in Hamburg when on a research assignment to the East German Archives in Potsdam he discovered the 'September Program' of 1914 which summarised German war-aims. This enabled Fischer to confirm his conclusions that the Wilhelmine Empire bore the chief responsibility for the outbreak of war in August 1914 as well as its duration. See Imanuel Geiss, 'The Outbreak of the First World War and German War Aims', *Journal of Contemporary History*, Vol. 1, No. 3 (July 1966), pp. 75–91.

John C. G. Röhl (b. 1938) of Anglo-German parentage was educated at Stretford Grammar School and at Corpus Christi College, Cambridge. This led to a distinguished career in contemporary German history and a professorship at Sussex University where his last major publication is a multi-volume, monumental study of the life and times of Kaiser Wilhelm II. Professor Röhl is a vigorous critic of the recent work of the Cambridge professor Sir Christopher Clark.

Hartmut Pogge von Strandmann (b. 1938) is a German-born historian who first began university studies in Hamburg with Fritz Fischer and then moved to Oxford where he became a full professor in modern history having produced numerous pioneering books and articles focussed on the ideologies and personalities of the German *haute bourgeoisie* prior to and during and after the Great War. As with his colleague John Röhl he is a decided opponent of the work of Christopher Clark. See the Bibliography for his key works.

Volker R. Berghahn (b. 1938) was born in Berlin and as a university student studied in California and England. He took his PhD at the London School of Economics in 1964 and soon became Professor of History at Coventry from where he re-settled in the USA first at Brown University and finally at Columbia where he occupied the prestigious Seth Low Chair. Professor Berghahn's academic record singles him out as arguably the most distinguished trans-Atlantic scholars of modern history of our times. See the Bibliography.

Franz Schnabel (1887–1966) was a distinguished liberal Roman Catholic scholar who throughout his academic life opposed Prussian militarism and National Socialism. He was thus selected by the US occupation authority to head the post-1945 de-Nazified Department of History at the University of Munich in 1947. There he lectured weekly to over one thousand students in the *Auditorium Maximum* on Prusso-German 19th century and contemporary history. He was the outstanding historical political pedagogue of the immediate post-war era.

Hermann Kantorowicz (1877–1940) was a notable professor of jurisprudence at Kiel during the Weimar Republic and is renowned posthumously for the publication by Imanuel Geiss of his *Gutachten zur Kriegschuldfrage* (legal opinion on guilt for the outbreak and duration of the First World War). During the Third Reich Professor Kantorowicz occupied a chair at Oxford. See John A. Moses, 'The War Guilt Question. A Note on Politics and Historiography in the Weimar Republic', *Australian Journal of Politics and History*, Vol. 61, No. 1 March 2015, pp. 128–34.

Walther-Peter Fuchs (1905–97) was a leading German Reformation historian at the University of Erlangen. Prior to and during the war he had endorsed the Hitler regime but as was the case with Fritz Fischer he underwent a 'Damascus Road Experience' and became dedicated to explaining how the German people were seduced by National Socialism. For him a major contributory factor was the *statist ideology*, derived from Lutheranism, that inspired most of the German history professors. The political-pedagogic legacy of the guild (*die Zunft*) of historians from the mid-19th until the mid-20th century had fostered a culture of unquestioning obedience to the 'powers-that-be' which in the Third Reich had led to a disastrously submissive political attitude on the part of the educated elite who should have known better.

Professor Waldemar Besson (1929–71) was originally trained as a historian at the University of Tübingen under the émigré Professor Hans Rothfels and prior to his graduation studied at the University of Santa Barbara in California where he became impressed with American democracy. This resulted in his doctoral thesis on President F. D. Roosevelt whom he admired. Besson followed that up with a detailed study of the Nazi take over in his home state of Württemberg. Concerned always to relate history to politics, Besson in the early 60s moved to Erlangen where established the chair of political science and attracted many democratically committed students. In 1966 he accepted the call to the new university of Konstanz where he continued both as an outstanding teacher and commentator on current affairs. His neat message to his countrymen at that time was: 'Germany must dance at three weddings simultaneously: one in Washington, one in Moscow and one in Brussels.'

Bernd Felix Schulte (b. 1947) was prior to his university training an artillery officer in the *Bundeswehr*. After his period of service he studied for a doctorate under Fritz Fischer in Hamburg and became thereafter a dedicated private scholar with means to enable him to tour the nation investigating the private archives of leading generals in the Imperial Germany army as well as politicians of that era. His research publications have been as staggering as they are sensational in their findings which corroborated and sharpened the initial revelations of Fritz Fischer and Imanuel Geiss.

Helmut Bley (b. 1935) began his academic career as a research assistant for Hamburg professor Egmont Zechlin (1896–1992) who was initially a convinced opponent of Fritz Fischer but then became reconciled with his hitherto ostracised colleague. Herr Bley had always inclined to the Fischer camp and made his reputation with pioneering work on the German colonial administration of South West Africa and other African protectorates of the Reich. In the process he became an aficionado of August Bebel's career in opposition to the Reich government, its antediluvian constitution and especially its colonial administration.

August Bebel (1840–1913) led the Social Democratic Party from 1869 until his death. While in the Reichstag, Bebel became renowned for his fiery opposition to the regime's reactionary and oppressive policies, so much so that he became known as the *Gegen Bismarck* (the counter Bismarck). Herr Bebel was strongly influenced by Karl Marx whose views he tried to bring into alignment with his party friends, the famous revisionist Eduard Bernstein and Karl Kautsky, the SPD ideologue. Their vision of Germany was vastly at odds with that of the upper bourgeoisie and the ruling elite.

Carl Legien (1861–1920) was born in Thorn West Prussia and raised in an orphanage. When old enough he served in the Prussian army as an officer's batman, learning by osmosis the skills of command and organisation. These were to stand him in good stead as leader of the German social democratic oriented trade unions from 1890 until his death. As a long-time member of the Second Internationale he campaigned for world peace but in 1914 opted to support the fatherland as he believed the official propaganda that Germany was under attack from Tsarist Russia. He consistently opposed the idea of a general strike as a needless provocation of the ruling classes who would not hesitate to employ the army against striking worker. See John A. Moses, *Trade Unionism in Germany from Bismarck to Hitler* (1984).

Epilogue

The argument of the foregoing has been that in order to achieve clarity on the question why the fledgling Commonwealth and all the other overseas dominions of Great Britain joined in the war against Imperial Germany it is absolutely essential to comprehend the *peculiar* character of Imperial Germany (Blackbourn & Eley). One needs to be reminded that with its authoritarianism, militarism, rabid anti-socialism, anti-Semitism and bureaucratic culture it was the forerunner of the rogue state of Nazi Germany.[1] This exercise also demands that we are informed about imperial Germany's hybrid monarchical-parliamentary constitution and the ideology upon which it was based, namely to ensure the dominance of Prussian ruling classes 'for imaginable time.' That is to say such issues as the nature of the State itself and the self-perception of the Statesmen need seriously to be examined.

It will not do simply to argue that all Great Powers of a century ago were virtually the same kind of rapacious, materialistic and imperialist political entities like 'beasts of prey' in the international jungle (Golo Mann) because they were all sustained by highly competitive capitalist economies. On the contrary, each was culturally unique and inhabited by citizens and/or subjects who had imbibed values which shaped their particular *habitus,* meaning their general mode of behaviour towards each other in their class divisions, and especially towards foreign nations. Each nation possesses a unique spirit which is expressed in its cultural achievements and institutions. These are identified in particular by its poets and writers who include both novelists and historians. Obviously these perceptive people usually come from an educated elite but, despite their relatively small number within the overall national community, they exert an undeniable shaping force on its education and general culture. In short, this literary-artistic coterie is the essential generator, identifier, and mentor to the nation, indeed a prophetic school, and is consequently the source of considerable political influence.

Attention is drawn here to the apologetic writing of a most high-profile neo-Rankean historian Professor Hans Delbrück (1849–1929) who after the ignominious defeat in 1918, vigorously and unapologetically defended Prusso-German culture against the West. His rancour at the defeat was understandable, but he persisted in his conviction that the West had nothing to teach the culturally and morally superior Germans.[2] The post-war Weimar Republic which drew heavily on modern western European political traditions was considered by many of Delbrück's generation as a culturally alien impost on the German people. That, of course, was not the view of most Social Democrats. Consequently, Germany remained a politically and culturally divided society until forty-four years after the Second World War when the final re-unification took place after the collapse of the infamous Berlin wall. Ultimate unification externally as a nation state and also internally as an egalitarian society, admirable though it is, had proved a costly achievement indeed.

Prusso-German 'Peculiarity'

It should be clear that the way in which each nation conducts politics is the product of their unique culture. Some shared common roots, deriving, for example, from the European Enlightenment which facilitated political dialogue among them. This was the case regarding the western European and trans-Atlantic peoples because they could communicate in a mutually comprehensible political discourse.

In the cases of central and eastern European countries, however, the Enlightenment in its western form with its political consequences had been largely rejected by the ruling classes and the bourgeoisie because it was considered to contain the seeds of revolution. Prusso-Germany, Austria-

Hungary and Russia all found the liberal political doctrines and trends of the West to be politically volatile. First, on the domestic front it would have meant sharing political power with the lower classes and secondly it would have negated all dreams of imperialistic expansion which were precious to both the ruling elite and the *Bildungsbürgertum*. They resisted demands for social and political change coming from the proletariat as dangerously revolutionary. German conservative and bourgeois politicians and self-styled opinion-makers like the war-time Thomas Mann, for instance, had become most eloquent in erecting a wall of arguments for the rejection of Western political ideas. The notions behind the liberal parliamentary system which rested on the sovereignty of the people in contrast to the doctrine of the divine right of kings was emphatically opposed east of the Rhine.

As has been shown, the Prusso-German *habitus* or *spirit* of the educated elite is attributable to their commitment to Hegelianism and Neo-Rankeanism. This indeed moulded the distinctly German spirit resulting in the self-isolation of the *Bildungsbürgertum* and the aristocracy from the West; indeed the West was perceived largely as being mired in a decadent materialism; none of its institutions was deemed worthy of adoption. Indeed the West became increasingly an entity destined to be overtaken by the more youthful, vigorous and intellectually superior Prusso-German *Kultur*. Rejection of all things Anglo-Saxon and French, for example, had become paradigmatic.[3] And in this regard the German *Academy*, *Army* and *Navy* were in total agreement. Most German professors endorsed unreservedly the military culture like a chorus in a Greek play. Only very few pacifists were able to articulate a contrary position. Indeed, it is remarkable that there really were some courageous pacifist intellectuals at all, not to mention thousands of social democratic subjects.

The record in this respect is overwhelmingly depressing. As the late Professor Adolf Gasser from his Swiss democratic vantage point had made clear during the early phase of the Fischer Controversy, one fails completely to comprehend the nature of Prusso-Germany if one ignores the fact that it was a State geared to prioritise the military. In this regard, Professor

Gasser echoed the assessment of his Munich colleague, Franz Schnabel (see above, especially chapter 2). While one might possibly understand how the Prussian militaristic political culture could justify itself and especially win the approval of the middle and upper classes, it ruled out considering modern political alternatives. This is why the German bourgeoisie and aristocracy have been reproached by liberals such as Franz Schnabel of suffering from a perennial *Konzeptsionslosigkeit,* that is, the inability to conceive of other more humane and peaceful solutions to surviving the admittedly challenging geo-political position in Central Europe in which Prusso-Germany found herself. Instead of exploring the possibility of non-violent solutions to foreign policy issues Prusso-German statesmen placed their reliance exclusively on the established military arrangements whereby the *army in being* was the essential foreign policy tool. As it evolved in the Bismarckian constitution the army remained essentially a *State within the State.*[4]

It was this constitutional situation that deeply worried the spokesmen of the working class, that is the trade unionists and the leaders of the Social Democratic Party as well as of the Roman Catholic Centre Party which had a strong working-class constituency, especially in the Rhineland, and, as well, the progressive Liberals. All these championed democratic solutions to both domestic social policy and foreign/colonial policy issues. They repeatedly warned through their members in the Reichstag that national policy in these areas was leading to internal polarisation as well as the alienation of neighbouring Powers. And since these warnings were always associated with demands for constitutional change they were largely ignored by the ruling elite.

The most dramatic example was the parliamentary crisis in the wake of the infamous Zabern affair when the numerically strongest parties in the Reichstag (Social Democrats, the Centre Party and the Progressive Liberals) moved a vote of no confidence in the government for its unequivocal support for the army following upon the latter's outrageous behaviour towards the civilian population in the garrison town of Zabern (or Saverne) in 1913. The Reich cabinet, which was chosen from outside the Reichstag, and hence not subject to its control, simply ignored the will of the House and unequivocally supported the army.

The Zabern affair was indeed the most brutal affirmation of the will of the ruling classes *not* to pay any attention to democratic-parliamentary principles. In fact one could confidently argue that if the Zabern affair had resulted in the constitutional changes demanded by the majority of the Reichstag there would not have been a war in August 1914. It may not be forgotten that imperial Germany was the home of the largest democratic party in the world by 1912, namely the Social Democratic Party, and it together with the Centre Party and the Progressive Liberals formed the absolute majority in the Reichstag. More cohesive collaboration among the three 'opposition' parties, of course was hindered because of their divergent ideological/religious differences. This was only gradually put aside to enable more collaboration as the nature of the war, far from being one of self-defence as initially proclaimed, gradually became understood for what it really was, namely as an *Eroberungskrieg*, that is a war of conquest for the benefit of the militaristic ruling classes. These believed that apart from extensive annexations and increase in Prusso-German power abroad, that it would also serve to shore up the existing social-political order.

The Kaiser's Germany: A Society Divided

What has most recently appeared from the pen of the eminent German social democratic historian, Professor Helmut Bley of Hanover, is confirmation of all of the above in his study of August Bebel (1840–1913) who led the Social Democratic Party in the Reichstag from 1862 until his death.[5] This man was the closest politician in Germany who could and should have been designated 'leader of His Majesty's loyal Opposition', such was the significance of his long parliamentary career. Indeed, during his life time he was called the *Gegenkaiser*, the 'anti-Kaiser' so impressive was his record in the Reichstag and as Party leader. What professor Bley has revealed is that from 1904 until 1913 Bebel had been secretly warning the British government about the potential dangers of German militarism. He did this in private conversations with the British Honorary Consul in Zürich, Heinrich Angst, a Swiss national. In his discussions with Angst, Bebel emphasized the bellicosity of the Prussian military and the dangerous class character of the Junker state. These judgements by Bebel corresponded with the content of his Reichstag speeches expressing concern about the increasing self-isolation of the German Empire especially after the diplomatic humiliation in the first Morocco crisis of 1905/06. This concern was intensified at the 1911 Morocco crisis, although the party at first underestimated it for its tactical use in the 1912 Reichstag election.[6]

Nevertheless, with the 1912 national elections the German public had made clear to the ruling classes that they were by no means at ease under the prevailing constitutional arrangements. The return of the Social Democratic Party with a simple majority in the Reichstag of 110 seats was a dramatic increase on the 1907 election in which the SPD had polled only 43 mandates. If they could have combined with the *Zentrum* with 91 and the *Progressive Liberals* with 42 the 'opposition' parties could under different circumstances have formed government. One is justified in speculating that the course of history may have been very different. The difficulty was that all of these parties had irreconcilable ideological differences that made it impossible for them to coalesce more cohesively than they had done in 1913 when they combined in their vote of no confidence in the government over its handling of the Zabern affair. That crisis illustrated that the Reich was nothing more or less than a disguised military oligarchy. If anything the obvious concerns of the population about this situation made the military even more determined to exploit every available opportunity to clamp a lid on any future democratic ambitions. And the July-August crisis of 1914 in the Balkans presented itself as a most opportune time for such a scenario. The circumstances seemed to be God-sent to enable the Reich leadership to solve all its domestic problems and realise its ambitious foreign policy program altogether.

The Militaristic Hegemony of the
German Ruling Classes

One needs really to be prepared to enter into the world of ideas of the German ruling classes in order to comprehend the outbreak of the Great War and its massively tragic duration. Although Sir Eyre Crowe had warned as early as 1907 that Germany could be the source of serious international disturbance, no one could have imagined in August 1914 what would actually ensue. And when one takes on board the utterances of German leaders especially after the failure of the Schlieffen Plan to achieve its ambitious goals by the end of 1914, one is astounded at the determination of the German government to persevere in the face of ever greater international opposition rather than to negotiate a peace without annexations which was demanded by the Reichstag majority. One wonders at the capacity of the German ruling classes at that time to grasp realities.

Instead of drawing sober conclusions the German leadership persisted in the conviction that they could still realise the 'September Program' , at least in part. The irrationality and the poverty of alternative ideas that prevailed is something that today's German historians find extremely difficult to comprehend. The values of their ancestors seem to belong to an alien race, and yet they all derived from ideas propounded by such notable Germans as Martin Luther, Gottfried von Herder, G.W.F. Hegel, Leopold von Ranke and Heinrich von Treitschke, and these are all personages who contributed to shaping the world view of none other than Adolf Hitler. The future dictator imbibed ideas from all these thinkers, albeit very selectively, while he was serving a prison term in Landsberg (from 1 April until 20 December 1924) where he wrote *Mein Kampf,* his autobiographical/programmatic reflections. And here one needs to be aware of the 'roots of continuity.' In short, the German intellectual leaders through their endorsement of the war-aims 1914–18 contributed significantly to their own decline as Professor Fritz Ringer had so convincingly portrayed.

It is essential also to appreciate the toxic potency of Prusso-German political culture and to comprehend the role it played in shaping the catastrophic 20th century. This is where Franz Schnabel's regret that no significant Whig tradition developed in Germany among the educated bourgeoisie is most relevant. Hans Delbrück's above-mentioned post-war apologia for the Bismarckian-Wilhelmine system even after it was so manifestly discredited remains a puzzle to the Western liberal mind to this day.

Antipodean Self-Assessment in the Imperial Context

The idea that the remote Dominions of Australia and New Zealand were insulated by distance from the consequences of disputes originating in Central Europe is, in the light of both technical and ideological realities, quite untenable. As sovereign nations, both Australia and New Zealand needed their leading thinkers to evince sufficient intellectual rigour to comprehend the Prusso-German mind of a century ago. At the present time it seems that 'confusion hath now made his masterpiece' as a consequence of a perennial Australian intellectual anarchy which is something that foreign academic visitors are quick to discern.

As indicated by the example of Professor Helmut Bley at the present time, German academics of liberal or social-democratic persuasion in contrast to right-wing revisionists have been since 1945 focussed on exposing the key elements of past German nationalism and evaluating the consequences. That political circumstances resulted in both the military excesses of the Second World War and the Holocaust is beyond all doubt. One of the most articulate critics of the so-called *Spirit* which animated German *Kultur* was the late Kurt Sontheimer (1928–2005), a genuine liberal. He investigated the key advocates of a unique German spirit and found the most succinct expression of the German spirit in their statements made during the Great War. He observed that the then intellectual mentors had been at pains to project German war policy as the quintessential expression of the German spirit. And the key one is revealed in the way German philosophers, historians and theologians defined 'freedom'. Here, of course, the language becomes less concrete and increasingly more mystical.

German 'freedom' was in no way to be confused with the Western idea of rights and obligations of the citizen which stress the protection of individuals against the State; rather the German idea of freedom did not require a revolution against the State but promoted the idea of the inner reconciliation of the individual consciousness with that of duties towards the State as Hans Delbrück's above-mentioned book stressed. The Hegelian roots of this idea are very obvious. One became more free to the extent that one submitted to the ordinances of the State. Why? Because the State is not like an economic association like an agricultural cooperative that functions for the benefit of its members, but a divine institution that functions in history in accordance with the will of the Creator God. This made German *Kultur* very different from and superior to all the European or trans-Atlantic neighbours, hence, *Gott mit uns*.

One needs to enquire what the content of this *Kultur* was, indeed, what were the true Germanic virtues that constituted the pillars of German *Kultur*. The Berlin legal scholar and historian, Otto von Gierke (1841–1921), listed the following: German loyalty (*Treue*) which traced its roots back to the primeval times of the Germanic tribes and was still strong in the present. Following this came the unique German concept of duty (*Pflicht*) and the seriousness of one's comprehension of life (*Lebensauffassung*) combined with a simplicity of uprightness, truthfulness and sense of justice. Further, courage (*Mut*) that knew no fear was most highly prized but above all else was the religious certainty and belief in a higher purpose of life and the guidance of almighty God in the fate of human beings.

It is essential to grasp that all these virtues were peculiarly Germanic virtues and define the uniqueness of German *Kultur* and existence (*Sein*). They were different from the essence (*Wesen*) of every other national culture. Equipped with such virtues the German was able to distinguish the negative qualities of egoism, materialism, pacifism, dissension and the pettyfogging shop keeper's spirit (*Krämergeist*) all of which were allegedly major Anglo-Saxon attributes. In all respects the German spirit was culturally superior, and very importantly, was convinced of a mission from almighty God to displace all foreign civilisations and replace them with the incomparably more virtuous and stronger German *Kultur*. As a consequence, the German spirit was assumed to manifest the following four distinct characteristics: First, it was German idealistic thinking that generated the creative energy which produces life. Secondly, the German spirit was by definition a spirit of the community (*Gemeinschaft*). It was the basis of national cohesiveness and the preparedness for service to the whole. It guided and shaped the life of the *Volk*. Thirdly, the German spirit insofar as it was not penetrated and tainted by foreign ideas was capable of the highest achievements in all spheres of social life. For this reason its potential should not be limited to the mere national sphere but claimed also universal validity. Fourthly and finally, in order for the German spirit to be fully effective it must demonstrate its strict unity and unshakeable solidarity (*Geschlossenheit*) especially in delineating itself from everything foreign, especially the western liberal model of society. As such the 'German spirit' evinced an ideological character that served to justify the frankly authoritarian character of all social relationships. It perceived itself as virtually invulnerable though it could be weakened to the extent that it might give in to a foreign spirit. So the 'German spirit' served as the source and embodiment of everything good for German politics and German life. And very importantly it is a means of agitation and never merely discussion. It wanted nothing to do with the spirit as an instrument and medium for truth but rather always asserted the spirit as the creator and guarantor of an authoritarian political ordering of society. In short the 'German spirit' was the core of nationalist ideology.[7]

As already stressed, these were the ideas or principles enunciated initially by leading German thinkers from the time of Hegel (1770–1831) and Goethe (1782–1832). They came to full fruition at the outbreak of the

Great War and dominated internal German discussion throughout the war as leading German minds such as Friedrich Meinecke and Ernst Troeltsch in particular reported in great detail during the Weimar Republic (1919–1933). These mere fourteen years may be seen as the first great challenge to the old 'German spirit' because with the military defeat and humiliation of the Reich the opportunity was opened for a massive revision of German values and the final appropriation of western political ideas. This happened with the adoption of the Weimar constitution of 1919 but that very western and democratic instrument was never wholeheartedly accepted, especially by the German *petite bourgeoisie* and the *Bildungsbürgertum*. There was a hankering for a revitalisation of the true German spirit which they misguidedly imagined they had found in the Nazi movement and in the person of its leader, Adolf Hitler. In 1934 very few of the latter classes could have suspected that the leader (*Führer*) would become a misleader or seducer (*Verführer*) of the nation. Indeed, Hitler's evil genius consisted in his ability to convince the masses that he incorporated the true 'German spirit' for which a complete rejection of all western political values was essential. Hence the public support for all Nazi efforts to 'throw off the chains of the dictated peace of Versailles'.

Instead of a return to 'glorious times' the Third Reich of Adolf Hitler led the nation to perdition. As Kurt Sontheimer observed, 'It is a tragedy brought about by the Germans themselves to note with what ease the Third Reich was able to incorporate the 'German spirit' and use it as a spearhead in the service of the most inhumane policies'. And here Sontheimer makes the damning indictment of naming the Third Reich as the pinnacle of German anti-western separate development (*Sonderentwicklung*), 'From now on the German separate consciousness had lost every justification. There is absolutely no reason why anyone would try to work on even a purified restoration of it.'[8]

The Fischer Controversy

Re-Visited in London, 2011

On the occasion of the fiftieth anniversary of the publication of Fritz Fischer's *Griff nach der Weltmacht* in 1961 the German Historical Institute in London organized a conference to review the legacy of the controversy unleashed by the Professor Fischer and his school to take stock of the subsequent research.[9] This was an event of considerable historiographical importance because it subjected the revolutionary findings of the Fischer school to microscopic scrutiny. And in view of the thesis promulgated by Sir Christopher Clark that the Powers simply woke up after a sonambulist stumble to find themselves at war this collection of essays constitutes a corrective in the on-going discussion/debate.

Andreas Gestrich in his introductory essay to this volume which he edited together with Professor Hartmut Pogge von Strandmann, provides a critical overview of the impact that the Hamburg Professor Fritz Fischer's pioneering/revolutionary research has had after fifty years. As one who was an eye-witness in Germany from the beginning of the controversy I appreciate the diligence that these two English-based German scholars demonstrate here. They have surveyed the many analyses of subsequent scholars of various ideological persuasions from conservative to socialist, from many countries. This has been a copy book exercise in objectivity and even-handedness. Of course, the conservative commentators have understandably mostly been German. These are people like Herfried Münkler who, in the tradition of Fischer's leading contemporary critic, Professor Gerhard Ritter, are unhappy with the allocation of the main war-guilt to Germany. Other scholars, too, also have pointed to Fischer's primary concern with German war-aims and his alleged failure to pay adequate attention to those of other powers. Consequently, a more comparative approach is being recommended.

This, however, in the findings of Gestrich and von Strandmann far from invalidates Fischer's main argument, namely that Germany did not suddenly after the outbreak of war in August 1914 come up with an ambitious catalogue of annexationist war-aims, but rather that the now famous 1914 September Program of war aims was really the distillation of submissions from various influential economic pressure groups who had been weaving plans for German expansion for some considerable time. And these were not only Pan German enthusiasts and imperialist dreamers, but also hard headed businessmen. Furthermore, it had undoubtedly been the desire of the German army for some considerable time to launch a preventive war against France and Russia, and this was documented in the evolution of what became the Schlieffen Plan. In this regard, too, the so-called war-council of late 1912 (see chapter three) which had been 'discovered' and evaluated by John Röhl, was indeed a totally frank example of the determination of the Kaiser and his generals to launch a preventive war at the appropriate time. So in the questions of war-aims and war planning Fischer and his school were/are substantially correct. Germany bears the chief responsibility for the outbreak and duration of the Great War.

Interestingly, none of the scholars involved in the current debate has thought to emphasise the *peculiarity* of the formation of Prusso-German thinking about the nature of the State and of the way history is believed to unfold. This is, of course, a sphere of enquiry that not many scholars wish to enter. But it has been observed here that the mind of the educated and aristocratic German was very different from that of other 'civilised' nations, as Kurt Sontheimer has so forcefully explained. It was the theologians and university professors who exemplified it more frankly in their war-time sermons and appeals. They comprised that section of the *Bildungsbürgertum* whose stock-in-trade was to influence and formulate/articulate public opinion with their ideas. And it is by examining their doctrines and the assumptions upon which they were based that ultimately determined how and why the 'Germans' saw the world in such a dangerously different way from their neighbours.

Finally, I wish to point to a phenomenon which, as far as I know, no other German trained historian has considered. And here I am reminded of what the late Edward Hallett Carr (1892–1982) said about historical 'facts' in his book *What is History* (1961): 'The belief in a hard core of historical facts existing objectively and independently of the interpretation of the historian is a preposterous fallacy, but one very hard to eradicate'. As stated at the beginning, how a historian interprets facts or indeed, identifies 'facts' is a very subjective process. It depends on a variety of elements in one's training or education that become embedded in one's psyche. It was something I noticed in my personal encounter with German historians of differing religious and ideological commitments.

Firstly, let me comment on Franz Schnabel whose critical work on the 'aggrandisement of Prussia' was so influential in student re-education in post-1945 Munich. Why did Schnabel develop such a deep abhorrence of Prussianism? My take on that question is that he was inwardly formed by his liberal Roman Catholicism and the influence of his French mother. That is to say, from his birth onwards he did not have personally to experience the brutality of Prussian authoritarianism to find it abhorrent. It simply grated against every fibre in his being. And, as well, it was re-enforced by the memory of the Prusso-German victory over France in 1870. This was evident from his lectures in which with ironical subtlety he occasionally referred to the German invasions of France. No one then knew of his half-French parentage. Despite this Schnabel's critique of Prusso-Germany was never emotional; it derived from a highly refined comprehension of the 'Whig tradition' which of course, he had learned from his study of British history and philosophy, especially of John Locke (1632–1704) who was known as 'the Father of Liberalism.' I 'witnessed' this 'fact' in Schnabel's lectures and it was then re-enforced by reading his publications. So Franz Schnabel was a liberal German in the core of his being having intellectually endorsed the 'Whig tradition'. It was providential that he was still alive and well when US forces liberated the southern part of Germany. Known already as an opponent of the Nazi regime, Schnabel was sought out and installed as first post-war professor of history at the University of Munich. The political-pedagogic influence on his students has been immeasurable.

In the case of the Protestant Fritz Fischer at Hamburg from 1947 until 1978, we are dealing with a 'convert' to liberalism because in his youth Fischer had been essentially a 'blood and soil' nationalist which means that he had been educated to believe in the mystical and superior uniqueness of the German *Volk*. In short, along with thousands of other young men, he was ripe for membership in the Nazi Party when it came to power. Then via the financial support of the Nazi Institute for the History of the New Germany (Reichsinstitut für Geschichte des neuen Deutschlands).[10] Fritz Fischer began his academic career by completing his doctorate and post-doctorate (*Habilitation*) in Prussian church history which opened the way to an academic post. The intervention of the war in 1939, however, saw Fischer recruited into the *Wehrmacht* education section. His task was to instruct German soldiers about the allegedly deleterious Jewish influence upon the British and American political systems. It was a kind of 'Why-We-Fight' exercise. At the end of the war Fischer had been captured by the Americans and interned in a camp with *Waffen SS* personnel whose unrepentant attitudes revolted him. Fischer's residual Lutheran Christianity still had the capacity to move his conscience. After some confusion about his identity, US re-education officers finally recognized who Fischer was and engaged him in a revisionist historical program.

As Fischer revealed to me he had been via this experience converted to an Anglo-Saxon liberal world view. Then, after several years as a prisoner of war, Fischer was released in 1947 to take up the chair in Hamburg to which he had been nominated already in 1942.[11] I never had cause to question the authenticity of Fischer's 'conversion'. Such an experience would have been replicated many thousands of times in other educated people. In any case his first major public statement at the first post-war German Historians' Congress held in Munich in 1949 contained already the seeds of his future ideological re-assessment of modern German history. In that extensive address Fischer delineated why Germany had separated herself spiritually from the West and attributed that to the failure of a liberal or Whig tradition to take root in Germany.[12]

Fischer's subsequent re-assessments of the course of German history in his many extensive publications have been examples of pioneering methodological innovation, especially from within the German tradition. As Paul Kennedy once quipped to me, 'Fischer out-rankered Ranke' in *showing how it actually was*. A final observation: By examining the different formation of each these two liberal historians' explanation for the course of German history we have an insight into the unique circumstances that influence one's historiography. In the case of Schnabel, it was his birth and liberal Catholic humanistic values; with Fischer, born a Protestant and educated in the *volkisch* German tradition before becoming a Nazi he was enabled through his war-time experience to experience a *metanoia*, that is a transformative change of heart or repentance in the theological sense. Fischer had embarked on the pilgrimage from Teutonic racialist obscurantism to enlightened Western liberalism. And it was this that enabled the critique that issued into the 'Fischer Controversy' today.

Fazit/Conclusions

1) If historians do not search out the cultural differences between peoples and evaluate them when investigating the crucial decision-making processes they are crippled in their ability to draw reliable conclusions and to make mature judgments.

2) The pioneering research of Peter Overlack on the operational plans of the German Navy in the Pacific has revealed a hitherto inadequately understood strategic threat to Commonwealth security during the Great War of 1914–1918. Knowledge of this episode is essential for comprehending the acute danger in which the Antipodean Dominions found themselves in 1914.

3) The chapters by John Moses have shown that German 'peculiarity' resulted from the way in which the educated elite, the *Bildungsbürgertum*, had located itself in a virtual 'parallel universe' distinct from the West. The self-isolation of this class stifled the growth of liberal, democratic values in Germany. Only after the 'liberation' in 1945 by superior Allied forces could these values be re-kindled. Germany's current membership in the 'West' has been the end result of a very costly learning process.

Bibliography

Abbreviations

ANU   Australian National University
CUP   Cambridge University Press
HUP   Harvard University Press
ISAA   Independent Scholars Association of Australia
MUP   Melbourne University Press
OUP   Oxford University Press
PLW   *Public Lectures on the War*
PUP   Princeton University Press
SUP   Sydney University Press
WUP   Wesleyan University Press
YUP   Yale University Press

Unpublished Primary Sources

Extensive use was made of archives, especially by Dr Peter Overlack in his sections on the German naval forces in the Pacific. These were as follows:

Bundesarchiv-Militärarchiv, Freiburg
Bundesarchiv, Koblenz
Politisches Archiv des Auswärtigen Amts, Bonn
Bundesarchiv, Potsdam
Privatarchiv, Heltorf (Spee Archiv)
Australian Archives, Victoria
Australian War Memorial Archive, Canberra

A fully itemised list of files and other primary sources consulted is provided in Peter Overlack, 'The Imperial German Navy in the Pacific 1900–1914 as an Instrument of *Weltpolitik,* with special Reference to Australasia in its Operational Planning', PhD, University of Queensland, 1995.

Books

Afflerbach, Holger, *Falkenhayn, Politisches Denken und Handeln im Kaiserreich*, Oldenbourg, Munich, 1994.

––– (ed.), *The Purpose of the First World War: War Aims and Military Strategy*, Berlin, 2015.

––– & David Stephenson (eds), *An Improbable War*, Berghahn Books, New York, 2007.

Alff, Wilhelm (ed.), *Deutschlands Sonderung von Europa 1862–1964*, Aufsätze von Adolf Gasser et al., Peter Lang, Frankfurt, 1984.

Anderson, Margaret Lavinia, *Practising Democracy: Elections and Political Culture in the German Empire*, PUP, Princeton, 2000.

Anievas, Alexander (ed.), *Cataclysm 1914: World War 1 and the Making of Modern World Politics*, Brill: Leiden & Boston, 2018.

Angell, Norman, *The Great Illusion: A Study of the Relations of Military Power in Nations to their Economic and Social Advantage*, Putnam, New York/London, 1910.

Atkinson, Alan, *The Europeans in Australia: A History* 3 Vols. OUP, Melbourne & UNSW Press, 1997–2014.

–––, *The Commonwealth of Speech: An Argument about Australia's Past, Present and Future*, Australian Scholarly Publishing, Melbourne, 2002.

Bahne, Patrick & Alexander Camman (eds), *Die Debatte um Hans-Ulrich Wehlers 'Deutsche Geschichte'*, Beck'sche Reihe, Munich, 2009.

Baird, Julia, *Victoria the Queen: An Intimate Biographyof the Woman who ruled an Empire*, Random House, New York, 2016.

Bean C. E. W. (ed.), *The Official History of Australia in the War of 1914–1918*, IX Vols., Angus & Robertson, Sydney, 1922–1942.

Bell, G.K.A., *Randall Davidson*, OUP, London, 1935.

Benz, Wolfgang & Werner Bergmann (eds), *Vorurteil und Völkermord: Entwicklungslinien des Antisemitismus*, Herder, Freiburg/Basel/Wien, 1997.

Berghahn, Volker R. (ed.), *Militarismus*, Kiepenhauer & Witsch, Cologne, 1975.

Berry, J. A. & A. T. Strong (eds), *PLW*, George Robertson & Co., Melbourne 1915.

Besson, Waldemar & Freiherr Hiller von Gaetringen (eds), *Geschichte und Gegenwartsbewusstsein: Festschrift für Hans Rothfels zum 70. Geburtstag*, Vandenhoek & Ruprecht, Göttingen, 1963.

Blackbourn, David & Geoff Eley, *The Peculiarities of German History: Bourgeois Society and Politics in 19th Century Germany*, OUP, Oxford/New York, 1984.

Bley, Helmut, *Bebel und die Strategie der Kriegsverhütung 1904–1913*, Offizin Verlag, Hannover, 2014.

Böhme, Klaus, *Aufrufe und Reden deutscher Professoren im ersten Weltkrieg*, Reclam, Stuttgart, 1975.

Boland, T. P., *James Duhig*, University of Queensland Press, St Lucia, 1968.

Born, Karl Erich, *Staat und Sozialpolitik seit Bismarcks Sturz*, Steiner Verlag, Wiesbaden, 1957.

Brändle, Maximillian (ed.), *The Queensland Experience: The Life and Work of 14 Remarkable Migrants*, Phoenix Publications, Brisbane, 1991.

British White Book: Official Correspondence between the European Powers during the Fourteen Days preceding Britain's Declaration of War, August 4th, 1914, William Brooks & Co, Sydney, 1914.

Bucholz, Arden, *Moltke, Schlieffen and Prussian War Planning*, Berg Publishers, New York/Oxford, 1991.

Bülow, Bernhard von, *Imperial Germany*, Cassell, London, 1913.

Carey, Hilary M., *God's Empire – Religion and Colonialism in the British World, c.1801–1908*, Cambridge, CUP, 2011.

Casson, Majory R., *George Cockburn Henderson – A Memoir*, The Library Board of South Australia, Adelaide, 1964.

Charlton, Peter, *Pozieres – Australians on the Somme*, Methuen Hayes, Sydney, 1986.

Chickering, Roger, *We Men who Feel most German: A Cultural Study of the Pan German League, 1886–1914*, Allen & Unwin, Boston, 1984.

Clark, Christopher, *The Iron Kingdom: The Rise and Downfall of Prussia 1600–1947*, The Belknap Press of HUP, Cambridge, Mass., 2006.

———, *The Sleepwalkers: How Europe went to War in 1914*, Harper Perennial Edition, 2014.

Clark, Manning, *The Quest for an Australian Identity*, University of Queensland Press, St Lucia, 1980.

———, *Manning Clark on Gallipoli*, MUP, Carlton, 2005.

Cochrane, Peter, *Australians at War*, ABC Books, Sydney, 2001.

Connor, John, *Anzac and Empire: George Foster Pearce and the Foundation of Australian Defence*, CUP, Cambridge, 2011.

Conze, Werner & Jürgen Kocka (eds), *Bildungsbürgertum im 19. Jahrhundert*, 4 Vols., Klett-Kotta, Stuttgart, 1985–1989.

Crawford, R. M., *'A Bit of a Rebel', The Life and Work of George Arnold Wood*, University of Sydney Press, Sydney, 1975.

Creighton, Mandell, *The Church and the Nation: Charges and Addresses*, Hardpress Reprint, 2012.

Curran, Tom, *The Grand Deception: Churchill and the Dardanelles*, Andrew G. Bonnell (ed.), Big Sky Publishers, Newport, NSW, 2015.

Davidson, Jim, *Samoa mo Samoa: The Emergence of the Independent State of Western Samoa*, OUP, Melbourne/New York, 1967.

Davis, H. W. C, *The Political Thought of Heinrich von Treitschke*, Constable, London 1914.

Dawson, Willam Harbutt, *The Evolution of Modern Germany*, Fisher Unwin, London, 1914.

Dehio, Ludwig, *Germany and World Politics in the Twentieth Century*, Chatto & Windus, London, 1960.

Delbrück, Hans, *Regierung und Volkswille: Ein Grundriss der Politik*, Deutsche Verlagsanstalt für Politik, Berlin-Charlottenburg, 1920.

–––, *Government and the Will of the People – Academic Lectures* (trans. with notes and glossary of political names and terms by Roy S. MacElwee), OUP, New York, 1923.

–––, *Delbrück's Modern Military History*, Arden Bucholz (ed. and transl.), University of Nebraska Press, Lincoln & London, 1997.

Dorpalen, Andreas, *Heinrich von Treitschke*, New Haven, YUP, 1957.

Düllfer, Jost & Karl Holl (eds), *Bereit zum Krieg*, Vandenhoek und Ruprecht, Göttingen, 1986.

Ekins, Ashley (ed.), *1918: Year of Victory – The End of the Great War and the Shaping of History*, Exisle publishing Ltd, Auckland, 2010.

Elias, Norbert, *Studien über die Deutschen*, Suhrkamp, Frankfurt/M., 1989.

–––, *Civilizing Process: The History of Manners and State Formation and Civilization*; trans. by Edmund Jephcott, Blackwells, Oxford and Cambridge USA, 1994.

Engel-Janosi, Friedrich, *The Growth of German Historicism*, John Hopkins, Baltimore, 1944.

Evans, *Raymond, Loyalty and Disloyalty: Social Conflict on the Queensland Homefront, 1914–18*, University of Queensland Press, St Lucia, 1993.

Erdmann, Karl-Dietrich (ed.), *Kurt Riezler: Tagebücher, Dokumente*, Vandenhoek & Ruprecht, Göttingen, 1972.

———, *Toward a Global Community of Historians: The International Historical Congresses and the International Committee of Historical Sciences 1898–2000*, Berghahn Books, New York/ Oxford, 2005.

Ferguson Niall, *The Pity of War*, Barnes & Noble, New York/London, 1998.

Fischer, Fritz, *Griff nach der Weltmacht: Die Kriegszielpolitik des kaiserlichen Deutschlands 1914–18*, Droste Verlag, Düsseldorf, 1961. [English: *Germany's Aims in the First World War*, with and introduction by Hajo Holborn and James Joll, W. W. Norton Company, New York, 1967.

———, *Krieg der Illusionen. Die deutsche Politik von 1911 bis 1914*, Droste, Verlag, Düsseldorf, 1969.

———, *Bündnis der Eliten:Zur Kontinuität der Machtstrukturen in Deutschland 1871–1945*, Droste Verlag, Düsseldorf, 1979.

———, *Hitler war kein Betriebsunfall*, Beck'sche Reihe, Munich, 1992.

Fischer, Gerhard, *Enemy Aliens: Internment and Home Front Experience in Australia 1914–1920*, University of Queensland Press, St Lucia, 1989.

——— (with Nadine Helmi), *Internment at Trial Bay during World War 1*, New South Wales Migration Heritage Centre, Ultimo, 2005.

Fletcher, Roger, *Revisionism and Empire: Socialist Imperialism in Germany 1897–1914*, Allen & Unwin, London, 1984.

Flinker, Martin, *Thomas Manns politische Betrachtungen im Lichte der heutigen Zeit*, Mouton & Co., 's-Gravenhage, 1959.

Foster, Leonie, *High Hopes: The Men and Motives of the Australian Round Table*, MUP, Melbourne, 1986.

Frances, Raelene & Bruce Scates (eds), *Beyond Gallipoli: New Perspectives on Anzac*, Monash University Publishing, Melbourne, 2016.

Freud, Sigmund, *Zeitgemässes über Krieg und Tod, Warum Krieg?: Der Briefwechsel mit Albert Einstein*, Reclam, Stuttgart, 2012.

Fuchs, Eckhardt, *Thomas Buckle: Geschichtsschreibung und Positivismus in England und Deutschland*, Leipziger Universitätsverlag, Leipzig, 1994.

Fussell, Paul, *The Great War and Modern Memory*, OUP, London/Oxford/New York, 1975.

Fukyama, Francis, *The End of History and the Last Man*, Free Press, Macmillan, Canada, New York/Toronto, 1992.

Fulbrook, Mary, *A Concise History of Germany*, CUP, Cambridge/New York, 1992.

Fulbrook, Mary, *Subjectivity and History: Approaches to Twentieth-Century German Society,* German Historical Association Annual Lecture, London, 2016.

Garton, Stephen, *The Cost of War: Australians Return,* OUP, Melbourne, 1996.

Gatzke, Hans W. *Germany's Drive to the West (Drang nach Westen): A Study of Germany's Western War Aims during the First World War,* The Johns Hopkins Press, Baltimore, 1950.

Gaunson, Bruce, *At War with the Kaiserreich: Australia's Epic in the Great War.* Hybrid Publishers, Melbourne, 2018.

Geiss, Imanuel & Berndt Jürgen Wendt (eds), *Deutschland in der Weltpolitik des 19. und 20. Jahrhunderts: Fritz Fischer zum 65. Geburtstag,* Bertelsmann Universitätsverlag, Düsseldorf, 1973.

Geiss, Imanuel (ed.), *Julikrise und Kriegsausbruch: [Dokumentensammlung]* 2 Vols., Verlag für Literatur und Zeitgeschehen, Hannover, 1964.

———, *Nation und Nationalismen: Versuche über ein Weltproblem*, edition lumiere, Bremen, 2007.

Gestrich, Andreas & Hartmut Pogge von Strandmann (eds), *Bid for World Power? New Research on the Outbreak of the First World War,* OUP, Oxford/New York, 2017.

Gilson, Richard, *Samoa, 1830–1910: The Politics of a Multicultural Community,* OUP, Melbourne/New York, 1970.

Gladwin, Michael, *Captains of the Soul: A History of Australian Army Chaplains*, Big Sky Publications, Newport N.S.W. 2016.

Gollan, Robin, *Radical and Working Class Politics: A Study of Eastern Australia, 1850–1910*, Melbourne, MUP, 1960.

Gooch, George, P., *Studies in German History*, Longmans, Green, London & New York, 1948.

Görlitz, Walter, *Kleine Geschichte des deutschen Generalstabes,* Haude & Spener Verlagsbuchhandlunge, Berlin, 1977.

Goss, Roisin Anne, 'Eugene Hirschfeld: A Life', PhD Thesis submitted to the School of History, Philosophy, Religion and Classics, University of Queensland, 2010.

Grab, Walter, *Norddeutsche Jakobiner: Demokratische Bestrebungen zur Zeit der französischen Revoilution*, Europäische Verlagsanstalt, Frankfurt/M., 1967.

Griffin, James (with Paul Ormonde), *Daniel Mannix: Beyond the Myths,* Garratt Publishing, Melbourne, 2012.

Great War, The: 10 Contested Questions, [with a Foreword by Geraldine Doogue] ABC Books, Sydney, 2015.

Groh, Dieter, *Negative Integration und Revolutionäre Attentismus. Die deutsche Sozialdemokratie am Vorabend des ersten Weltkrieges,* Propyläen, Berlin, 1973.

Grosse Kracht, Klaus, *Die zankende Zunft: Historische Kontroversen in Deutschland nach 1945,* Vandenhoek & Ruprecht, Göttingen, 2005.

Gutsche, Willibald, *Wilhelm II: Der letzte Kaiser des deutschen Reiches,* Deutscher Verlag der Wissenschaften, Berlin, 1991.

Hammer, Karl, *Deutsche Kriegstheologie 1870–1918: Dokumente,* Deutscher Taschenbuch Verlag, Munich, 1970.

———, *Weltmission und Kolonialismus: Sendungsideen des 19. Jahrhunderts im Konflikt,* Deutscher Taschenbuch Verlag, Munich, 1981.

Hempenstall, Peter, *Pacific Islanders under German Rule: A Study in the Meaning of Colonial Resistance,* ANU Press, Canberra, 1978.

Hewitson, Mark, *Germany and the Causes of the First World War,* Berg Publishers, Oxford & New York, 2004.

Hillgruber, Andreas, *Germany and the Two World Wars* (trans. by William C. Kirby), HUP, Cambridge, Mass., 1981.

Historikerstreit: Dokumentation der Kontroverse um die Einzigartigkeit der nationalsozialistischen Judenvernichtung, Piper Verlag, Munich, 1987.

Holborn, Louise W. et al., *German Constitutional Documents since 1871,* Praeger, New York, 1970.

Hölscher, Lucian, *Weltgericht oder Revolution, Protestantische und Sozialistische Zukunftsvorstellungen im Deutschen Kaiserreich,* Klett Kotta, Stuttgart, 1989.

Horne, John & Alan Kramer, *German Atrocities, 1914. A History of Denial,* YUP, New Haven/London, 2001.

——— (ed.), *A Companion to World War I,* Wiley-Blackwell, Oxford, 2012.

Huber, Ernst Rudolf, *Deutsche Verfassungsgeschichte seit 1789,* 6 Vols. Kohlhammer, Stuttgart, 1957–81.

———, *Dokumente zur deutschen Verfassungsgeschichte,* Kohlhammer, Stuttgart/Berlin, 1978.

Huber, Wolfgang and Gerhard Liedke (eds), *Christentum und Militarismus,* Ernst Klett Verlag, Stuttgart 1974.

———, *Von der Freiheit: Perspektiven für eine solidarische Welt,* Verlag C. H. Beck, Munich, 2012.

Hucko, Elmar, M. (ed.), *The Democratic Tradition: Four German Constitutions,* Berg Publishers, Leamington Spa/ New York, 1987.

Hudson, Wayne, *Australian Religious Thought,* Monash University Press, Melbourne, 2016.

Hueffer, Ford Madox, *Between St Dennis and St George,* New York, 1971 (Haskell House re-print of the 1915 edn.).

Hüppauf, Bernd (ed.), *Ansichten vom Krieg: Vergleichende Studien zum Ersten Weltkrieg in Literatur und Gesellschaft,* Forum Academicum, Königstein Ts., 1984.

Hutchison, William R. & Lehmann, Hartmut (eds), *Many are Chosen: Divine Election and Western Nationalism,* Fortress Press, Minneapolis, 1994.

Iggers, Georg, G., *The German Conception of History,* WUP, Middletown., Conn., 1968.

Inglis, Kenneth, S., *Sacred Places: War Memorials in the Australian Landscape,* MUP, Carlton Sth, 1999.

Jäckel, Eberhard, *Hitler's World View: A Blueprint for Power,* WUP, Middletown Conn., 1972.

Janz, Oliver, *1914 Der Grosse Krieg,* Campus Verlag, Frankfurt/New York, 2013.

Jarausch, Konrad, *The Enigmatic Chancellor: Bethmann Hollweg, and the Hubris of Imperial Germany,* YUP, New Haven & London, 1973.

Jasper, Willi, *Lusitania: The Cultural History of a Catastrophe* (trans. by Stewart Spencer), YUP, New Haven & London, 2016.

Jenkins, Julian, *Christian Pacifism Confronts German Nationalism – the Ecumenical Movement and the Cause of Peace in Germany, 1914–1933,* The Edward Mellen Press, Lampeter, 2002.

Jones, Larry Eugene and James Retallack eds, *Between Reform Reaction and Resistance: Studies in the History of German Conservatism from 1789 to 1945,* Berg Publishers, Providence/Oxford, 1993.

Kahler, Erich, *The Orbit of Thomas Mann,* PUP, Princeton, 1969.

Kantorowicz, Hermann, *Der Geist der englischen Politik und das Gespenst der Einkreisung Deutschlands,* Rowohlt Verlag, Berlin, 1929. (English edn.: *The Spirit of British Policy and the Myth of the Encircle*ment, Allen & Unwin, London, 1931.)

Kennan, George F., *The Decline of Bismarck's European Order: Franco-Russian Relations 1875–1890,* PUP, Princeton, 1979.

Kehr, Eckart, *Economic Interest, Militarism and Foreign Policy, Essays on German History*, Berkeley, 1977 (translation of the 1965 Ullstein edition of *Der Primat der Innenpolitik*).

Keller, Ernst, *Der unpolitische Deutscher: Eine Studie an den Betrachtungen von Thomas Mann,* Franke Verlag, Bern/Munich, 1965.

Kennedy, Paul Michael, *The Rise and Fall of British Naval Mastery*, Charles Scribner's Sons, New York, 1976

———, *The Rise of the Anglo-German Antagonism 1860–1914*, George Allen & Unwin, London, 1980.

Kessler, Harry Graf, *Aus den Tagebüchern 1918–1937,* Deutsche Taschenbuch Verlag, Munich, 1965.

Kiesewetter, Hubert, *Von Hegel zu Hitler: Eine Analyse der Hegelischen Machtstaatideologie und der politischen Wirkungsgeschichte des Rechtshegelianismus,* Hoffmann & Campe, Hamburg, 1974.

Klein, Fritz (ed.), *Deutschland im Ersten Weltkrieg,* 3 Vols VEB, Berlin–East, 1969.

Kramer, Lloyd, and Sarah Maza (eds), *A Companion to Western Historical Thought,* Blackwells, Oxford. 2006.

Kremers, Heinz (ed.), *Die Juden und Martin Luther: Martin Luther und die Juden,* Neukirchner Verlgag, Neukirchen-Vluyn, 1987.

Krill, Hans-Heinz, *Die Ranke Renaissance,* de Gruyter, Berlin, 1962.

Krockow, Christian Graf von, *Die Deutschen in ihrem Jahrhundert, 1890–1990,* Rowohlt Verlag, Reinbek, 1990.

Krumeich, Gerd & Gerhard Hirschfeld, *Deutschalnd im ersten Weltkrieg,* Fischer Verlag, Frankfurt am Man, 2013.

———, *Juli 1914: eine Bilanz. Mit einem Anhang: 50 Dokumente zum Kriegsausbruch,* Verlag Schönigh, Paderborn, 2014.

Lattke, Michael, *Paul Anton de Lagarde und das Judentum,* University of Queensland, St Lucia, 2014 (online).

Laue, Theodore von, *Leopold Ranke – The Formative Years,* PUP, Princeton, 1950.

Lenger, Friedrich, *Werner Sombart, 1863–1941, eine Biographie,* C.H. Beck, Munich, 1994.

Leipold, Andreas, *Deutsche Seekriegsführung im Pazifik in den Jahren 1914 und 1915,* Wiesbaden, Harrasowitz, 2012.

Leonhard, Jörn, *Die Büchse der Pandora:Geschichte des ersten Weltkrieges,* C.H. Beck Verlag, Munich, 2014.

Lukins, Tanya, *The Gates of Memory. Australian People's Experience and Memories of Loss and the Great War,* Curtin University Books, Fremantle, 2004.

MacCallum, M. W., *Reflections on the War,* Angus & Robertson, Sydney, 1915.

McCaughey, Davis, *Piecing Together a Shared Vision: the 1987 Boyer Lecture,* The Australian Broadcasting Commission, Sydney, 1988.

McClelland, Charles, E., *The German Historians and England: A Study in Nineteenth Century Views,* CUP, Cambridge, 1971.

MacDougall, Hugh A. (ed.), *Lord Acton on Papal Power,* Sheed & Ward, London, 1973.

Macintyre, Stuart, *A History for a Nation: Ernest Scott and the Making of Australian History,* Carlton, Victoria, MUP, 1994.

Mack, Burton L, *Who Wrote the New Testament? The Making of the Christian Myth,* Harper Collins, New York, 1950.

McKenna, Mark, *The Tradition of Australian Republicanism,* The Department of the Parliamentary Library, Canberra, 1996.

–––, *Australian Republicanism: A Reader,* Mark McKenna & Wayne Hudson (eds), MUP, Carlton, 2003.

–––, *Notes from the Underground: Writing the Biography of Manning Clark,* Melbourne School of Historical Studies, The University of Melbourne, 2008.

–––, *An Eye for Eternity: The Life of Manning Clark,* Miegunyah Press, Carlton, Vic., 2011.

McKernan, Michael, *The Australian People and the Great War,* Nelson, West Melbourne, 1980.

Macleod, Jenny, *Reconsidering Gallipoli,* Manchester University Press, Manchester, 2004.

McMeekin, Sean, *July 1914: Countdown to War,* Basic Books, New York, 2013.

McQuilton, John, *The Australian People and the Great War from Tarrawingee to Tamgalalanga,* MUP, Carlton Sth, 2001.

Maier, Charles S., *The Unmasterable Past: History, Holocaust and German National Identity,* Cambridge, Mass., 1988.

Mann, Thomas, *Die Betrachtungen eines Unpolitischen,* Fischer Taschenbuch Verlag, Frankfurt/M, 1988.

Marriott, James & James Grant Robertson, *The Evolution of Prussia: The Making of an Empire,* The Clarendon Press, Oxford, 1915.

Meaney, Neville, *A History of Australian Defence and Foreign Policy 1901–1923* Vol. I, *The Search for Security in the Pacific*, SUP, Sydney, 2009.

Meinecke, Friedrich, *Weltbürgertum und Nationalstaat*, Oldenbourg Verlag, Munich, 1907 (English edn.: Cosmpolitanism and the National State, Princeton, 1979).

———, *Die Idee der Staatsräson*, Oldenbourg Verlag, Munich 1924 (English edn.: *Machiavellism*, YUP, New Haven, 1957).

———, *Die Entstehung des Historismus*, Oldenbourg Verlag, Munich, 1936 (English edn.: *Historism: The Rise of the New Historical Consciousness*, Herder & Herder, New York, 1972).

Miller, Ignaz, *Mit vollem Risiko in den Krieg:Deutschland 1914 und 1918: zwischen Selbstüberschätzung und Realitätsverweigerung* Neue Zürcher Zeitung, Zürich, 2014.

Miller, J. D. B., *Norman Angell and the Futility of War*, Macmillan, Basingstoke, Hampshire, London, 1986.

Mogk, Walter, *Paul Rohrbach und das 'Grössere Deutschland: Ethischer Imperialismus im Wilhelminischen Deutschland'*, Wilhelm Goldmann Verlag, Munich, 1972.

Mombauer, Monika (ed.), *The Origins of the First World War; Diplomatic and Military Documents*, Manchester University Press, Manchester, 2013.

Mommsen, Wolfgang, *Max Weber and German Politics, 1890–1920*, University of Chicago Press, Chicago/London, 1974.

———, *Imperial Germany 1867–1918: Politics, Culture and Society in an Authoritarian State* (trans. by Richard Deveson) Arnold, London, 1995.

Morgan, J.H., *The German War Book, Being 'The Usages of War on Land'*, issued by the Great General Staff of the German Army (trans. with a critical introduction by J. H. Morgan), John Murray, London, 1915.

Mosse, George L. *The Nationalism of the Masses; Political Symbolism and Mass Movements in Germany from the Napoleonic Wars through to the Third Reich*, Howard Fertig, New York, 1975.

Moses, A. Dirk, *German Intellectuals and the Nazi Past*, CUP, Cambridge, 2007.

Moses, John A. & Paul M. Kennedy (eds), *Germany in the Pacific and Far East, 1870–1918*, University of Queensland Press, St Lucia, 1977.

———, *Trade Unionism in Germany from Bismarck to Hitler* 2 Vols, I, 1862–1918 II, 1919–1933, George Prior Publishers, London, 1982.

———, *Prussian German Militarism in Australian Perspective and the Thought of George Arnold Wood*, Peter Lang, Bern / Frankfurt am Main, 1991.

Moses, John A. & Paul M. Kennedy (eds), *The Reluctant Revolutionary: Dietrich Bonhoeffer's Collision with German History*, Berghahn Books, NewYork, 2014.

––– (with George F. Davis), *Anzac Day Origins: Canon D. J. Garland and Trans-Tasman Commemoration*, Barton Books, Canberra, 2013.

Muehlon, Wilhelm, *Ein Fremder im eigenen Land: Erinnerungen und Tagebuchaufzeichnung eines Krupp-Direktors 1908–1914*, Wolfgang Benz (ed. and intr.), Donat Verlag, Bremen, 1989.

Müller, Karl-Alexander von, *Mars und Venus: Erinnerungen, 1914–1919*, Gustav Kilpper, Stuttgart, 1954.

Neale, R.S., *Writing Marxist History: British Society and Culture since 1700*, Basil Blackwell, Oxford, 1985.

Neitzel, Sönke, *Kriegsausbruch: Deutschlands Weg in die Katastrophe 1900–1914*, Zurich, 2002.

Nicolai, Georg F., *The Biology of War*, (1918) Classic Reprint, 2012.

Nippel, Wilfried, *Johann Gustav Droysen: ein Leben zwischen Wissenschaft und Politik*, C.H. Beck, Munich, 2008.

Notes and Records of the Royal Society of London, Royal Society, Royal Society, London, 1938.

Otte, Thomas G., *July Crisis: The World's Descent into War, Summer 1914*, CUP, Cambridge, 2014.

Oxford Companion to Australian Military History, The, Peter Dennis et al. (eds), OUP, Melbourne, 1995.

Pogge von Strandmann & Immanuel Geiss, *Die Erforderlichkeit des Unmöglichen: Deutschland am Vorabend des ersten Weltkrieges*, Europäische Verlagsanstalt, Frankfurt am Main, 1965.

Popper, Karl, *The Open Society and its Enemies*, Routledge & Kegan Paul, London, 1945.

Pugsley, Christopher, *Gallipoli – The New Zealand Story*, Reed Publishing NZ, Auckland, 1998.

–––, *The Anzac Experience: New Zealand, Australia and Empire in the First World War*, Reed Publishing NZ, Auckland, 2004.

Ramsden, John, *Don't Mention the War: the British and Germans since 1890*, Little Brown, London, 2006.

Rauh, Manfred, *Parliamentisierung des deutschen Reiches*, Droste Verlag, Düsseldorf, 1977.

Rees, Peter, *Bearing Witness: The Remarkable Life of Charles Bean, Australia's Greatest War Correspondent*, Allen & Unwin, Sydney, 2015.

Reid, Richard & Brendan Kelson, *Sinners, Saints and Settlers: A Journey through Irish Australia*, National Museum of Australia Press, Canberra, 2011.

———, *Not just Ned: A True History of the Irish in Australia*, National Museum of Australia Press, Canberra, 2011.

Retallack, James, *Red Saxony. Election Battles and the Spectre of Democracy in Germany 1860–1918*, OUP, 2017.

Reynolds, Henry, *Unneccesary Wars*, New South Publishing, Sydney, 2016.

Ringer, Fritz, *The Decline of the German Mandarins: The German Academic Community 1890–1933*, HUP, Cambridge, Mass., 1969.

Ritter, Gerhard, *Stein: Eine politische Biographie*, 2 Vols. Deutsche Verlagsanstalt, Munich, 1931.

———, *Sword and Scepter*, 4. Vols, University of Miami Press, Coral Gables, Florida, 1969–73 (trans. of *Staatskunst und Kriegshandwerk: Das Problem des Militarismus in Deutschland*, Verlag R. Oldenbourg, Munich, 1964–68).

Robson, Lloyd L., *The First AIF: A Study of its Recruitment, 1914–1918*, MUP, Carlton Sth, 1970.

Röhl, J. C. G., *From Bismarck to Hitler*, Longman, London, 1970.

——— (ed.), *1914: Delusion or Design? The Testimony of two German Diplomats*, Elek, London, 1973.

———, *Wilhelm II: Into the Abyss of War and Exile, 1900–1941*, CUP, Cambridge, 2014.

———, & Guenther Roth, *Aus dem grossen Hauptquatier: Kurt Riezlers Briefe an Käthe Liebermann 1914–15*, Harrasowitz Verlag, Wiesbaden, 2016.

Röhr, Wolfgang, *Hundert Jahre deutsche Kriegsschulddebatte*, VSA Verlag, Hamburg, 2015.

Ruedorffer, J. J., *Grundzüge der Weltpolitik in der Gegenwart*, Deutsche Verlagsanstalt, Stuttgart, 1916. (Pseudonym for Kurt Riezler.)

Sabro, Martin et al. (eds), *Zeitgeschichte als Streitgeschichte: Grosse Kontroversen seit 1945*, Verlag C. H. Beck, Munich, 2003.

Scates, Bruce, *Return to Gallipoli: Walking in the Battlefields of the Great War*, CUP, Melbourne, 2006.

Schieder, Wolfgang (ed.), *Erster Weltkrieg, Ursachen, Entstehung und Kriegsziele*, Kiepenhauer & Witsch, Cologne/ Berlin, 1969.

Schnabel, Franz, *Deutsche Geschichte im 19. Jahrhundert*, 4 Vols, Herder, Freiburg, 1936 (1959).

Schöllgen, Gregor, ed. *Escape into War? The Foreign Policy of Imperial Germany,* Berg Publishers, New York, 1990.

Schorske, Carl E., *German Social Democracy, 1905–1917,* HUP, Cambridge Mass., 1955.

Schrecker, John E., *Imperialism and Chinese Nationalism: Germany in Shantung,* HUP, Cambridge, Mass., 1971.

Scott, Ernest, *The Official History of Australia in the War of 1914–1918,* Vol. IX, Angus & Robertson, Sydney, 1936.

Schulte, Bernd F., *Rückbesinnen und Neubestimmen: Beiträge zur Deutschen Frage, 1850 bis 1989,* Forum Film, Abteilung Geschichte und Zeitgeschehen, 2000.

———, *Aufstieg oder Niedergang: Deutschland zwischen Mittelalter und Postmoderne,* Hamburger Studien zu Geschichte und Zeitgeschehen, Hamburg, 2008.

———, *Deutsche Policy of Pretention: Der Abstieg eines Kriegerstaates 1971– 1914,* Hamburger Studien zu Geschichte und Zeitgeschehen, 2009.

———, *Das deutsche Reich von 1914: Europäische Konföderation und Weltreich,* Hamburger Studien zu Zeitgeschichte und Zeitgeschehn, Hamburg, 2012.

Schulze, Winfried, *Deutsche Geschichtswissenschaft nach 1945,* Deutscher Taschenbuch Verlag, Munich, 1989.

Schwabe, Klaus, *Wissenschaft und Kriegsmoral: Die deutschen Hochschullehrer und die politischen Grundfragen des ersten Weltkrieges,* Musterschmidt Verlag, Göttingen, 1969.

Seal, Graham, *Inventing ANZAC: The Digger and National Mythology,* University of Queensland Press, St Lucia, 2004.

Seeberg, Reinhold, *Geschichte, Krieg und Seele,* Georg Richters, Erfurt, 1916.

Shaw, Barry, ed. *Brisbane at War 1899–1918,* Brisbane History Group, Brisbane, 2017.

Sieg, Ulrich, *Germany's Prophet: Paul de Lagarde and the Origins of Modern Antisemitism,* Brandeis University Press, Waltham MA., 2013.

Smith, Helmut Walser, *German Nationalism and Religious Conflict: Culture, Ideology, Politics 1870–1914,* PUP, Princeton, 1995.

Smith, Woodruff D., *The Ideological Origins of Nazi Imperialism,* OUP, New York/Oxford, 1986.

Sombart, Werner, *Händler und Helden: Patriotische Besinnungen,* Dunker & Humboldt, Munich, 1915.

Srbik, Heinrich Ritter von, *Geist und Geschichte* 2 Vols., Verlag Bruckmann, Munich, 1950.

Stanley, Peter (ed.), *Why did Australia go to the Great War?* Proceedings of a Symposium held at the University of NSW, Canberra, 8 May 2013, Conflict & Society, Canberra, 2018.

Steinberg, Jonathan, *Yesterday' Deterrent: Tirpitz and the Birth of the German Battle Fleet,* Macdonald, London, 1965.

———, *Bismarck. A Life,* OUP, New York, 2011.

Steiner, Zara S. & Nielson, Keith, *Britain and the Origins of the First World War*, 2nd edn., Palgrave Macmillan, London, 2003.

Steinmetz, George, *The Devil's Handwriting: Precoloniality and the German Colonial State in Quingdau, Samoa, and Southwest Africa,* The University of Chicago Press, Chicago/London, 2007.

Stephens, David and Alison Broinowski, *The Honest History Book,* University of NSW Press, 2017.

Stevens, David (ed.), *Maritime Power in the 20ᵗʰ Century – The Australian Experience*, Allen & Unwin, Sydney, 1988.

———, *In All Respects Ready. Australia's Navy in World War One*, OUP, Melbourne, 2014.

Stevenson, Robert C., *To Win a Battle: The 1ˢᵗ Australian Division in the Great War, 1914–18,* CUP, Cambridge, 2013.

Stevenson, Robert C., *War with Germany*, OUP, Oxford, 2015.

Stern, Fritz, *The Politics of Cultural Despair: A Study in the Rise of the Germanic Ideology*, University of California Press, Berkeley, 1961.

———, *Bethmann Hollweg und der Krieg,* Mohr & Siebeck, Tübingen, 1968.

———, *Dreams and Delusions,* Weidenfeld & Nicholson, London, 1988.

———, *Einstein's German World,* Penguin Books, London, 2001.

Stockings, Craig and John Connor (eds), *Before Anzac Dawn: A Military History of Australia to 1915*, UNSW Press, Sydney, 2013.

Strong, Archibald, T., *Australia and the War,* George Robertson & Co, Melbourne 1915.

Strong, Rowan, *Anglicanism and the British Empire c.1700–1850,* OUP, Oxford, 2007.

Stürmer, Michael (ed.), *Das kaiserliche Deutschland: Politik und Gesellschaft 1870–1918,* Droste Verlag, Düsseldorf, 1970.

Taylor, A. J. P, *The Course of German History: A Survey of the Development of German History since 1815,* Routledge, London, 1945.

Thompson, Alistair, *ANZAC Memories: Living with the Legend*, OUP, Melbourne, 1994.

Thompson, Wayne C., *In the Eye of the Storm: Kurt Riezler and the Crises of Modern Germany*, Iowa State University Press, Iowa, 1980.

Vagts, Alfred, *A History of Militarism: Civilian and Military*, Hollis, London, 1959.

Veblen, Thorsten, *Imperial Germany and the Industrial Revolution*, Macmillan, New York, 1915.

Verhey, Jeffrey, *The Spirit of 1914: Militarism, Myth and Mobilisation in Germany*, CUP, Cambridge, 2000.

Vermeil, Eduard, *Germany's Three Reichs: Their History and Culture*, A. Dakers, London, 1945.

Vondung, Klaus (ed.), *Das wilhelminische Bildungsbürgertum*, Vandenhoeck & Ruprecht, Göttingen, 1976.

———, *Die Apokalypse in Deutschland*, Deutscher Taschenbuch Verein, Munich, 1988.

Wank, Solomon (ed.), *Doves and Diplomats*, Greenwood Press, Westport, Conn./London, 1978.

Wehler, Hans-Ulrich, *Krisenherde des Kaiserreiches*, Vandenhoek und Ruprecht, Göttingen, 1970.

Wieland, Lothar, *Belgien 1914: Die Frage des belgischen 'Franktireurkrieges' und die deutsche öffentliche Meinung von 1914 bis 1936*, Peter Lang, Frankfurt/M, Bern/New York, 1984.

Wilcox, Craig, *Australia's Boer War: The War in South Africa 1899–1902*, OUP, Melbourne, 2002.

Willms, Johannes, *Bismarck: Dämon der Deutschen: Anmerkungen zu einer Legende*, Kindler Verlag, Munich, 2011.

Winkler, Heinrich A., *Germany: The Long Road West*, OUP, Oxford/New York, 2006–2007.

Winter, Jay, et al. (eds), *The Cambridge History of the First World War*, Cambridge, 2014.

Wolff, Theodor, *Tagebücher 1914–1919*, eingeleitet und herausgegeben von Bernd Sösemann, 2 Vols. Harald Boldt Verlag, Boppard am Rhein, 1984.

Wormell, Deborah, *Sir John Seeley and the Uses of History*, CUP, Cambridge/New York, 1980.

Yates, Keith, *Graf Spee's Raiders: Challenge to the Royal Navy 1914–1915*, Naval Institute Press, Annapolis, 1995.

Zarnow, Gottfried, *Die Geburt der Weltkriege*, Verlag für politische Bildung, Düsseldorf, 1957.

Book Chapters and Journal Articles

Anderson, Margaret Lavinia, 'A German Way of War?' *German History,* Vol. 22 No. 2 2004.

Badash, Lawrence, 'British and American Views of the German Menace in World War 1', *Notes and Records of the Royal Society of London,* Vol. 34, 1979–80.

Blänsdorf, Agnes, 'Der Weg der Riezler Tagebücher: Zur Kontroverse über die Echtheit der Tagebücher Kurt Riezlers' *Geschichte in Wissenschaft und Unterricht,* No. 10, 1984.

Bongiorno, Frank & Grant Mansfield, 'Teaching and Learning Guide for: Whose War was it Anyway? Some Australian Historians and the Great War', *History Compass,* Vol. 7, No. 2, March 2009.

Brändle, Maximillian, 'Henry Tardent 1853–1929', in *The Queensland Experience: The Life and Work of 14 Remarkable Migrants,* Maximillian Brändle (ed.), Phoenix Publications, Brisbane 1991.

Broinowski, Alison, 'Australia's Tug of War: Militarism versus Independence', in *The Honest History Book,* David Stephens & Alison Broinowski (eds), UNSW Press, Sydney 2017.

Chickering, Roger, 'Problems of a German Peace Movement, 1890–1914', in Solomon Wank (ed.), *Doves and Diplomats,* Greenwood Press, Westport, Conn./London 1978.

Cooper, Anthony, 'Australian Historiography of the First World War: Who is Deluded?', *Australian Journal of Politics and History,* Vol. 40, No. 1, April 1994.

Düllfer, Jost, 'Militarismus, Realpolitik und Pazifismus': Aussenpolitik und Aufrüstung in der Sicht deutscher Hochschullehrer (Historiker) im späten Kaiserreich', *Militärgeschichtliche Mitteilungen,* Vol. 1, 1986.

Eley, Geoffrey, 'Germany, the Fischer Controversy, and the Context of War: Re-Thinking German Imperialism, 1880–1914' in *Cataclysm 1914,* Alexander Anievas (ed.), pp. 23–36.

Faber, Karl-Georg, 'Realpolitik als Ideologie', *Historische Zeitschrift,* Vol. 203, August 1966.

Fletcher, Brian H., 'Anglicanism and National Identity in Australia, 1900–1914', *Journal of Religious History,* Vol. 25, No. 3, October 2001.

Gammage, Bill, 'Anzac's Influence on Turkey and Australia', *Journal of the Australian War Memorial,* 18 April 1991.

Gasser, Adolf, 'Der deutsche Hegemonialkrieg von 1914', in *Deutschland und die Weltpolitik des 19. und 20. Jahrhunderts,* I. Geiss & B. J. Wendt (eds), Droste Verlag, Düsseldorf, 1973.

Geiss, Imanuel, 'Kurt Riezler und der erste Weltkrieg', in *Deutschland in der Weltpolitik des 19. und 20. Jahrhunderts,* I. Geiss & B. J. Wendt (eds), Droste Verlag, Düsseldortf, 1973.

Hildebrand, Klaus, 'Der deutsche Eigenweg: Über das Problem der Normalität in der modernen Geschichte Deutschlands und Europas', in Manfred Funke et al. (eds), *Demokratie und Diktatur: Geist und Gestalt politischer Herrschaft in Deutschland und Europa,* Droste Verlag, Düsseldorf, 1987.

Hirschfeld, Gerhard, 'From one War to the Other: The Impact of the First World War on the Second World War', in, *Bid for World Power? New Research on the Outbreak of the First World War,* Andreas Gestrich & Hartmut Pogge von Strandmann (eds), German Historical Insitute London, Oxford, OUP, 2017.

Hoffmann, Christhard, 'Geschichte und Ideologie: Der Berliner Antisemitismusstreit 1879/81', in Wolfgang Benz & Werner Bergmann (eds), *Vorurteil und Völkermord: Entwicklungslinien des Antisemitismus,* Herder, Freiburg/Basel/Wien, 1997.

Iggers, Georg G., 'The Professionalization of Historical Studies and the Guiding Assumptions of Modern Historical Thought', in *A Companion to Western Historical Thought,* Lloyd Kramer and Sarah Maza (eds), Blackwells, Oxford 2006.

Jenkins, Julian, 'German War Theology and Germany's *Sonderweg*: Luther's Heirs and Patriotism', *Journal of Religious History,* Vol. 15, No. 3 June 1989.

Jones, David, 'Ripples from a distant War: The Port of Brisbane in the Great War', *Brisbane at War 1899–1918,* Barry Shaw (ed.), Brisbane History Group Papers No. 26, 2017, pp. 89–100.

Keyserling, Hermann, 'On the Meaning of the War', *Hibbert Journal,* Vol. 13, No. 3, 1916.

Leonhard, Jörn, 'Construction and Perception of National Images: Germany and Britain, 1870–1914', *The Linacre Journal,* No. 4, December 2000.

Mann, Golo, '1914 – The Beast in the Jungle. Dr Fischer's Thesis', *Encounter,* November 1965.

Mansfield, Grant, *'Unbounded Enthusiasm*: Australian Historians and the Outbreak of the Great War', *Australian Journal of Politics and History,* Vol. 53, No. 3, September 2007.

Mombauer, Monika, 'The Fischer Controversy after Fifty Years', Special Issue of the *Journal of Contemporary History,* 48/2, April 2013.

Mommsen, Wolfgang J., 'Der Geist von 1914: Das Program eines politischen Sonderwegs der Deutschen', in *Nation und Geschichte,* Wolfgang, J. Mommsen (ed.), Piper Verlag, Munich, 1990.

———, 'The Spirit of 1914 and the Ideology of a German *Sonderweg',* in *Imperial Germany 1867–1918: Politics, Culture and Society in an Authoritarian State,* Arnold, London 1995 (trans. by Richard Deveson).

Moses, John A., 'The British and German Churches and the Perception of War 1908–1914', *War and Society,* Vol. 5, No. 1, 1987.

———, 'Australian Anglican Leaders and the Great War, 1914–1918: The 'Prussian Menace', Conscription and National Solidarity' *Journal of Religious History,* Vol. 25, No. 3, October 2001.

———, 'Archibald T. Strong (1876–1930): An Australian Empire Patriot and the Great War', *Australian Journal of Politics and History,* Vol. 53, No. 3, September 2007.

———, 'The Prusso-German Idea of War: The Values of a Rogue State', *History Compass,* Vol. 19, No. 12, December 2012.

———, 'The Faith of Canon David John Garland (1864–1939) – An Australian Gladstonian Imperialist', *St Mark's Review,* Vol. 225, No. 3, August 2013.

———, 'German Bourgeois Pacifists and World War I: The Example of Professor Dr Georg Nicolai', *ISAA Review,* Vol. 13, No. 1, 2014.

———, 'The University of Queensland's Reaction to the Great War', *Journal of the Royal Historical Society of Queensland,* Vol. 22, No. 9, May 2015.

———, , 'Alfred von Tirpitz: Architect of the Imperial German Battle Fleet', in *The War at Sea: Proceedings of the King-Hall Naval History Conference,* Andrew Forbes (ed.), Sea Power Centre, Canberra, 2015.

Overlack, Peter, 'German Commerce Warfare Planning for the Australian Station, 1900–1914', *War & Society,* Vol. 14, No. 1, May 1966.

———, 'Queensland's Annexation of Papua: A Background to Anglo-German Friction,' *Journal of the Royal Historical Society of Queensland,* Vol. 10, No. 4, 1979.

Overlack, Peter, 'Australian Defence Awareness and German Naval Planning in the Pacific, 1900–1914, *War & Society,* Vol. 10, No. 1, May 1992.

———, 'The Past Re-Captured and Lost: Irish and German Political Romanticism Compared', in *Papers of the Seventh Irish-Australian Conference 1993,* Crossing Press, Sydney, 1994.

———, 'German Interest in Australian Defence 1900–1914: New Insights into a Precarious Position on the Eve of War', *Australian Journal of Politics and History,* Vol. 40, No. 1, 1994.

———, 'An Instrument of Culture: The Imperial German Navy, the Academics and Germany's World Mission', in *Power, Conscience and Opposition, Essays in Honour of John A. Moses,* A. Bonnell, G. Munro & M. Travers (eds), Peter Lang, Bern/ New York, 1996.

———, 'The Force of Circumstance: Graf Spee's Options for the East Asia Cruiser Squadron in 1914', *Journal of Military History,* Vol. 60, No. 4, October 1996.

———, 'German Commerce Warfare Planning for the Australian Station 1900–14', *War & Society,* Vol. 14, No. 1, May 1996.

———, 'Marconi versus Telefunken: the Anglo-German Struggle for the Australian Airwaves before 1914', *Journal of the Australian Naval Institute,* January–March 1997.

———, 'Captive in Brisbane: The Diary of a German Captain's Wife', *Journal of the Royal Historical society of Queensland,* Vol. 16, No. 7, August 1997.

———, 'The 1916 Easter Rising in the Australian Press: Background & Response', *Journal of Australian Studies,* Vol. 21, No. 54/ 55, 1997.

———, 'Documents on Australian Maritime Strategy', in *In Search of a Maritime Strategy: The Maritime Element in Australian Defence Planning since 1901,* David Stevens (ed.), ANU Press, Canberra, 1997.

———, 'The Function of Commerce Warfare in an Anglo-German Conflict to 1914', *Journal of Strategic Studies,* Vol. 20, No. 4, December 1997.

———, 'Australasia and Germany: Challenge and Response before 1914', in *Maritime Power in the Twentieth Century. The Australian Experience,* David Stevens (ed.), Allen & Unwin, Sydney, 1998.

———, 'Bless the Queen and Curse the Colonial Office' – Australian Reaction to German Consolidation in the Pacific', *Journal of Pacific History,* Vol. 33, No. 2, September 1998.

Overlack, Peter, 'Asia in German Naval Planning Before the First World War: The Strategic Imperative', *War & Society,* Vol. 17, No. 1, May 1999.

———, 'Australian Reactions to German Interests in the Netherlands Indies and Timor prior to 1914: A Strategic Imperative', in *The German Empire and Britain's Pacific Dominions 187 1–1919. Essays on the Role of Australia and New Zealand in World Politics in the Age of Imperialism,* J. A. Moses & C. Pugsley (eds), Regina Books, Claremont, CA, 2001.

———, 'A Vigorous Offensive: Core Aspects of Australian Maritime Defence Concerns before 1914', in *Southern Trident. Strategy, History and the Rise of Australian Naval Power,* Allen & Unwin, Sydney, 2001.

———, 'The Commander in Crisis: Graf Spee and the German East Asia Cruiser Squadron in 1914', in *The Face of Naval Battle. The Human Experience of Modern War at Sea,* J. Reeve and D. Stevens (eds), Allen & Unwin, Sydney, 2003.

———, 'Japan as a Factor in German Asian Policy before World War 1', in Europe's Pasts and Presents. Proceedings of the 14th Biennial Conference of the Australian Association for European History, 2003, Australian Humanities Press, Adelaide, 2004.

———, 'German Assessments of British–Australian Relations, 1901–1914', *Australian Journal of Politics and History,* Vol. 50. No. 2, 2004.

———, 'German War Plans in the Pacific, 1900–1914', *The Historian,* Vol. 60, No. 3, Spring, 1998.

Palmer, Nettie, 'The Protectors of Small Nationalities', *The Socialist,* 12 February 1915.

Quarterly Review, No. 443, April 1915.

Ringer, Fritz, '*Bildung:* The Social and Ideological Context of the German Historical Tradition,' *History of European Ideas,* Vol. 10, No. 2 1989.

Schlenke, Manfred, 'Nationalsozialismus und Preussen: eine historische Bilanz aus Anlass der 60. Wiederkehr des Tages von Potsdam (21 März 1933)', in Peter-Michael Hahn et al., *Potsdam: Märkische Kleinstadt,* de Gruyter, Berlin 1955.

Sontheimer, 'Deutscher Geist als Ideologie: Ein Beitrag zur Theorie vom deutschen Sonderbewusstsein', in Manfred Funke et al. (eds), *Demokratie und Diktatur: Geist und Gestalt politischer Herrschaft in Deutschland und Europa,* Droste Verlag, Düsseldorf, 1987.

Stevens, David, 'The German Naval Threat in the Indo-Pacific 1914–15', *The Strategist,* 31 July 1915.

Tampke, Jürgen, 'Imperial Germany's Military Strategy in the South Pacific', *Australian Journal of Politics and History,* Vol. 40, No. 2, April 1994, pp. 96–102.

Tucker, T. G. 'British and German Ideals', in *PLW,* George Robertson & Co., Melbourne, 1915.

Turner, L. C. F., 'Australian Historians and the Study of War', *Historical Disciplines and Culture in Australasia, An Assessment,* John A. Moses (ed.), University of Queensland Press, St Lucia 1979.

Vom Brocke, Bernard, 'An die Europäer' – Der Fall Nicolai und die Biologie des Krieges', *Historische Zeitschrift,* Vol. 240, 1985.

Vom Bruch, Rudiger, 'Universität, Staat und Gesellschaft', *Archiv für Sozialgeschtichte,* Bd. 20, 1980.

Vondung, Klaus, 'Deutsche Apokalypse 1914', in *Das wilhelminische Bildungsbürgertum,* Vandenhoek und Ruprecht, Göttingen 1976.

Wehler, Hans-Ulrich, 'Der erste totaler Krieg: Woran das deutsche Reich zugrunde ging – und was daraus folgte', *Die Zeit,* Nr 35, 20 August 1998, Nr 35/1998.

Wernecke, Klaus, 'Aussenpolitik ohne Unterbau. Christopher Clarks Mächte auf dem Weg in den Ersten Weltkrieg', *Sozialismus,* 2013, H. 12.

Williamson, George S., 'A Religious *Sonderweg?* Reflections on the Sacred and the Secular in the Historiography of Modern Germany', *Church History,* Vol. 75, No. 1, March 2006, pp. 139–56.

Withycombe, Robert, 'Australian Anglicans and Imperial Identity, 1900–1914', *Journal of Religious History,* Vol. 25, No. 3, October 2001.

Notes

Preface

1 See his novel, *Keiner kommt davon, Ullstein Verlag,* Frankfurt/ Berlin, 1957, meaning, 'None shall Escape', that is, the impending nuclear holocaust. It was subsequently translated as the *Seventh Day,* 1959.

2 Succinctly explained in Georg G. Iggers, *The German Conception of History,* WUP, Middletown, Conn., 1968.

3 It should be noted that Bismarck had based his foreign policy on the annexation of the French provinces of Alsace and Lorraine in 1870, thus incurring the implacable resentment of France. His conception of foreign policy then was always to be aligned with two other great powers and to be militarily ready to march against any other powers which threatened the delicate balance. In short, international relations for Bismarck presumed that war could break out at any time, consequently the army had always to be maintained in a state of readiness for conflict.

4 This subject has been neglected by Australian historians, but see the chapters by Peter Overlack.

5 Clive Hamilton, *Silent Invasion: China's Influence in Australia,* Melbourne: Hardie Grant Books, 2018.

6 The most contentious example of failure in this respect has been the Whitlam government's policy towards the struggle of the East Timorese against Indonesian occupation when the Commonwealth succumbed to the then Jakarta regime. See Katsumi Ishizuki, 'Australian Policy towards East Timor', *The Round Table: Commonwealth Journal of International Affairs,* Vol. 93 No. 374, 2004, pp. 271–85.

Introduction

1 In 1909 Angell wrote a book entitled *Europe's Optical Illusion*. It was then re-issued the following year as *The Great Illusion: A Study of the Relations of Military Power in Nations to their Economic and Social Advantage,* Putnam, New York/ London, 1910. See also J. D. B. Miller, *Norman Angell and the Futility of War,* Macmillan, Basingstoke, Hampshire, London, 1986.

2 Still edifying is the book by E. H. Car, *What is History?,* Macmillan, London, 1961.

3 This is the only example of an Anzac monument, at least in Queensland, that depicts a digger in action. Appropriately, the monument was dedicated in May 1924 by the Reverend Robert Moline, MC, BSB who was then priest-in-charge of St Mary's Anglican Church in Atherton and priest-bother in the Brotherhood

of St Barnabas. Moline was a Cambridge graduate (Emmanuel College) and decorated for bravery in action in the Great War having been awarded the Military Cross. He had served as a junior officer in a Rifles regiment. Of additional interest is the fact that the unveiling of the statue was performed by the Shire chairman of Atherton Mr Frederick Grau who was from a German immigrant family of devout Roman Catholics. *Cairns Post*, 8 May 1924.

4   See the various works of Raymond Evans and his associates, formerly of the Department of History at the University of Queensland.

5   That is, *unvoreingenommen von irgendwelchen Fachkenntnissen.*

6   The Germans have an apposite saying about voicing uninformed opinions: *Vor Inbetriebnahme des Mundwerks, Gehirn einschalten*, meaning, 'before opening one's mouth one needs to switch on one's brain.'

7   John A. Moses, 'Australia's Academic Garrison 1914–1918', *Australian Journal of Politics and History*, Vol. 36 No. 3 1990, pp. 361–76; John A. Moses, *Prussian-German Militarism 1914–1918*, in *Australian Perspective and The Thought of George Arnold Wood*, Peter Lang, Bern/Frankfurt am Main, 1991.

8   Dr Gerhard Fischer, a German-born and educated linguistic scholar who taught at the University of New South Wales ventured to publish on German-Australian relations and in particular about the internment of German nationals in Australian during the First World War. See *Enemy Aliens: Internment and the Home Front Experience in Australia 1914–1920*, University of Queensland Press, St Lucia, 1989; and (with Nadine Helmi), *Internment at Trial Bay during World War 1*, NSW Migration Heritage Centre, Ultimo, 2005.

9   See below chapter 7 and Moses, *Prussian-German Militarism*; Moses, 'An Australian Empire Patriot and the Great War: Professor Archibald T. Strong (1876–1930)' *Australian Journal of Politics and History*, Vol. 53, No. 3, September 2007, pp. 407–19; Stuart Macintyre, *A History for a Nation: Ernest Scott and the Making of Australian History*, Melbourne, 1994. In this context see the pioneering work of Neville Meaney, *A History of Australian Defence and Foreign Policy 1901–1923* Vol. I, *The Search for Security in the Pacific*, SUP, Sydney, 2009.

10 On 2 April 1917 Wilson went before the joint houses of Congress to seek a *Declaration of* War against Germany in order that the world be made safe for democracy. See 65th Congress, 1st Session, Senate Document No. 5.

11 See volume 11 of the *Official History of Australia in the War of 1914–1918*: Angus & Robertson, Sydney, 1921–1942.

Chapter 1: 'Lest we Forget' – Christianity and Australian Culture

1   Peter Rees, *Bearing Witness: The Remarkable Life of Charles Bean, Australia's Greatest War Correspondent*, Allen & Unwin, Sydney, 2015, pp. 124–8.

2   John A. Moses, 'Australian Anglican Leaders and the Great War, 1914–1918: The "Prussian Menace", Conscription and National Solidarity', *Journal of Religious History*, Vol. 25, No. 3, October 2001, pp. 306–22; Robert Withycombe, 'Australian Anglicans and Imperial Identity, 1900–1914', *Journal of Religious History*, Vol. 25 No. 3 October 2001, pp. 286–305; Brian H. Fletcher, 'Anglicanism and National Identity in Australia', *Journal of Religious History*,

Vol. 25 No. 3, October 2001, pp. 324–45. The scholarly insights of these papers and their significance in the discussion about Australian involvement in the Great War are totally ignored by such recent publications as, *Beyond Gallipoli: New Perspectives on Anzac,* Raelene Frances and Bruce Scates (eds.), Monash University Publishing, Melbourne, 2016. Clearly, the contributors to this volume occupy a parallel universe in contrast to those cited above in this footnote.

3   G. L. Mosse, *The Nationalisation of the Masses; Political Symbolism and Mass Movements in Germany from the Napoleonic Wars through to the Third Reich;* H. Fertig, New York, 1975; and *Fallen Soldiers: Re-shaping memory of the World Wars,* OUP, New York, 1990. See also Walter Grab, *Norddeutsche Jakobiner: Demokratische Bestrebungen zur Zeit der französischen Revolution,* Europäische Verlagsanstalt, Frankfurt/M, 1967.

4   Keith Yates, *Graf Spee's Raiders: Challenge to the Royal Navy 1914–1915,* Naval Institute Press, Annapolis, 1995.

5   Peter Overlack, 'The Imperial German Navy in the Pacific 1900–1914 as an instrument of *Weltpolitik,* with special reference to Australasia in its operational planning' (PhD thesis, Department of History, University of Queensland, 1995). Dr Overlack has published much of this thesis in article form in journals of military and naval studies. His work is of fundamental importance in understanding the direct imperial German threat to Australasian security during the First World War.

6   Wayne Hudson, *Australian Religious Thought,* Monash University Press, Melbourne, 2016.

7   See the concise discussion of Orangeism in Moses/ Davis, *Anzac Day Origins,* pp. 102–4.

8   See Mandell Creighton, *The Church and Nation: Charges and Addresses,* Hardpress reprint, 2012.

9   John A. Moses, 'The Faith of Canon David John Garland (1864–1939) – An Australian Gladstonian Imperialist', *St Mark's Review,* No. 225, August 2013 (3), pp. 71–84.

10   Leonie Foster, *High Hopes: The Men and Motives of the Australian Round Table,* MUP, 1986.

11   For example, William Hutchison & Hartmut Lehmann (eds.), *Many are Chosen: Divine Election and Western Nationalism*: Fortress Press, Minneapolis, 1994.

12   In particular see Hilary M. Carey, *God's Empire – Religion and Colonialism in the British World, c.1801–1908,* CUP, 2011; Rowan Strong, *Anglicanism and the British Empire c.1700–1850,* OUP, 2007.

13   Richard Gilson, Samoa, *1830–1910: The Politics of a Multicultural Community,* OUP, Melbourne/New York, 1970; Jim Davidson, *Samoa mo Samoa: The Emergence of the Independent State of Western Samoa*: OUP, 1967; and Peter Hempenstall, *Pacific Islanders under German Rule: A Study in the Meaning of Colonial Resistance,* ANU Press, Canberra, 1978.

14   Burton L. Mack, *Who Wrote the New Testament? The Making of the Christian Myth,* Harper Collins, New York, 1950.

15   From the poem, *The Recessional,* where it occurs in the first stanza:

God of our fathers, known of old,
Lord of our far-flung battle-line,
Beneath whose awful hand we hold
Dominion over palm and pine –
Lord God of Hosts, be with us yet
Lest we forget, lest we forget.

Chapter 2: Towards Understanding the Rise of the Prusso-Germany:
The Unknown Empire

1 Cited after Roger Chickering, 'Problems of a German Peace Movement, 1890–1914', in Soloman Wank (ed.), *Doves and Diplomats*, Greenwod Press, Westport, Conn,/London, 1978, pp. 42–54.

2 A.J.P. Taylor, *The Course of German History: A Survey of the Development of German History since 1815*, Routledge, London, 1945; Eduard Vermeil, *Germany's Three Reichs: Their History and Culture*, A. Dakers, London, 1945. For a more recent assessment of Prussia, see Christopher Clark, *Iron Kingdom: The Rise and Downfall of Prussia 1600–1947*, The Belknap Press of HUP, Cambridge, Mass., 2006.

3 On Seeley see Deborah Wormell, *Sir John Seeley and the Uses of History*, CUP, Cambridge/New York, 1980.

4 J. A. R. Marriott & James Grant Robertson, *The Evolution of Prussia The Making of an Empire*, The Clarendon Press, Oxford, 1915; William Harbutt Dawson, *The Evolution of Modern Germany*, Fisher Unwin, London, 1914; Thorsten Veblen, *Imperial Germany and the Industrial Revolution*, Macmillan, New York, 1915.

5 See Moses, *Prussian-German Militarism* and Stuart Macintyre, *A History for a Nation: Ernest Scott and the Making of Australian History*, Carlton, MUP, 1994; Moses, 'Archibald T. Strong', pp. 407–19.

6 Robin Gollan, *Radical and Working Class Politics: A Study of Eastern Australia, 1850–1910*, Melbourne: MUP, 1960.

7 Maximilian Brändle, 'Henry Tardent 1853–1929', *The Queensland Experience: The Life and Work of 14 Remarkable Migrants*, Maximillian Brändle (ed.), Phoenix Publications, Brisbane, 1991, p. 77.

8 Ibid., p. 82.

9 John A. Moses, *Trade Unionism in Germany from Bismarck to History*, 2 Vols., Barnes & Noble, New York, 1984.

10 *Deutsche Geschichte im 19. Jahrhundert* Vol. I, Herder Verlag, Freiburg, 1959, pp. 95–7. Translation by present writer.

11 Imanuel Geiss, *Nation und Nationalismen: Versuche über ein Weltproblem*, edition lumiere, Bremen, 2007, pp. 54–5. 'Ein Staat wie das Bismarckische Preussen-Deutschland ist durch seinen Ursprung mit fatalistischer Notwendigkeit dem Untergang geweiht ... Auf dem Schlachtfeld geboren, das Kind des Staatsstreichs, des Krieges und der Revolution von oben, muss es ruhelos vom Staatsstreich zu Staatsstreich, vom Krieg zu Krieg eilen, und entweder auf dem Schlachtfeld

zerbröckeln oder der Revolution von unten erliegen. Das ist Naturgesetz.'

12 Johannes Willms, *Bismarck: Dämon der Deutschen: Anmerkung zu einer Legende*, Kindler Verlag, Munich, 2011. Jonathan Steinberg, *Bismarck. A Life*, OUP, New York, 2011. Note that Italy because of her unique geographical position as a giant peninsula could never be involved in an anti-British coalition simply because of her acute vulnerability to naval attack.

13 Moses, *Trade Unionism in Germany*, Vol. I, pp. 139–62 *passim*; Carl E. Schorske, *German Social Democracy 1905–1917*, HUP, Cambridge, Mass. 1955.

14 Fritz Fischer, *Krieg der Illusionen*, Droste Verlag, Düsseldorf, 1969, pp. 231–50, *passim*.

15 John Röhl, *Wilhelm II: Into the Abyss of War and Exile, 1900–1941*, CUP, 2014, p. 911. See also Fischer, *Krieg der Illusionen* (chapter 9), pp. 231–88, *passim*.

16 See Helmut Bley, *Bebel und die Strategie der Kriegsverhütung 1904–1913*, Offizin Verlag, Hannover, 2014, pp. 17–18. Here, the Social Democratic history professor points out that apart from mainly Hans-Ulrich Wehler, Wilhelm Deist and Dieter Groh, very few colleagues had drawn attention to the Zabern crisis as an unmistakeable warning signal to the army leadership that their special position in the Reich constitution was being challenged. They were nothing less than ecstatic during the July crisis soon after since it most definitely presaged the war that had all been hankering for which in their estimation would bolster and enhance their political standing.

17 Hans-Ulrich Wehler, *Krisen Herde des Kaiserreiches*, Vandenhoek und Ruprecht, Göttingen, 1970. Wehler entitled chapter II. 'Symbol des halbabsolutischen Herrschaftssystems: Der Fall Zabern von 1913/14 als Verfassungskrise des Wilhelminischen Reiches', pp. 65–84. That is, the Zabern affair was a symbol of the permanent dysfunctionality of the Kaiserreich, described as *half absolutist*. Wolfgang Mommsen agreed in his *Imperial Germany 1867–1918: Politics, Culture, and Society in an Authoritarian State* (trans. by Richard Deveson), Arnold, London, 1995 in which he highlighted the disjunction between the political and social structures within Germany.

18 Bernd F. Schulte, *Das Deutsche Reich von 1914: Europäische Konföderation und Weltreich*, Hamburger Studien zu Zeitgeschichte und Zeitgeschehen, Hamburg, 2012.

19 Guenther Roth and John Röhl, *Aus dem Grossen Hauptquatier: Kurt Riezlers Briefe and Käthe Liebermann 1914–15*, Harrasowitz Verlag, Wiesbaden, 2016.

20 Wayne C. Thompson, *In the Eye of the Storm: Kurt Riezler and the Crises of Modern Germany*, Iowa State University Press, Iowa, 1980.

21 See A. Dirk Moses, *German Intellectuals and the Nazi Past*, CUP, Cambridge, 2007, p. 105, chapter 5, where the phenomenon of the German who had to flee the fatherland into exile but who still identified himself with German liberal culture.

22 See the most important findings of Dr Bruce Gaunson in this regard: *At War with the Kaiserreich: Australia's Epic in the Great War*, Hybrid Publishers, Melbourne, 2018.

Chapter 3: German War Aims in the Pacific

1   Christian Morgenstern (1871–1914), the poem is 'Die unmögliche Tatsache', that
    is 'The impossible Fact.' The final stanza is:

    Und er kommt zu dem Ergebnis [And he comes to the conclusion]

    Nur ein Traum war das Erlebnis [His mishap was an illusion,]

    Weil, so schliesst er messerscharf, [For he reasons pointedly]

    Nichts sein kann, was sein sein darf. [That which must not, cannot be.]

2   Dr Tampke was a German-born student at Macquarie University graduating BA
    in 1971 and who then completed a doctorate at ANU in 1975. Subsequently, he
    taught at UNSW until retirement.

3   Cited after Roger Chickering, *We Men who Feel most German: A Cultural Study of
    the Pan-German League*, 1886–1914, Allen & Unwin, Boston, 1984, pp. 12–13.

4   John E. Shrecker, *Imperialism and Chinese Nationalism: Germany in Shantung*,
    HUP, Cambridge, Mass. 1971, p. 180. Coal was mined from the Wei-hsein field
    from 1902.

5   See below chapters 8, 9 and 10 by Peter Overlack for detailed analysis of imperial
    German naval activities for the Far East and Pacific.

6   Alison Broinowski, 'Australia's Tug of War: Militarism versus Independence'
    in *The Honest History Book,* David Stephens & Alison Broinowski (eds.),
    UNSW Press, Sydney, 2017, pp. 271–86. This chapter makes such assertions as
    'Conservative Australian leaders have always preferred subservience to autonomy,'
    p. 273. The argument is that 'Republicans and egalitarians, on the other hand,
    resented Australians being called up to fight for Britain …' Such reasoning
    is flawed because it leaves out of the equation the fact that other Great Power
    harboured designs on Britain's Pacific dependencies. Most Australians have
    preferred to live in a body politic where the rule of law and basic human rights
    prevailed. That is essentially why Australasian leaders have supported 'Britain's
    wars'. Empire membership ensured liberty.

7   Newton in *Honest History,* 16–31. A more elegant example of the fallacy of
    presentism would be hard to imagine. In short, many of the contributors to this
    volume share in this fallacy which means they write history how they would
    prefer it to have been rather than as it actually was.

8   Davis Mc Caughey, *Piecing Together a Shared Vision,* The 1987 Boyer Lectures,
    Sydney: The Australian Broadcasting Corporation, 1988. On pp. 15–16 he
    writes, 'An Irish historian recently wrote: 'To the Irish all history is applied
    history, and the past is simply a convenient quarry which provides ammunition
    to use against enemies in the present. They have little interest in it for its own
    sake. That is a terrible indictment. It suggests that it is not the truth of the matter
    that is sacred, only the use to which the material may be put. Of course, it is well
    known that all history is written or perceived from a particular point of view. The
    past is always appreciated in a particular perspective. … [But] … there is all the
    difference in the world, between, on the one hand, knowing that your knowledge
    is partial, and, on the other, using the past as a quarry from which to build a
    secure house for yourself in the present.'

9   On 3 August, the British ambassador to Berlin, Sir Edward Goschen put the

question to Reich Chancellor Bethmann Hollweg as to what guarantees the German government would give regarding the future of the French and Belgian colonies in the event of a French defeat, and the answer was evasive. The Australian government picked this up and construed it to mean that Germany would feel free to dispose over all the overseas territories of other defeated Powers. See *The British White Book*.

10 On the Tirpitz Plan see John A. Moses, 'Alfred von Tirpitz: Architect of the Imperial German Battle fleet' in *The War at Sea*, Andrew Forbes (ed.), Sea Power Centre-Australia, Canberra, 2015, pp. 23–34. Tirpitz continues to attract interpreters as the recent appearance of studies by the German scholars, Michael Epkenhans and Michael Salewski as well as the American Patrick J. Kelly indicate. Their details are to be found in the Bibliography.

11 Davis McCaughey, *Piecing together a shared Vision,* 1987, Boyer Lecture.

12 See for example: 'Australasia and Germany: challenge and response before 1914' in *Maritime Power in the Twentieth Century – the Australian Experience*, David Stevens (ed.), Allen & Unwin, Sydney, 1998, pp. 22–39. Here the context of the Great Power naval rivalry and its impact on Australian and New Zealand politicians at the time is painstakingly recorded. Curiously, the advocates of 'presentism' do not wish to know about all this.

13 David Blackbourn and Geoff Eley, *The Peculiarities of German History: Bourgeois Society and Politics in 19ᵗʰ Century Germany,* Oxford/New York: OUP, 1984. One should note, however, that Professor Eley has now reversed his assessment of imperial Germany and has taken on board the criticism of Professor Jürgen Kocka.

Chapter 4: Recounting the Rise of the Prussian Menace and German War Aims 1914–1918

1 Andreas Gestrich & Hartmut Pogge von Strandmann (eds.), *Bid for World Power: New Research on the Outbreak of the First World War*, OUP, Oxford/New York, 2017.

2 Wilfried Nippel, *John Gustav Droysen: ein Leben zwischen Wissenschaft und Politik*, C.H. Beck, Munich, 2008, p. 175.

3 See Heinrich von Srbik, *Geist und Geschichte*, Verlag F. Brückmann, Munich, 1950, vol. I, p. 189.

4 See St Paul's Epistle to the Romans, chapter XIII.

5 For a more extensive explanation of this phenomenon see John A. Moses, *Reluctant Revolutionary: Dietrich Bonhoeffer's Collision with Prusso-German History*, Berghahn Books, New York, 2009 & 2014) See especially the chapter, 'The "Peculiarity" of German Political Culture', pp. 1–26.

6 It is well known Moslem teaching from the Hadith (tradition) that, '[There] is a palace in Paradise and in it are seventy courts of ruby ... And in each court [there are] seventy houses of green emerald stone, in every house seventy beds. On every bed, seventy mattresses of every colour and on every mattress a woman.'

7 Hans Delbrück, *Regierung und Volkswille: Ein Grundriss der Politik*, Deutsche Verlagsgesellschaft für Politk, Berlin-Charlottenburg, 1920. See Delbrück's

account of the causes of the war and the responses of his English colleague James Headlam-Morley in *The Contemporary Review*, March 1921, pp. 322–45.

8 Adolf, Gasser, *Ausgewählte historische Schriften 1933–1983*, Helbig & Lichtenhahn, 1983, pp. 51–3. Gasser's critique of the *Kaiserreich* is directed at the fact that it was dominated behind the scenes by the military. He observed that those men were not necessarily all rabid imperialists but they were *infantile* in their understanding of the real world. This indictment is endorsed by Kurt Riezler in his correspondence from Army HQ with his fiancé. On 28 August 1914 he confided to her that there was much enthusiastic discussion about the most desirable way to re-order Europe. However, Riezler noted: 'The military are of course completely raving (ganz rabiat) and want to annex half of the world'. See Roth & Röhl, *Aus dem grossen Hauptquatier*, p. 126.

Chapter 5: Historicism: The Forgotten Ideology Behind Weltpolitik

1 The 1912 elections saw the SPD returned with a majority of 110 mandates in a house of 397 seats. Of the 30 parties represented the Catholic Centre (*Zentrum*) party polled 91 seats while the progressive liberals (*Fortschrittliche Volkspartei*) listed 42.

2 The research on this question is considerable. See Gregor Schöllgen (ed.), *Escape into War? The Foreign Policy of Imperial Germany*, Berg Publishers, New York, 1990.

3 George F. Kennan, *The Decline of Bismarck's European Order: Franco-Russian Relations 1875–1890*, PUP, Princeton, 1979, Introduction.

4 First published by Alan Lane, London 2012, now in paperback by Harper Perennial, 2014.

5 The order of *Knight Bachelor* was bestowed in 2015. In 2008 Clark succeeded Sir Richard Evans as *Regius Professor* at Cambridge. He was awarded the *Order of Merit* of the Federal Republic of Germany in 2010 for services to Anglo-German relations as well as the *Deutscher Historiker Preis* in the same year. Any improvement in Anglo-German understanding, is of course, to be welcomed. The question is whether one may cosmetically re-write the history of a tortured past in order to improve international relations in the present. In Queensland, where Clark was raised he was honoured by the *Premier's Prize* and received the same accolade in New South Wales in 2007. In the United Kingdom Clark received the *Wolfson Historian's Prize* 2007, as well as other awards.

6 Wolfgang Röhr, *Hundert Jahre deutsche Kriegschulddebatte*, VSA Verlag, Hamburg, 2015, p. 122.

7 See Georg G. Iggers, 'The Professionalisation of Historical Studies and the Guiding Assumptions of Modern Historical Thought' in *A Companion to Western Historical Thought* Lloyd Kramer and Sarah Maza (eds.), Blackwell, Oxford, 2006 – paperback. In a penetrating observation about Hayden White's views, Iggers states on page 239 that giving precedence to the shaping power of narrative rather than to research would mean the destruction of the professional ethos of the historian.

8 Klaus Wernecke, 'Aussenpolitik ohne Unterbau. Christopher Clarks Mächte auf dem Weg in den Ersten Weltkrieg' *Sozialismus*, 2013, H. 12.

9   See the remarks of Professor Oliver Janz of Berlin (*Freie Universität*), *1914 Der Grosse Krieg*, Campus Verlag, Frankfurt/New York, 2013. On page 17 he writes that the German imperial government bears a considerable part (*einen erheblichen Teil*) of the historical responsibility for the outbreak of a general war as Fischer wrote in 1961 is largely uncontested: *Dass die deutsche Reichsführung einen erheblichen Teil der historischen Verantwortung für den Ausbruch des allgemeinen Krieges trug, wie Fischer 1961 schrieb, ist weitgehend unbestritten.*

10 The literature on this is considerable, but note Thomas Mann, *Die Betrachtungen eines Unpolitischen* (1918), trans. by Walter D. Morris, as *Reflections of a non political Man* (New York, 1983). Of specific relevance here is Eckhardt Fuchs, *Henry Thomas Buckle: Geschichtsschreibung und Positivismus in Deutschland*, Leipzig, 1994, where Fuchs recalls the critique by F. C. Dahlmann of Buckle. The great pioneer of Historicism celebrated German *Kultur* as opposed to superficial Anglo-Saxon 'civilisation'. See also Jeffrey Verhey, *The Spirit of 1914: Militarism, Myth and Mobilisation in Germany*, CUP, Cambridge, 2000.

11 Ludwig Dehio, 'Ranke und der deutsche Imperialismus' *Historische Zeitschrift* CLXX, 1950, pp. 307–28. This appeared in an anthology of Dehio's essays in English entitled *Germany and World Politics in the Twentieth Century*, Chatto & Windus, London, 1960, pp. 38–71.

12 The question of German Anglophobia is dealt with in the monumental work of Paul Michael Kennedy, *The Rise of the Anglo-German Antagonism 1860–1914*, George Allen & Unwin, London 1980.

13 This entire subject has been penetratingly dealt with by Georg G. Iggers, *The German Conception of History*, WUP, Middletown Conn., 1968. Iggers has subsequently added numerous books and articles not only on German historiographical traditions but also other European and Chinese traditions in historical writing. For a more recent and concise example of Iggers' incisive observations, see his, 'The Professionalization of Historical Studies and the Guiding Assumptions of Modern Historical Thought' in *A Companion to Western Historical Thought*, Lloyd Kramer and Sarah Maza (eds.), Blackwells, Oxford, 2006.

14 Published in English as *Historism: The Rise of the New Historical Outlook* (trans. by J. E. Anderson): Herder & Herder, New York, 1972. See slso: *Weltbürgertum und Nationalstaat*, Munich, 1907, translated as *Cosmopolitanism and the National State*, Princeton, 1979, and *Die Idee der Staatsräson*, Munich, 1924), translated as *Machiavellism*, YUP, New Haven, 1957. For a guide to the various definitions of historicism see Iggers, *The German Conception*, pp. 287–90. See also, Friedrich Engel-Janosi, *The Growth of German Historicism*, Johns Hopkins Press, Baltimore, 1944.

15 Meinecke, *Die Entstehung*, pp. 2–3.

16 Ibid., pp. 4–5.

17 Ibid. See also Waldemar Besson, 'Historismus' in Waldemar Besson (ed.), *Das Fischer-Lexikon Geschichte*, Frankfurt am Main, 1961, p. 106.

18 Meinecke, *Die Entstehung*, p. 5.

19 Ibid.

20 Srbik, *Geist und Geschichte I*, p. 140.

21 Meinecke, *Die Entstehung*, p. 141.

22 Ibid.p. 410, and *Weltbürgertum*, p. 249.

23 Meinecke, *Die Entstehung*, p. 410.

24 Ibid., p. 420.

25 Ibid., p. 421.

26 Meinecke, *Weltbürgertum*, p. 239.

27 Ibid., p. 239.

28 Meinecke, *Die Idee*, p. 239.

29 Ibid., p. 411

30 At that time Eyre Crowe was moved to circulate his memorandum among colleagues pointing out that German foreign policy was driven by a ruthless will to expansion that would eventually violate the peace of Europe. Christopher Clark dismisses Crowe's warnings as simply petulant anti-Germanism (see Clark, *The Sleepwalkers*, pp. 162–5). History was to prove Sir Eyre Crowe to be right in every respect. Crowe was a good example of a civil servant who by virtue of being half German by birth and having received his early schooling in Germany had a better insight into the German mind than most of his colleagues.

31 Popper, *The Open Society*, p. 35.

32 These are very evident in Ranke's journalistic contributions to the *Historisch–Politische Zeitschrift* which he edited, 1832–1836. His conservatism and historicism were illustrated pre-eminently in two famous articles, namely *Die Grossen Mächte* (1833) and *Das Politische Gespräch* (1836). See the English translations in Georg G. Iggers and Helmut von Moltke, *The Theory and Practice of History by Leopold von Ranke*, Bobbs Merrill, Indianapolis/New York, 1973.

33 Meinecke, *Die Idee*, pp. 452–4.

34 Ibid., p. 455.

35 Ranke, *Die Grossen Mächte*, in the Iggers & Moltke edn., p. 100; Theodore von Laue, *Leopold Ranke – The Formative Years*, PUP, Princeton, 1950, pp. 181–218, *passim*.

36 Ranke, *Die Grossen Mächte*, 37: 'Der Krieg, sagt Heraklit, ist der Vater der Dinge. Aus dem Zusammentreffen engegengesetzter Kräfte in den grossen Momenten der Gefahr – Ungluck, Erhebunge, Rettung – gehen die neuen Entwicklungen am entschiedentsten hervor.'

37 Von Laue, *Leopold Ranke*, p. 87.

38 John A. Moses, 'The Fischer Controversy Revisited'. Essentially the Fischer school removed the discipline from being the fiefdom of Prusso-file conservatives to become accessible to colleagues of liberal and social democratic persuasion.

39 Cited after Karl-Georg Faber, 'Realpolitik als Ideologie, *Historische Zeitschrift*, Vol. 203, August 1966 p. 8. Ketteler continued his definition in prophetic vein by adding: 'Who knows what sort of world vocation Russia or the North American states will one day assume? Every false principle which one exploits to one's own advantage will surely later be turned against him who subscribes to it'.

40 Srbik, *Geist und Geschichte*, Vol. I, pp. 347–8. Here the Austrian scholar

regretfully noted that the triumph of Prussia over Austria in founding the Reich should have been considered a preliminary step only to an expanded unification of all Germanic tribes. Von Srbik had deplored the Nazi incorporation of Austria into the Reich as something that had to have disastrous consequences. Although he believed in Germanic unity, he was highly sceptical of the way that Hitler achieved it.

41 Faber, 'Realpolitik als Ideologie', p. 3. The phrase, 'set the points' is an allusion to points of a railway track. When the points are set, the train automatically proceeds in the direction intended.

42 Ibid., p. 19.

43 Ibid.

44 Franz Schnabel, *Deutsche Geschichte im 19. Jahrhundert* vol. I, pp. 100–1.

45 Georg G. Iggers, *The German Conception of History*, p. 19. Adolf Hitler was an avid reader of von Treitschke. See Eberhard Jäckel, *Hitler's World View: A Blueprint for Power*, WUP, Middletown, Conn., 1972.

46 Sribik, *Geist und Geschichte* I, pp. 385–98. Here the Austrian historian portrays the political-pedagogic role of von Treitschke's historiography as catastrophic. See also Hans Kohn, *Heinrich von Treitschke*, YUP, New Haven, 1957; Andreas Dorpalen, *Heinrich von Treitschke*, YUP, New Haven 1957; H.W. C. Davis, *The Political Thought of Heinrich von Treitschke* Constable, London, 1914.

47 J. E. E. D. Acton had observed in a letter, April 1887 to Bishop Mandell Creighton who had recently published his celebrated history of the Papacy, that 'power tends to corrupt, and absolute power corrupts absolutely'. Quoted after *Lord Acton on Papal Power*, H. A. MacDougall (ed.), Sheed & Ward, London, 1973, pp. 230–1.

48 Hans-Heinz Krill, *Die Ranke Renaissance,* de Gruyter, Berlin, 1962, pp. 1, 139.

49 Krill, *Die Ranke Renaissance*, p. 174. The allusions to Schiller's *Menschheitsnation*, that is Germany as leader of world civilisation in the cultural sense as well as Hegel's idea of the *world-historical nation* could not be more obvious.

50 Ibid., p. 175. Lenz pointed to British policy towards the Boers in southern Africa to illustrate this.

51 Ibid., Cf Roger Fletcher, *Revisionism and Empire: Socialist Imperialism in Germany 1897–1914,* George Allen & Unwin, London, 1984, pp. 150–4.

52 Cf. Wolfgang Mommsen, *Max Weber and German Politics 1890–1920*, University of Chicago Press, Chicago & London, 1974, pp. 36–40.

53 Krill, *Die Ranke Renaissance*, p. 176.

54 Ibid., p. 185.

55 J. J. Ruedorffer, *Grundzüge der Weltpolitik in der Gegenwart* (Stuttgart: Deutsche Verlagsanstalt, 1916), 219. The literature on Riezler is extensive, but see Wayne Thompson, *In the Eye of the Storm; Kurt Riezler and the Crisis of Modern German History,* University of Iowa Press, Iowa City, 1988. Further, see the discussion in chapters 4 and 5.

56 Krill, *Die Ranke Renaissance*, p. 185.

57 The concept of *Risikoflotte*, that is, 'risk fleet' implies that the German navy

should be large enough to take on in battle any combination of enemy navies who would by virtue of German strength run the risk of defeat. That is, the German navy should be large enough to constitute a massive risk for any enemy power (read: *England*). It also meant that such a large fleet would make Germany *bundnisfähig*, that is an attractive alliance partner under the motto: 'It is better to allied to Germany rather than to find oneself in vulnerable isolation.'

58 Fritz Stern, *Dreams and Delusions: The Drama of German History*, Weidenfeld & Nicholson, London, 1988.

59 Gregor Schöllgen (ed.), *Escape into War? The Foreign Policy of Imperial Germany*, Berg, Oxford, 1990. See therein, Schöllgen, 'Germany's Foreign Policy in the Age of Imperialism – A Vicious Circle?', pp. 121–34.

60 Bernd F. Schulte, *Das deutsche Reich von 1914: Europäische Konföderation und Weltreich*, Hamburger Studien zur Zeitgeschichte und Zeitgeschehen, Hamburg, 2012, pp. 9–18.

61 The recent work of the American historian of German-Turkish relations, Sean McMeekin, re-evaluates the Russian role in the July – August crisis of 1914 to claim that Russian manoeuvring is to blame for the breakdown of negotiations. See his *July 1914: Countdown to War*, Basic Books, New York, 2013.

62 For the documentation and commentary see Bernd F. Schulte, *Das deutsche Reich von 1914: Europäische Konföderation und Weltreich*, Hamburger Studien zur Zeitgeschichte und Zeitgeschehen, Hamburg, 2012. See Appendix 3.

63 Words of the Kaiser himself expressing his impatience with Austria-Hungary in failing to deal quickly enough with Serbia. See Fritz Fischer, *Griff nach der Weltmacht, Die Kriegszielpolitik des kaiserlichen Deutschlands 1914–18*, Droste Verlag, Düsseldorf, 1961, p. 58.

64 Bethmann Hollweg in *Kurt Riezler Tagebücher, Dokumente*, Karl-Dietrich Erdmann (ed. and intr.), Vandenhoek & Ruprecht, Göttingen, 1972, p. 185.

65 Jeffrey Verhey, *The Spirit of 1914: Militarism, Myths, Mobilisation in Germany*, CUP, 2000; Bernhard vom Brocke, 'Wissenschaft und Militarismus', in William Calder III et al., *Wilamowitz nach 50 Jahren* Wissenschaftliche Buchgesellschaft, Darmstadt, 1985, pp. 649–719.

66 Klaus Schwabe, *Wissenschaft und Kriegsmoral: Die deutschen Hochschullehrer und die politischen Grundfragen des ersten Weltkrieges*, Musterschmidt Verlag, Göttingen, 1969.

67 Cited after G. K. A. Bell, *Randall Davidson* Vol. 2 OUP. London, 1935, p. 741; John A. Moses, 'The British and German Churches and the Perception of War 1908–1914', *War and Society*, Vol. 5, No. 1, May 1987, pp. 23–44.

68 The reference is to Friedrich Nietzsche's famous tract, *On the Uses and Abuses of History for Life* (1874).

69 There is a considerable literature on the *Bildungsbürgertum*, but see Fritz Ringer, *The Decline of the German Mandarins: The German Academic Community 1890–1933*, HUP, Cambridge Mass., 1969. No doubt all Powers had educated their subjects to feel superior to their neighbours and rivals, but each within the frame work of their unique cultural heritage.

70 Manfred Schlenke, 'Nationalsozialismus und Preussen: eine historische Bilanz

aus Anlass der 60. Wiederkehr des Tages von Potsdam (21 März, 1933)', in Peter-Michael Hahn et al., *Potsdam: Märkische Kleinstadt*, de Gruyter, Berlin, 1955, pp. 307–26.

Chapter 6: *Kulturkrieg* 1914–18: British and Australian Professors Confront their German Counterparts about the War

1   The impact of the *Kulturkrieg* on American academics and their response is dealt with by Carol S. Gruber, *Mars and Minerva: World War I and the Uses of Higher Learning in America*, Lousiana State University Press, Baton Rouge, 1975. The reaction of British Academics is covered by Stuart Wallace, *War and the Image of Germany: British Academics 1914–1918*, John Donald, Edinburgh, 1988. For Germany the pioneering study is by Klaus Schwabe, *Wissenschaft und Kriegsmoral: Die politischen Grundfragen des ersten Weltkrieges*, Musterschmidt Verlag, Göttingen, 1969.

2   See Moses, 'The British and German Churches', pp. 45–62. The gathering at Konstanz was attended by some 80 delegates representing 12 countries and 30 different Christian denominations. Their purpose was to found a *World Alliance for Promoting International Friendship through the Churches*. The outbreak of war dramatically interrupted this endeavour but stalwart spirits in the major belligerent countries managed to resume contact via Switzerland were able to finalise the foundation of the organisation. It was a milestone in the world ecumenical movement.

3   The telegrams and other correspondence relating to this incident are held in the archival collection of Dr Friedrich Siegmund-Schultze (1855–1969) now housed in the *Evangelisches Zentralarchive*, Berlin. The file designated DII6 contains a report composed by the American delegation dated 6 August 1914 which states: 'Under safe conduct from the Kaiser, who had conveyed by the assistant Court Preacher [Siegmund-Schultze] his interest in the conference, and with the special protection of the Grand Duchess of Baden, the delegates passed through the lines of bayonets by day and the lurid glare of searchlights sweeping the heavens for hostile air-ships by night, leaving Flushing just an hour before the German warships menaced the Channel, passed safely over the mines in the Thames, to continue the conference in London where the English delegates were saddened by the news that their own land was at war.'

4   'Theologians and the War', *The Times*, 30 September 1914. An abbreviated earlier version of the German 'Appeal ...' appeared in the *Westminster Gazette* on 9 September 1914. See also, Charles E. Bailey, 'The British Protestant Theologians in the First World War: Germanophobia Unleashed', *Harvard Theological Review*, Vol. 77, No. 2, 1984, pp. 201–4. for a useful but curiously slanted interpretation of the 'war of words'. Investigations into this episode require some degree of sophistication in the history of theological thought. One needs to know how the theologians in each of the belligerent nations acquired their respective 'mindsets'. The full English language text of the address of the German theologians, 'To Evangelical Christians Abroad' is appended to the 'Reply from Oxford to the German Address to Evangelical Christians' in a pamphlet entitled, *To the Christian Scholars of Europe and America*, Oxford, 1914.

5   Moses, 'The British and German Churches', p. 39.

6   Held in the Archives of the University of Queensland, Series UQA52/1914 and the Archives of the University of Adelaide, Senate Minutes, Docket 530/14.

7   See 'Scholars Protest against War with Germany', *The Times,* 1 August 1914, p. 6; 'Britain's Destiny and Duty: Declaration of Authors: A Righteous War', *The Times,* 18 September 1914, p. 3. Further, 'Reply to the German Professors: Reasoned Statement by British Scholars', *The Times,* 21 October 1914.

8   Vom Brocke, 'Wissenschaft und Militarismus', p. 657. The full text is on p. 718.

9   Translation in C. F. T. Brooke & H. S. Canby, *War Aims and Peace Ideals,* YUP, New Haven, 1916, p. 6. In 'Wissenschaft und Militarismus' vom Brocke provides a detailed investigation and apologia for these two declarations, pp. 657–65.

10   Vom Brocke, 'Wissenschaft und Militarismus', p. 652. G.F. Nicolai, the renowned medical scientist at Berlin, had tried to mobilise colleagues in German universities to sign a counter declaration specifically to the *Aufruf and die Europäer* repudiating the war, but could only muster three signatures apart from his own. In private some of Nicolai's friends sympathised with his views but did not wish to be publicly associated with him. However, in 1917, Nicolai finally succeeded in getting his famous pacifist study published in Switzerland, namely, *Die Biologie des Krieges* (The Biology of War). The work was promptly confiscated in Germany although some 100 copies could be secretly distributed. See vom Brocke, 'An die Europäer. Der Fall Nicolai und die Biologie des Krieges', *Historische Zeitschrift,* Vol. 240, 1985, pp. 363–75.

11   Vom Brocke, 'Wissenschaft und Militarismus', p. 692, cited in note 62.

12   P. M. Kennedy, *The Rise and Fall of British Naval Mastery,* Charles Scribner's Sons, New York, 1976, p. 230. Here Kennedy cites an observation by Viscount Esher who after 1905 predicted that 'The years 1793–1815 will be repeated, only Germany, not France, will be trying for European domination.'

13   Ibid., pp. 205–37, *passim,* where Kennedy documents the realities of Britain's global strategic over-extension which was caused by the challenge mounted by the German navy under Admiral Alfred von Tirpitz. His aim had been to concentrate as many *battleships* as Germany could produce in the shortest possible time in the North Sea.

14   *Quarterly Review,* No. 443, April 1915, p. 314.

15   The concept 'revolutionary *attentisme*' comes from Dieter Groh, *Negative Integration und revolutionäre Attentismus: Die deutsche Sozialdemokratie am Vorabend des ersten Weltkrieges,* Suhrkamp, Frankfurt/M 1973. Here Groh characterises the German socialists prior to 1914 as men who believed, as their ideological mentor Karl Kaustsky taught, that world history was in any case moving towards the great proletarian revolution as Marx presaged. One only had to wait watchfully for it to eventuate and then assume political power on behalf of the international working class, hence *revolutionary attentisme.* One must observe here, that, of course, the German educated middle class, the *Bildungsbürgertum,* believed in *world revolutionary attentisme* which derived logically from their Hegelian-neo-Rankean world view. The great world empires were moving inexorably towards a violent reckoning for world hegemony. The one which was the most culturally superior which meant of course, superior also in armaments, would inevitably impose its will on the moribund and

decadent powers which had, as it were, reached their peak and were now in a state of inexorable decline. This had been the predominant view among educated Germans at that time. One only had to be prepared to meet the challenge when it came, as come it must. The outcome of such a conflict would be tantamount to a revolution in the world order.

16 Cited in Lawrence Badash, 'British and American Views of the German Menace in World War I', *Notes and Records of the Royal Society of London*, Vol. 34, 1979–1980, p. 104.

17 On Wood, see R. M. Crawford, *'A Bit of a Rebel'*, SUP, Sydney, 1975 and Moses, *Prussian-German Militarism*. Information on Henderson is provided by Majory R. Casson, *George Cockburn Henderson – a Memoir*, The Library Board of South Australia, Adelaide, 1964.

18 The Hon. Secretary of the Executive of the University War Committee circularised, 8 May 1915, the Registrars of the Universities of Queensland, Sydney, Tasmania, Adelaide, Perth and Dunedin, advising them of the formation of the Melbourne War Committee, inviting them to do the same. Most had already taken similar initiatives. See Archives of the University of Melbourne, 'War Committee' file, p. 27.

19 The public lecture series organised by this committee were published as *PLW*, Richard J. A. Berry and Archibald T. Strong (eds.), with the authority of the Council of the University of Melbourne, George Robertson & Co, Melbourne, 1915.

20 For example, Professor Steele of the Department of Chemistry at the University of Queensland had been seconded to Britain to become director of munitions production and had in all directed six plants as reported in the Brisbane *Daily Mail*, 22 March 1919.The professor of physics at Adelaide offered inventions to the authorities in Britain to be used in combating U-Boat attacks. This was in accordance with the resolution of the scientific staff of 15 June 1915, 'that the council be asked to approach the Federal and State governments with the suggestion that members of staff of the university work to aid or supplement wherever possible, the work of the scientific, technical or professional branches of the government departments during the war, on matters connected with imperial defence, in which assistance may be useful.' *Council Minutes*, University of Adelaide, Vol. 10, p. 306.

21 On the impact of Angell's thought, see Howard Weinroth, 'Norman Angell and the Great Illusion: An Episode of Pre-War Pacifism', *Historical Journal*, Vol. 17, No. 3 1974, pp. 55–74.

22 Friedrich von Bernhardi's book, *Deutschland und der nächste Krieg* (Germany and the next War), 1912, had gone through six editions by 1913 and had been translated into English. As Fritz Fischer observed, these were not the wild wish dreams of an exhuberant Pan-German, but encapsulated precisely the thinking of the German power elite. See *Griff nach der Weltmacht*, p. 50.

23 Archibald T. Strong, *Australia and the War*, George Robertson, Melbourne, 1915, p. 8.

24 For example, Strong claimed to have addressed public meetings nearly every night during the conscription campaigns, delivering recruiting speeches in

Melbourne, in many of the suburbs and in country districts. He supplied literature to the government for two of its war loans and for the recruiting campaign after the failure of the second conscription referendum. Strong even suggested to the later acting prime minister William A. Watt when he was on the Parliamentary War Committee, the organisation of a scheme for propaganda on war and peace issues. When this was formed, Strong played an active part in its work. See Moses, 'Archibald T. Strong', pp. 407–19.

25 For example, Nettie Palmer, wife of Vance Palmer, ventured to attack Strong's arguments in favour of prosecuting the war as fallacious. See her, 'The Protector of Small Nationalities', *The Socialist,* 17 December 1915.

26 From Wood's lecture, 'The Immediate Responsibility for the War', *Hermes,* Vol. 21, No. 2, 1915, pp. 48–56. See Moses, *Prussian-German Militarism,* pp. 75–89.

27 Crawford, *'A Bit of Rebel',* pp. 197–200, *passim.*

28 Wood, 'The Immediate Responsibility for the War' in Moses, *Prussian-German Militarism,* pp. 83–4.

29 Ibid., p. 76.

30 Wood, 'German History and the War', in Moses, *Prussian-German Militarism,* pp. 94–5.

31 Ibid., p. 104.

32 Crawford, *'A Bit of a Rebel',* p. 291. Wood had read Bismarck's memoirs in the 1898 English translation. As well he had read Moritz Busch, *Bismarck. Some Secrets of his History,* Macmillan, New York, 1898.

33 Wood, 'German History and the War', p. 98.

34 Ibid., p. 101.

35 Ibid., p. 103.

36 Ibid., pp. 105–6.

37 Gerhard Fischer, *Enemy Aliens: Internment and Homefront Experience in Australia, 1914–1918,* University of Queensland Press, St Lucia, 1989.

Chapter 7: German and Australian Perceptions of the War in 1914

1 See Gerhard Fischer, *Enemy Aliens* who argues from a strictly German point of view, that Australian policy-makers 'militarised' the nation through their anti-Germanism. Australia became a more racist and chauvinist community. This argument was advanced without making any effort to assess how Australian decision-makers formed their image of Imperial Germany and the threat she posed to Empire security.

2 Bill Gammage, 'Anzac's Influence on Turkey and Australia', *Journal of the Australian War Memorial,* 18 April 1991, pp. 13–19.

3 See Moses, *Trade Unionism in Germany,* Vol. 1, chapters 9 and 10.

4 Ernest Scott, *Australia during the War,* Angus & Robertson, Sydney, 1936, p. 858.

5 John Robertson, *Anzac and Empire. The Tragedy and Glory of Gallipoli,* Heinemann, Melbourne, 1981, p. 267.

6 Rudiger vom Bruch, 'Universität, Staat und Gesellschaft', *Archiv für*

Sozialgeschichte, Bd. 20, 1980, pp. 526–44, discusses the range of literature on the nexus between university and state in Germany. Specifically relevant here is Klaus Schwabe, *Wissenschaft und Kriegsmoral: Die deutschen Hochschullehrer und die politischen Grundfragen des ersten Weltkrieges,* Musterschmidt Verlag, Göttingen, 1969. See the 'Ideas of 1914', pp. 21–45, *passim.*

7 Franz Schnabel, *Deutsche Geschichte im 19. Jahrhundert,* Herder, Freiburg, 1950, Vol. I, pp. 100–1; Vol. III, pp. 144–59, *passim.*

8 Georg, Friedrich Nicolai, *The Biology of War,* The Century Company, New York, 1919, pp. xiii–xiv. Here the famous pacifist professor of medicine at the University of Berlin, one of the few notable professorial opponents of the war, lists the disciplines of all 93 of the intellectuals who signed the pro-war manifesto, *To the Civilised World (An die Kulturwelt)* in which the signatories declared their solidarity with the policy that led to the invasion of Belgium. This was the earliest of in a series of such manifestos which illustrated to what extent German intellectuals shared the nationalist, anti-pacifist paradigm. See Klaus Böhme, *Aufrufe und Reden deutscher Professoren im ersten Weltkrieg,* Reclam, Stuttgart, 1975.

9 vom Brocke, 'Wissenschaft und Militarismus'. In greater detail than in Klaus Schwabe (fn 6) vom Brocke investigates the German ideas of 1914 and the responses which these called forth from French, British and American academics. This refers to the so-called *Kulturkrieg* or 'war of civilizations.'

10 Eckart Kehr, *Economic Interest, Militarism and Foreign Policy,* University of Calfiornia Press, Berkeley, 1977 (translation of the 1965 Ullstein edn. of *Der Primat der Innenpolitik*). See p. 74 in the chapter 'Class Struggle and Armament Policy in Imperial Germany.'

11 Ibid., p. 23 in the chapter, 'Anglophobia and *Weltpolitik.*'

12 Ibid., pp. 25–6.

13 Ibid., p. 26.

14 Ibid., p. 27. Compare, Paul M. Kennedy, *The Rise of the Anglo-German Antagonism, 1860–1914,* Allen & Unwin, London, 1980, pp. 251–88, *passim.*

15 Kehr, *Economic Interest,* 'Anglophobia and *Weltpolitik*', pp. 34–49, *passim.* Cf, Joseph Schumpeter, *Imperialism and Social Classes,* Augustus. M. Kelley, Fairfield NJ, 1989.

16 Fritz Ringer, '*Bildung*: The Social and Ideological Context of the German Historical Tradition', *History of Education Ideas,* Vol. 10, no. 2, 1989, p. 193.

17 Ibid., p. 194.

18 Friedrich Meinecke, *Machiavellism: The doctrine of Raison d'état in der neueren Geschichte,* being the translation of *Die Idee der Staatsräson in der neueren Geschichte,* Routledge & Kegan Paul, London, 1957. See in particular the chapter which covers the influence of Hegel, Fichte, Ranke and Treitschke, pp. 343–408.

19 For a succinct introduction to this question see Julian Jenkins, 'German war Theology and Germany's *Sonderweg*: Luther's Heirs and Patriotism', *Journal of Religious History,* Vol. 15, No. 3, June 1989, pp. 292–310.

20 Jonathan *Steinberg, Yesterday's deterrent: Tirpitz and the Birth of the German Battle Fleet,* Macdonald, London, 1965, pp. 208–21. On German cultural

pessimism see Fritz Stern, *The Politics of Cultural Despair: A Study in the Rise of Germanic Ideology*, University of California Press, Berkeley, 1961, pp. 267–98.

21 Roger Fletcher, *Revisionism and Empire: Socialist Imperialism in Germany 1897– 1914*, Allen & Unwin, London, 1984, pp. 168–82, *passim*.

22 See Hermann Kantorowicz, *Der Geist der englischen Politik und das Gespenst der Einkreisung Deutschlands*, Rowohlt Verlag, Berlin, 1929. Kantorowicz courageously refuted the notion, widespread in Germany during the 1920s and later, that Britain had virtually plotted the so-called encirclement of Germany. This work was translated with a preface by Gilbert Murray by W. H. Johnson as *The Spirit of British Policy and the Myth of the Encirclement*, Allen & Unwin, London, 1931.

23 See the present writer's *The Politics of Illusion: The Fischer Controversy in German Historiography*, George Prior, London, 1974, pp. 7–44, *passim*. This deals with the application of this ideology to German foreign policy. See also Rudiger vom Bruch, 'Krieg und Frieden – Zur Frage der Militarisiserung der deutschen Hochschullehrer und Universitäten im späten Kaiserreich, in Jost Düllfer, & Karl Holl (eds.), *Bereit zum Krieg*, Vandenhoek & Ruprecht, Göttingen, 1986, and Jost Düllfer, 'Militarismus, Realpolitik und Pazifismus: Aussenpolitik und Aufrüstung in der Sicht deutschen Hochschullehrer (Historiker) im späten Kaiserreich', *Militärgeschichtliche Mitteilungen*, I, 1986, pp. 37–58, in which it is shown how virtually impossible it was for German intellectuals to take a pacifist position seriously, so committed were they to the Hegelian doctrine of the power-state.

24 Compare vom Brocke, 'Wissenschaft und Militarismus', pp. 650–64, *passim*.

25 Wolfgang, J. Mommsen, 'Der Geist von 1914: Das Program eines politischen *Sonderwegs* der Deutschen', in Wolfgang J. Mommsen, *Nation und Geschichte*, Piper Verlag, Munich, 1990, p. 91.

26 Klaus, Vondung, 'Deutsche Apokalypse 1914', in Klaus Vondung (ed.), *Das wilhelminische Bildungsbürgertum*, Vandenhoek & Ruprecht, Göttingen, 1976, p. 156.

27 Mommsen, Wolfgang, 'Der Geist von 1914', p. 91. Rudolf Kjellen, *Grossmächte der Gegenwart*, B. G. Teubner, Leipzig/Berlin, 1914. Here the Swedish professor's analysis proved very shrewd. He noted that on the one hand that the Prusso-German power elite wanted to assert their *Kultur* throughout the world but raised doubts as to whether the broad masses were seriously interested in supporting this objective.

28 Mommsen, 'Der Geist von 1914', p. 91.

29 Fischer, *Griff nach der Weltmacht*, pp. 820–56.

30 Werner Sombart, *Händler und Helden:Patriotische Besinnung*, Dunker & Humboldt, Munich, 1915, p. 92.

31 Ibid., p. 93.

32 Christian Graf von Krockow, *Die Deutschen in ihrem Jahrhundert 1890–1990*, Rowohlt Verlag, Reinbek, 1990, p. 100.

33 Kurt Sontheimer, 'Der deutsche Geist als Ideologie' in Manfred Funke et al. (eds.), *Demokratie und Diktatur:Geist und Gestalt politischer Herrschaft in Deutschland, Festschrift für Karl-Dietrich Bracher*, Droste, Düsseldorf, 1987, p.

38.; and Lothar Wieland, 'Der deutsche Englandhass im ersten Weltkrieg und seine Vorgeschichte', in Wilhelm Alff (ed.), *Deutschlands Sonderung von Europa 1862–1945,* Peter Lang, Frankfurt/M, 1984, p. 340.

34 See Ford Madox Hueffer, *Between St Dennis and St George,* New York, 1971, Haskell House re-print of the 1915 work, pp. 225–85, *passim,* for a contemporary complaint about English authors who did not understand the German mind and consequently could not see that it was impossible to negotiate with the *Kaiserreich* as one might with another Western power.

35 A. J. P. Taylor, *The Trouble Makers: Dissent over Foreign Policy 1792–1939,* Indiana University Press, Bloomington, 1958. See especially chapter 5 on the Great War, pp. 152–66, *passim.* On page 136, Taylor skewers the Union for Democratic Control for their lack of perception regarding the thrust of German foreign policy prior to the war. Particularly guilty was E. D. Morel for saying that there had been nothing in German policy prior to 1914 to arouse British suspicions or excite alarm. Clearly Morel had not seen the Eyre Crowe Memorandum of 1907 or chose to ignore it.

36 Mommsen, Wolfgang, 'Der Geist von 1914', pp. 92–3. for two highly informative confirmations of the unique cultural self-perception of imperial Germany, see Charles, S. Maier, *The Unmasterable Past: History, Holocaust and German National Identity,* HUP, Cambridge, Mass. 1988 and Richard J. Evans, *In Hitler's Shadow. West German Historians and the Attempt to Escape from the Nazi Past,* Pantheon Books, New York, 1989.

37 See above chapter 6. Leading Australian professors from most universities at the time became centrally involved such as B. D. Steele and A. Gibson from Queensland and professors H. Barraclough and Edgeworth David of Sydney in either munitions production or the improvement of war technology. This indicates that they had at least access to the 'corridors of power'. Others such as the acting head of the department of English in Adelaide, A. T. Strong or G. C. Henderson of Adelaide functioned as active propagandists for conscription while professor J. J. stable of the Department of English at Queensland became especially active as a government censor.

38 J. McKellar Stewart, 'Nietzsche and the Present German Spirit' in R. J. A. Berry & A. T. Strong (eds.), *Public Lectures and the War,* George Robertson & Co, Melbourne, 1915, p. 138.

39 W. M. MacCallum, *Reflections on the War,* Angus & Robertson, Sydney, 1915, p. 8. MacCallum was Challis Professor of Modern Literature at the University of Sydney and had studied at Glasgow, Leipzig and Berlin.

40 T. G. Tucker, 'British and German Ideals' in *PLW,* p. 10

41 MacCallum, *Reflections,* p. 23.

42 T. H. Laby, 'The Dominions and the War in *PLW,* p. 180. The reference is to the British *White Paper,* Despatch No. 85.

43 F. W. Eggleston, 'The Significance of Empire' in *PLW,* p. 37.

44 Ibid., p. 41.

45 Tucker, 'British and German Ideals', in *PLW,* p. 2.

46 Ernest Scott, 'The Nature of the Issue', in *PLW,* pp. 24–5.

47 The text of this paper is reproduced in Moses, *Prussian-German Militarism,* pp. 119–30.

48 Scott, 'The Nature of the Issue', p. 26.

Chapter 8: Did Australia face an existential threat in 1914? German war planning and the realities of Australia's position

1 The issue has continued for two decades, initially starting with Gerhard Fischer's '"Negative integration" and an Australian road to modernity: interpreting the Australian homefront experience in World War I', *Australian Historical Studies,* Vol. 26, 104 (April 1995), pp. 452–76. More realistic are the essays in John Moses and Christopher Pugsley (eds.), *The German Empire and Britain's Pacific Dominions 1871-Essays on the Role of Australia and New Zealand in World Politics in the Age of Imperialism*: Regina Books, Claremont Calif., 2000.

2 H. Herwig & D. Trask, 'Naval Operations Plans between Germany and the United States of America 1898–1913', *Militärgeschichtliche Mitteilungen,* Heft 2, 1970, p. 9.

3 Willi Boelcke, 'Die Marine als Werkzeug preußisch-deutscher Außen-und Wirtschaftspolitik', *Marine-Rundschau,* Bd. 78, 10, 1981, p. 558. On the transition from world- to great-power see Gregor Schöllgen, 'Die Großmacht als Weltmacht. Idee, Wirklichkeit und Perzeption deutscher "Weltpolitik" im Zeitalter des Imperialismus', *Historische Zeitschrift,* Bd. 248, 1989, pp. 79–100.

4 G. Schmoller, 'Die wirtschaftliche Zukunft Deutschlands und die Flottenvorlage', in G. Schmoller, M. Sering, A. Wagner (eds.), *Handels- und Machtpolitik. Reden und Aufsätze im Auftrage der Freien Vereinigung für Flottenvorträge,* Klett-Cotta, Stuttgart 1900, I, p. 33.

5 Jehuda Wallach, *Das Dogma der Vernichtungsschlacht. Die Lehren von Clausewitz und Schlieffen und ihre Wirkungen in zwei Weltkriege,* Bernard & Graefe, Frankfurt/Main, 1967, p. 227.

6 Walther Görlitz (ed.), *Der Kaiser ... Aufzeichnungen des Chefs des Marinekabinetts Admiral Georg Alexander von Müller über die Ära Wilhelms II,* Göttingen, Musterschmidt, 1965, p. 37. A long term flow of events and perspectives is provided by Wolfgang Mommsen, *Großmachtstellung und Weltpolitik. Die Außenpolitik des Deutschen Reiches 1870–1914,* Ullstein Verlag, Frankfurt/M., Berlin, 1993.

7 Volker Berghahn, 'Flottenrüstung und Machtgefüge', in Michael Stürmer (ed.), *Das kaiserliche Deutschland. Politik und Gesellschaft 1870–1918*: Droste, Düsseldorf 1970, p. 381; see also R. J. S. Hoffmann, *Great Britain and the German Trade Rivalry 1875–1914,* Russell, New York, 1964.

8 See Adolf von Trotha, *Großadmiral von Tirpitz. Flottenbau und Reichsgedanke,* Korn, Breslau, 1934), pp. 51f.; Ulrich von Hassell, *Tirpitz. Sein Leben und Wirken mit Berücksichtigung seiner Beziehungen zu Albrecht von Stosch,* Chr. Belsersche Verlagsbuchhandlung, Stuttgart, 1920, pp. 119–20.

9 Tirpitz' neo-Rankean world-view is discussed in Hans-Heinz Krill, *Die Ranke-Renaissance-Max Lenz und Erich Marcks* de Gruyter, Berlin, 1962, pp. 196f. On Mahan's influence see R.H. Beadon, 'The Sea Power of Germany and the

Teaching of Mahan', *Journal of the Royal United Service Institution*, 68, 1923, pp. 500–7. Influential to an understanding the link has been J. S. Sumida, *Inventing Grand Strategy and Teaching Command: The Classic Works of Alfred Thayer Mahan reconsidered*, Johns Hopkins University Press, Baltimore/London 1998. More recently see Patrick J. Kelly, *Tirpitz and the Imperial Germany Navy*, Indiana University Press, Bloomington, 2011; Jan Rüger, *The Great Naval Game. Britain and Germany in the Age of Empire*, CUP, Cambridge, 2009 examines the political-cultural aspects. A broader sweep is presented in Dirk Bönker, *Militarism in a Global Age. Naval ambitions in Germany and the United States before World War I*, Cornell University Press, Ithaca/London, 2012.

10 Hans Delbrück, 'Deutsche Ängstlichkeit', *Preußische Jahrbücher*, Bd. 149, August 1912, pp. 362–3.

11 Peter Winzen, 'Der Krieg in Bülows Kalkül: Katastrophe der Diplomatie oder Chance zur Machtexpansion?', in J. Düllfer & K. Holl (eds.), *Bereit zum Krieg. Kriegsmentalität im Wilhelminischen Deutschland 1890–1914*, Vandenhoek & Ruprecht, Göttingen, 1986, pp. 161–93.

12 Bundesarchiv-Militärarchiv (German Federal Military Archive) Freiburg (henceforth BAMA), RM5/v 5792, encl. Richthofen-Tirpitz, Diederichs. Also included were copies of 'The Military Forces of Australasia'; 'Report on the Military Forces of the Colony of New South Wales, 1899'; 'Report of the Council of Defence (Victoria), 1900'; 'Report on the Defence Forces of New Zealand, 1900'; 'Report on the Queensland Military Forces, 1900'; 'Report on the Marine Defence Force, 1899–1900' (Queensland).

13 On the Two-Power Standard see A. J. Marder, *From Dreadnought to Scapa Flow: The Royal Navy in the Fisher Era, 1904*–1919, Vol. 1 *The Road to War*, OUP, Oxford, 1970, pp. 123–5. The Admiralty study is RM5/v 1160, Kapitänleutnant Rehder, 'Die Entwicklung der englischen Colonialmarinen. Augenblicklicher Stand der Frage und Betrachtungen über die Entwicklungsmöglichkeiten, sowie über die Beteiligung der Colonialflotten in einem deutsch-englischen Krieg', June 1914.

14 Holger Herwig, *Politics of Frustration: The United States in German Naval Planning, 1889–1941*, Little, Brown, Oxford, 1976, pp. 61–2.

15 The importance of Constantinople was that from here a Power 'would exercise its pressure on Egypt and indirectly on India.' *Deutsche Volkswirtschaftliche Correspondenz*, Nr. 81, 8 Oktober 1912, in Klaus Wernecke, *Der Wille zur Weltgeltung*, Droste Verlag, Düsseldorf, 1970, p. 289.

16 *Deutschland im Orient nach dem Balkankrieg* (Berlin, 1913), p. 14, in Wernecke, p. 292. Jäckh was editor of the *Neckar-Zeitung* and had a close relationship with Bülow.

17 C. Smythe, 'German Statesmen of the Hour', *Sydney Morning Herald*, 16 September 1911.

18 Müller-Tirpitz, 8 February 1905, cited in Volker Berghahn, *Germany and the Approach of War in 1914*, Macmillan, London, 1973, p. 53.

19 H. Herwig, 'Verfehlte Weltpolitik: Drei Aspekte deutsch-amerikanischer Beziehungen 1888–1941', in J. Hütter, R. Meyers, D. Papenfuss, Hrsg., *Tradition und Neubeginn. Internationale Forschungen zur deutschen Geschichte*

im 20. Jahrhundert, Carl Heymanns Verlag, Köln, 1975, p. 55, based on BA-MA, Nachlaß Vanselow, F 7612, 'Kriegsziele der Marine', Holtzendorff's memorandum of 26 November 1916, in Holger Herwig, 'Admirals versus Generals: The War Aims of the Imperial German Navy, 1914–1918', *Central European History*, Vol. 5, No. 3 (Sept. 1972), pp. 215–16.

20 In early 1914 intensive negotiations involving the ambassadors in London and Lisbon, the Colonial Office, the Warburg and Deutsche Banks, resulted in a German-Portuguese agreement for the acquisition of more than half of the then territory of the Portuguese Nyassa Company, which would create a core for *Mittelafrika*. Wernecke, *Der Wille zur Weltgeltung*, pp. 296–8.

21 PA-AA, 'Der Weltkrieg', Nr. 15, Bd. 2, Bl. 44, Holtzendorff to Bethmann Hollweg, 26 November 1916.

22 Emphasis on battleship construction did not mean that the Navy's overseas function was rejected, rather it was a practical recognition of immediate needs and the limited resources available. The battleship fleet represented the first step in the development of a world-fleet once the European situation had been 'stabilised' to Germany's advantage.

23 BA-MA Nachlaß Levetzow, N239/19, Bd. 2, Denkschrift Trotha, 'Aufgaben der Marine nach dem Kriege', 1 July 1917.

Chapter 9: German surveillance activity in Australia and local defence concerns – growing fears

1 The files of the German Navy in the *Bundesarchiv-Militärarchiv* Freiburg are designated BAMA; RM *(Reichs-Marine)* followed by volume number. The files of the Bundesarchiv Berlin are designated BA-Berlin, those of the Political Archive of the Foreign Office (Politisches Archiv des Auswärtigen Amtes) Berlin PA-AA, and the Melbourne depository of the Australian Archives, AA Victoria.

2 Quoted in the *Frankfurter Zeitung*, 18 January 1904.

3 RM5/v 5972, Commander Cruiser Squadron-Chief of Admiralty Staff, 21 June 1911. On Britain's vulnerability, see C. E. Fayle, *Seaborne Trade,* vol. 1, *The Cruiser Period: History of the Great War Based on Official Documents* Murray, London, 1920. The main German plans are: BAMA RM5/v 5970, 'Der Handelsangriff an den Quellen der feindlichen Einfuhr, dargestellt an einem Angriff unseres Kreuzergeschwaders auf die englische Wolleinfuhr aus Australien', memorandum by Kap. Lt. Freiherr von Bülow, 1902; RM5/v 5899, 'An welchen Punkten werden die englischen Haupthandelslinien im Gebiet der australasischen Meere dem Kreuzkrieg die grössten Aussichten auf Erfolg bieten', memorandum by Ob. Lt. z.S. Hermann, 18 February 1910; also the operational plans of the East Asia Cruiser Squadron for the Australian & East Asian Stations in the RM5/v series. That Germany was recognised as a threat to Australian security is shown in the easily accessible information concerning the danger posed by merchant vessels capable of conversion to auxiliary cruisers. This is but one example, which was discussed at length in Federal Parliament in 1911. (See *Commonwealth Parliamentary Debates,* vol. 60 (1911), pp. 423–4, 624, 714–15, 1144–6.) This topic was also the subject of regular press comment from 1904. Already in 1911 it was believed that all German merchantmen with a speed

over 13 knots carried gun mountings and ammunition, with at least one, *Kaiser Wilhelm der Grosse,* on Australian routes. (PA-AA, R 19268, Kiliani-Bethmann Hollweg, 18 July 1913, enclosing clipping of the *Sun.* A full documentation of the Anglo-Australian response is in this series.)

4   RM5/v 5972, Ingenohl-Fischel, 30 November 1909, p. 66.

5   RM5/v 3682, Chief of Admiralty Staff to Chief of Cruiser Squadron, 25 April 1902.

6   RM5/v 5705, Kiliani to Bethmann Hollweg, 11 March 1913.

7   RM5/v 6693, Senior Officer Australian Station to Chief of Admiralty Staff, Apia, November 1901.

8   RM5/v 5709, Buri to Bülow, 20 September 1901.

9   PA-AA, R 19270, 'Australien-Vertrauensmänner', undated, unsigned.

10 RM5/v 5346, Admiralty Staff-Commander *Condor,* 21 June 1906, p. 9.

11 RM5/v 5346, Admiralty Staff-Commander *Cormoran,* November 1910, p. 167.

12 RM5/v 3662, Irmer to Bülow, 6 August 1909.

13 RM5/v 3662, Foreign Secretary to Chief of Admiralty Staff, 4. March 1910. The character of Eugene Hirschfeld is somewhat enigmatic. Major Serle of the Department of Military Intelligence in Brisbane wrote in 1920 that 'Hirschfeld claimed when first interned privileges as a Colonel in the German Army.' AA Victoria, MP 367/10, 567/3/4740, Serle to Department of Defence, 29 June 1920.

14 RM5/v 3662, Irmer to Bethmann Hollweg, 25 November 1909.

15 AA Victoria, MP84, 1877/4/7, Department of defence to Secretary, Department of External Affairs, 28 September 1911.

16 RM5/v 5900, Senior Officer Australian Station to Chief of Admiralty Staff, 14 October 1912.

17 RM5/v 3662, Commander *Cormoran* to Chief of Admiralty Staff, 14 March 1913.

18 AA Victoria, Bl97 567/3/4138, Department of Defence to W. G. Higgs, 11 November 1919.

19 RM5/v 3662, Senior Officer Australian Station to Chief of Admiralty Staff, 14 June 1910, 'Verhandlung über die Verpflichtung des Herrn Walter de Haas als Hauptberichterstatter des Australischen Stations.'

20 *Kölnische Zeitung,* 8 January 1903.

21 *Frankfurter Zeitung,* 19 September 1906.

22 RM5/v 5711, Commander *Condor* to Kaiser, 19 April 1907.

23 RM5/v 5704, Commander *Condor* to Kaiser, 2 June 1908.

24 RM5/v 5704, Müller to Tirpitz, 25 September 1908.

25 RM5/v 5607, Irmer to Bülow 22 October 1908.

26 *Sydney Morning Herald,* 28 April 1909.

27 RM5/v 6005, Commander *Condor* to Kaiser, 2 May 1909.

28 RM5/v 6005, Commander *Planet* to Kaiser, 8 June 1909.

29 RM5/v 1160, Irmer to Bethmann Hollweg, 15 December 1909.

30 Ibid.

31 BA Berlin, RKA 10.01 8937, Irmer to Bethmann Hollweg, 5 October 1909.

32 Ibid.

33 RM5/v 6006, Commander *Planet* to Kaiser, 15 April 1910.

34 RM5/v 5704, Commander *Planet* to Kaiser, 8 June 1909.

35 RM5/v 5703, Irmcr to Bethmann Hollwcg, 10 January 1910.

36 RM5/v 6006, Commander *Planet* to Kaiser, 15 April 191

37 RM5/v 5707, 'Die geplante Landesverteidigung des australischen Commonwealth und ihre Beteiligung an der nationalen Verteidigung Grossbritannien', Admiralty Staff Project No. 10, 1909.

38 Ibid.

39 RM5/v 5707, Irmer to Bethmann Hollweg, 1 November 1909

40 RM5/v 6007, Commander *Cormoran* to Kaiser, 12 June 1911.

41 RM5/v 6007, Commander Planet to Kaiser, 24 April 1911. The main cause for this pervading malaise was the lack of respect for any authority in the character of the average Australian. Captain Siemens made equally incisive comments on developments in the naval construction program in Australia. In an assessment of the Henderson Plan, he pointed out the unpleasant financial shock which was likely to descend upon the Australian people, and it was questionable whether the enthusiasm for naval construction would continue apace when the accounts came in. In 1911, after the Australian Government spent £3.5 m on the Fleet Unit, Admiral Sir Reginald Henderson was tasked with providing a naval blueprint for Australia. Over a 20 year timetable the RAN was to expand to 8 battle cruisers, 10 protected or light cruisers, 18 destroyers, and 12 submarines, with a personnel increase to 15,000 men including 5,000 reserves. See inter alia A. W. Jose, *The Royal Australian Navy: Official History of Australia in the War of 1914–18*, Vol. IX, Sydney, Angus & Robertson, Sydney, 1928; James Curran and Stuart Ward (eds.), *Australia and the Wider World: Selected Essays of Neville Meaney*, SUP, Sydney, 1913, chapter 8.

42 *The Standard*, 12 May 1912.

43 RM5/v 1160, 'Die Entwicklung der englischen Kolonialmarinen. Augenblicklicher Stand der Frage und Betrachtungen über die Entwicklungsmöglichkeiten der Kolonialflotten in einem deutsch-englischen Krieg', June 1914.

44 See R. Hyam, *Britain's Imperial Century, 1815–1914: A Study in Empire and Expansion*, Macmillan, London, 1976, p. 129.

45 RM5/v 1160, 'Die Entwicklung'.

46 RM5/v 5708, Commander *Cormoran* to Kaiser, 12 August 1913.

47 Ibid.

48 RM5/v 5705, Buenz to Bethmann Hollweg, 28 September 1912.

49 RM5/v 1160, Müller to Tirpitz, 9 November 1913. See also the sub-chapter 'A 'Reconstructed Empire'? Imperial Initiatives and Dominion Responses', in J. Eddy and D. Schreuder, eds, *The Rise of Colonial Nationalism*, Allen & Unwin,

Sydney, 1988, pp. 39ff.

50 RM5/v 1160, Irmer to Bethmann Hollweg, 9 November 1913.

51 Ibid.

52 RM5/v 1160, Müller to Navy Office, 11 January 1912.

53 RM5/v 1160, Rehder, 'Die Entwicklung'.

54 *Frankfurter Zeitung*, 4 March 1909.

55 *New Zealand Herald*, 24 June 1904. See the author's article 'Bless the Queen and curse the Colonial Office', *The Journal of Pacific History*, Vol. 33, No. 2, September 1998, pp. 133–52.

56 *Sydney Morning Herald*, 11 January 1905.

57 *The Globe*, 5 March 1905.

58 *Daily Telegraph*, 3 May 1905.

59 RM5/v 5971, Commander *Condor* to Chief of Admiralty Staff, 20 April 1907.

60 See among others Holger Herwig, *'Luxury' Fleet: The Imperial German Navy, 1888–1918*, Allen & Unwin, London, 1980 and 'The German Reaction to the Dreadnought Revolution', *International History Review*, 13, 1991, pp. 273–83; Ivo N. Lambi, *The Navy and German Power Politics, 1862–1914*, Allen & Unwin, London, 1984.

61 *Sydney Morning Herald*, 15 December 1909.

62 *Sydney Morning Herald*, 25 May 1909.

63 *The Age*, 4 June 1909.

64 RM5/v 5711, Commander *Condor* to Chief of Admiralty Staff, 3 July 1910.

65 RM5/v 6693, 'Denkschrift: Die Kriegführung Deutschlands gegen England auf der Australischen Station betreffend', November 1901.

66 W. R. Creswell, 'Considerations Affecting the Naval Defence of the Commonwealth ...', in Meaney, *A History of Australian Defence*, p. 179.

67 Ibid., p. 180.

68 CPD, Vol. XLIV, Senator Chataway, 3 November 1910, p. 5578.

69 G. P. Gooch and Harold Temperley, *British documents on the origins of the war: 1898–1914*, H.M. Stationery Office, London, 1926–29, Vol. X, ii, No. 270, Memo. Sir Eyre Crowe on Timor and the Anglo-German secret convention of 1898, January 1912, p. 429–33.

70 *Sydney Morning Herald*, 4 August 1911.

71 *Sydney Morning Herald*, with its early warning 11 November 1904, and with some self-satisfaction 4 August 1914.

72 RM5/v 5971, 'Denkschrift zu den Befehlen für das Kreuzergeschwader und S. M. Schiffe auf dem Ostasiatischen und Australischen Station', December 1911.

73 *Sydney Morning Herald*, 26 May 1911.

Chapter 10: German Naval War Planning Against Australia, 1900–1914

1   'An welchen Pünkten werden die englischen Haupthandelslinien im Gebiet der australischen Meere dem Kreuzerkrieg die größten Aussichten auf Erfolg bieten und nach welchen Gesichtspünkten wäre dieser Kreuzerkrieg zu führen?', Batavia, 18 February 1910, Bundesarchiv-Militärarchiv Freiburg (henceforth RM designations), RM5/v 5899, p. 295.

2   Politisches Archiv des Auswärtigen Amtes (henceforth PA-AA) 'Der Weltkrieg', Nr. 15, Bd. 2, p. 44, Holtzendorff to Bethmann Hollweg, 26 November 1916.

3   P.M. Kennedy (ed.), *The War Plans of the Great Powers, 1880–1914*, Allen & Unwin, London, 1979, pp. 1–2.

4   RM47 /v 525, Unsigned Admiralty report, 9 November 1914.

5   Arthur J. Marder, *From the Dreadnought to Scapa Flow*, Vol. 1, p. 4. See the author's article, 'The Function of Commerce Warfare in an Anglo-German Conflict to 1914', *Journal of Strategic Studies*, Vol. 20, December 1997, Nr. 4, pp. 94–114.

6   RM5/v 5925, 'Denkschrift über den Kreuzerkrieg gegen England', April 1911, Bl. 2.

7   In 1914, the East Asia Squadron numbered a total of six major warships: *Scharnhorst*-class cruisers SMS *Scharnhorst* and SMS *Gneisenau*; *Dresden*-class cruisers SMS *Dresden* and SMS *Emden*; the *Bremen*-class cruiser SMS *Leipzig*; the *Königsberg*-class cruiser SMS *Nürnberg*.

8   P. Hislam, *The Admiralty of the Atlantic. An Enquiry into the Development of German Sea Power Past, Present and Prospective*, Longmans, Green, London, 1908, p. 178.

9   P. A. Silburn, *The Colonies and Imperial Defence,* Longmans, Green London, 1909, p. 283.

10   Gerhard Fischer, 'Negative Integration and an Australian road to modernity: interpreting the Australian home front experience in World War 1', *Australian Historical Studies*, Vol. 104, April 1995, specifically pp. 455–9.

11   RM5/v 5971, 'Denkschrift zu den Befehlen für das Kreuzergeschwader und S.M. Schiffe auf dem ostasiatischen und australischen Station', undated but probably December 1911 from marginalia, p. 173. A later comment recommended ongoing observation of the position of enemy forces in peacetime which would contribute considerably to success. War Cases were allocated alphabetically to the expected enemy powers.

12   RMS/v, 5899, Korvettenkapitän Emsmann, 'Ausführungsbestimmungen auf der Australischen Station. Zu den Operationsbefehlen fiir das Kreuzergeschwader und S.M. Schiffe im Auslande vom 1 Februar 1900', 20 June 1900, p. 8. Instructions for the Governor of New Guinea are in 'An das Kaiserliche Gouvernement von Deutsch Neu-Guinea', Bl. 12, Anlage 1. Instructions for the Consul-General in Sydney are in RM5/v 5972, 'An das Kaiserlich Deutsche Generalkonsulat Sydney', Bl. 15, Anlage 2; Emsmann to Diederichs, 20 July 1900, Bl. 4.

13   'An den Kaiserlich Deutsche Konsulat Auckland', 20 June 1900, being detailed directives for Auckland in RMS/v 5899, Bl. 24.

14   The 'U' (*Umladungsplätze*) or transshipment/ assembly anchorages extended from the Indian Ocean around the Canadian-US and Mexican Pacific rim to South

America. Secrecy measures and recognition signals for Henry Reed Bay were quite involved and are detailed in RM5/v 5899, Anlage 1a.

15 The Marshall Islands were acquired in 1885 and administered from Jaluit by an Imperial Commissioner.

16 RM38/v 126, '0-Befehle für die Auslandsschiffe 1914', p. 7. However, in Article V of the Hague Convention, days of grace did 'not affect merchant-ships whose build shows that they are intended for conversion into war-ships'. See the Hague Convention 'Status of Enemy Ships', *Papers Relating to the Foreign Relations of the United States, With the Annual Message of the President Transmitted to Congress December 3, 1907,* US Government Printing Office, Washington D.C., 1907, Part I, pp. 1247ff.

17 RMS/v 6693, 'Denkschrift, die Kriegführung Deutschlands gegen England auf der Australischen Station betreffend', November 1901, p. 9.

18 Ibid.

19 RMS/v 6693, *Seeadler* in the western Pacific, required no support vessel, as the coal depots at Matupi, Ponape and Yap were at its disposal, as well as coal carried by the postal steamers which could be met under way: 'Ausführungsbestimmungen für den Australischen Station', November 1901, p. 5.

20 The East Asian Station was divided into five support regions *(Etappen)* based on Tsingtao, Yokohama, Shanghai, Manila and Batavia, each with a coordinating naval officer.

21 RM5/v 5970, 'Der Handelsangriff an den Quellen der feindlichen Einfuhr, dargestellt an einem Angriff unseres Kreuzergeschwaders auf die englische Wolleinfuhr aus Australien', p. 64.

22 Ibid.

23 RM5/v 5698, Bl.157, 'Mobilmachungsübersicht des Kreuzergeschwaders', encl. Geissler-Kaiser, 15 November 1903.

24 RM5/v 5899, Bl.110, 'Gemäß ... der Allerhöchsten Befehle an S.M. Schiffe im Auslande für den Kriegsfall', Prittwitz-Kaiser, 18 September 1904.

25 RM5/v 6255, 'Vorarbeiten zur Durchführung der Operationsbefehle auf der Australischen Station', 1904.

26 RM5/v 6693, 'Denkschrift zu den Allerhöchsten Befehlen an S.M. Schiffe im Auslande für den Kriegsfall', 6 March 1906, p. 143.

27 In 1903, 1,245 ships with 2,520,000 tons passed Aden; Colombo 3,285 ships with 4,265,481 tons; Singapore 2,632 ships with 3,369,000 tons. The Colombo-Fremantle route had 520 British ships carrying 1,280,000 tons; the Fremantle-Melbourne route 2,300,000 tons; and Melbourne-Sydney 2,800 ships carrying 3,700,000 tons. In 1902 coastal traffic consisted of 6,603 incoming steamers carrying 8 million tons, and 451 sailing ships carrying 594,188 tons; and 6,484 outgoing steamers carrying 8.2 million tons, and 492 sailing ships carrying 772,000 tons.

28 RM5/v 6693, Büchsel, 'Denkschrift zu den Allerhöchsten Befehlen an SM Schiffe auf der Ostasiatischen und der Australischen Station', 6 March 1906.

29 RM5 / v 6004, Breusing to Büchsel, 9 June 1906, p. 115.

30 RM5/v 6693, Büchsel, 'Denkschrift ...' 6 March 1906; Senior Officer Australian Station to Consul-General Sydney, 'Preparations for Implementation of Operational Orders on the Australian Station, Pt. 2 War case D – War against England', Appendix 11 to S.G.B. Nr. 89, Apia September 1904.

31 RM5/v 6255, 'Operational Orders for Overseas Ships', pp. 9lff.

32 RM5/v5972, Ingenohl to Fischel, 21 December 1909, Bl. 31.

33 PA-AA, R19287, Irmer to Bülow, 19 March 1909.

34 RM5/v 5971, 'Denkschrift', Bl. 173.

35 RM5/v 5899, 'An welchen Pünkten', p. 295.

36 Ibid. In 1901–2, Australia exported 1,250,00 bales, and of these 301,000 (24% were for sale in London and transported as Australian capital; 949,000 (76%) were already sold in Australia and transported as capital of the (British) purchaser.

37 Ibid. Approximately one-seventh of the total trade in the years 1898–1900 was carried in sailing vessels, whose courses ran predominantly with the west winds around Cape Horn, returning to Australia around the Cape of Good Hope. In 1906 the Australian merchant marine counted 1644 sailing vessels totalling 128,288 tons.

38 Ibid.

39 RMS/v 5899, Kranzbühler to Fischel, 18 March 1910, p. 207.

40 Already the previous November Kranzbühler had written to Hahl requesting that in the event of war, immediate supplies be shipped to Daja-Hafen for the resupply of the ships in the Pacific: RMS/v 5900, Kranzbühler to Hahl, 30 November 1909; RM5/v 5899, Kranzbüihler to Fischel, 18 March 1910; RM5/v 6255, 'Vorarbeiten zur Durchführung der Operationsbefehle auf der Australischen Station', p. 207; p. 229ff. lists materiel requirements.

41 RMS/v 5899, Kranzbühler to Fischel, 11 November 1910, p. 265.

42 RMS/v 6004, Tirpitz to Baudissin, 22 October 1908; Baudissin to Dernburg, 3 November 1908, p. 225. Of considerable importance was the fact that the newer ships' daily coal consumption at 'economy' speed equalled that of the older ones at full speed, and that their armaments were superior to the British P-class cruisers on the Station.

43 RMS/v 5899, Kranzbühler to Fischel, 11 November 1910, p. 265.

44 'Military-political Reports' of the cruiser commanders, particularly in RMS/ v 6004.

45 PA-AA, R 19287, Irmer to Bülow, 26 March 1909.

46 RM5/v 6007, Commander *Cormoran* to Kaiser, 12 June 1911. Konter-Admiral Rieve, Sectional Head in the Admiralty, prepared a summary of this report with comment, which was forwarded to the Kaiser. RM5/v 5707, Rieve to Kaiser, 15 August 1911.

47 RM5/6679, 'Entwurf einer Ms-Übersicht des Kreuzergeschwaders für den Kriegsfall C (England)', 1910, p. 31.

48 RM5/v 6255, Memorandum 18 February 1910, 'At which Points do the main German Trade Routes in Australian Waters offer Cruiser Warfare the greatest

Prospects for Success and from which Standpoints should this be implemented?',
pp. 295ff.

49 RM5/v 5925, 'Denkschrift über den Kreuzerkrieg im Kriege gegen England',
April 1911, p. 2.

50 Ibid.

51 RMS/v 5972, Krosigk to Heeringen, 21 June 1911, encl. 'Bericht des Leiters über
das an Bord S.M.S. *Nürnberg* in den Monaten Juli bis September abgehaltene
strategische Kriegsspiel', p. 308.

52 RM5/v 5899, Senior Officer Australian Station to Kaiser, 'Gemäss ... der
Allerhöchsten Befehle an S.M. Schiffe im Auslande für den Kriegsfall', 18
September 1904, p. 110.

53 RM5/v 6008, Ebert to Heeringen, 23 April 1912.

54 RM5/v 5973, 'Strategische Bedeutung des Südseegebietes', Spee to Pohl, 9
October 1913, p. 260.

55 RM5/v 5900, Spee to Pohl, 29 October 1913, p. 118.

56 Cited without reference from German Admiralty documents by Erich Raeder in
the official history, *Der Kreuzerkrieg in den ausländischen Gewäßern*, Bd. 1, *Das
Kreuzergeschwader*, 2te Auflage, Mittler, Berlin, 1927, p. 68.

57 See the author's detailed consideration of Graf Spee's options, based in part on
his unpublished private papers, 'The Commander in crisis. Graf Spee and the
East Asian Cruiser Squadron in 1914', in John Reeve & David Stevens (eds.),
The Face of Naval Battle. The Human Experience of modern War at Sea, Allen &
Unwin, Sydney, 2003, pp. 78–91. The Japanese factor plays a major part in this.
The most detailed account from a Japanese perspective is Akira Hayashima,
*Die Illusion des Sonderfriedens:deutsche Verständigungspolitik mit Japan im ersten
Weltkrieg*, Oldenbourg, München, 1982.

58 RM5/v 5925, 'Denkschrift über den Kreuzerkrieg gegen England', April 1911, p. 2.

59 Ibid.

60 J.C.R. Colomb, 'Our Naval Arrangements in the Other Hemisphere', *Fortnightly
Review*, Vol. LXVII, 1900, p. 263.

61 A. W. Jose, *The Royal Australian Navy, 1914–1918*, Angus & Robertson, Sydney,
1938, p. 11.

62 Ibid., pp. 19, 41, 153.

63 'Der Weltkrieg', in PA-AA, Nr. 15, Bd. 2, p. 44, Holtzendorff to Bethmann
Hollweg, 26 November 1916.

64 BA Koblenz, Nachlaß Solf, 1053/48, Bl.195, 'Sitzungsprotokolle-Koloniale
Kriegsziele'.

65 *Sydney Morning Herald*, 26 May 1911.

Appendices

1 John A. Moses 'The War-Guilt Question: A Note on Politics and Historiography
in the Weimar Republic' *Australian Journal of Politics and History*, Vol. 61, No. 1
March (2015), pp. 128–34.

2　Gerhard Ritter's historiographical ideas have been examined closely by his former student Professor Klaus Schwabe, in *Gerhard Ritter ein politischer Historiker in seinen Briefen*, Boldt, Boppard am Rhein, 1984; Karl-Dietrich Erdmann, *Toward a Global Community of Historians: The International Historical Congresses and the International Committee of Historical Sciences 1898–2000*, Berghahn Books, New York/Oxford, 2005.

3　See in Moses & Kennedy (eds.), *Germany in the Pacific and Far East 1870–1918*, University of Queensland Press, St Lucia, p. 198.

4　Gerhard Ritter, *Sword and Scepter*, Vol. III.

5　Fritz Fischer, *Krieg der Illusionen*, Droste Verlag, Düsseldorf, 1969, p. 781. See Bethmann Hollweg's memoirs entitled, *Reflections on the World War*, Thornton Butterworth, London, 1920.

6　Cited by Fritz Fischer, *Krieg der Illusionen*, p. 783 from Helmut von Moltke, *Betrachtungen und Erinnerungen* Hamburg, 1914, p. 11.

7　Cited after Fritz Fischer in *Krieg der Illusionen*, from Fritz Stern, *Bethmann Hollweg und der Krieg*, Tübingen, 1968, p. 30.

8　The content of this book which was never translated into English, précised by the present writer in his book, *The Politics of Illusion: The Fischer Controversy in German Historiography*, Barnes & Noble, New York, 1974.

9　Cf. Bernd F. Schulte, *Das deutsche Reich von 1914: Europäische Konföderaion und Weltreich* Verlag Abteilung Geschtichte und Zeitgeschen, Hamburg, 2012.

10　The most notable expression of this mind-set is to be found in the famous inaugural address of Max Weber on his accession to a professorial chair at the University of Freiburg in May 1895. See Wolfgang J. Mommsen, *Max Weber and German Politics 1890–1920*: Chicago University Press, Chicago/London, 1984, pp. 35–48 *passim*.

11　Alexander Kidd, 'The Brisbane Episcopate of St Clair Donaldson 1904–1921', PhD Thesis University of Queensland, 1996.

12　Hilary Carey, *God's Empire: Religion and Colonialism in the British World c.1801–1908*, CUP, 2011; Rowan Strong, *Anglicanism and the British Empire c.1700–1850*, OUP, 2007; Geoffrey R. Treloar, *Lightfoot, the Historian: The Nature and Role of History in the Life and Thought of J. B. Lightfoot (1828–1889) as Churchman and Scholar*, Mohr & Seebeck, Tübingen, 1998.

13　There is a considerable literature on this subject, but see John Jay Hughes, *Absolutely Null and Utterly Void* and *Stewards of the Lord*, Sheed and Ward, London/Sydney, 1968.

14　See John A. Moses & Kenneth J. Cable (eds.), *From Oxford to the Bush: Essays on Catholic Anglicanism in Australia*, Broughton Press, St Lucia, 1997, pp. 213–55 *passim*.

15　James Griffin (with Paul Ormonde), *Daniel Mannix: Beyond the Myths*, Garratt Publishing, Melbourne, 2012.

16　This issue is covered by T. P. Boland, *James Duhig*, University of Queensland Press, St Lucia, 1986, pp. 144–5.

17　Richard Reid, & Brendan Kelson, *Sinners, Saints and Settlers: a Journey through*

Irish Australia, National Museum of Australia Press, Canberra, 2010; Richard Reid, *Not just Ned: a true History of the Irish in Australia,* National Museum of Australia Press, Canberra, 2011.

18 See Moses, 'Australian Anglican Leaders and the Great War', pp. 306–23, and Robert Withycombe, 'Australian Anglicans and Imperial Identity' *Journal of Religious History,* Vol. 25, No. 3, October 2001, pp. 286–305. (This issue of the JRH is focussed on 'Religion and National Identity'.)

19 John Röhl (ed.), *1914 – Delusion or Design? The Testimony of Two German Diplomats,* Elek, London, 1973.

20 See above in chapter 3.

21 Moses, 'The British and German Churches', pp. 23–44.

22 John A. Moses, 'Church and State in Post Reformation Germany, 1530–1914' in *Church and State in Old and New Worlds,* Hilary M. Carey & John Gascoigne (eds.), Brill, Leiden/Boston, 2011, pp. 77–97, *passim.*

23 It is now clear that the German aim was to impose their Teutonic *Kultur* on Europe and the colonial world whereas the already established British aim was to raise up independent self-governing dominions which allowed the local culture to flourish under the rule of law which the Westminster system guaranteed.

24 John A. Moses, 'The University of Queensland's Official Reaction to the Great War, 1914–15', *Queensland History Journal,* Vol. 22, No. 2, May 2015, pp. 664–76.

25 In his Inaugural Address to the Brisbane Diocesan Synod in June 1915, Donaldson had reiterated his conviction that, 'Our Empire stands as living protest against German ideals'. See the discussion in Moses & Davis, *Anzac Day Origins,* pp. 152–8 *passim.*

26 Emphasis added. This section contains the essential burden of Archbishop Donaldson's imperial pedagogy.

Epilogue

1 Willi Jasper, *Lusitania: The Cultural History of a Catastrophe,* YUP, New Haven & London, 2016 (trans. by Stewart Spencer). This is arguably the best analysis of the Prusso-German separate path (*Sonderweg*) currently available in English. It explains frankly why the German ruling classes perceived themselves to be so superior to all other Great Powers and why they justified such atrocities as the rape of Belgium, the sinking of the *Lusitania* and unrestricted submarine warfare. In particular it further explains why the Kaiser and his government rejected the demands of the majority of the Reichstag in July 1917 to sue for peace without annexations.

2 Hans Delbrück, *Government and the Will of the People,* Academic Lectures, OUP, New York, 1923. Professor Delbück was renowned for his most famous publication, *Geschichte der Kriegskunst im Rahmen der politischen Geschichte* (History of warfare in the framework of political history) 4 Vols, 1920, 3rd edn.

3 Kurt Sontheimer, 'Der deutsche Geist als Ideologie' in *Demokratie und Diktatur: Geist und Gestalt politischer Herrschaft in Deutschland und Europa,* Manfred Funke et al. (eds.), Droste, Düsseldorf, 1987, pp. 35–45.

4   Manfred Messerschmidt, 'Die Armee in Staat und Gesellschaft – Die Bismarckzeit' in *Das kaiserliche Deutschland: Politik und Gesellschaft 1870–1918*, Michael Stürmer (ed.), Droste Verlag, Düsseldorf, 1970, pp. 89–112.

5   Helmut Bley, August Bebel und die Strategie der Kriegsverhütung, 1904–1913, Offizin Verlag, Hannover, 2014.

6   Ibid., p. 13.

7   Karl Eric Born, *Staat und Sozialpolitik seit Bismarcks Sturz*, Steiner Verlag, Wiesbaden 1957, p. 4 noted that, 'Even the *Kaiserreich* had an ideology. As its advocates we may name the Prussian, national liberal school of historians (L. Häusser, Droysen, Treitschke, Sybel) and the broader circles of the educated middle class. […] But in this ideology there was no room for the workers. It spoke of the achievements of the princes […] of the efficiency and bravery of the army, of the commitment to duty of the public servants of the achievements of German science and art, of the diligence of the Burgers and finally of the entrepreneurial spirit of the German business community, *but not of the worker.*'

8   Sontheimer, 'Der deutsche Geist als Ideologie', pp. 40–5.

9   Andreas Gestrich & Hartmut Pogge von Strandmann (eds.), *Bid for World Power? New Research on the Outbreak of the First World War*, German Historical Institute London, OUP, 2017, p. v.

10 Helmut Heiber, *Walter Frank und sein Reichsinstitut für Geschichte des neuen Deutschlands* Deutsche Verlagsanstalt, 1966.

11 John A. Moses, 'The Fischer Controversy Re-Visited', in *Europe's Expansions and Contractions*, Evan Smith (ed.), Australian Humanities Press, Unley SA, 2010, pp. 43–62.

12 Fritz Fischer, 'Der deutsche Protestantismus und die Politik im 19. Jahrhundert', *Historische Zeitschrift*, Vol. 181, 1951, pp. 473–518.

Index

This index is divided into two sections: People *&* **General**.
Page references in italics refer to illustrations.

General

282–3, 290–1 *see also* Australia,
national identity and character;
German Empire, characteristics
National Liberal Party xviii, 36, 38,
39, 285
National Socialism *see* Nazism
nationalism xviii, 2, 7, 18, 64, 67–8,
73–7, 200, 227–8, 289
nationality, freedom of 271–2
natural law 73
Nauru 47
naval construction *see under* German
Navy; Royal Australian Navy;
Royal Navy
navy
British *see* Royal Navy
German *see* German Navy
Navy League 48, 202
Nazism xviii, xxii, 8, 26, 30, 34–5, 63,
65–6, 94, 113–14, 133, 210, 282,
292, 296
NDL *see* North German Lloyd
Neo-Rankeans 71, 72, 84, 85–9, 92–3,
130, 206, 284
Netherlands 152, 172, 203, 209–10,
267 *see also* Dutch East Indies
Neu-Mecklenburg (New Guinea) *see*
New Ireland (New Guinea)
New Britain (New Guinea) 47, 178
New Caledonia 184, 200
New Guinea 19, 47, 148, 151–2, 169–
71, 174, 177–9, 184, 198, 200 *see
also names of islands and cities*
New Hebrides 194
New Ireland (New Guinea) 47, 178
New Zealand xxii–xxiv, 13–14, 17, 23,
24, 28, 190, 289 *see also names of
cities and places*
attitudes to WWI xxii–xxiv, 26, 112,
116, 169
defence and national security 20,
51–3, 119, 150–1, 173, 177–9,
182, 190, 200
exports 181, 189
foreign policy xix–xx, 166, 169
Newcastle (NSW) 182

nickel 200
Norddeutsche Lloyd (NDL) *see* North
German Lloyd
North America 82(n39), 152
North German Lloyd 155–8, 178–9,
185, 187, 223
North Korea xxiii
North Sea 19, 45, 50, 147, 149, 154,
166, 175–6, 193, 197, 228
Norway 209
Noumea 183, 186
Nürnburg, SMS (German cruiser) 192,
193, 194, 274

Orange-ism 15–16, 21
Ostenneyer & von Rompey 156
Ottoman Empire 19, 259, 267 *see also*
Turkey

Pacific Region xix, xx, 7–8 19–20,
26, 45, 48, 87, 96, 147, 150–4,
163, 166, 169–200 *see also under*
German Navy; *individual countries
and islands*
pacifism 39, 63, 64, 101, 106, 121,
128, 134, 146(n8), 284
Palau (Caroline Islands) 192
Palawan (Philippines) 183
Pan German League 48, 202
Pan Germanism 36, 39, 67, 98, 106,
173, 204, 207–10, 228, 294
Panama Canal 149
parliamentary democracy *see* democracy
patriotism 18, 64, 134, 248, 266 *see
also* Christian patriotism
peace conferences, Christian 97
peace-keeping xxiii–xxiv
peace terms 45, 266–8, 271–2, 292
People's Republic of China xxiii
Persia 171
Perth (WA) 194 *see also* Fremantle
(WA)
Philippines 186, 189
Phoebe, HMS (Royal Navy cruiser) 179
phosphate 200
Planet, SMS (German naval vessel)

161, 163–4, 165, 178, 274

Pohnpei (Micronesia) *see* Ponape
(Micronesia)

Poland 85, 88, 209, 267

political culture *see also* Ideas of 1914
Australia 4–6, 28, 32, 118–19,
135–42, 233, 252–3
German Empire xviii–xxii, 6–8,
27, 32–8, 55–6, 67–94, 118–19,
121–38, 232–7, 283–9
Great Britain 6–7, 121–36, 236–7
Prussia xviii, 27, 32–5

politicians, German 9

Ponape (Micronesia) 177–8

Port Moresby (Papua) 179

ports *see also names of individual ports*
Australia and New Zealand 50,
52–3, 152, 159–60, 169–71, 177,
179–84, 194–5
blockades 182–3, 198

Portugal 169, 172, 200

postal steamers 158, 178–9

Potsdam 26, 94, 203 210

power elite 2, 38, 43, 57, 68, 70, 90,
98–9, 102–3, 106(n22), 115,
118–30, 202, 206, 227, 284–9,
297 *see also* intellectual class; Junker
class; *Machtstaat* (Power State)

Pozières (France) 63

prayer in time of war 250–2, 271

Presbyterian Church 4, 15

presentism 53–6

Progressive Liberals 285–7

Progressive People's Party 38

Protestantism 4, 13, 15–16, 17, 21, 24,
93, 234

Prussia xviii, xxi, 26–7, 88, 128, 208
see also under German Empire;
Prussianism
army xxi, 32–6
constitution 27, 59
domination of German Empire 27,
33–6, 64, 81–4
elections 35, 60
history, 17th–18th centuries 33–4
Hohenzollern dynasty   *see*

Hohenzollern dynasty

Prussianism xviii, xxii, 5, 7, 27, 30–4,
36, 79, 94, 100–2, 111, 138, 228,
234–6, 295 *see also under* German
Empire; nationalism

Prusso-German Empire *see* German
Empire

Qingdao *see* Tsingtao (China)

Rabaul (New Guinea) 190

racism xx, 7–8, 64, 65, 83, 118(n1),
121, 228

radio telegraphy 158, 184, 195

railways 90, 148, 157, 164, 171, 218,
220, 223, 234, 261, 266

rationalism 73

raw materials 50–1 *see also* coal
supplies; food supplies; wool trade

Realpolitik 71, 80–3, 110–11, 128

Recessional (by Rudyard Kipling) 25(n15)

Red Sea 149, 193

Reichstag xxi, 10, 38, 43

religion and State *see* Church and State

Riga 74

Roman Catholic Centre Party *see*
Centre Party

Roman Catholicism 21, 23, 232

Roman Catholics
Australia 4, 11, 13, 14, 15, 231–3
Germany xvii, xviii, 10, 24, 32, 97
see also Centre Party

Romania 40

Rome, Ancient 245–6, 248, 264–5

Round Table movement 6, 9, 22, 231

Royal Arthur, HMS (Royal Navy
cruiser) 179

Royal Australian Navy 147, 153–5,
159–73, 191, 196, 274
naval construction 161, 167, 191

Royal Navy 19, 20, 45, 49, 51, 54,
148, 150, 153–5, 165–8, 172–3,
176, 179, 181–2, 185–6, 193, 204
see also battleships
Admiralty 102, 168, 196, 199
Australian Squadron 160, 161, 171,

About the Authors

John Moses is a graduate of the University of Queensland, Department of History under its then Head, the late Professor Gordon Greenwood. In 1961 he continued post-graduate studies in Germany at the Universities of Munich 1961–63 and then in Erlangen, 1963–65 where he graduated D.Phil. before returning to Brisbane to join the Department of History. Here he served until retirement in 1989, having spent frequent lengthy study leaves in Germany as an Alexander von Humboldt Fellow. Through his acquaintance with numerous German historians John Moses became familiar with their role as political-historical mentors. He followed their various controversies with an insider's interest. Among these was the famous 'war-guilt debate' unleashed by Professor Fritz Fischer in Hamburg in the early 'sixties as well as debates with the Marxist-Leninist historians who held posts in the then German Democratic Republic. He has published widely on German labour history, Marxism-Leninism, German colonialism in the Pacific, German historiography, the Church Struggle under both the Nazis and the Communists, as well as on the origins of Anzac commemoration in Australia. He is currently an Adjunct Professor at St Mark's National Theological Centre in Canberra and a practising Anglican priest.

Peter Overlack held a DAAD (German Academic Exchange) Scholarship, and as recipient of a University of Queensland Postgraduate Award completed his Doctoral thesis in 1995 on the East Asia Cruiser Squadron as an instrument of German *Weltpolitik*. He has been widely published on German and Australian naval, colonial, strategic and intellectual history in journals such as the *Australian Journal of Politics & History*, *War & Society*, *Journal of Australian Studies*, *Journal of Military History* (USA), *Journal of Strategic Studies* (UK), and *The Historian* (USA), as well as being a contributor to several books and participating in international conferences. From an early age his interest in history was sparked by the lives of ancestors who included ship captains for the Lloyd and plantation managers in the Dutch Indies. He is currently a secondary teacher and freelance writer in Brisbane.

Printed in Australia
AUHW011035110419
310979AU00003B/10

9 781925 801613